The Social History
of American Education

The Social History
of American Education

Edited by
B. Edward McClellan
and William J. Reese

91-182

University of Illinois Press

Urbana and Chicago

Library of Congress Cataloging-in-Publication Data

The Social history of American education.

1. Education—United States—History.
2. Educational sociology—United States.
3. Educational equalization—United States.
I. McClellan, B. Edward (Bernard Edward), 1939–
II. Reese, William J.
LA205.S63   1988 $370_9.973$ 87-5893
ISBN 0-252-01461-8 (cloth; alk. paper)
ISBN 0-252-01462-6 (paper; alk. paper)

Contents

Introduction

Historians of American education who have reflected on the development of their own discipline have been of virtually one voice in declaring the early 1960s a turning point in the study of the nation's educational past. Before the 1960s historians of education had worked out of a largely celebratory tradition that viewed the development of the nation's vast educational system as nothing less than the unfolding of American democratic promise. In the way that political historians (who had their own celebratory tendencies) measured progress and marked off eras by reformist presidential administrations, educational historians took as their framework the growth and transformation of formal schooling, especially public schooling. When they looked to the distant past, before formal education had become a standard feature of growing up, they frequently limited their search to a quest for the roots of a now familiar and influential public school system. When they looked at more recent times, they applauded the growth of modern schooling and extolled its virtues while rarely highlighting its vices.

New intellectual stirrings in the 1960s began the demise of this celebratory tradition. A growing sensitivity to conflict and discontinuity led to deep skepticism about the progressive assumptions in both educational and political history and suggested that unduly narrow perspectives had blinded many historians to the rich diversity of the American past. The political discontent that soon followed these intellectual stirrings only accentuated the trends toward a more critical and broadly focused history.

In the field of educational history, the break from the past was effectively announced by the publication of Bernard Bailyn's *Education in the Forming of American Society: Needs and Opportunities for Study* (1960). Bailyn argued that historians of education, most of whom taught in schools of education, had acquired a stake in glorifying the cause of public education and dignifying the role of the professional educator. Thus, the history they wrote tended to be both uncritical and narrowly focused on the growth of formal schooling. What was required to bring education into the mainstream of historical study, Bailyn asserted, was a recognition that education meant more than schooling. By altering their focus, by studying the whole process by which culture was transmitted from one generation to another, historians would come to have a more complex and more accurate view of the educational past, a vision that made a place for discontinuities as well as continuities, for conflict as well as harmony.

Perhaps because he did not continue his research in the history of education, Bailyn's direct influence was relatively short-lived, except in the work of several colonial historians. Indeed, a quarter of a century after the publication of his celebrated work, his greatest impact appears to have come not from his broad focus or from his vague methodological prescriptions but simply from the respectability he gave to education as an object of proper historical study. His call for returning education to the mainstream of historical inquiry was answered eagerly by a generation of talented graduate students in both history departments and schools of education. Once drawn to the study of education, however, these students adopted a focus of their own and set out in directions that Bailyn had not mapped. Heavily influenced by the political unrest of the 1960s, they became a part of a broader intellectual movement that gave birth to what has been labelled "the new social history."

The new social history was distinguished both by its critical view of American institutions and by its bold application of social-scientific methodologies to historical study. Often moved by a sympathy with the poor and the working classes, practitioners of the new social history subjected the motives of powerful Americans, including school leaders, to a rigorous scrutiny. At the same time, they attempted to rescue from obscurity the experiences of common people whom earlier generations of historians had neglected.

The first work of the new social history of education, and arguably the most influential book in the field since 1960, was Michael B. Katz's *The Irony of Early School Reform: Educational Innovation in Mid-Nineteenth Century Massachusetts* (1968). Katz made a frontal assault on the celebratory tradition in American educational history, portraying school reformers as self-interested representatives of propertied classes who attempted to impose their schemes on a reluctant populace and make the school into an agency that would at once promote their own economic well-being and render workers and immigrants socially safe.

Fully as important as Katz's controversial argument was his methodology. Especially in his treatment of an 1860 vote to abolish the Beverly high school, Katz departed from the traditional approaches of educational historians and employed a quantitative political analysis to argue his case for the class basis of conflict over educational reform.

Katz's conclusions have been much disputed, but there can be little doubt that his work foreshadowed the research agenda that has dominated the field since the late sixties. Like Katz, most historians of education have continued to focus on schooling—some colonialists constitute an important exception—but by emphasizing the social context of formal instruction, they have attempted to avoid the narrowness that Bailyn found in the work of their pre-1960 predecessors. Although their conclusions have often differed sharply from Katz's, these historians have shared a keen interest in the relationship of the school to social equality and individual liberty. Moreover, many of them have employed increasingly sophisticated quantitative techniques to explore a range of questions that earlier generations of educational historians had barely raised. Taken together their work has given the field an unprecedented vitality.

The extraordinary scholarly renaissance that began with the work of Bernard Bailyn has found as one of its primary outlets the pages of the *History of Education Quarterly*. Established as the successor to the *History of Education Journal* in 1961, the *Quarterly* has at once reflected and encouraged the new scholarship. Along with its sponsoring association, the History of Education Society, the *Quarterly* has been—to use the words of Lawrence Veysey—a "meeting-ground" for a generation of scholars who have done much to return the study of the nation's past to the mainstream of historical inquiry.

The collection that follows brings together articles from the *History of Education Quarterly* in an effort to make available to students as well as to professional historians a cross section of the best scholarship in the social history of American education. The volume covers the whole span of American history and treats both popular and higher education. The articles do not reflect any one particular interpretative point of view or any one methodology; instead, they have been chosen to indicate the rich variety that has characterized recent scholarship in the field.

The publication of this volume gives recognition to many authors who have contributed to the *History of Education Quarterly* in the past. In hopes that it might also encourage scholars of the future, all royalties from the sale of the volume will be used to support the *Quarterly* as it continues its efforts to publish work of significance in the field of educational history. In this way, the remarkable accomplishments of the last quarter of a century can contribute in a tangible way to what we can all hope are the even better years that lie ahead.

PART I

The Colonial Period

Introduction

THE COLONIAL ERA has been a particularly puzzling period for American educational historians. The challenge, as Bernard Bailyn pointed out in *Education in the Forming of American Society* (1960), has been to find significant patterns of educational change in the enormous variety of colonial life. Bailyn believed that earlier scholars had failed to meet this challenge because they had focused too narrowly on formal instruction, and he called for a research agenda that would take a broader view and examine education in all its varied institutional contexts. By observing the changing educational functions of various institutions, Bailyn hoped, historians would be able to find the patterns of change that had so long eluded them.

Since Bailyn's dramatic pronouncements, historians of colonial education have given as much attention to the family, the community, the church, and apprenticeship as they have to the school. Yet, progress toward an overview of the period has been slow. This has been especially true for the history of elementary or popular education, where instruction remained far less formal than it was in the higher branches of learning. Not only have sources been scarce and difficult to interpret, but historians have discovered that patterns of transmitting elementary values and skills across generations have varied enormously from colony to colony. Clear trends, therefore, have been difficult to trace, large generalizations difficult to make.

Although historians of popular education have failed to achieve a clear overview of the era, they have nevertheless produced a number of impressive case studies. Following Bailyn, these historians have given special attention to the institutional contexts in which education took place, but they have also traced the intricate connections of education to the diverse religions and cultures of the period. Their work has greatly illuminated the subtle processes of colonial education, and it may yet point the way to an understanding of the larger patterns of educational change that Bailyn sought to comprehend.

Historians of elite education have had a somewhat easier task. The education of elites in the colonial era was a separate and well-defined process in which formal instruction played a central role. Since that process lacked the varied and shifting institutional contexts of popular education, historians could safely focus their research on schools. Even accounting for the enormous variety in secondary and higher education, this specific institutional focus has been a great advantage and has allowed the history of elite education to achieve a level of clarity that has so far eluded historians of popular education.

The luxury of having a specific institutional focus has not, however, led historians of elite education to frame their studies narrowly. Especially since the 1960s, they have been keenly sensitive to both the social systems that operated within educational institutions and the larger social structures of which educational institutions were a part. Although the new social history has sometimes been identified with the effort to study history "from the bottom up," these historians have shown that its methods may also be employed effectively to study the most elite institutions and social groups.

The articles that follow reflect the effort of recent historians to probe some of the puzzles posed by both popular and elite education in the colonial era. N. Ray Hiner's essay explores popular education in seventeenth-century Massachusetts. Hiner's major purpose is to trace the impact of religious belief on education, but he also succeeds in providing a rich description of the social institutions and processes in which Puritan education was embedded.

Articles by Jon Teaford, Kathryn McDaniel Moore, and Jurgen Herbst focus on that part of colonial education designed to train an elite of students for positions of leadership in the society. The problems they explore are related in one fashion or another to the growing heterogeneity of the elites that secondary schools and colleges were expected to serve in the eighteenth century. Teaford traces the decline of the Latin grammar school and the emergence of competitive forms of secondary education. Moore explores the social basis of student-faculty conflict at Harvard and Yale at a time when those institutions were becoming more heterogeneous. Jurgen Herbst examines the social and cultural forces that led Americans to begin to separate public and private education, a distinction that had been unknown to that point but was to have an important impact on the subsequent history of higher education.

1

The Cry of Sodom Enquired Into: Educational Analysis in Seventeenth-Century New England

N. Ray Hiner

CHARLES CHAUNCY knew he was striking a responsive chord when in a commencement address at Harvard in 1655 he drew on the Third Epistle of John to declare, "I have no greater joy than to hear that my children walk in truth." (1) The seventeenth-century Puritans who shook off the dust of the English Babylon and ventured into the "howling wilderness" of the New World clearly expected that this act of faith would insure the salvation of their children. The Scriptures told them this was so: as God promised Abraham, so he assured the inhabitants of the New Israel that he would "make thee exceeding fruitful," and "establish my covenant between me and thee and thy seed after thee in their generations for an everlasting covenant. . . ." (2) Hardly a complacent group, the Puritans understood very well that the "old deluder Satan" was abroad in New England and would do his utmost to thwart the salvation of as many souls as possible, even those of the children of the covenant. Thus, they promptly established regular public worship, encouraged family and community attention to the nurture of literacy, exercised controls over apprenticeship, and built schools and colleges—all actions designed, in part, to create the conditions most favorable for the reception of God's grace. In the end, the Puritans knew their difficult struggle would culminate in victory. They could afford to be optimistic; they had God's promise that grace was hereditary: God would honor his covenant and their children would be saved.

But as Edmund Morgan has shown, the Puritans discovered much to their dismay that grace was not necessarily hereditary, at least not in New England. (3) Many children, even children of the elect, would not or could not demonstrate to their parents' or ministers' satisfaction that they had received in full measure the blessings of the new covenant. The reasons for the Pu-

The research for this article was funded in part by a University of Kansas General Research Grant. I also wish to acknowledge the helpful suggestions of Mr. John Estes.

N. Ray Hiner is professor of history and education at the University of Kansas.

ritans' failure to transmit this essential element of their culture are complex. The remarkable prosperity, political uncertainties, the growing heterogeneity and mobility of the population, and other demographic factors contributed to the disintegration of the organic unity of the early consensual communities. (4)   But beyond these factors, the Puritans obviously set an unusually high educational standard for themselves when they expected their children to duplicate in detail their own personal, intense, religious experiences. Some failures were inevitable. For this reason it can be argued that the Puritans were actually quite successful educators. Given the conditions of seventeenth-century New England, Puritan culture was uncommonly persistent and has continued to influence American culture.

However, this argument misses a basic point: the Puritans themselves felt strongly that they had failed. From their perspective, their children's coldness and apostasy threatened to strike a mortal blow to the very integrity and viability of the entire Puritan enterprise in the New World. This threat was perceived very keenly by the religious leaders of New England, and their lamentations were eloquent and ubiquitous. When they dealt with this problem in their writings and sermons they expressed alarm and a profound disappointment with the "rising generation." "Look into families," cried Samuel Willard, "and see what disorders there are, children rising up against parents, and carrying themselves disobediently. . . ." "Look into the towns, and you shall see disorder, young men despising the aged and carrying themselves contemptuously towards them." (5)   Samuel Danforth shared Willard's concern. The new generation, he charged, had only "a careless, remiss, flat, dry, cold, dead frame of spirit." "They that have ordinances, are as though they had none, and they that hear the word, as though they heard it not." Those who receive the sacraments and are "exercised in the holy things" use them "by the by, as matters of custom and ceremonies so as not to hinder their eager prosecution of other things which their hearts are set upon." (6)   Increase Mather put it succinctly:"The body of the rising generation is a poor, perishing, and (except the Lord pour down his spirit) an undone generation." (7)   Conditions appeared even worse when it became obvious that the first generation of saints was passing rapidly from the scene. We are losing "the pillars of this generation," cried Mather in 1679. "All New England" shook when they fell to the ground. (8) The possible consequences of this lamentable degeneracy frightened Puritan leaders. "Will it not move you," Richard Mather asked Puritan mothers, "to think that the children of your bowels should everlastingly perish, and be in inconceivable misery world without end?" (9)   How painful it must have been for the Puritans to contemplate the terrible possibility of their children's damnation. But they were also afraid that unless spiritual conditions in New England improved, God would withdraw his special blessing and protection and vent his wrath upon all its people, young and old alike. God could bear to see some things in Sodom which he could not bear to see in Zion. (10) William Stoughton warned solemnly that if New England should "so frustrate and deceive the Lord's expectations" that God revoked his "covenant-interest," then all would be lost indeed—"ruin upon ruin, destruction upon destruction would come, until one stone were not left upon another." (11)

As Puritan leaders pondered the dreadful fate of their apostate children and considered the declining state of their religious utopia, they undertook a thorough-going analysis and evaluation of their entire educational system. No major element of the Puritan system of cultural transmission escaped scrutiny; its purposes, its structure, its processes, and its teachers were examined carefully. (12) How did these Puritan analysts conceptualize their educational system? What did they identify as its basic purposes and goals? How did they describe the nature of the beings they sought to educate? What did they believe were the most efficacious settings and conditions for education? Whom did they identify as the most important teachers in this system, and what were their primary pedagogical tools and processes? What solutions did this analysis produce, and to what extent were these solutions based on a refined and broadened conception of the educational process itself?

The Puritans never lacked a clear and explicit educational purpose. They sought to create a regenerate man, a converted man, a person whose being had been transformed by the infusion of God's mercy and grace. By the 1640s, the New England churches had developed a "test" that was used to determine if a man had in fact received the covenant of grace. (13) When an individual applied for full membership in a congregation, he was expected to demonstrate by means of a public, spiritual autobiography that he had successfully traversed all the steps of the process of conversion. The first step of this "morphology of conversion" required the spiritual neophyte to become aware of the omnipotence of God and God's law which, in turn, led him to a consciousness of his own depravity and a fear of his certain damnation. At this point, the meaning of God's promise of salvation through Christ became clear to him. He then experienced an internal struggle between a strong desire to believe in this promise and a perverse tendency to doubt its validity. Emerging from this spiritual conflict with a deep assurance that he had received God's mercy and escaped the eternal agonies of hell, the regenerate man became sensitive to the horrible tragedy of sin in the world and felt committed to obey God's commandments with a new energy. This morphology of conversion epitomized the ultimate purpose of the Puritan educational system and served as its rigorous "final examination." The Puritans sought nothing less than a radically transformed personality, a personality produced by a complex, demanding process of careful introspection and self-analysis. (14)

From an educational point of view, it is highly significant that the Puritans viewed conversion as a process with identifiable stages. Their predestinarian tradition that God had selected only certain individuals to be saved might have closed the door to any efforts by men to intervene with educational activity. Yet, as Norman Pettit has observed, once conversion was conceived as a process rather than a point in time, the stage had been set for the triumph of "the concept of preparation," which permitted man to play a role of his own, over the concept of "salvation by seizure," which gave man little or no part to play. (15) The idea of conversion as a process provided the Puritan leaders room for conceptual maneuver as they struggled to respond creatively to their generational crisis. It created the intellectual space through which they transported a large portion of their conscious educational apparatus into a position of theological respectability. So Thomas Shepard, Jr. could proclaim quite boldly in 1673 that the only way New England could recover from "any degree of sliding back from God," and thus escape God's wrath, was "by a more thorough, conscientious, religious, effectual care for the nurture of the rising generation." (16)

Beyond the creation of a regenerate man, the Puritans had other educational goals, equally explicit. Most of these were encompassed by the characteristics of the "civil man," another well-known seventeenth-century cultural ideal. A civil man was one whose behavior and reputation established that he had fulfilled the "Dutiful Child's Promise" to "as much as in me lies, keep all God's holy commandments." (17) He respected authority, obeyed the laws of the community, and accepted his responsibilities as parent, provider, husband, and master. (18) The Puritans certainly expected their children to become civil adults, but the just and honorable behavior of the civil man did not in itself constitute evidence of regeneracy. To be sure, continual uncivility was a sure sign of unregeneracy, but civility itself was a trumpet with an uncertain sound. Increase Mather noted in 1678 the presence of many who were "civil, and outwardly conformed to good order," yet he lamented that these same men often had never known "what the New Birth means" and would therefore be unable to enter the Kingdom of God. (19) In other words, the Puritan analysts looked first to an individual's motives and were satisfied with good behavior only if it occurred for the proper reasons. In the Puritan taxonomy of educational objectives the encouragement of specific civil behavior was subordinate to the development of regeneracy, a changed psychological or spiritual condition. In social-scientific terms, the Puritans viewed enculturation, the process by which the central values of a culture are internalized by the child, as more critical than socialization, the process by which a child learns the ways of a society so that he can function within it. (20) Although they did see an organic relationship between regeneracy and civility, this relationship was unmistakably hierarchical. If a man became regenerate, proper behavior would follow "naturally" because his changed personality would require it. Puritans sought to develop in the individual an inner monitor or conscience that would compel him to think, feel, and act in acceptable ways with a minimum of external controls. Hence Increase Mather's entreaty, "Let us make converting work our main design." (21)

It is within this context of educational purpose that the Puritan analysis of the nature of the child is best understood. To the Puritan, the child was obviously not born regenerate. Indeed, without the unmerited gift of God's transforming love, every man was an imperfect being—so imperfect, in comparison with the ultimate perfection of God, that the Puritan did not hesitate to label the child a corrupt being who carries within his heart "a bundle of folly" wherever he goes. (22) He was born in sin, a child of wrath by nature. (23) Although this pessimistic assessment of the moral condition of the child irritates our modern sensibilities, it should also be noted that few educators have recognized a greater potential for change in the child. (24) Puritans believed the child with careful nurture and God's grace could become regenerate—as nearly perfect as was possible for a human being to become. The children of the elect were thought to possess unusual promise; they were the direct inheritors of their parents' covenant with God. According to Increase Mather, a promise of "converting grace," of "blessed salvation" was reserved for the children of the covenant. (25) Yet it was precisely this assumption, that children of Godly parents had a prerogative in "seeking the Lord," which was being challenged in the late seventeenth century. Puritan writers during this period might logically have admitted that their optimistic assumptions about their children's great mutability needed to be modified. Instead they chose to emphasize the equally logical and theologically more comfortable proposition that it was not their ideas about the nature of the child which were at fault, but their pedagogy and those who were responsible for it. Puritans reminded themselves continually that God had entrusted children to them to be cared for and educated. "He doth put them out to us. . . ." explained Deodat Lawson, "as Pharaoh's daughter did Moses to the Hebrew woman, his mother, saying as she did . . . 'Take this child, and nurse it for me. . . .' " God would surely hold them to a strict accounting of how well they had met their obligation to their children. (26) The question asked by the Puritan writers was not, Should we reconsider our view of the child?, but rather, Have we been diligent enough in our teaching?, and, How can we make our instruction more effective? The Puritans refused to become educational pessimists; they continued to believe in the great potential of their children, occasionally in the face of strong evidence to the contrary. (27)

Perhaps a major source of the Puritans' optimism was their resolute faith in the educational efficacy of a Christian community and its two primary institutions, the family and the church. They were certain that if they allowed their children to run wild in the woods free from the care and concern of families and fellow Christians, the result would not be the "new Jerusalem, but a Gog and a Magog." (28)   Since it was clear that the God who had said, "Let us make man after our own image," had made man a "sociable creature;" so it was also evident to the Puritan writers that families were "the nurseries of all societies." (29)   Eleazar Mather insisted, as would have most Puritans, that

... families are the seminaries of church and commonwealth. Keep the Lord with you in families, and keep him in all societies; let him go thence, and he will go quickly from the rest. Here begins all apostacy and degeneration; the ruin of churches and country springs from thence. Ruin families and ruin all. So, on the other hand, keep God there, and keep him everywhere. The generation to come will reap the fruit of family education; such children as you bring up, such parents will they be. ...(30)

Even though the family was very important to the Puritans, they did not discuss its educational role in isolation from other institutions. Families were expected to be "little churches" which prepared children to receive the spiritual benefits provided by the larger church, and the church was relied upon to reinforce the educational efforts of the home. (31)   Family and church were related symbiotically in the minds of the Puritans.

The church provided its strongest assistance to the family when the congregation was a harmonious body, when its members were "comforted in the mutual faith of each other, walking in the gospel simplicity without visible addition or diminution from the precept or pattern in the Mount." (32)   Puritan writers were appalled by the spirit of discord and dissension they saw springing up in their churches, not only because of its repugnant theological implications, but also because of its pernicious influence on the young. (33)   How could they be a good example to their children when they could not live peaceably together? (34)   They saw the urgent need to lay aside "all dividing and contentious animosities" and "come to love one another." (35)   In the first generation, those who refused to accept the congregational consensus could simply be banished from the community, Anne Hutchinson style. But as the century progressed, and as the forces contributing to the deterioration and decay of church unity became more complex and diffused, this solution no longer sufficed and compromise was often resorted to as a substitute for consensus. (36)   The Puritan writers understood very quickly the importance of this unsettled polity for the education of their children, although they were not able to discover how to restore the supposed halcyon atmosphere of the early years.

The introduction of the half-way covenant in the 1660's was in part an effort by the Puritan leadership to respond to the challenge of educating their children in these unstable conditions. This compromise allowed the unconverted children of church members to retain a limited church membership and present their own children for baptism. The sacrament of communion, however, was reserved for converted members. In one sense the half-way covenant was an admission of educational failure. But it was also an educational innovation designed to meliorate a serious generational and political problem. Faced with the growing number of pious but unconverted offspring and an increasingly heterogeneous population, many Puritan clergymen decided that a strict standard for church membership and baptism would cripple the church as an educational institution and isolate it further from the life of the community. (37) Consequently, Thomas Shepard, Jr., a supporter of the half-way covenant, held that the churches could not be kept completely pure. He agreed with his father who had said that churches did not consist solely of "angels and saints," but also "many chaffy hypocrites and oft times profane persons." Their presence was desirable because they and their children might then "enjoy the special watch and care of the whole church, which otherwise they must want." (38) The educational function of the half-way covenant was buttressed by the introduction of the mass covenant renewal which required every church member to stand and reaffirm his pledge to God and his fellow Christians. Children were often expected on these occasions to "own the covenant" and declare their intention to prepare themselves to enter full communion. (39)

The third and least important member of the symbiotic triad of Puritan educational institutions was the school. Of course, the Puritans are noted for their early support of colleges and lower schools, but in their writings these institutions occupied a distinctly subordinate role in the education of Puritan children. Colleges, or "schools of learning," received relatively more attention than did the lower or "inferior schools" in large measure because the colleges trained the ministers needed to replace the first-generation leaders. Churches could not properly fulfill their vital educational role without the guidance of a well educated ministry. Without colleges, an uneducated ministry; without an educated ministry, declining churches; without strong churches, unconverted children; ergo colleges were one of the means necessary to insure the transmission of grace to the next generation. (40)

The scattered and brief nature of references to lower schools by Puritan writers in the seventeenth century lends some support to Samuel E. Morison's contention that the Puritans supported schools for reasons other than "to out-smart Satan." At least as important, he says, was their desire to provide "training for citizenship and service in a civilized state." (41) Puritans did expect their schools to aid the development of both regeneracy and civility, but neither goal was discussed in very specific terms until late in the seventeenth century. By the 1690's, however, an increasing concern for the cultivation of civility ultimately focused greater attention on the lower schools. In 1699 Cotton Mather was praying, "Save us our Lord Jesus Christ; save us from the mischief and scandals of an uncultivated offspring." According to Mather, Christ was pleased when children were "well-formed with and well-formed in the rules of civility, and not . . . clownish, and sottish, and ill-bred sort of creatures." But "an unmannerly brood" was "a dishonor to religion." A barbarous progeny could be avoided if children were given a more careful instruction in civil matters, if they were taught to "read, and write, and cipher, and . . . put into some agreeable callings. . . ." The family had an important role in cultivating this civility, but schools also had a major responsibility. So Mather pleaded with his fellow New Englanders to increase their support for schools lest their posterity be betrayed "into the very circumstances of savages." (42) Mather's admission that the lack of civility was a serious concern which had to be dealt with by the schools was a tacit admission that the unchurched and unconverted had become so numerous by the end of the seventeenth century that "education for salvation" by churches and families had failed to reach all members of the community. Education for social control by the schools became necessary to keep the unregenerate civilized on a minimum level. Regardless of its origin, an intensified concern for civility tended to enlarge the cultural importance of the schools.

If a Christian community provided the most efficacious setting for the education of children, Puritan analysts reasoned that everyone in such a community was a potential "teacher," if only by force of his example. All members of Puritan communities were urged to make certain they had "the special presence of God" in themselves. They were also cautioned to watch their conversations and behavior, for fear that the young would be tempted to follow an improper model. (43) Even magistrates and servants were obliged to recognize their educational responsibilities. Magistrates were reminded "how powerfully" their examples would "diffuse the fear of God into all that are about or under them." "Holiness and virtue," proclaimed Cotton Mather, "grow into fashion when such men become exemplary for it." (44) Servants were asked to consider themselves as "hand-maids of the Lord" when they dealt with children. (45)

Although everyone in a Puritan community was expected to be a "teacher," parents and ministers bore the heaviest teaching burdens. Scarcely a sermon or an essay on "educational" topics failed to include exhortations and specific instructions to parents concerning their obligations to educate their children. Puritan parents were told they must first search their own souls to be certain they themselves were in a state of grace. (46) Apostasy among the rising generation, warned Eleazar Mather, was a sure sign of a weariness of spirit among the former generation. "The second generation seldom or never prove to be total apostates," he asserted, "but the first are deep, secret heart revolters." Yet Mather assured parents their situation was not hopeless. For the sake of the new generation and their own souls, they could through careful prayer and repentance recover their lost zeal. Thus revived and renewed in spirit, they could offer their children good examples. As parents, Mather said, "you must lead them to Christ by example as well as by counsel. You must live religion as well as talk religion. . . ." (47)

At this point parents were considered ready to direct their attention to more formal instructional processes. Some of the best opportunities for parents to introduce their children to the basic principles and duties of the Christian faith came during regular family worship when they led their children in daily scripture reading and prayer. Here they could teach their children that there was one God; that man was born in sin; and that Christ offered himself for man's sins. Here children could be made aware of their obligations to keep the sabbath, brought to understand the sacraments of Baptism and the Lord's Supper, and urged to accept covenant obligations. (48) Parents were also encouraged strongly to pray with their children as well as for them. Cotton Mather advised parents to take their children with them into their "secret chambers" and permit them to kneel alongside. "Let the child hear the groans," he said, "and see the tears, and be a witness of the agonies, wherewith you are travailing for the salvation of it." Your children "will never forget what you do; it will have a marvelous force upon them." (49)

Another important element of family instruction was the catechism. "Let us carefully attend catechising of our families," exhorted Deodat Lawson, and thereby provide them "a methodical knowledge of God, Christ, and the way of salvation." (50) Although the catechism deserves much of the criticism it has received from modern educational theorists, it can be viewed as an early example of a linear teaching program. The child usually received rather immediate negative or positive reinforcement and he was allowed to progress at his own rate through a series of discrete steps. Moreover, by the end of the seventeenth century Puritan writers placed a greater emphasis on positive reinforcement in the teaching of catechism. Parents were told to be "frequent" in their catechising, but not "tedious or overlong," and they were encouraged to employ "some small rewards and encouragements to quicken them in learning the truths and duties of religion." (51) The fami-

ly catechism did not exist in pedagogical isolation; it was reinforced by public catechism and supported by other teaching tools in both the family and
the church. Even so, the tendency of catechism to produce rote memoriza-
tion undoubtedly inhibited the attainment of the Puritans' primary educational goal of internalized understanding of their faith. But the Puritan analysts were not altogether insensitive to this pedagogical weakness. Parents
were warned to avoid an undue coldness and formality and encouraged to
work instead for a sound understanding in all their instructional activities,
in Bible-reading and prayer, as well as in the catechism. (52)

In addition to guiding family worship and providing formal religious
instruction, parents were expected to be constantly on the alert to reprimand
their children for behavior contrary to God's commandments. (53)   They
were admonished not to hesitate to discipline their children even if it meant
corporal punishment, because one likely cause of degeneracy was a growing
indulgence among parents. (54)   Yet parents were advised by ministers to
temper their discipline "with kindness, and meekness, and loving tender-
ness, that our children may fear us with delight and see that we love them,
with as much delight." "Good" Puritan parents exercised a strong, but
"sweet authority" over their children. (55)

Parental obligations did not end with instruction and discipline; the
child's social environment also had to be considered. Since a man's "society" was likely his for eternity, evil company could trap children in the
"snares of death." (56)   According to Benjamin Wadsworth, young people
should be kept out of taverns and not permitted "to be abroad unseasonably
on nights, lest they're drawn into numberless hazards and mischiefs
thereby." (57)   Cotton Mather sounded the alarm against the devil's efforts
to "decoy young men" into what seemed to be "good fellowship" and
"merry meetings" such as "those husking meetings, whereat so many of
your young people in the country do debauch themselves." No experience of
the Puritan child, not even a merry meeting, was so insignificant that
parents could afford to ignore its educational potential. Mather advised
parents to be ready for all opportunities "to be instilling your instructions
into the souls of your little folks." Children, he explained, "are narrow
mouth'd vessels, and things must be drop after drop instilled into them."
(58)

Hardly any attention was devoted to mothers in the seventeenth-century
recitations of parental duties. Benjamin Wadsworth did caution mothers to
be very careful as soon as they knew they were with child. After birth, he also
advised that "mothers . . . if able, should suckle their children." "Those
mothers," he complained, "who have milk, and are so healthy as to be able
to suckle their children, and yet thro' sloth or niceness neglect to suckle
them seem very criminal and blameworthy." (59)   The mother's influence

was certainly not unimportant, but the father had the primary responsibility for instructing and guiding his children in the way to salvation. The master was "the soul of the family," declared Deodat Lawson, "the correlate of every relation there. Husband of the wife, father of the children, master of the servants, governor of the governed." "Every child and servant acts by, from, and under him." The master of the family existed in a "public capacity" and thus was required to "give account of persons" committed to his charge. (60)   There was little ambiguity in Puritan educational theory about where the power and accountability for family education resided.

If the Puritan father had a relatively equal teaching partner, it was not his wife, but his minister. The father's educational endeavors were designed to develop a "readiness" in his children to receive the more direct means of salvation provided by the minister as he guided the spiritual life of his flock. The father was commanded to bring his children to public worship, and he was urged to question them at home about the minister's sermons. "When the minister's work in public is done," said Eleazar Mather, "the family work begins." (61)   The minister could not be effective in his work if the children had not been made sensitive to the meaning of what he offered them; yet, the father's strivings would very likely come to nought if his children could not receive the blessings of a public ministry. The parent and minister were teachers whose success was profoundly dependent on the effectiveness of the other. The home without the church provided only half an education; and children without a father or a minister were only half taught, and most likely unconverted. Therefore, any tendency among parents to shirk their educational duties, or any inclination to leave the propogation of the faith to ministers and magistrates, caused great concern among ministers. (62)   They knew they could not be effective in their work without the active support of parents.

The Puritan minister's basic teaching tool was the sermon. Through it the pastor explained the word of God, applied God's teaching to individual and community life, and recommended spiritual remedies. Here the minister focused and combined his insight and skill in logic, rhetoric, pedagogy, literary theory, and theology to produce a basic means through which God often acted to regenerate the individual. (63)   By modern standards it seems remarkable that the Puritans expected their children to attend these sermons and to benefit from them. (They probably did overestimate the intellectual capacity of their very young children.) However, as noted earlier, the main points of the sermon were supposed to be translated for the children by the father, and the child had usually been introduced to many of the concepts mentioned in the sermons as he learned his catechism.

If many sermons were in fact too abstruse for children, the Puritan minister had other forms of spiritual sustenance to offer the young sent to his ecclesiastical nursery. He explained the meaning of the sacraments of baptism and communion; he reinforced the instruction of the home by directing public catechism; he supervised the religious instruction provided in the schools; and he oversaw "the lives and conversations" of the children of the covenant who were expected to welcome his sincere Christian counsel and admonition. (64)   Some clergymen also prepared handbooks and catechisms designed specifically for children. Examples of this genre were John Cotton's catechism, *Spiritual Milk for Boston Babes* . . . (1656), which was eventually included in *The New England Primer* (1690), and James Janeway's *A Token for Children* (1700). Janeway's work, a popular English moral handbook often reprinted in America, depicted "The Exemplary Lives and Joyful Deaths of Several Young Children." (65)   The didactic purpose of these "biographies" was explicit. In his preface to his young readers, Janeway explained,

> You may now hear (My dear lambs) what other good children have done, and remember how they wept and prayed by themselves; how earnestly they cried out for an interest in the Lord Jesus Christ. May you not read how dutiful they were to their parents? How diligent at their books? How ready to learn the scripture, and their catechism? Can you forget what questions they were wont to ask? How much they feared a lie, how much they abhorred naughty company, how holy they lived, and how dearly they were loved, how joyfully they loved?
>
> Do you do as these children did? How dost thou spend thy time? Is it in play and idleness with wicked children? Dare you take God's name in vain, or swear, or tell a lie? Dare you do anything which your parents forbid you and neglect what they command you? Do you dare to run up and down the Lord's day? Or do you keep in to read your book to learn what your good parents command you? What do you say child? Which of these two sorts are you of? (66)

As condescending and trite as these questions may seem to modern tastes, they certainly presented the child with clear moral choices described in behavioral terms. Janeway recommended in his preface to parents that they make their children read his book "a hundred times," and "ask them what they think of those children, and whether they would not be such."

Puritan divines also used the lives (and deaths) of members of their own communities as raw material for the religious instruction of their spiritual catechumen. When the pious young John Tappan of Boston died unexpectedly in 1672 at the age of nineteen, Samuel Wakeman used his funeral oration as an opportunity to point out that this "young man's legacy to the rising generation" was the purity and sobriety of his life. He was a civil, sober man, a delightful child to his parents who could repeat good sermons; his life was an admonition to all. (67)   Nor did the ministers hesitate to employ the lives of more colorful and less upstanding individuals as vehicles for instruction. Consider *The Cry of Sodom Enquired Into* preached by Samuel Danforth, "Upon Occasion of the Arraignment and Condemnation of Benjamin Good for His Prodigious Villany," and including "A Solemn Exhortation to Tremble at God's Judgement and to Abandon Youthful Lusts." (68) The villany that led ultimately to Mr. Good's condemnation consisted of two acts of buggery or bestiality, the final one occurring after he had been put under "the yoke of government and service (which might have bridled and restrained him from wickedness)." But, we are told by Danforth, he broke away from his master and attained a "licentious liberty," finally committing his vile deed in broad daylight in an open field at noon-day. Appalling indeed! But also instructive, for as Danforth informed his audience, the youth had confessed he had early "lived in disobedience to his parents in lying, stealing, sabbath breaking, and was wont to fly away from catechism." He admitted he had not listened to the voice of God and had been extremely addicted to sloth and idleness. Danforth made certain the educational import of the young man's experience was not lost on his young listeners. He warned children to be obedient to their parents, to beware of evil company, and to listen to the word of God. He followed these warnings with injunctions to parents to watch carefully over their children and servants, to instruct them diligently, to provide them solemn charges and reproofs, and to pray for them. (69) In like manner ministers often spoke directly to the young on special days of fasting and prayer for the rising generation. (70)

The appearance of "young men's associations" late in the seventeenth century provided still another pedagogical opportunity for ministers. Cotton Mather championed these groups and he presented a charter or agreement signed by the young men of one community as a model for others. The youths agreed:

I It shall be our endeavor to spend two hours from seven to nine on the evening of every [ ] in praying together by turns; one to begin, and other to conclude the meeting; and between the two prayers having a sermon repeated; whereto the singing of a psalm shall be annexed.

II If after the stated exercises of the evening are over, there be any residue of time, we will confer upon some questions. Every one of us in his turn, is to be provided with a question, altho the answer to it shall be left wholly free unto every one as he shall see cause to say more or less concerning it.

III We resolve to be charitably watchful over one another; and therefore . . . will not unkindly divulge one another's infirmities, but yet lovingly inform one another what we shall know or hear to be a fault; so we will never manifest ourselves offended at any our number that shall bestow a Christian reproof upon us for any of our own miscarriages. (71)

The agreement also outlined the requirements for membership and described procedures for the collection of money.

Mather's support of organizations for young men illustrates a growing consciousness among Puritan analysts of the presence of youth and a general trend toward a somewhat greater differentiation by age in discussions of the rising generation. Whereas sermons preached earlier in the century usually addressed the rising generation as one group, the Janeway handbook included few biographies of children over twelve; *The New England Primer* was designed primarily for young children; and the young men's associations were created specifically for the education of youth. Cotton Mather was addressing young people in 1694 when he warned, "To stand barren among the people of God for three years together is by much too much, but it is likely that some of you have stood so for more than three times three. Let me inquire of you I pray, How old are you? It may be twelve, or fifteen, or twenty years old, and what? A slave of the Devil all the while! That is too long!" (72)   Deodat Lawson was thinking of essentially the same age-group when he complained in 1693 that there were many youth of twelve, fourteen, and sixteen years of age who could "read little and understand less of the Holy Scriptures. . . ." (73)   Thomas Foxcroft noted that each age of man had its own peculiar passion and sin when he delivered a sermon to "a society of young men meeting privately for religious instruction on Lord's-Day-Evenings." The passion of old age is covetousness, explained Foxcroft to his adolescent audience; ambition is the sin of middle age; and sensuality "the emphatical blemish of wanton youth." (74)

This heightened concern for youth expressed in the writings and sermons of the late seventeenth and early eighteenth centuries demonstrates the gradual evolution of a more precise and refined conception of the educational process: both children and youth had distinctive social and psychological needs, and this distinctiveness required the introduction of teaching strategies and materials not always provided by the traditional educational apparatus. (75) Ministers, especially, were challenged to develop the new strategies and materials because children and youth of all ages, whether unchurched or church-going, needed careful ministerial guidance and direction to protect them from the temptations and sins of an increasingly secular social environment.

By the end of the seventeenth century, Puritan analysts had examined the basic components of their system of cultural transmission—its purposes, its settings and institutions, its teachers and students, and its processes. The comprehensive scope and the penetrating nature of this analysis make it clear that a large portion of Puritan education was a conscious process. Yet as comprehensive as Puritan educational analysis was, it had its weaknesses, some of which were rooted in the nature of Puritanism itself. In their analysis Puritan writers emphasized the interlocking and shared educational obligations of home, church, and community, of parents, ministers, and citizens. Certainly this perspective was appropriate in the relatively homogeneous communities of the early years, but when the population became more heterogeneous and when consensus became difficult if not impossible, the highly interdependent educational system became very vulnerable. When either the home, the church, the community, or to some extent the school, failed to accomplish its educational tasks, it weakened the capabilities of the other and consequently threatened the effectiveness of the entire system. Even the education of children of the saints, which included ample spiritual milk from the home and church, could be diluted seriously by the absence of support from an orthodox community. Similarly, the family, a cornerstone of the Puritan educational edifice, provided little help to the unchurched and unconverted youth since their parents were very likely unconverted themselves. The school could provide literacy and the most elementary spiritual instructions, but it was not designed to furnish the direct means of salvation. Puritan analysts were obviously aware of these weaknesses, but the remedies they proposed were for the most part quite limited in nature, given the profound nature of the problems they faced. The church was the only Puritan educational institution equipped to fill the educational vacuum that had appeared by the end of the seventeenth century. Yet as scholars have long noted, the Puritans were slow to adopt an aggressive evangelical policy for their churches. In this context the development of the half-way covenant, the mass covenant renewal, community fast days for the young, and young men's associations did represent serious efforts by churches and ministers to respond creatively to the challenge posed by the presence of a diverse population. But the results of these innovations did not satisfy the Puritans themselves, and indeed they did not revolutionize the church as an educational institution.

The reluctance of the Puritans to restructure their churches as educational institutions was related in part to an inconsistency between their primary educational objective and their approach to pedagogy. Conversion, the Puritans' overriding educational objective, was essentially affective in nature, but Puritan pedagogy, or preparation for conversion, was largely cognitive. Of course the Puritan sermon contained its own kind of highly controlled passion, and Puritan parents were loving parents who expressed the full range of human emotions. Yet when the Puritan child had acquired a knowledge of the fundamentals of his faith, when he had before him the examples of pious parents, and when he had heard the word of God explicated in public worship, it was more or less assumed that conversion would follow in God's own time. The idea of conversion as a process never led the Puritan writers to conclude that the salvation of their children could be produced by educational efforts alone. God, not ministers or parents, chose the time and place to infuse the child with the precious gift of grace. In other words, the critical affective elements of conversion came from God, not pedagogy. However, the pedagogical changes introduced during the Great Awakening reveal that the Puritans of the seventeenth century had not exhausted the educational alternatives open to them, even within the confines of their traditional theology. (76) Even so, these later innovations were developed within the analytical framework built by the seventeenth-century writers. If there were great harvests in the 1730's and 1740's, if the church was revitalized as an educational institution in the eighteenth century, it was in part because Puritan analysts had carefully tilled the educational soil in the seventeenth. In this sense, Puritan children were truly the inheritors of their fathers' deep faith and diligent inquiry.

Notes

1. Charles Chauncy, *God's Mercy Shewed to His People* (Cambridge 1655), p. 12.
2. Genesis 17:6-7. Also see Thomas Shepard, *The Church Membership of Children* (Cambridge, 1663), p. 1; Eleazer Mather, *A Serious Exhortation to the Rising Generation in New England* (Boston, 1678), p. 18; and Increase Mather, *A Call From Heaven to the Present and Succeeding Generations* (Boston, 1679), p. 7.
3. Edmund S. Morgan, *The Puritan Family* (revised ed. New York, 1966), p. 185.
4. See Michael Zuckerman, *Peaceable Kingdoms: New England Towns in the Eighteenth Century* (New York, 1970); Kenneth A. Lockridge, *A new England Town: The First Hundred Years* (New York, 1970); John Demos, *A Little Commonwealth: Family Life in Plymouth Colony* (New York, 1970), and Clarence L. Ver Steeg, *The Formative Years, 1607-1763* (New York, 1964).
5. Samuel Willard, *Useful Instructions for a Professing People in Times of Great Security and Degeneracy* (Cambridge, 1673), p. 75.
6. Samuel Danforth, *A Brief Recognition of New England's Errand into the Wilderness* (Cambridge, 1671), p. 13.
7. Increase Mather, *Pray for the Rising Generation* (Cambridge, 1678), p. 14.
8. See Increase Mather's "Note to the Reader" in *A Call From Heaven.*
9. Richard Mather, *A Farewell Exhortation to the Church and People of Dorchester in New England* (Cambridge, 1657), p. 13.
10. Samuel Willard, *Covenant Keeping, the Way to Blessedness* (Boston, 1682), p. 80.
11. William Stoughton, *New England's True Interest* (Cambridge, 1670), p. 16.
12. According to Bernard Bailyn's apt phrase, education in all of English America was "wrenched loose from the automatic, instinctive workings of society, and cast as a matter for deliberation in the forefront of con-

sciousness." See his *Education in the Forming of American Society: Needs and Opportunities for Study* (New York, 1960), p. 21.

13. Edmund S. Morgan, *Visible Saints: The History of a Puritan Idea* Ithaca, N.Y., 1963), pp. 66-71, 88.

14. Howard M. Feinstein, "The Prepared Heart: A Comparative Study of Puritan Theology and Psychoanalysis," *American Quarterly*, 22 (Summer, 1970), 168.

15. Norman Pettit, *The Heart Prepared: Grace and Conversion in Puritan Spiritual Life* (New Haven, 1966), 155.

16. Thomas Shepard, Jr., *Eye Salve* (Cambridge, 1673), p. 43.

17. Paul Leicester Ford, ed., *The New England Primer* (New York, 1962). This is a reprint of a facsimile edition published by Dodd, Mead, and Company, New York.

18. See Morgan, *The Puritan Family*, p. 1.

19. Increase Mather, *Pray for the Rising Generation*, p. 14.

20. My definition of socialization is drawn from Frederick Elkin's *The Child and Society; The Process of Socialization* (New York, 1960), p. 4.

21. Increase Mather, *A Call From Heaven*, p. 85.

22. Increase Mather, *Solemn Advice to Young Men* (Boston, 1695), p. 13.

23. Richard Mather, *A Farewell Exhortation*, p. 9; and Joseph Belcher, *Two Sermons Preached in Dedham* (Boston, 1710), pp. 15-16.

24. For examples of recent criticisms of the Puritan view of the child, see Zuckerman, *Peaceable Kingdoms*, pp. 72-83; and Clarence J. Karier, *Man, Society, and Education* (Glenview, Illinois, 1967), pp. 14-18.

25. Increase Mather, *A Call From Heaven*, pp. 9-11.

26. Deodat Lawson, *The Duty and Property of a Religious Householder* (Boston, 1693), p. 31.

27. I am indebted to Perry Miller for my understanding of the Puritans' "cosmic optimism." See his *The New England Mind: The Seventeenth Century* (Boston, 1961), pp. 37-38; and Perry Miller and Thomas H. Johnson, comp., *The Puritans* (New York, 1938), pp. 60-61.

28. Cotton Mather, *The Way to Prosperity* (Boston, 1690), pp. 34-35; and Chauncy, *God's Mercy Shewed to His People*, pp. 15-16.

29. Cotton Mather, *A Family Well-Ordered* (Boston, 1699), p. 3.

30. Eleazar Mather, *A Serious Exhortation to the Rising Generation*, p. 20.

31. Lawson, *The Duty and Property of a Religious Householder*, p. 50.

32. Joshua Scottow, *Old Men's Tears for Their Own Declensions* (Boston, 1691), p. 4; and Eleazar Mather, *A Serious Exhortation to the Rising Generation*, p. 25.

33. Willard, *Useful Instructions for a Professing People*, p. 75.

34. Increase Mather, *A Call From Heaven*, pp. 81-82.

35. Cotton Mather, *Optanda* (Boston, 1692), p. 69.

36. Zuckerman, *Peaceable Kingdoms*, pp. 6-7.

37. Robert G. Pope, *The Half-Way Covenant: Church Membership in Puritan New England* (Princeton, N.J., 1969), pp. 7-9, 237, 275-276; and Ross Worn Beales, Jr., "Cares for the Rising Generation: Youth and Religion in Colonial New England" (Ph.D. diss., University of California, Davis, 1971), pp. 84-86.

38. In 1663, Thomas Shepard, Jr. (1635-1677) arranged the posthumous

publication of his father's (1605-1649) essay, *The Church Membership of Children.* In a lengthy preface to this essay, the younger Shepard made it clear that his father's earlier views were directly relevant to the question of the half-way covenant (see the "Preface to the Reader" and pp. 14, 25). Also see Samuel Danforth, *A Brief Recognition of New England's Errand into the Wilderness* (Cambridge, 1671), pp. 16-17.

39. See Increase Mather's *The Necessity of Reformation* (Boston, 1670), p. 12; and his *A Call From Heaven,* p. 89. The mass covenant renewal is discussed perceptively by Pope, *The Half-Way Covenant,* pp. 241-246. Although the half-way covenant and mass covenant renewal may have been educationally viable, the presence of large numbers of unconverted persons in the churches had its own educational disadvantages, for they presented examples to children unworthy of emulation. Perhaps it was this concern which led Cotton Mather to recommend in 1710 that groups of approximately twelve families from within each church meet as "associated families" "once a fortnight" to pray, sing psalms, and repeat and discuss sermons. Such groups, he said, "should look upon themselves as bound up in one bundle of love, and count themselves as obliged in very close and strong bonds to be serviceable unto one another." (42)   That this description of associated families can be taken as a reasonably accurate definition of the aims and nature of the original seventeenth-century churches themselves is eloquent testimony to the difficulty of educating the children of saints in a church which included "chaffy hypocrites" and "profane persons." Mather obviously did not wish to include them in his associated families. See Cotton Mather, *Bonifacius: An Essay Upon the Good* (Boston, 1710), pp. 82-83.

40. See Chauncy, *God's Mercy Shewed to His People,* pp. 29, 31; Increase Mather, *The Necessity of Reformation,* p. 14; Shepard, *Eye Salve,* p. 45; and Richard Mather, *A Farewell Exhortation,* pp. 7-8.

41. Samuel Eliot Morison, *The Intellectual Life of Colonial New England* (2nd ed., Ithaca, N.Y., 1956), pp. 67, 69. Also see Chauncy, *God's Mercy Shewed to His People,* p. 15; Increase Mather, *A Call From Heaven,* pp. 72-73; and Shepard, *Eye Salve,* p. 6.

42. Cotton Mather, *A Family Well-Ordered,* pp. 17-18, and pp. 1, 5 of "addenda" (with separate pagination).

43. Willard, *Covenant Keeping,* p. 103.

44. Cotton Mather, *Optanda,* pp. 40-41.

45. Cotton Mather, *Corderius Americanus: An Essay Upon the Good Education of Children* (Boston, 1708), p. 12.

46. See Increase Mather's *Pray for the Rising Generation,* p. 19; and his *A Call From Heaven,* p. 20.

47. Eleazar Mather, *A Serious Exhortation to the Rising Generation,* pp. 20-21.

48. See Benjamin Wadsworth's *Exhortations to Early Piety* (Boston, 1702), p. 30; and his *The Well-Ordered Family or Relative Duties* (Boston, 1712), pp. 53-55. Also note Richard Mather, *A Farewell Exhortation,* p. 11; Lawson, *The Duty and Property of a Religious Householder,* pp. 23-24; and Cotton Mather, *A Family Well-Ordered,* pp. 18-19.

49. Ibid., pp. 35-36.
50. Lawson, *The Duty and Property of a Religious Householder*, p. 26; and Richard Mather, *A Farewell Exhortation*, p. 12.
51. Wadsworth, *The Well-Ordered Family*, pp. 63-64.
52. Ibid., p. 62; and Lawson, *The Duty and Property of a Religious Householder*, pp. 25-26.
53. Ibid., p. 28.
54. Ibid., pp. 28-30.
55. Cotton Mather, *A Family Well-Ordered*, pp. 22-23; and Wadsworth, *The Well-Ordered Family*, pp. 55-56.
56. Cotton Mather, *Early Religion Urged* (Boston, 1694), p. 29.
57. Wadsworth, *A Well-Ordered Family*, p. 58.
58. See Cotton Mather, *Addresses to Old Men, Young Men, and Little Children* (Boston, 1690), p. 70; *Early Religion Urged*, p. 31; and *A Family Well- Ordered*, pp. 20-21.
59. Wadsworth, *A Well-Ordered Family*, p. 45.
60. Lawson, *The Duty and Property of a Religious Householder*, pp. 30-31.
61. Eleazar Mather, *A Serious Exhortation to the Rising Generation*, p. 20. Also see Richard Mather, *A Farewell Exhortation*, p. 13; Cotton Mather, *A Family Well-Ordered* p. 20; and Wadsworth, *A Well-Ordered Family*, p. 61.
62. *Ibid.*, pp. 83-84.
63. For a comprehensive discussion of the importance of the sermon in Puritan life and thought, see Perry Miller, *The New England Mind: The Seventeenth Century*, pp. 290-392.
64. See Willard, *Covenant Keeping*, pp. 115-117; Cotton Mather's *A Family Well-Ordered*, Addenda, p. 1; and *Bonificius*, pp. 95-102.
65. See Lawrence Cremin, *American Education: The Colonial Experience, 1607-1783* (New York, 1970), pp. 130, 394, 484; and Morison, *The Intellectual Life of New England*, pp. 79-82.
66. James Janeway, *A Token for Children* (Boston, 1700).
67. Samuel Wakeman, *A Young Man's Legacy to the Rising Generation* (Cambridge, Mass., 1673), pp. 42-44.
68. Samuel Danforth, *The Cry of Sodom Enquired Into* (Cambridge, Mass., 1674).
69. Ibid., pp. 8-9, 19, 23-24.
70. See Increase Mather, *Pray for the Rising Generation;* Cotton Mather's *Early Religion Urged* and *Cares About Nurseries* (Boston, 1702), pp. 47-88; Wadsworth, *Exhortations to Early Piety*, pp. 1-30; and Belcher, *Two Sermons Preached in Dedham.*
71. Cotton Mather, *Early Religion Urged*, pp. 115-117.
72. Ibid., p. 49.
73. Lawson, *The Duty and Property of a Religious Householder*, p. 57.
74. Thomas Foxcroft, *Cleansing Our Way in Youth* (Boston, 1719), pp. 15 ff. For an interesting account of the history of the "ages of man" concept, see Philippe Aries, *Centuries of Childhood: A Social History of Family Life*, trans. Robert Baldick (New York, 1962), pp. 15-32.
75. Ross Beales argues convincingly that young people in colonial New England experienced a prolonged period of "adolescent" dependence.

For an enlightening comparison of colonial "youth" and modern "adolescence," see his "Cares for the Rising Generation," pp. 20-23.

76. For discussions of the educational significance of the Great Awakening, see Lawrence Cremin's *American Education*, pp. 310-321; and Ross Beales, "Cares for the Rising Generation," pp. 92-122.

2

The Transformation of Massachusetts Education, 1670–1780

Jon Teaford

IN MARCH 1711, Cotton Mather declared that, "A lively Discourse about the Benefit and Importance of *Education*, should be given to the Countrey." "The Countrey," he asserted, "is perishing for want of it; they are sinking apace into Barbarism and all Wickedness." (1) Mather was convinced that formal education was being neglected in eighteenth-century Massachusetts, and for two centuries after Mather's death historians accepted his verdict. As early as 1835, Lemuel Shattuck described the late seventeenth and early eighteenth centuries as a *"dark age"* of learning. (2) Later historians used similar phrases. By the close of the nineteenth century, Edward Eggleston wrote the epitaph for early eighteenth-century education, "a period of darkness and decline." (3)

Mather's dictum stood unchallenged until 1934 when Clifford Shipton offered a less dismal view of eighteenth-century New England education. In "Secondary Education in the Puritan Colonies," Shipton argued that New England schools were improving rather than deteriorating during the period. Moreover, according to Shipton, the concern for education that typified the early Puritan remained strong throughout the eighteenth century. Shipton concluded by denying that there had ever been a "permanent collapse of secondary education in Puritan New England such as earlier studies indicated." (4)

More recently, Robert Middlekauff has reinforced Shipton's findings. In *Ancients and Axioms: Secondary Education in Eighteenth-Century New England*, Middlekauff found that "the community's devotion to literacy and classical learning" survived "the decline of religion and the commercialization of society which occurred in the eighteenth century." (5) Thus Middlekauff speaks of the "persistence of the Puritan tradition in education," declaring that "long after the Puritans disappeared, their educational tradition survived, a legacy to their commitment to intelligence and to humane values." (6)

Jon C. Teaford is professor of history at Purdue University.

It is only after the Revolution that Middlekauff found alterations in the Puritan tradition of education. According to Middlekauff, classical learning played the dominant role in secondary education from the founding of the first New England schools in the 1630s to the time of the American Revolution. But after the Revolution the dominant position of classical learning was seriously challenged by "useful" learning—science, mathematics, geography, writing, the modern languages. Middlekauff attributes this shift from tradition to the experience of the American Revolution. He writes: "Though New England's chief institutions survived the Revolution almost totally unaltered, its cast of mind did not. . . . Freedom made Americans self-conscious; it engaged their attention to the problem of what they were; it stretched their sense of what they might become. So preoccupied, they became eager in the search for fresh ideas about the future." (7) Among these fresh ideas were new thoughts on the purpose and nature of education. And out of this post-Revolutionary search for fresh ideas came support for an altered system of education, a system of education that offered an expanded curriculum of nonclassical subjects.

Yet Shipton and Middlekauff's interpretation is not a definitive answer to the question of educational decline. The debate continues, and both sides have presented convincing arguments supported by a mass of evidence. The many presentments for neglect of schooling seem to substantiate the view of Shattuck and Eggleston, while the vitality of private education during the eighteenth century seems to favor the interpretation offered by Shipton and Middlekauff. Each side has accumulated a multitude of examples supporting its position. Those who agree with Shattuck and Eggleston can point to the decadence of the classical tradition in a town such as Newton, and in rebuttal Shipton and Middlekauff may note the vitality of the grammar school in nearby Cambridge. Thus any adequate description of what was happening in New England education must pursue a course that will resolve the contradiction between past interpretations.

But before attempting any analysis, it is necessary to examine what is meant by "Puritan tradition," for it is possible that at least some of the differences among historians may be based on confusions over the precise meaning of the concepts they employ. Though dissenters in religion, seventeenth-century Puritans were orthodox in their views on education. They were as devoted to the renaissance model of education as any Anglican, and they too emphasized instruction in the ancient languages, especially Latin. The renaissance model, however, did not neglect the mastery of the English tongue. The educator John Brinsley expressed the prevailing seventeenth-century view when he listed first among the goals of education, "to teach scholars how to be able to read well, and write true orthography in a short time." (8) Yet one of the chief reasons for teaching English reading and writing to the younger students was that this elementary knowledge would supposedly aid the child in acquiring proficiency in Latin. The schoolmaster Richard Mulcaster, speaking of elementary instruction in English reading and writing, stated that, "the entry to language and the judgment thereof by grammar is the end of the Elementary." (9) Rather than concern himself with this preparatory education, the accomplished and respected schoolmaster devoted his primary effort to classical instruction. Brinsley wrote that teaching reading and writing to the little children of the town must be "borne with patience and wisdom, as an heavy burden." (10) Brinsley was not completely resigned to bearing this burden and instead suggests, "There might be some other school in the town for these little ones. . . . It would help some poor man or woman, who knew not how to live otherwise, and might do that well, if they were rightly directed." (11) Instruction in the vernacular was assigned a low priority and could be left to the poor and incompetent, thus enabling the trained and educated schoolmaster to devote himself to the more important calling of teaching Latin. (12)

The first Puritan colonists carried this renaissance model of education to New England. As early as 1642, the legislators of the Massachusetts Bay Colony enacted a law requiring that all children be taught to "read & understand the principles of religion & the capitall lawes of this country." (13) Five years later, the Massachusetts Bay General Court ordered that every town of one hundred or more families must support a grammar school. (14) By 1651, eight Massachusetts communities had established classical grammar schools. (15) Thus the early New England colonists dedicated themselves to establishing in the New World a standard of education comparable to that of the Old.

Yet New England education did not remain static during the colonial period. Rather, by the last decades of the seventeenth century there appeared the first signs of change. Beginning in the 1670s, a growing number of towns failed to maintain grammar schools, and many of those towns which had earlier funded schools now closed them. Townspeople bickered over the necessity of a classical education and attempted to evade requirements set by the magistrates. During these closing years of the seventeenth century, the courts frequently presented towns for failing to support grammar schools. The judges who presided over the county courts did not overlook the town's neglect of grammar schooling but adhered to the educational standards of the original colonists.

The Massachusetts Council was equally relentless in enforcing the educational standards of the law of 1647. As Robert Middlekauff writes: "The Council took a simple but firm stand: it would listen to pleas for the suspension of the school laws but it would not suspend them." (16) A majority of the members of the lower house favored suspension in 1705 and passed a resolve freeing towns from punishment for neglect of grammar schooling. The Council, however, "voted a nonconcurrance," holding firm in defense of traditional standards of education. (17) Thus in the late seventeenth and early eighteenth centuries, the courts and Council persisted in their adherence to the Puritan tradition of education, despite the negligence of the towns and the lenience of the representatives.

This neglect of grammar schooling may represent either a change in attitude toward the education or a necessary compromise with external factors. For Shattuck and Eggleston, this neglect is indicative of an emerging anti-intellectual attitude among the people of Massachusetts. Shipton and Middlekauff, however, deny any change of attitude and instead contend that the neglect of grammar schooling was a temporary symptom of the tribulations plaguing Massachusetts between 1675 and 1713. Indian warriors harassed the inland towns of Massachusetts, periodically destroying frontier settlements and disrupting any attempts at permanent schooling. Defense tended to receive top priority and not education. Towns were taxed heavily to ensure the defense of the colonies, and thus funds available for schools dwindled. According to Shipton and Middlekauff, once the Indian threat subsided, widespread neglect of grammar schooling ceased. Shipton and Middlekauff have also argued that a shortage of schoolmasters rather than a decline in educational zeal forced many of the schools to close. To substantiate this contention, they cite the small number of Harvard graduates, and consequently the small number of potential schoolmasters during the years 1675 to 1713. (18)

Yet the Indian threat and the shortage of schoolmasters cannot fully explain the widespread neglect of grammar schooling during the Colonial period. The greatest number of presentments occurred during the war years, but presentments continued, though in diminished numbers, during the years of peace. After 1713, the threat of Indian attacks on Middlesex County towns ended, and yet from 1721 to 1763 the Middlesex County Court found it necessary to issue 18 presentments against delinquent towns. (19) During these same years following the Peace of Utrecht, there was an ample supply of Harvard graduates. In the decade from 1721 to 1730, Harvard graduated 381 students, the highest number for any decade in the period from 1700 to 1763. (20) Yet during this same decade the Court of Quarter Sessions of Middlesex County alone heard six cases of towns failing to employ a grammar school master. By 1726, there was such an abundance of schoolmasters that one unemployed master found it necessary to advertise for a school offering his services to "Any Town that wants a School-Master to Teach Latin, Read and Write English, and learn Arithmetic & c." (21) Thus the neglect of Massachusetts' grammar schools cannot be seen as a temporary aberration characteristic only of a short period of disorder. Something beyond the mere circumstances of the Indian wars seemed to have influenced the course of New England education.

Some historians, including Bernard Bailyn, have argued that the relative poverty of many inland Massachusetts towns prevented them from fulfilling their obligations to education. According to this hypothesis, the townspeople of the inland and frontier settlements did not forsake the ideal of the grammar school, but often failed to realize this ideal owing to lack of funds. Bailyn contends that there was no change in attitude toward education during the Colonial period but rather a compromise with financial realities. Thus Bailyn argues:

There took place not an abandonment of the original high ideals, not a general regression of educational and intellectual standards, but a settling into regional patterns determined by the more ordinary material requirements of life. The most sensitive institution was the grammar school, and the greatest pressures upon its continuation were in inland isolated hamlets. In inland communities where two generations contact with cultural centers had been few and the physical demands of everyday life severe, the laws relating to any but the most elementary schooling were neglected and evaded. (22)

One cannot deny that mere living on the frontier was a hardship. Many of the inland towns had been outposts in the warfare of 1675 to 1713, and during these years suffered devastation. Thus Bailyn's explanation of the neglect of grammar schools on the frontier is probably valid. (23) But he is mistaken when he says that the neglect of grammar schools conforms to "regional patterns determined by the more ordinary material requirements of life." The communities presented usually were not victims of grinding poverty, nor were they necessarily isolated from cultural centers. And the "physical demands of everyday life" in these delinquent towns do not seem to have been unusually severe.

As noted before, between 1721 and 1763, the various towns of Middlesex County were presented 18 times for failing to support a grammar school. Yet Middlesex County was also the seat of one of the chief cultural centers of New England, Harvard College. Three of the delinquent towns lay within ten miles of the Harvard campus. Further, the chart below reveals that according to provincial tax assessments most of the towns presented were not poor struggling communities.

In ten of the cases, the communities presented were above the median according to wealth. In three cases the towns presented were among the top third of Massachusetts towns in wealth. Eight of the towns were below the median, and in only three of the cases were the towns in the bottom third. Thus among the towns presented in Middlesex County, the majority were of above average wealth, and only a few could perhaps meet Bailyn's description.

In other counties we also find examples of relatively wealthy towns being presented for failing to employ a grammar school master. For example, in 1741, Springfield, Massachusetts, was presented for not maintaining a grammar school. According to the provincial tax assessment, Springfield was among the wealthiest ten percent, paying a tax to the province of £262.1os. (25) Likewise Haverhill, in Essex County, was presented in 1751 for not keeping a grammar school. That same year Haverhill paid a provincial tax of £223.2s. ranking as the 28th wealthiest town out of a total of 170 in Massachusetts. (26)

Chart of Towns Presented in Middlesex County (24)

1721–1763

Town	Year	Rank According to Wealth
Newton	1762	45th out of 207
Groton	1748	43rd out of 160
Billerica	1727	41st out of 127
Framingham	1750	55th out of 160
Chelmsford	1726	43rd out of 124
Chelmsford	1724	43rd out of 113
Chelmsford	1721	43rd out of 112
Billerica	1724	45th out of 113
Billerica	1721	45th out of 112
Chelmsford	1742	75th out of 158
Weston	1737	81st out of 147
Sherburn	1761	114th out of 197
Littleton	1748	101st out of 160
Hopkinston	1757	121st out of 183
Westford	1750	107th out of 160
Stow	1758	124th out of 184
Stow	1749	115th out of 160
Stoneham	1737	120th out of 147

From town records, it is possible to discover a number of examples of towns which failed to keep grammar schools yet spent large sums on other projects which they seem to have held more important and necessary. Framingham was presented in March 1717 for failing to maintain a grammar school. Again in 1749 the grand jury presented the town for having failed to support a grammar school for some years and imposed a fine of 11 pounds and 7 shillings. Framingham finally hired as grammar school master, a Benjamin Webb (Harvard, 1743), in 1751, paying him 35 pounds "lawful money" per year. In other words, it cost the town 35 pounds "lawful money" (about 120 pounds old tender) to maintain a grammar school. If Bailyn's interpretation is valid, this sum must have laid an impossible financial burden on the town. Yet the truth is otherwise. In 1745, the townspeople appropriated for ordinary town expenses the sum of 750 pounds old tender, and in 1735 the town built their second meeting house at a total cost of 900 pounds old tender. This meeting house was the pride of Framingham. It rose three stories, stretched 55 by 42 feet, and had two stairways. One less story or one less stairway would probably have paid for a grammar school, and yet the townspeople seem to have felt that the money would be spent more wisely in aggrandizing the meeting house than in providing a classical education. The accounts of generous spending in the Framingham records prove that the town was not without funds. But the townspeople did not choose to lavish their money on a grammar school. (27)

Poverty, cultural isolation, and the disorders of war cannot adequately explain the widespread neglect of grammar schooling in late seventeenth- and eighteenth-century Massachusetts. As in the case of Framingham, long-settled and relatively wealthy towns close to the cultural centers of New England frequently failed to maintain grammar schools. Neither financial reality nor the Indian threat forced these prosperous communities to neglect grammar schooling. Instead, the delinquent towns by their own volition allowed their grammar schools to lapse. It seems then that the growing neglect of grammar schools should be attributed to a change in the attitude of the people of Massachusetts toward classical education. The townspeople of Massachusetts no longer seem to recognize the necessity and worth of grammar schooling. That devotion to the ideal of the classical grammar school, so apparent during the first decades of settlement, by the eighteenth century seems to have been gradually disappearing.

The records of the county courts for the second half of the eighteenth century seem to reflect this changing attitude. In the early eighteenth century, the numerous presentments were witness to the courts' vigorous enforcement of the school laws. But by the 1760s and 1770s, there were fewer and fewer presentments. Twenty-nine presentments appear in the Middlesex County Court Records for the years between 1700 and 1720, while in the period from 1760 to 1780 there were only two presentments. From 1763 through the Revolutionary War, none of the towns of Middlesex County were presented for failing to maintain grammar schools. There are two possible explanations for this drop in presentments. Either the towns had decided to comply with the school laws or the courts had abandoned their efforts to enforce these laws. Robert Middlekauff argues for the first of these alternatives. (28) Yet in fact violation of the school laws did not cease. A majority of Massachusetts towns continued to violate the grammar school requirement. According to the census of 1763–1765, 144 towns in Massachusetts contained 100 families or more. (29) Yet Middlekauff's own estimate is that only 65 Massachusetts towns maintained grammar schools in 1765. (30) If one accepts this estimate, then 55 percent of the towns were violating the grammar school law, while only a minority complied.

Since there was no census for Massachusetts before 1763–1765, it is impossible to know exactly how many towns contained 100 families or more during the earlier decades of the eighteenth century. Therefore, it is difficult to compare the percentage of towns violating the school law during the 1760s with the percentage of the presentment-ridden period from 1700 to 1720. Figures for Middlesex County alone, however, give some suggestion of the percentage of towns delinquent in the first decade of the eighteenth century. A list of polls of Middlesex County in 1708 indicates that nine towns in the county contained more than 100 families. (31) Of these nine, Walter Small estimates that only five had attempted to found a grammar school, but only four succeeded. (32) Thus only four out of nine, or 44 percent, were complying with the school law in 1708. If Middlesex County is representative of all of Massachusetts in 1708, then the percentage of towns violating the school law during the first decade of the eighteenth century may have been very near equal to the percentage for the 1760s.

The towns of Middlesex County had a better record of compliance during the 1760s than that of Massachusetts as a whole. In the years 1763–1765, at least eight Middlesex towns of 100 houses or more failed to maintain grammar schools. (33) About 33 percent of the towns of Middlesex County having over 100 families were violating the school law, while 67 percent were fulfilling their legal obligation. Though eight towns were delinquent, the county court only presented two towns in the 1760s. In the 1770s, no towns were presented, but prior to the opening of the Revolution in 1775 at least nine Middlesex towns were delinquent. (34)

Since there was widespread evasion and no increase in compliance it must be concluded that the drop in presentments was due to a slackening of enforcement. The county courts were no longer dedicated to enforcing total compliance but increasingly overlooked violations of the school laws. As a result of the courts' indifference, the school laws had virtually become a dead letter. The courts had long been the staunch defenders of the grammar school tradition, but by the time of the American Revolution, they had abandoned the Puritan cause of classical learning.

By the second half of the eighteenth century, the General Court had also abandoned the classical cause. Through the late seventeenth and early eighteenth centuries the General Court attempted to foil delinquent towns by increasing the fine for neglect, thereby making it commensurate with the salary of a grammar school master. After 1718, however, the General Court did not raise the penalty for neglect. Yet up until the Revolution the average salary of a grammar school master continued to increase. Thus it became much cheaper for a town to pay the penalty than to hire a schoolmaster. Further, during the eighteenth century no new methods of enforcement or punishment were enacted to coerce towns into compliance. Instead the General Court consistently disregarded the numerous violations of the school law.

There are even signs of the Council forsaking the grammar school idea. From 1700 to 1713, many petitions for remission of fines were received from ravaged frontier towns plagued by recurrent Indian attacks. The Council refused to accede to those petitions. In 1767, however, the Council readily concurred with a resolution excusing Sturbridge from paying for not maintaining a grammar school. Yet in contrast to the frontier towns of Queen Anne's War, Sturbridge claimed to have suffered only from unspecified "Difficulties of . . . Scituation" and "Great Charges in Settling a minister." (35)

During the Revolution, the grammar school tradition collapsed entirely. Throughout Massachusetts, grammar schools closed their doors, and the courts made no attempt to enforce the school laws. (36) The neglect of grammar schools during the Revolution is somewhat reminiscent of the neglect of grammar schools during the Indian wars of 1675 to 1713. During both the Revolution and the Indian wars the burdens of defense bore heavily on the grammar schools. Yet there was one very important difference between the two wartime periods of neglect. At the time of the Indian wars, the county courts and General Court attempted to force towns to maintain the classical tradition of education. The courts and Provincial Congress during the Revolution made no such attempts to save the grammar schools from neglect. The bench overlooked the widespread violations of the school laws and refused to issue any more stringent reprimands or penalties. Both the courts and Congress made no attempt to save the waning grammar school tradition. Instead they watched it perish with seeming unconcern.

Thus by the 1760s and 1770s, the hard core of support for the Puritan tradition of classical grammar schools had virtually disappeared. The former defenders of the grammar school tradition had either abandoned the cause or at least become a great deal more tolerant of the tradition's enemies. The tradition was moving toward extinction, and very few people were attempting to keep it from reaching that fate. Both the courts and legislature were content to allow the grammar school tradition to die a slow and gradual death.

As noted before, for Shattuck and Eggleston, this waning devotion to classical education signified a dark age of learning. Yet education includes more than Latin grammar, and one cannot describe a period as a "dark age" simply because the popularity of Homer and Cicero were in decline. In order to test Shattuck and Eggleston's view that New England education was in a state of decline, it is necessary to discard their classical bias and examine English and vocational education as well as grammar schooling.

Like their British counterparts, the first grammar schools in New England usually taught reading and writing to the younger children, while placing prime emphasis on Latin instruction. There were no schools specializing in instruction in English, and beyond the level of the most rudimentary skills no schooling in nonclassical subjects was available. Beginning in the late seventeenth century, there arose in Massachusetts a number of town-supported writing schools and private vocational schools providing instruction in subjects neglected by the classical grammar schools. Thus during the late seventeenth and eighteenth centuries, the neglect of grammar schooling is accompanied by the expansion of English and vocational schooling.

The first to offer a more advanced English education were the private writing masters. As early as 1667, Will Howard was licensed "to keep a wrighting schoole, to teach children to writte and to keep accounts." (37) In 1684, the townspeople of Boston voted to establish the first town-supported writing school, later known as the "Writing School in Queen Street." (38) In 1700, the townspeople established a second writing school, the North Writing School, and, in 1720, a third one, the South Writing School. (39) These writing schools primarily taught writing and cyphering. Some masters also seem to have provided instruction in reading to those students who needed it. (40) Despite this seemingly elementary curriculum, it is important to note that the writing schools were not elementary schools designed to teach young scholars prior to their entry into grammar school. Contrary to the belief of Middlekauff, the writing schools as well as the grammar schools were what today might loosely be called secondary schools. (41) As seen in the chart below, the average range of ages of 104 boys attending the South Writing School during the years of 1761 to 1765 was 7 to 14. Likewise the grammar school scholars averaged in age from 7 to fourteen. The average writing school student then was not a child learning only the rudiments of reading and writing. Instead he was a boy acquiring the commercial skills of penmanship and cyphering prior to entering an apprenticeship.

Ages of Boys Attending the South Writing School
during the period 1761–1765 (42)

Years	Number of Students Born That Year	Age Range During the Period 1761–1765
1747	2	14–18
1748	6	13–17
1749	7	12–16
1750	13	11–15
1751	11	10–14
1752	10	9–13
1753	11	8–12
1754	12	7–11
1755	8	6–10
1756	5	5–9
1757	8	4–8
1758	2	3–7
1759	1	2–6

Further, there is some evidence which suggests that the entrance requirements for the writing schools and grammar schools may have been virtually the same. John Proctor, master of North Writing School, stated at a meeting of selectmen, April 15, 1741, "that he refus'd none of the Inhabitants Children, but such as could not Read in the Psalter." (43) And Harrison Gray Otis recalled in a letter written late in his life that the "probationary exercise" required for admittance to the grammar school was "reading a few verses in the Bible." (44) Thus instead of preparing boys for entry into a classical curriculum, the writing schools seem to have offered a secondary education paralleling that of the grammar schools.

The establishment of writing schools was an important innovation in Massachusetts education. As noted earlier, writing and arithmetic had occupied a very subordinate position in the curriculum taught by the grammar school master. Some grammar school masters in both England and New England were even known for their poor penmanship. Grammar school masters were university graduates trained in the classical languages, not the intricacies of the calligrapher's art. In his *Ludus Literarius,* Brinsley had devoted a chapter to explaining the way in which a grammar school master could teach his students to write "though himself be no good penman." (45) In the same book Brinsley noted that, "few Masters or Ushers are fit penman to write such copies as are necessary." (46) But in the writing schools such as those established in Boston before the close of the seventeenth century, writing and arithmetic were taught by masters skilled in penmanship and accounts. Now, provided with professional instructors, writing and arithmetic were no longer neglected. Future bookkeepers were taught to cast accounts and future scriveners were instructed in the various ornate hands popular in the seventeenth and eighteenth centuries. The flourishing trade of Boston demanded an educated commercial class with a mastery of figures and a legible hand, and with the establishment of writing schools this demand was satisfied.

The numerous private schools of eighteenth-century Massachusetts offered instruction in other vocational subjects. In 1709, Owen Harris placed an advertisement in the *Boston News-Letter* for his school offering instruction in "Writing, Arithmetick in all its parts; And also Geometry, Trigonometry, Plain and Sphaerical, Surveying, Dialling, Gauging, Navigation, Astronomy; The Projection of the Sphaere, and the use of Mathematical Instruments." (47) Other private school masters of eighteenth-century Boston taught fortification, gunnery, "Bookkeeping after the Italian Method of Double Entry," "Foreign Exchanges, either in French or in English," "divers sorts of Writing, viz., English and German Texts; the Court Roman, Secretary and Italian Hands." (48) All these subjects were also taught in evening schools "for the Benefit of those who cannot attend by Day." Thus the private schools of eighteenth-century Boston provided instruction in a wide range of vocational subjects alien to the traditional classical curriculum.

There are no figures on how many children attended these private schools, but there are a few records which suggest that these schools trained a fairly large number of students. For example, at the private schoolmaster Samuel Grainger's funeral, there were "about 150 Children who were under his Tuition walking before the Corpse." (49) This estimate of enrollment is consistent with the fact that Grainger employed an usher to aid in the teaching. In the town writing schools an usher was hired only if there were at least 150 to 200 pupils. This figure of 150 to 200 pupils is approximately equal to the total number of grammar school students in the town of Boston. Therefore if estimated private school attendance is added to the figures for writing school attendance, the total number of students studying a nonclassical curriculum dwarfs the number enrolled in the grammar schools.

A comparison of the attendance figures for Boston's town-supported grammar and writing schools also reveals the increased popularity of the vocational as opposed to the classical curriculum. Enrollment in the grammar schools declined during the eighteenth century, while writing school attendance soared. In 1727, there were 210 scholars in the grammar schools and 220 in the writing schools. (50) A comparison of these figures with the average enrollment figures for the years 1765–1767 reveals that during this 40-year period grammar school enrollment dropped 16 percent, while writing school enrollment rose 241 percent. (51) During this same period, the population of Boston increased approximately 19 percent. There was, then, an increasing demand for instruction in the skills of penmanship and cyphering accompanied by a declining interest in the traditional classical studies.

As early as the late seventeenth century, then, there appeared signs of the change in education that Robert Middlekauff believes was the result of the American Revolution. The Puritan emphasis on classical learning was giving way to an emphasis on vocational learning. Prior to the Revolution, instruction was available in a long list of nonclassical subjects as well as in the traditional curriculum of Latin and Greek. The change Middlekauff sees after the Revolution is therefore merely the culmination of prerevolutionary educational developments.

Advances in English and vocational education were not limited to Boston. During the late seventeenth century, writing schools began to appear in many Massachusetts communities. For example, in the town records of Chelmsford there is the following entry:

Agust the 26th 1699. the selectmen of said towne Apointed Samuel Fletcher Junr Schoolmaster to Learne young persons to write; on the Day Above said Selectmen Apointed for Scooldames: Moses Barretts wife and Joshua Fletchers wife. (52)

In Chelmsford, as in Boston, it seems that a knowledge of the alphabet and the rudimentary skills of reading were taught by school dames, while the older boys continued their English education under the tutelage of a writing master.

The multiplication of town supported writing schools was accompanied by the appearance of a number of private vocational schools throughout the commercial towns of Massachusetts. Newspaper advertisements indicate that private vocational schools offered instruction in at least Salem, Marblehead, and Newburyport. (53) Thus while Boston set the pace in educational development, the other towns of Massachusetts were not far behind.

The views of the townspeople of Worcester were representative of prevailing attitudes toward education in the inland communities of eighteenth-century Massachusetts. While the townspeople of Worcester faithfully promoted English education, they were very vocal in their opposition to classical learning. Twice, in 1728 and 1736, the town was presented for failing to employ a grammar school master. When Worcester eventually hired a grammar school master, it did so only out of fear of further punishment. For in 1740 the townspeople voted that "the body of the town keep a grammar school the whole year, and save the town from presentment." (54) In the 1760s, the townspeople of Worcester explicitly rejected the grammar school tradition. The town meeting of Worcester in 1766 instructed their representative to the General Court, "That the law for keeping of Latin grammar schools be repealed and that we be not obliged to keep more than one in a county and that to be kept at the county charge." (55) And in 1767 they again directed their representatives to:

Use your endeavors to relieve the people of the Province from the great burden of supporting so many Latin grammar schools, whereby they are prevented from attaining such a degree of English learning as is necessary to retain the freedom of any state. (56)

These instructions to Worcester's representative exemplify the reversal of educational priorities among eighteenth-century New Englanders. The early Puritans believed that if the schoolmaster was required to spend much of his time teaching the young children to read and write, it would prevent him from giving adequate instruction in the classical languages. Instruction in reading and writing were, if possible, relegated to a school dame, thereby allowing the schoolmaster to devote himself to the more important subjects of the classical curriculum. In Worcester's instructions to its representative, however, the townspeople did not ask that English education be sacrificed for the sake of Latin instruction, as they would have done in the 1630s. For the people of Worcester, English education was of top priority and not classical learning.

The transformation of Massachusetts education during the Colonial period is then a reversal of priorities. Devotion to the traditional classical curriculum gradually gave way to ever increasing support for vocational and English learning. By 1780, the grammar schools were faltering while the town writing schools and private vocational schools were flourishing. But contrary to the view of Robert Middlekauff, the classical curriculum of the grammar school did not give way to the diversified curriculum due to a change in attitude resulting from the Revolution. Instead the change in attitude gradually evolved during the century prior to the Revolution. It was during this century that the writing and vocational schools were founded, and the grammar schools sorely neglected. The disorder arising from the war may have accelerated the neglect of grammar schooling. Yet regardless of the Revolution, changing priorities in education would have eventually demanded some compromise between the English and classical curriculums.

NOTES

1. Cotton Mather, *Diary* (New York: 1957), II, 51.
2. As quoted in William Lincoln, *History of Worcester, Massachusetts* (Worcester, 1862), p. 248.

3. Edward Eggleston, *The Transit of Civilization* (New York, 1901), p. 235. Similar views are expressed by George H. Martin, *Evolution of the Massachusetts Public School System* (New York, 1902), p. 69; and Walter Small, *Early New England Schools* (Boston, 1914), p. 57.

4. Clifford K. Shipton, "Secondary Education in the Puritan Colonies," *New England Quarterly,* VII (1934), 661.

5. Robert Middlekauff, *Ancients and Axioms: Secondary Education in Eighteenth-Century New England* (New Haven, 1963), pp. 8–9.

6. *Ibid.,* p. 195.

7. *Ibid.,* pp. 114–15.

8. John Brinsley, *A Consolation for Our Grammar Schooles* (New York, 1943), p. 52.

9. Richard Mulcaster, *The First Part of the Elementarie* (London, 1582), p. 55.

10. John Brinsley, *Ludus Literarius* (Liverpool, 1917), p. 13.

11. *Ibid.*

12. There is evidence that early American schoolmasters shared Brinsley's attitude toward elementary instruction in English reading and writing. Both Ezekial Cheever, New Haven's first schoolmaster, and his successor, Bowers, complained of having to devote too much time to instructing abecedarians. See Samuel Eliot Morison, *Puritan Pronaos* (New York, 1936), p. 97.

13. *Records of Massachusetts Bay in New England* (Boston, 1854), II, 6.

14. *Records of Massachusetts,* II, 203.

15. According to Samuel Eliot Morison: Boston (1636), Charlestown (1636), Salem (1637), Dorchester (1639), Cambridge (1642), Roxbury (1646), Watertown (1651), Ipswich (1651), Morison, *Pronaos,* pp. 96–97.

16. Middlekauff, p. 33.

17. *Massachusetts Acts and Resolves,* (Boston, 1869), VII, 593.

18. Shipton, "Secondary Education," *N.E.Q.,* VII (1934), 653; Middlekauff, p. 35.

19. Chelmsford (1721, 1724, 1726, 1742), Billerica (1721, 1724, 1727), Weston (1737), Stoneham (1737), Littleton (1748), Groton (1748), Stow (1749, 1758), Westford (1750), Framingham (1750), Hopkinston (1757), Sherburn (1761), Newton (1762).

20. Computed from the figures recorded in *Sibley's Harvard Graduates,* volumes VI, VII, and VIII.

21. *Boston News-Letter,* Sept. 30, 1726, quoted by Vera Butler, *Education as Revealed by New England Newspapers Prior to 1850* (Philadelphia, 1940), p. 271.

22. Bernard Bailyn, *Education in the Forming of American Society* (Chapel Hill, 1960), pp. 81–82.

23. Most frontier towns, however, did not have 100 families and therefore were not required to maintain a grammar school. In 1765, only one of the six towns of Berkshire County had over 100 families.

24. Rank of the towns according to wealth computed on the basis of the provincial tax assessments recorded in the *Massachusetts Acts and Resolves.*

25. *Acts and Resolves,* II, 1028.

26. *Ibid.,* III, 584.

27. The information on Framingham gathered from D. Hamilton Hurd, ed., *History of Middlesex County* (Philadelphia, 1890), pp. 616–35.

28. Middlekauff, pp. 35–36.
29. Based on the census figures found in *Collections of American Statistical Association* (Boston, 1847), I, 148–56.
30. Middlekauff, p. 40.
31. Small, *New England Schools,* pp. 30–31.
32. *Ibid.*
33. Newton, Sherburn, Medford, Stow, Holliston, Tewksbury, Pepperell, and Acton. This is a tentative estimate based on town and county histories and town records. Not enough information was obtainable on Reading, Hopkinton, or Groton to know whether they maintained grammar schools or not.
34. Based on the census of 1776. The census of 1776 did not count the number of families. The average number of people per family in Middlesex County in 1765 had been 5.66. Therefore I have assumed that towns having over 566 inhabitants in 1776 had 100 families or more. According to my survey the delinquent towns were: Tewksbury, Holliston, Medford, Acton, Shirley, Townsend, Stow, Dunstable, and Dracut. Not enough information was obtainable on Groton, Reading, Hopkinton, and Wilmington.
35. *Acts and Resolves,* XVIII, 196.
36. For example, Braintree dismissed its grammar school master on April 24, 1775, and Topsfield did likewise on May 9, 1775. Leominster maintained a grammar school from 1765 to 1775, but in the latter year, the townspeople cut the school appropriation from 40 pounds to 12 pounds and voted to eliminate all classical instruction. Neither Braintree, Topsfield, nor Leominster were reprimanded by the court or Provincial Congress for their neglect of grammar schooling.
37. *Boston Town Records,* (Boston, 1881), VII, 36.
38. *Ibid.,* VII, 171.
39. *Ibid.,* VII, 240.
40. See, for example, *Boston Town Records,* VII, 164; and *Boston Town Records,* XII, 108.
41. Robert Middlekauff believes that the writing schools were designed to teach young children prior to their entry into grammar school. He writes, "Boston's citizens took satisfaction in their hierarchy of schools. It was one in which the functions and the constituencies of two kinds of schools remained distinct. At the first level, in the writing schools, young boys learned to read, write, and cypher; at the next, in the grammar schools, their older brothers, themselves graduates of the writing schools, studied Latin and Greek." (Middlekauff, p. 54).
42. Based on the list of students found in D. C. Colesworthy's *John Tileston's School* (Boston, 1887), pp. 49–55, and on the birth records as found in volume 24 of *A Report of the Record Commissioners of the City of Boston* (Boston, 1894).
43. *Boston Selectmen's Records* (Boston, 1881), VII, 288. Also the following entry appears in the *Boston Town Records* for May 8, 1741: "We have made enquiry into the Circumstances of the North Writing School, which consists of about Two Hundred and Eighty Scholars, A Master and Usher. . . . We don't find that any Children of the Town have been refused, that could Read in the Psalter. . . ." *Boston Records,* XII, 279).
44. Samuel Eliot Morison, *Life and Letters of Harrison Gray Otis* (Boston, 1913), p. 6.
45. Brinsley, p. 27.
46. *Ibid.,* p. 32.

47. *Boston News-Letter*, March 21, 1709, quoted by Butler, *Education as Revealed by Newspapers*, p. 218.
48. At least 113 advertisements announcing the opening of new private schools appeared in Boston newspapers from 1700 to 1775.
49. *Boston News-Letter*, Jan. 17, 1734, quoted by Robert Seybolt, *The Private Schools of Colonial Boston* (Cambridge, 1935), p. 16.
50. *Papers relating to the History of the (Episcopal) Church in Massachusetts* (n.p., 1873), p. 230, quoted by Shipton, "Secondary Education," *N.E.Q.*, VII (1934) 660.
51. Attendance figures for 1765-1767 found in Robert Seybolt's *Public Schools in Colonial Boston* (Cambridge, 1935), p. 64.
52. Hurd, *Middlesex County*, pp. 259-60. There are numerous examples of rural towns providing instruction in writing and arithmetic beyond the dame school level. On March 2, 1713, the townspeople of Framingham voted, "Lieutenant Drury and Ebenr Harrington to be school masters to instruct the youth of Framingham in writing; and the selectmen are appointed to settle school dames in each quarter of the town, which masters and mistresses are to continue until August next." (Hurd, *Middlesex County*, pp. 635-36). In the town of Leominster in the years 1751 and 1752, the people voted to choose a committee of three "to provid sum meat persons for winter and summer schooling, six weeks for a writing-school and the rest to be laide out for school dames." (Hurd, *History of Worcester County* [Philadelphia: 1889], p. 1216). In the year 1756, Leominster appropriated funds "to be expended for paying a master to keep a writing-school three months during the winter and the balance for hiring school dames as the selectmen should direct" (Hurd, *Worcester County*, p. 1216). The town of Bedford in 1758 a "writing school" in the center of town four months and a "women's teaching-school" six months in the quarters of the town (Hurd, *Middlesex County*, p. 824). At the time of his death in 1771, Captain Ephraim Brigham left Marlborough a permanent fund of 111 pounds, the interest of which was to be "annually expended in hiring some suitable person to keep a school in the middle of the town, to teach young people the arts of writing and cyphering" (Small, p. 236).
53. See, for example, advertisements in the following issues: *Essex Gazette*, July 21, 1772; Feb. 15, 1774; Oct. 25, 1774; and *Essex Journal and New Hampshire Packet*, Oct. 25, 1776.
54. Lincoln, *Worcester*, p. 249.
55. *Ibid.*, pp. 249-50.
56. *Ibid.*, p. 250. (I thank Professor Richard D. Brown for calling my attention to this item.)

3

The War with the Tutors: Student-Faculty Conflict at Harvard and Yale, 1745–1771

Kathryn McDaniel Moore

MOST HISTORICAL DESCRIPTIONS of the relationship between tutors and students in early American higher education have tended to emphasize elements of consensus and community. (1) Historians such as Morison and Smith have suggested that the relationship was basically close and cordial, characterized by shared values and fostered by the small, homogeneous nature of the institution. (2) While not discounting the basic validity of this description, current research has begun to examine what one scholar has characterized as the "rising curve of collective student disorder." (3) By focusing on conflict as opposed to consensus new insights are provided about collegiate institutions, their modes of reaction to and acceptance of change, and a truer picture of their effectiveness as agents of society emerges. Moreover, by this approach students themselves must be taken seriously as more than passive recipients but rather as a force in their own right of institutional and even societal change. (4)

But once having acknowledged the need to take students into account a second set of issues arises; namely, explaining the causes of their behavior. Here again new research probes for answers. Novak's recent book on student revolt during the years 1798–1815 examines the workings of "generational consciousness" and its impact on collegiate authority. (5) This approach provokes many useful questions but it also has limitations. One in particular is pertinent to the research described below; namely, by defining and then focusing on student activism as the embodiment of a generational ideology more mundane but perhaps more immediate sources of conflict are overlooked, such as the characteristics of the students, the college teachers and officials, and their day-to-day relationships.

Kathryn McDaniel Moore is director and professor, Center for the Study of Higher Education, Pennsylvania State University.

It is possible that a basic cause of student discontent and rebellion during the eighteenth century lay in the system of social superiority upheld by the colleges and enforced by the tutors. But rather than seeking the explanation in an overarching ideology or even in college laws and customs, an alternative hypothesis is that there were social demographic differences between students and tutors and that these differences figured importantly in subsequent interactions. That is to say, it might have mattered as much who a student or tutor was as what he believed, and at least it is necessary to have both kinds of information. Thus, answers have been sought to three questions: 1) who were the college tutors?; 2) who were the students most often in conflict with tutors?; and 3) based on 1 and 2, are there any significant differences in the characteristics of both groups that tend to confirm or deny the conclusion that social distinctions were an important source of student-tutor conflict?

The study is based on an analysis of the published biographical data of the graduates of Harvard and Yale colleges, faculty records, student diaries and other materials available for the years 1745-1771. This period was chosen for a number of reasons. First, it was a time of considerable growth. Enrollments at both institutions reached levels they were not to attain again until the end of the century. Moreover, in each college these years encompass a single presidency, the Clap years at Yale and the Holyoke years at Harvard. Thus, serious fluctuations in presidential leadership through changeover is not an issue. It should also be noted that the rising tide of revolutionary fervor, while present and undoubtedly influential, is taken as a constant for both colleges and does not enter directly into consideration.

The analysis of demographic characteristics is not a new technique in historical studies, although it has only recently been used in major ways to analyze higher education. Research by Harris and others make it clear that the question of social class and status differentials among college graduates is a particularly useful one. (6) In order to examine whether or not such differences existed between tutors and students at Harvard and Yale two principal variables were used: father's occupation and student's occupation as recorded in the graduate's published biographies. During this period there were relatively few occupational categories; however, knowledge of an individual's occupation can be used to indicate (within limits) general income level, educational attainment, social position and sometimes political and religious preferences. In specific, father's occupation is a reasonably good predictor of whether or not a boy attended college and perhaps for what reasons.

Other demographic variables that figured in the analysis were place of residence, age at admission to college, and religious preference. Place of residence was taken as an indicator of the provinciality of the college and a possible basis of discrimination for or against students of particular regions. Age at admission is interesting in itself and also as a determinant of age gaps between tutors and students. Finally, religious preference is useful for analyzing the extent to which differential treatment was accorded of minority sects.

In the context of these general parameters, the first question to be examined is: Who were the college tutors? In the literature the typical picture of the tutorship is that of an "ill-compensated, low-status" temporary position made up of "youngsters for whom teaching was only a bypath to more desired careers. . . ." (7) In Shipton's words, it was a "miserable life." (8) However, subsequent studies have indicated that that is not the whole picture. According to Smith's research, as the Harvard tutorship developed over time, terms of service lengthened and a more favorable career climate emerged. By 1758 terms of nine years or more were common and even lifetime careers like Henry Flynt's were a possibility. (9)

When Smith's analysis of the tutorship at Harvard was extended to include another fifteen years, many previous conclusions held true. As Table 1 indicates, the average term (excluding Flynt's 55 years) continued to be nine years. The average age of the tutors at the beginning of their service was 27 years. Typically, they entered Harvard at the usual age of 16; graduated at 20 or 21, and then occupied themselves for some six or seven years before assuming a tutorship. Common activities for this interim period included keeping school (60 percent), other college offices, especially butler or librarian (50 percent) and continued education on the Hopkins or other fellowship (25 percent).

Of the 15 Harvard tutors who served during the period 1745–1771, 40 percent were eldest sons. As Table 2 indicates, their fathers' occupations were equally divided between the ministry (29 percent), farming (29 percent) and trade or manufacture (29 percent). The only other professional father was a Harvard professor. With regard to the tutor's own oc-

Table 1

Comparison of Characteristics of Harvard and Yale Tutors, 1745–1771

	Harvard N = 15	*Yale N = 36*
Average years as a tutor	9 years	3 years
Average age at start of tutorship	27 years	24 years
Average number of years between BA and tutorship	7 years	4 years
Activities prior to tutorship*		
a. kept school	9 (60%)	9 (25%)
b. fellowship	4 (27%)	11 (31%)
c. college officer	7 (47%)	2 (6%)

*Percentages total more than 100 because some tutors engaged in more than one activity.
Source: Clifford K. Shipton, *Sibley's Harvard Graduates* (Cambridge, Mass. 1936–1976). and Franklin B. Dexter, *Yale Biographies and Annals* (New York, 1885).

cupations, six (40 percent) made their careers in education with four being solely tutors, one a professor, and one a Harvard president. The ministry claimed five or one third of the tutors (a slightly larger percentage than the college average of 25 percent), and one fifth (three) became doctors or lawyers. Only one became a farmer. These data confirm Smith's contention that education was developing as a career. It is also indicative of the increasing attractiveness of the tutorship itself. By 1771 it had become a position which a selected group of men were willing to take up several years after their baccalaureates and pursue as a career for another nine or more years.

The Yale tutorship appears to have been a rather different experience. In the first place there were 36 or twice as many tutors during the same period, even though Yale enrollments were generally smaller than Harvard's. The average tenure was three years, and the waiting period between the bachelor's degree and the tutorship was only four years. Although Yale tutors entered college at the same age as their Harvard counterparts, they were younger when they took a tutorship, and they served a much shorter time. The primary interim occupations of the tutors were either keeping school, usually the one in New Haven (25 percent), or the Berkeley or Dean fellowships (31 percent). Only two of the 36 tutors held any other college office prior to their tutorship. Thus, a typical career line of the Yale tutor lay through winning a scholarship, while at Harvard it tended to be through other college offices.

Background information is available for 28 of the 36 Yale tutors. As Table 2 indicates, of this number, 46 percent of the Yale tutors had fathers who were ministers, with 21 percent in trade and 25 percent in the military or other public service. Occupational and other information was available for 32 of the 36 tutors. Of these, twenty (63 percent) went into

Table 2

Occupations of Harvard and Yale Tutors and Their Fathers

		Father's Occupations		Tutor's Occupations	
		Harvard	Yale	Harvard	Yale
1.	Ministry	4 (29%)	13 (46%)	5 (33%)	20 (63%)
2.	Farming	4 (29%)	2 (7%)	1 (7%)	1 (3%)
3.	Trade	4 (29%)	6 (21%)	–	1 (3%)
4.	Public Service	1 (7%)	7 (25%)	–	–
5.	Education	1 (7%)	–	6 (40%)	3 (9%)
6.	Law	–	–	2 (13%)	7 (22%)
7.	Medicine	–	–	1 (7%)	–
	Total	14 (100%)	28 (90%)	15 (100%)	35 (100%)

Source: Clifford K. Shipton, *Sibley's Harvard Graduates* (Cambridge, Mass., 1936–1976), and Franklin B. Dexter, *Yale Biographies and Annals* (New York, 1885).

the ministry with eleven (55 percent) following in their own fathers' footsteps. Seven tutors (19 percent) became lawyers while three (nine percent) had careers in education. Clearly the tutorship at Harvard and Yale each conforms to one of the stated hypotheses about the colonial tutorship. But based on these two colleges alone it is not possible to tell which representation in the literature is the more accurate for colonial colleges generally.

Scholarly debate regarding the second question: who were the students most often in conflict with the tutors, has to do specifically with the social class origins of such students. One contention which has been supported by Flacks and Keniston with regard to student conflict in the twentieth century and by Morison, Wertenbaker and Shipton for the eighteenth century is that student troublemakers tend to come from wealthy, permissive, upperclass families. (10) This is the theory that undergirds various studies of student protesters of the 1960's and of the student disrupters of campuses in the 1760's through 1830's. (11) Recently, however, research on indigent and rural students in several New England colleges during the antebellum period has shown how the increasing heterogeneity of student bodies began to erode the old system of discipline and belief, not so much by direct attack, although that was there, but by the sheer presence of new students as a group with whom colleges had to come to terms. (12) As Allmendinger states: "Disorder came from the mundane realities of student life and from the peculiar institutional weaknesses of the collegiate community in the early nineteenth century." (13)

In order to examine these alternative hypotheses information was collected on those students punished at Yale from 1745 to 1771. The broad outlines of student activism and indiscipline during the Clap years is wellknown, but less well studied in depth. The story is a familiar, even classic, one of a domineering, religiously orthodox president who waged a successful campaign for his views in the forum of public opinion only to be overthrown by determined student opposition on his own campus. Clap's personality and policies at Yale were the extreme opposite of Holyoke's at Harvard. In dealing with students Clap was inquisitorial, autocratic, religiously self-righteous and intolerant. His views on the purpose of Yale as a seminary to train a religious elite were well and widely known in his own day and were highly controversial in some quarters.

The data gathered from the faculty records and the Dexter biographies, indicate some of the parameters of the struggle between Clap, his handpicked tutors and the Yale students. (14) The sample of Yale students who were investigated included only those students whose names appear in the faculty records for more than one punishable offense. The numbers of single entries runs to approximately two hundred lawbreakers, but this includes notations for many minor offenses and fines. The number of recorded multiple offenders, whose crimes were usually more serious as well as more numerous, is fifty-five. This number excludes thirteen students who were reported as expelled. These students could not be included because Dexter's biographies, unlike Shipton's, do not include permanent expellees. In addition, one has the distinct impression that under Clap expulsion was truly a permanent state. This is in contrast to Harvard's unwritten policy of treating an expulsion as an extended suspension or rustication. Thus, the Yale multiple offenders are those students who committed two or more punishable offenses but who nevertheless succeeded in graduating, usually with their class.

Principal comparisons were made with the population of Yale graduates as summarized by Bailey. (15)   The most interesting comparisons concern residency, father's and student's own occupations. With regard to residency, Bailey reported that 78 percent of the total population of graduates came from Connecticut with the remainder coming from Massachusetts, New York and Long Island, Rhode Island and a miscellany of other places. The multiple offenders differ somewhat in that only 64 percent are Connecticut residents and 36 percent are from out of the colony.

With respect to father's occupation, the data are not comprehensive for either the general population or the offenders. Bailey can account for only 40 percent of the fathers' occupations. Data on the multiple offenders can account for 60 percent of their fathers' occupations. (16) Table 3 shows a comparative representation of fathers' occupations for the graduates and the multiple offenders. As the data indicate, the student offenders are different from their classmates in some important ways. First, almost twice the percentage of graduates' fathers were

Table 3

Father's Occupations of Yale Graduates and Multiple Offenders

	Graduates[*]	Multiple Offenders
Ministry	287 (35%)	6 (18%)
Farming	229 (28%)	5 (15%)
Trade	69 (8%)	13 (38%)
Public Service	36 (4%)	5 (15%)
Education	2 (1%)	–
Law	93 (11%)	–
Medicine	67 (8%)	2 (6%)
Manufacture	7 (1%)	2 (6%)
Miscellaneous	33 (4%)	1 (3%)
Total	823 (100%)	34 (100%)

[*]Recalculated from Bailey's statistics by eliminating the unknowns from the base. *Yale Review* (Feb., 1908): Also, Franklin B. Dexter, *Yale Biographies and Annals* (New York, 1885).

ministers compared to the offenders. This is further differentiated by the fact that of the six offenders' fathers who were ministers the majority were not Congregationalists; three were Anglican and one, a Baptist. The other important difference by father's occupation occurs in the category of trade. Nearly five times the percentage of offenders' fathers were engaged in trade compared with the general Yale population. Moreover, of this group of thirteen, ten were not merchants but sea captains. And indeed sea captains' sons form the single largest group of student offenders during the period.

An explanation of these discrepancies can be approached from two points of view. The first argues that Clap as a religious demagogue was notoriously intolerant and highly discriminatory in his treatment of students who did not profess his version of the Congregationalist faith. His treatment of the Cleaveland brothers deserves special note, but also his reluctant agreement to allow the Anglican students to have a separate worship. With regard to the sea captains' sons, it is likely that they were not perceived to be ministerial material and they probably did not comport themselves in the desired manner, thus the heavy hand of discipline fell upon them.

The other point of view is that there were apparently distinct groups of students who did not fit the primary mission of the college. Either they professed a different faith or they came from different backgrounds, particularly backgrounds which did not coincide with the beliefs and policies of the college governors. This difference led such students to oppose and attempt to thwart the government of the college. Their efforts were countered with the disciplinary measures available to the president and tutors in the college laws.

When the occupations of these student offenders are compared with the general Yale population, as indicated in Table 4, the result is fairly comparable. But the category of the ministry deserves note. Bailey calculated that for the entire century approximately 36 percent of the graduates became ministers. (See my recalculation of his figures in Table 4.) Calculations of the known occupations of the student offenders indicate that the percentage who entered the ministry was a comparable 33 percent. However, of the thirteen student offenders who became ministers, five were known to have failed in their calling because of intemperance, debt or bad character. Clap and his tutors would doubtless have felt some vindication of their treatment of these students in light of their apparent ability to identify "bad seeds."

These evidences of discriminant treatment of identifiable subgroups of students favors the possibility that family background was a better predictor of a student's disciplinary history than were his career "aspirations." This does not discount the fact that students could attend Yale and go on to succeed in becoming respected ministers, while some respected

Table 4

Occupations of Yale Graduates and Multiple Offenders

	Graduates*	Multiple Offenders
Ministry	729 (41%)	13 (33%)
Farming	115 (6%)	2 (5%)
Trade	230 (13%)	7 (18%)
Public Service	40 (2%)	3 (8%)
Education	67 (4%)	–
Law	346 (19%)	7 (18%)
Medicine	221 (12%)	7 (18%)
Manufacture	14 (1%)	–
Miscellaneous	28 (2%)	–
Total	1,790 (100%)	39 (100%)

*Based on a recalculation of Bailey's statistics by eliminating the unknowns (N = 225) from the base, *Yale Review* (Feb. 1908): 406. Also, Franklin B. Dexter, *Yale Biographies and Annals* (New York, 1885).

ministers' sons did ultimately lead ignominious lives. But these data still tend to support the notion that family background had an important effect upon the kind of experience a boy had while a student.

What do these findings contribute to an understanding of the conflictful side of the student-tutor relationship? The primary demographic differences between Yale tutors and students has to do with occupations. (See Tables 2 and 3 above). With respect to father's occupation, the interesting differences are in the catagories of minister and trade. While 46 percent of tutors' fathers were ministers, only 18 percent of the student of offenders had ministers for fathers. And both of these must be compared with 35 percent for the entire Yale population. Similarly, 38 percent of the students' fathers were traders, especially sea captains, as contrasted with 21 percent for the tutors and 8 percent for the entire population. It would seem that differences in background between tutors and offenders were dramatic and yet in predictable directions. Yale under Clap was primarily a Congregational seminary. Thus, it is understandable that Connecticut's Congregational ministers and their congregations especially would desire to send their sons there, the Great Awakening and its controversies to the contrary notwithstanding. The "best" of those sons, that is, those who fitted Clap's own preferences, would likely be chosen as tutors, the president's lieutenants. Moreover, their relative youth and rapid turnover in the tutorship would probably insure a closer following of the Clap policies. Contrast this with the maturity and length of service of the Harvard tutors who established themselves as a resident governing body by which they managed many college matters without Holyoke's immediate supervision.

It is also reasonable to assume that those students who were most likely to provoke and be provoked by the laws and customs of Clap's Yale would be those students who were in background and disposition most distinctly different from the mainstream. Few fit this better than the sea captains' sons or the sons of a different faith. In the first instance, the conflict in values is evident in the nature of the crimes for which they were punished. For the most part the crimes were either social or anti-authoritarian. These included, in order of frequency, card playing, tavern going, play-acting and riots, first; second, destruction of college property, while third in frequency but probably first in seriousness were acts of defiance, disobedience, or disrespect to college authorities.

In order to give life to these statistics; however, one must turn to the biographical detail about the students and tutors for whom the conflicts were real and vital. The Yale student who accumulated the most re-corded offenses was J. Denison (Y.C. 1756) whose name appears more than nine times in the faculty records. His father was a wealthy and pro-minent sea captain and West Indies trader. Denison entered Yale at 16. During his freshman year he was punished four times (usually by fines) for card playing, bell ringing, brandishing a pistol, and swearing and scuffling. His sophomore year he participated in three riots for which he was variously fined. His junior year he had several offenses for which he was deprived of the privilege of fagging underclassmen. And during his senior year he was convicted of stealing £10 from a fellow student and run-ning away. He was expelled for this last activity but was later degraded and restored. Upon graduation he joined his father in business and became a captain in his own right. (17)

The tie for second place for most notorious offender goes to Samuel Ely, (Y.C. 1764) whose father's occupation is unknown, and Winthrop Saltonstall (Y.C. 1756), the second son of General Gurdon Saltonstall (Y.C. 1726). Saltonstall appears to have confined himself primarily to a seige of bell ringing, but in his sophomore year he did run out on one punishment session which earned him a suspension for contempt. (18)

Ely stands out as a truly infamous character for whom Yale was a mere warmup. His crimes ranged from bell ringing in his freshman year to theft, cheating and card playing in his junior year. When senior year came his repeated offenses in combination with deficient scholarship got him rusticated for a full year. President Dwight who was a tutor at the time remembered him as "brazen-faced in his wickedness." Upon gradua-tion he became a minister but was soon dismissed for bad character. He next became something of a religious demagogue and was ultimately ar-rested and banished. (19) As these cases indicate, students could be as provoking as provoked. In extreme cases the college appears to have been long-suffering, especially if the family were prominent but even in the case of ne'er-do-wells like Ely.

Although it lacked a target for student rancor of the stature of Clap, Harvard also had its share of student-tutor conflicts. The excellent detail of the Shipton biographies is most helpful in uncovering the circumstances of many of these incidents. One of the best examples occurred in 1769 when the students launched a wholesale attack upon all the tutors. In typical Harvard style the battle was waged on both literary and physical fronts. The three tutors involved were Stephen Scales (H.C. 1763), Andrew Eliot (H.C. 1762) and Joseph Willard (H.C. 1765). (20) All three were minister's sons, but it was Willard, an eventual Harvard president, who conformed most uniformly to the older student pattern Allmendinger describes. Because of his stepfather's economic straits Willard worked as a schoolmaster before entering college. Consequently, he was 30 years old when he became a tutor while Scales and Eliot were 26 and 23 years old respectively. All three had reputations as able, even brilliant, scholars, but they were also known as haughty and supercilious. Needless to say it was the latter qualities which provoked the students to burn them in effigy one riotous evening. When the students were caught and punished, they revenged themselves by publishing a "number of scurrilous libels" in the form of a poem entitled, "A True Description of a Number of Tyrannical Pedagogues." The poem concludes with this advice to future students:

> "But if their tutors' mulcts grow wider every Hour,
> Wider their struts and arbitrare their Power,
> I would advise you Sons of Harvard then
> To let them know that you are sons of men." (21)

Perhaps because of the smaller number of tutors and their longer service there is more known about them as individuals than the Yale group. It seems safe to say that few if any tutors escaped some harassment from students, but one suspects that in general it was in direct proportion to the kind and degree of harassment they dealt students. The motivations for becoming a tutor and, indeed, for remaining for any extended time are difficult to discern. We do know that in general academic merit played a part. A large proportion of both Harvard and Yale tutors were recipients of scholarships and fellowships like the Hopkins and Berkeley which recognized scholarship and promise. Most of the Harvard tutors, as with the Yale group, prepared for the ministry, but those who made tutoring a career appear united in a dissatisfaction with the ministry. Either they developed a distaste for it or the parishioners who tried them out expressed a distaste for them. Few had as embarrassing an experience as one tutor, but it is indicative of a motive to persist in the tutor's role. One Sabbath Harvard tutor, Belcher Hancock, is reported to have discovered upon arrival to preach that a good part of the congregation had gone to another church "not being able to bear Mr. Hancock's Doctrines." (22)

It is also notable that several tutors at both colleges experienced various frailties, especially poor health. Yale in particular appears to have been hard on tutors; six died before the age of 30. Harvard for its part had to deal with two tutors who became notorious drunks. On the other side, tutors were not likely to miss desirable opportunities. It is surely no accident that Timothy Pitkin (Y.C. 1747) married one of Clap's daughters and William Kneeland (H.C. 1751) married one of President Holyoke's. In both cases the presidents lost a tutor because marriage was not permitted for any tutor.

These latter anecdotes point out the humanity of the educational enterprise in which students, tutors and presidents found themselves, but it does not deny the existence of pattern and system. First, family background counted for much more in this time than other "credentials." Thus, it is predictable that a tutor's career and a student's college experience might be predicated heavily upon assessments of that background. Second, there is no question that each college held and attempted to impart a distinct sense of mission to all members of its community. As chief officers in defense and promulgation of that mission, the tutors were carefully selected and directed in their efforts. Students who did not fit the college ideals were not chosen as tutors, neither were they afforded much room to challenge, disobey or thwart the college before its legal and social sanctions were invoked. And tutors were the primary agents in the administration of those sanctions.

While not yet a highly significant institution for status or career attainment, the college was nevertheless perceived as necessary by some, useful by others. Few were the men for whom the college itself became the focus of their life's work, but during the period under study Harvard was distinctive for the greatest stability and maturity of its tutor corps, while Yale had youth and zeal on its side. Despite clear differences in presidential leadership and tutorial characteristics there were serious struggles and discontents on the part of students at both institutions. The presence of conflict at both colleges speaks to the universality and significance of the confrontation. At both institutions the confrontation has as much if not not more to do with the manner by which the education was imparted by the tutors and the manner in which it was imbibed by the students. What is more, these disputes appear to be strongly, if not causally, linked to basic differences of social status between students and their tutors. Such differences reinforced, and were reinforced by, college custom and presidential direction.

NOTES

1. It should be noted, however, that Henry Adams was one of the earliest American historians to suggest that information about students would be a useful tool for understanding colleges and subsequently American society. Adams also contended that

"the relations between instructors and scholars were far from satisfactory," and that "the true grievance lay in the position of semi-hostility to the students taken by the college officers . . . The manner, not the act, of discipline was the cause of the evil." January 1872, as reprinted in Henry Adams, *Historical Essays* (New York, 1891), pp. 80-121.

2. Samuel Eliot Morison, *The Intellectual Life of Colonial New England* (Ithaca, N.Y., 1956) and Wilson Smith, "The Teacher in Puritan Culture," *Harvard Education Review,* 36 (1966): 402, respectively.

3. David Allmendinger, "The Dangers of Ante-Bellum Student Life," *Journal of Social History,* 7, 1 (Fall, 1973): 75.

4. Frederick Rudolph, "The Neglect of Students as a Historical Tradition," in Lawrence E. Dennis and Joseph Kauffman, *The College and the Student* (Washington, D.C., 1966), pp. 47-58.

5. Stephen J. Novak, *The Rights of Youth: American Colleges and Student Revolt 1798–1815* (Cambridge, Mass., 1977).

6. P.M.G. Harris, "The Social Origins of American Leaders: The Demographic Foundations," *Perspectives in American History,* 8 (1969): 159-346, also Sarah H. Gordon, "Smith College Students: The First Ten Classes, 1879-1888," *History of Education Quarterly,* 15, 2 (Summer 1975): 147-167.

7. Richard Hofstadter, *Academic Freedom in the Age of the College.* (N.Y., 1955), p. 24.

8. Clifford K. Shipton, *Sibley's Harvard Graduates,* IX (Cambridge, 1936), p. 68.

9. W. Smith, "The Teacher in Puritan Culture": 402.

10. Richard Flacks, *Youth and Social Change* (Chicago, 1971). Kenneth Keniston, *Radicals and Militants: Annotated Bibliography on Empirical Research on Campus Unrest,* (Lexington, Mass., 1973); Morison, *Intellectual Life,* and Thomas J. Wertenbaker, *Princeton, 1746–1896* (Princeton, 1946), and Shipton, *Sibley's Harvard Graduates, passim.*

11. See also Novak, *The Rights of Youth,* especially pages 38-57. For a detailed description of the characteristics of Harvard students who were involved in various acts against the college, its governors and property during the period 1636 to 1724, and for the eighteenth century generally see my "Old Saints and Young Sinners: A Study of Student Discipline at Harvard College 1636-1724," (Unpublished Phd. dissertation, University of Wisconsin, 1972). This research has tended to confirm the findings of other scholars regarding the upperclass backgrounds of student offenders.

12. David Allmendinger, *Paupers and Scholars* (New York, 1975).

13. Ibid. p. 110.

14. Franklin B. Dexter, *Yale Biographies and Annals* (New York, 1885); also "Record of the Judgments and Acts of the President and Tutors of Yale College 1751-1768," 3 vols., (handwritten ms. Yale University Archives). It should be noted that toward the end of Clap's term several tutors resigned in protest against his policies. But for the most part I have presumed the tutors were Clap's deputies.

15. William Bailey, "A Statistical Study of the Yale Graduates, 1701-92," *Yale Review* (1908): 400-426.

16. I concur with Bailey's assertion that farming is probably the least accurate estimate. In his survey 28 percent of the fathers were farmers; of the multiple offenders, 16 percent.

17. Dexter, *Yale Biographies,* 11, p. 415.

18. Ibid., 111, p. 68.
19. Ibid., 11, p. 429.
20. Shipton, *Sibley's Harvard Graduates,* XV, pp. 492-3, 224 and XVI, pp. 253-4.
21. Ms. Harvard University Archives, 1769.
22. Shipton, *Sibley's Harvard Graduates,* VIII, pp. 43-44.

4

The Eighteenth-Century Origins of the Split between Private and Public Higher Education in the United States

Jurgen Herbst

IN THE LATE eighteenth century are to be found the first beginnings of the to us so familiar division in American higher education between public and private institutions. Throughout most of the eighteenth century such distinction was unknown. Higher education and the preparatory Latin grammar schooling were viewed as intimately linked to the interests of state and church. This view applied to the three colleges existing in the first quarter of the century. Harvard, William and Mary, and Yale served as training centers for their provinces' political and professional leadership. They had been duly authorized and in part financially supported by their colonial legislatures. With the exception of Yale they were under the joint supervision and government of representatives of the colony's lay population and established church. These governmental arrangements reflected the Reformation concept of the unity of established secular and ecclesiastical government with the college, a concept which in turn rested on the assumed religious homogeneity of the province's population, Anglican in Virginia and Puritan in New England. (1) It was precisely this assumption of a religiously homogeneous population which could no longer be upheld in the eighteenth century. As it was being swept away by the appearance of Baptists and Quakers, Lutherans and Dutch Reformed as well as by the migration of Puritans and Anglicans into all the colonies, it could no longer provide guidelines for college founding and governance. As a consequence in colonies with existing colleges—Massachusetts, Virginia, and Connecticut—traditions of college governance came under fire, and the weakening alliance of state and church forced the colleges to redefine their own position. In colonies without an established church there emerged during the Great Awakening of the 1740s

Jurgen Herbst is professor of educational policy studies and of history at the University of Wisconsin—Madison.

a more particularistic perspective on college education as serving local or group interests and being largely without either financial support or direct governmental control from public authorities. (2)   It was under these conditions, also, that the first attacks appeared against the concept of a provincial college as a monopoly. These attacks were beaten back in 1762 in Massachusetts and in 1770 in Rhode Island. (3)   But when Queen's College opened in 1766 in New Jersey, a competing college appeared for the first time in one of the colonies, and a new development was inaugurated which, half a century later, would lead to the proliferation of the "private" colleges of the antebellum era.

The "typical" eighteenth century college—if one may postulate the existence of such an institution—operated under a policy of toleration, that is, nondiscrimination against students and professors of the various Protestant denominations. At the same time it showed preferment for the denomination of the college founders, that is, those who had founded and sponsored the college and who, more often than not, constituted a majority on the college governing board. Toleration with preferment could be found among already existing colleges, and it was instituted in the new foundations of the mid-eighteenth century. In the former, laymen and magistrates sitting on governing boards or speaking in legislatures argued the case for greater hospitality towards students and professors of all denominations. At Harvard they put orthodox Puritans and their allies on the defensive on the Board of Overseers. Under President Leverett the college accepted the endowments for two professorships from an English Baptist, and liberal Congregationalists gradually paved the way for the Unitarians of the next century. Using the official policy of toleration as an argument, ex-President Cutler of Yale, by 1727 an Anglican minister in Boston, claimed a seat on the Board of Overseers, although he failed to obtain it. (4)   At Yale President Clap fought a long and ultimately unsuccessful battle with his critics in the Assembly who wanted to insure greater legislative oversight of the college. A few weeks after Clap's forced retirement in 1766 the Assembly ordered an annual inspection of the college accounts, and in 1792 the state's governor and other civil officials were made trustees. (5)   In Virginia the struggle between the masters of the College of William and Mary and the gentry in control of the Board of Visitors brought victory to the latter, and here too diversity and toleration triumphed over the ideal of the territorial-confessional college. (6)

In newly created institutions the charters included prohibitions against the discrimination of students on religious grounds. Such phrases are contained in the 1746 and 1748 charters of the College of New Jersey (now Princeton), the 1754 charter of King's (now Columbia), the 1764 charter of the College of Rhode Island (now Brown), and the 1769 charter of Dartmouth College. The trustees of the College of Philadelphia (now the University of Pennsylvania) endorsed such a clause in 1764, nine years after the college charter had been authorized. Only the charter of Queen's College in New Jersey (now Rutgers) did not contain such a clause, presumably because the college was founded specifically for the benefit of members of the Dutch Reformed Church. But even here the 1770 charter declared that the college was "to promote . . . [the] advancement of a protestant religion of all denominations." At a majority of the newly founded eighteenth century colleges public officials were named *ex officio* to the governing boards and were thus to assure the public of its proper representation. Such appointments were most clearly announced in the charters issued by the Crown, if for no other reason than the Crown's interest in safeguarding the observance of a policy of toleration. At the College of New Jersey, at King's, Queen's and Dartmouth the governor of the province served as trustee. At the latter three colleges either the president or other members of the governor's council were included; at King's and Dartmouth also the speaker of the lower house, at King's and Queen's the Chief Justice or other judges of the Supreme Court and the Attorney General, and at King's the province treasurer and the mayor of the city of New York. Only the College of Philadelphia and the College of Rhode Island—two institutions in provinces known for their tolerance and liberality towards members of all faiths—had no *ex-officio* magistrates on their boards. (7)   By these non-discrimination clauses in college charters and by their inclusion *ex-officio* of magistrates on college governing boards most of the eighteenth century colonies tried to make sure that the interests of their people of all different Protestant denominations were protected in their respective provincial colleges against possible encroachment by the denomination which owned or governed the college.

But the non-discrimination clauses and the *ex-officio* participation of magistrates in college government were not always a sufficient answer to still the suspicions of those who objected to the basic assumption on which rested the policy of toleration. Toleration, the critics observed, went hand in hand with preferment for a particular church or denomination. In England the universities were Anglican institutions, and dissenters had found it necessary to open rival academies. In the colonies the College of New Jersey was founded by a group of presbyterian ministers who took a mediating position between Old Side orthodox and New Light liberal Presbyterians. It received no financial support from the colony, and was financially dependent on its students and presbyterian friends at home and abroad. (8)   In New York the Anglican founders of King's College, pointing to the real estate given them by Trinity Church, insisted that the religious services in the college be conducted according to the liturgy of the Church of England, and that the college president always be a member of that church. (9) In Rhode Island the Baptists as the initiators of the college insisted that their president always be a Baptist. (10) Toleration thus did not by any means guarantee equality to all denominational interests, and the critics of the policy vigorously assailed it. Best known among them was William Livingston, co-author and publisher of the *Independent Reflector* essays. Toleration, Livingston reasoned, was unworkable and infeasible. One could not assign to one particular church or denomination the ownership or government of a college, oblige this group to "tolerate" the presence and religious rights of other Protestants, and then assume that an equitable arrangement had been achieved. (11) The English policy of toleration as practiced in the colonies made one church or denomination "more equal" than the others, and therein lay its chief flaw.

Alternatives to the toleration with preferment policy were proposed by William Livingston, Ezra Stiles, and Theodore Frelinghuysen. Livingston introduced in 1754 a bill into the New York legislature for the establishment of a public college under the direct oversight of the Assembly. Such a college was to be an agency of the government, and its governing board was to function as a government committee. With his bill Livingston in fact outlined a prototype for what decades later would become the first American state university. (12) In the fifties, however, the proposal came to nothing. A second alternative model was suggested barely ten years later by Ezra Stiles on Rhode Island. Stiles, like Livingston a graduate of Yale College, was in 1763 a congregational minister in Newport, and had been asked by friends among the Baptists and Congregationalists to draft a charter for a provincial college. His was an idealistic vision of a truly inter-denominational college in which, through an intricate two board corporate governing scheme, a balance of denominational interests was to be achieved. Stiles did not believe in turning college government over to secular officials, nor did he even include magistrates *ex-officio* on the proposed college corporation. But he believed fervently in the possibilities for Christian cooperation and unity among Protestants of many denominations. He was, alas, far too optimistic. Rhode Island Baptists suspected "treachery" in Stiles' proposed charter, altered its provisions, and placed the management of the college securely into their own hands. (13) Frelinghuysen, finally, a leader among the Dutch Reformed of the middle colonies, shared Livingston's bitter opposition to the Anglican dominance at King's College. He resented what he called "the astonishing imposition of the encroaching party that would monopolize our intended college," and proposed instead that his fellow churchmembers give up chasing the utopia of interdenominational cooperation in college affairs and found a college of their own. This the Dutch Reformed did in the mid-sixties when Queen's College in New Jersey opened its doors to make it unnecessary for them to send "their youths intended for the ministry to a foreign country for education ... " (14) Unhappiness with the toleration and preferment model of college governance thus led to various other schemes. In New York we find an early germ for the later state university, in Rhode Island a suggestion for a multi-denominational college, and in New Jersey the first one-denominational college.

Frelinghuysen's project was the earliest of these to find concrete realization. With the chartering of Queen's College in 1766 the first steps were taken towards what became the nineteenth century private college. Faced with religious and ethnic pluralism the colonists in New Jersey discarded the concept of a provincial college monopoly established and safeguarded by the legislature. They acknowledged that, in the case of Queen's, they had authorized a college specifically and primarily for the benefit of the members of a particular church. Thus the new college was not to be a competitor with its neighbor at Princeton, but the latter's monopoly was nonetheless broken. After the Revolution the pattern set in New Jersey became familiar in other states as well. In Virginia a presbyterian academy, originally founded in 1776 as an alternative to the Anglican College of William and Mary, was incorporated as Hampden-Sydney College in 1783. A second newcomer appeared in 1782 as the degree-granting Liberty Hall Academy. It, too, had been founded by Presbyterians. These two schools challenged the monopoly of William and Mary, though, being presbyterian, they did not compete with the older college. Neither of them had public officials serving *ex officio* on their boards, and when Liberty Hall was incorporated as a college in 1813 (it is today known as Washington and Lee University) both colleges constituted early examples of the nineteenth century American private college. (15) But it wasn't until the 1830s and 1840s, as Tewksbury has shown, that the private denominational college came to flourish in large numbers. Then it nearly pre-empted the field and came to be viewed as *the* prototypical American college. (16)

Livingston's bill for a state college without ties to denominational religion also was to take on new life in the late eighteenth century. His suggestions bore fruit during the Revolution in the transformations of the College of Philadelphia into the University of Pennsylvania and of King's College into the University of the State of New York. (17) Other state universities were subsequently chartered in Georgia (1785), North Carolina (1789), Vermont (1791), Ohio (1802), South Carolina (1805), Maryland (1812), and Virginia (1819). (18) Together with the private denominational colleges these state universities came to constitute the two major traditions of American higher education in the nineteenth century. Stiles' vision of a multi-denominational Christian university, though proposed again by him and William Ellery in their 1770 draft charter for a college in Newport, remained but a dream. (19)   But even as such it was to exert a continuing appeal to those who, like Julian Sturtevant and Theron Baldwin of Illinois, sought to create a Christian state university as a cluster of denominational colleges under a multidenominational board responsible to the public. (20)   Finally, we must add a word concerning the lineal descendants of the eighteenth century college in the toleration with preferment tradition. Such institutions were founded in Maryland with Washington College in 1782 and St. John's College in 1784, in Kentucky with Transylvania University in 1783, and in New England with the congregational and presbyterian colleges of the 1790s and thereafter. These institutions bequeathed to the nineteenth century a concept of denominational stewardship for a community of Protestant Christians. Where this tradition continued it kept alive the confident assertion that men could indeed be their brother's keepers, an assertion born in this case of a unique mixture of the Enlightenment's confidence in man's reason and good will and of an Arminian faith in human ability to overcome selfishness and sin.

The nineteenth century, by and large, was not hospitable to the eighteenth century college. The private denominational college and the public state university became its rivals and eventually outgrew and overshadowed it. The eighteenth century college thus was a transitory phenomenon in the history of American higher education. As long as men of different Protestant persuasions were satisfied and willing to accept the concept of stewardship of one denomination in the education of their children, the eighteenth century college could function as a training ground for future professionals. But when with the revivals during the nineteenth century's first half denominational and sectarian differences assumed growing importance, many began to question the advisability and even feasibility of educating young men— and later young women—for public service and responsibilities in colleges under denominational oversight. Future magistrates and professionals, they argued, ought to be trained in publicly supervised institutions. The private colleges could then pursue their aims under their own control for those who preferred such more particularistic education for their children. When this bifurcation established itself, the eighteenth century college began to fade from view, and the to us so familiar distinction between private and public institutions of higher education became the norm. It was a distinction unknown to the eighteenth century when colleges, regardless of their relationship to specific churches or denominations, were considered public institutions created, as the Yale charter states it, for the instruction of youth in the arts and sciences that they "may be fitted for public employment both in church and civil state." (21) The eighteenth century college sought in vain to adjust itself to the strains of a pluralistic society. Its inability to contain its many disparate elements under denominational governance and yet to remain an institution serving the commonwealth was the cause of its decline.

Notes

The author gratefully acknowledges support received in preparation of this paper from the National Institute of Education. The opinions expressed do not necessarily reflect the position of the Institute, and no official endorsement by the National Institute of Education should be inferred.

1. See my "The First Three American Colleges: Schools of the Reformation," *Perspectives in American History*, 8 (1974): 7-52.
2. For the earliest example see the discussion of the College of New Jersey in G. Howard Miller, A Contracting Community: American Presbyterians, Social Conflict, and Higher Education (Michigan Ph.D. diss., 1970).
3. See Henry Lefavour, "The Proposed College in Hampshire County in 1762," *Proceedings,* Massachusetts Historical Society, 66 (1942): 53-79; Reuben A. Guild, *Early History of Brown University* (Providence, 1897), pp. 128-134.
4. See Samuel E. Morison, *Three Centuries of Harvard, 1636-1936* (Cambridge, 1936), pp. 66, 79.
5. Brooks M. Kelley, *Yale: A History* (New Haven, 1974), pp. 74, 103; on Clap's regime at Yale see Louis L. Tucker, *Puritan Protagonist: President Thomas Clap of Yale College* (Chapel Hill, 1962).
6. See Robert P. Thomson, "The Reform of the College of William and Mary, 1763-1780," *Proceedings,* American Philosophical Society, 115 (June, 1971): 187-213.
7. The charters of Princeton and Dartmouth can be found in Edward C. Elliott and M. M. Chambers, eds., *Charters and Basic Laws of Selected American Universities and Colleges* (N.Y., 1934); the charter of King's College is in Hugh Hastings, ed., *Ecclesiastical Records of the State of New York* (Albany, 1905), V, 3506-3514; the charters of Brown are in Reuben A. Guild, *Life, Times, and Correspondence of James Manning* (Boston, 1864), pp. 465-581; the Queen's College document was published in 1770 as *Charter of a College to be Erected in New Jersey* (N.Y.), and the 1755 charter and 1764 clause of the College of Philadelphia are printed in the U.S. Bureau of Educational Circular of Information No. 2, 1892 (Washington, 1893), on pp. 71-77, and 79-80.
8. Thomas J. Wertenbaker, *Princeton, 1746-1896* (Princeton, 1946), pp. 3-47.
9. See the charter in Hastings, *op. cit.*
10. Walter C. Bronson, *The History of Brown University, 1764-1914* (Providence. 1914), pp. 1-33.
11. See Milton M. Klein, ed., *The Independent Reflector* (Cambridge, Mass. 1963).
12. The bill may be found in the *Journal of the General Assembly of New York* (N.Y., 1766), II, 413-419.
13. Cf. the works by Bronson and Guild, cited above.
14. Frelinghuysen's statement was pseudonymously published as David Marin Ben Jesse, *A Remark on the Disputes and Contentions in this Province* (New York,

1755); on its authorship cf. Beverly McAnear, "American Imprints concerning King's College," *Papers of the Bibliographical Society of America,* 44 (1950); 327.

15. For Hampden-Sydney see Alfred J. Morrison, *The College of Hampden-Sidney: Calendar of Board Minutes, 1776-1876* (Richmond, Va., 1912), and for Washington and Lee, Ollinger Crenshaw, *General Lee's College: The Rise and Growth of Washington and Lee University* (New York, 1969).

16. See the summary table in Donald G. Tewksbury, *The Founding of American Colleges and Universities Before the Civil War* (reprint edition of 1965), pp. 32-54.

17. See John H. Van Amringe, "King's College and Columbia College," in *A History of Columbia University, 1754-1904* (New York, 1904), pp. 59-69, and Edward P. Cheyney, *History of the University of Pennsylvania, 1740-1940* (Philadelphia, 1940), pp. 121-146.

18. See table in Tewksbury, *op. cit.*

19. On the College of Newport project see Reuben A. Guild, *Early History of Brown University* (Providence, 1897), pp. 133-134 and my forthcoming essay in *Newport History.*

20. See Daniel Johnson, Puritan Power in Illinois Higher Education Prior to 1870. Ph.D. dissertation (University of Wisconsin—Madison, 1974).

21. For the Yale charter see Franklin B. Dexter, ed., *Documentary History of Yale University* (New Haven, 1916), pp. 20-23.

PART II

The Nineteenth Century

Introduction

BETWEEN THE REVOLUTION and the Civil War, Americans dramatically transformed the ways in which they educated their young. The major result of this transformation was to increase enormously the significance of schooling in both the life of the child and the life of the society. The change began quietly and did not initially alter the configuration of institutions that had educated colonial Americans. Between 1780 and 1830, parents simply began sending their children to schools and colleges more often. After 1830, a continued growth in enrollments was accompanied by a noisy campaign to create a system of public education to replace the mixture of pay schools and charity schools that were characteristic of the late eighteenth and early nineteenth centuries. By 1860, the vast majority of children in the Northeast were attending elementary schools, most of them public schools, and a small but growing number of them were advancing to secondary schools and colleges as well.

At the elementary level, the growth of schooling reflected an increasing tendency of parents to entrust the school with parts of the socialization process that had previously been carried out in more informal ways. Unlike their colonial predecessors, who had often regarded the school as a peripheral institution, postrevolutionary Americans began to view formal instruction as essential to the process of passing values and skills across generations. Although statistical evidence is not yet full enough to provide a precise measure of enrollment increase, there can be no doubt that it was dramatic. By the Civil War, nearly 90 percent of Massachusetts children between six and fourteen years of age were in school, and the rates for other northern states were almost as high. Moreover, these children were attending school more regularly and for considerably longer terms than had colonial children.

As the significance of formal instruction increased, a number of reformers began to condemn the hodgepodge of schools inherited from the colonial era. They sought to replace pay schools and charity schools, which had blended public and private support and often kept rich and poor in separate institutions, with a uniform system of common schools, which would be supported largely by tax monies and would bring together in one institution white children of all social stations. Beginning in the 1830s, reformers worked diligently to eliminate student fees, to improve school facilities, to encourage more centralized control, and to give the public school a virtual monopoly on the education of the young; and on every score but the last, they had succeeded impressively by the end of the century.

The vast majority of public schools in the nineteenth century offered no more than three to four years of strictly elementary training, and most students did not advance beyond those early years of basic instruction. Those who wished to go further, however, could choose to attend a private academy, a preparatory department of a college or university, or in some larger towns and cities a public high school. Beyond that, they could attend one of the nation's growing number of collegiate institutions.

The growth of secondary schools and colleges was considerably less dramatic than the growth of elementary schools, but even at these higher levels enrollment grew more rapidly than the population at large. In the first two-thirds of the nineteenth century, this growth took place primarily through the expansion of four-year liberal arts institutions; in the last third it was accompanied by the development of the university as a new and competing form of higher education.

For most of the century, public schools and colleges developed independently of each other. Students who wished to advance from the elementary school to the college rarely found a smooth route from one level to the next. Near the end of the century, however, public school leaders and college educators recognized their common interests and began to create the outlines of a well-articulated system of schooling that went all the way from the kindergarten to the graduate and professional school.

This impressive expansion of schooling undoubtedly enhanced the opportunities of many American children, but its benefits were never equally distributed. Black children were rarely admitted on an equal basis, and Indians were almost completely confined to special institutions run by missionaries or by agencies of the federal government. Immigrants were free to attend public schools, but they were often victims of harsh assimilationist schemes.

The impact of educational change on women was more complicated. Girls were admitted to public schools on an equal basis from the beginning, and they often used the school to great advantage. Moreover, schoolteaching become one of the few occupations open to women in the nineteenth century. At the same time, women found it difficult to advance to higher education. Most colleges remained exclusive male domains, and those open to women often tried to prepare them only for a world of domesticity.

The five articles reprinted in this section explore educational change in the nineteenth century with special emphasis on the dramatic expansion of schooling. David F. Allmendinger, Jr. and Ronald Story focus on the growth of college enrollment and trace its implications for student life. Allmendinger, whose essay is based primarily on a study of colleges in western New England, finds a continuation of the heterogeneity in college enrollments that had begun in the colonial era and explores the impact of that heterogeneity on college life. Story focuses on a single institution, Harvard College, where he finds a successful effort to avoid the kind of heterogeneity that was becoming common in many other colleges.

Articles by Michael B. Katz and Selwyn K. Troen treat the emergence and development of the public school. In a major revision of the argument he made earlier in the *The Irony of Early School Reform* (1968), Katz provides one of the best and most comprehensive statements yet on the creation of the public school. Troen's subject is more narrow; in a case study of educational change in St. Louis, he focuses on the social backgrounds of public school students and explores the factors that influenced decisions to enroll and withdraw from schools.

Finally, Anne Firor Scott treats the special world of women's education in an essay that explores the history of Troy Female Seminary in order to illuminate the purposes and results of higher education that was designed specifically for women.

5

New England Students and the Revolution in Higher Education, 1800–1900

David F. Allmendinger, Jr.

WITHIN THE SMALL BUILDINGS and gatherings of young men at New England colleges in the early nineteenth century, a social transformation began to work that would alter the experience of being a student. Unlike the conscious reforms introduced by the rise of universities after the Civil War, the transformation of the early nineteenth century proceeded without plan. No theorist designed it according to conscious pedagogical aims, and no institution either anticipated or really controlled the changes between 1800 and 1840. Only after 1840, when New England colleges already had assumed new forms, did a consciousness arise concerning what had transpired. The material conditions of collegiate life, the old communal arrangements that had controlled the behavior and intellectual activity of students through most of the colonial period had been demolished, creating a new disorder. Only after 1840 did plans arise for dealing with this disorder, a consequence of social changes sweeping over every New England institution of higher education. Long before the rise of universities, antebellum colleges had become places of dynamic change through the needs and workings of the student population itself.

A shift in the social origins of the student population caused this transformation. It began almost imperceptibly at the time of the American Revolution and then assumed unprecedented proportions after 1800. Into the New England colleges there came a flood of students from poor families. Never before had these families sent sons to college, nor could they afford to do so now; their sons came voluntarily to higher education, for the most part having made their own decisions. All ten New England colleges founded before 1822 experienced influxes of these poor young men, especially the newer, provincial institutions outside New Haven and Cambridge. It was the proliferation of these provincial colleges between 1765 and 1825 that permit-

David F. Allmendinger, Jr. is associate professor of history at the University of Delaware.

ted most of the poor to enter the student population. (1) At Amherst, about five hundred of the first thirteen hundred students between 1821 and 1845 relied on charity funds that had been established specifically for those preparing to enter the ministry. Elsewhere, about one-fourth of the whole student population must have relied on funds from sources outside their own families and colleges—from organized charities and from individual sources of self-help, like teaching, manual labor, or soliciting loans and gifts from friends. (2) After 1815, the founding of the American Education Society at Boston added to the flood of indigents. Between 1830 and 1840, when this society reached its greatest scale of charitable operations, ten to fifteen percent of the whole student population of New England had become its beneficiaries by producing evidence of total indigence. (3) New institutions like the American Education Society added to the self-determination of young men, making it easier for them to make their own decisions about proceeding to college.

This movement of poor young men into the student population was part of a massive emigration by the young from rural New England. They were joining an exodus of young people, most of whose origins can be traced to poor farm families; sons were abandoning farms in rural and hill communities, where population was pressing on the supply of arable land. (4) Those who found their way into the student population certainly accounted for only a small fraction of this emigration, and the numbers who went from farm to college were too small to suggest that this form of social mobility was common or easy in nineteenth-century New England. They were not significant in these ways. In terms of their impact on New England's colleges, however—where the entire student population ranged from only five hundred to two thousand before the 1840s—their significance was immense. (5) A fundamental demographic movement was under way in New England, with profound effects on the society and its institutions of higher education.

The power of New England colleges to control the consequences of such an invasion had never been more feeble than in the early nineteenth century. Scholarships had disappeared in America during the eighteenth century, leaving colleges without resources either to support large numbers of the poor or to select only those who could meet certain standards. (6) Under these conditions, the colleges simply lost control over impoverished students, who rapidly began to select themselves. All of this occurred, moreover, in a context of intense institutional competition for numbers of students sufficient to meet operating costs. As a result, student populations in rustic New England college towns came to be composed of a new mixture of young men from heterogeneous social origins, whose surest sign was the range of ages they represented. Boys in their teens now enrolled with large numbers of mature men; at the provincial New England colleges more than a third of the students in the early nineteenth century were graduated at twenty-five or older—a trend toward maturity that had begun at about the time of the

American Revolution and that ended after the Civil War. (7) In terms of their social composition, these little institutions assumed a new diversity and complexity all their own, quite beyond their power to control.

Student life as it had to be lived in the presence of the poor required certain changes in arrangements for the material needs of young men, for their boarding and lodging especially. Simply by their presence, the poor demolished the traditional collegiate community in New England, ending an ancient institution of control and discipline. The collegiate community had subjected its small membership to the discipline not only of a uniform curriculum, but of common living arrangements. While there had been exceptions throughout the eighteenth century, most members of these communities had been expected to gather permanently within their walls and to remain isolated from adult society for long periods; they were to dine together and share common lodgings in buildings sufficiently compact and secluded to permit officials to exercise a constant surveillance, *in loco parentis.* Between 1800 and 1840, essential features of the corporate collegiate community disappeared everywhere in New England, necessitating an entirely new style of student life, with both losses and gains for the quality of that life. (8)

The invasion of the poor shattered the order and uniformity, if not the content, of the classical curriculum. The poor came to college poorly prepared; no institution could expect now to enroll whole classes of young men possessing a uniform knowledge of required texts and subjects. Exceptions had to be made, special instruction offered. Nor could everyone be expected to proceed with the same course of studies at the same pace, for poor young men frequently had to leave school in order to find work. Their need for work disrupted the collegiate calendar and the uniform cycle of long school terms broken only by brief vacations. The poor, with their maddening absences for weeks on end, deranged the orderly progress of all students through the curriculum. While the poor were absent, students who could afford to stay in attendance simply had to mark time. When the poor returned, they required special attention to get them back in step. In terms of order and uniformity, the curriculum began to crack.

It did not survive much longer than the institution that had sustained it: the residential college. This crucial institution of the collegiate community was fragmented and then collapsed under the impact of the indigent invasion. College officials of the early nineteenth century had to abandon the assumption that students must be housed and fed in a secluded, self-contained community. They found it impossible to accommodate the range of tastes and needs that accompanied a mixture of social classes within a single, small institution. Alternatives to the residential college began to appear spontaneously. Students scattered into the adult society of college towns, taking rooms with families, in rooming houses, in hotels and inns, and finally in houses maintained by students themselves. The commons, too, declined and disappeared everywhere by the 1840s, releasing students to make their own arrangements for boarding—with families, in boarding houses, or in their own dining clubs. The austere practice of self-boarding in one's own room reappeared, and there is evidence of a revival of begging, referred to as seeking the "assistance of friends."

When the residential college declined, so too did the ideal of a democratic community of scholars whose members lived and studied together within the same walls. Rich and poor separated, finding their own accommodations. And while the social classes no longer mixed so intensely at any New England college, the new arrangements did make it possible for a student society of increasing variety and complexity to exist in these institutions of higher education. Choice and variety became qualities of student life, replacing the commonness of experience when all had been gathered and secluded together. (9)

The invasion of the poor and the fragmentation of the collegiate community altered student discipline between 1800 and 1840 and introduced a crisis of disorder in the colleges that eventually changed even the intellectual life of New England students. Before the nineteenth century, the routines and seclusion of the collegiate community had imposed a degree of unconscious order and discipline. In the presence of the nineteenth-century poor, seclusion became impossible and discipline difficult. The poor needed work and relied on sources of aid outside the college; they were driven beyond its walls to find support. Their mobility and independence made old methods of surveillance unworkable: how could one perform the duties of visitation over a student population that not only had scattered into its own enclaves—either in the towns or in unattended college buildings—but also spent long periods of each term away from the institution? The maturity of students and their mixture of ages made it difficult to enforce old legal codes: how could one apply rules designed for boys of fourteen to men in their thirties, some of whom might even be married? Officials of New England colleges confronted a crisis: a loss of control over the student population. And the old curriculum alone could not maintain this discipline without the institutional setting in which it once had functioned.

Evidence in student diaries and letters from the early nineteenth century suggests that at least some people perceived what was happening in these colleges as a form of student liberation. The more abundant evidence in faculty records suggests that officials perceived an advancing chaos that only a few could accept. To have accepted this disorder, this consequence of demographic change in the nineteenth century, these men must necessarily have been willing to accept institutional changes as fundamental as any introduced by the rise of universities in America. Their colleges would have had to abandon housing and boarding functions and renounce any role in discipline. In order to accommodate the independent poor without scholarship funds, they would have had to put aside the notion of an uninterrupted,

four-year course in residence and their preoccupation with constant attendance and performance in a classroom. They must have been willing to
forget the orderliness of predictable routines, and predictable sources of rev-
enue from constant numbers of students, with certain amounts of tuition
money to pay. If, on the contrary, they chose to reject these implications, a
new form of order would have to be created in the student population. This
was at least one problem shared by officials of all New England institutions
of higher education in the nineteenth century, whether in the colleges or in
the universities.

Though the transformation of the early nineteenth century would never be
reversed entirely, a new order did indeed emerge from this early period of
change. Through a massive and expensive effort to revive the residential
college—to recreate what had become a romantic conception of the collegiate community—students again found themselves being gathered together
under the discipline of an old, but reviving, institution. Ironically, the universities at New Haven and Cambridge succeeded best in reconstructing
buildings that expressed their desire to recreate the traditional English college. Still, consequences of the early nineteenth century survived: some students would continue to escape the residential college, and the social classes
would maintain their physical separation within these institutions. The prosperity of New England colleges after the Civil War also permitted them to
reinvent scholarships on a scale unprecedented for America. This meant that
for the first time since the eighteenth century, college officials could control
charitable funds and the selection of beneficiaries. At the same time,
they enhanced their power to select the entire student population, which
came increasingly from more affluent, homogeneous social origins after the
Civil War.

It was the invention of a new system of discipline, however, that contributed most to the creation of order in the student population and altered most
drastically the experience of being a student. Between 1825 and 1840, New
England colleges willingly abandoned the ancient system of discipline, under
which their officials had acted *in loco parentis*. Faculties relaxed their surveillance over details of the student's daily life; the old system of direct confrontation between officers and students over cases of discipline was quietly
discarded and never resurrected in pure form. In its place, all New England
colleges between 1825 and 1840 developed systems of grading and ranking
the academic performance of students, and then reporting these computa-
tions to parents. All colleges placed students under the discipline of competitive evaluation, devising ever more frequent and sophisticated methods of
testing and grading. Major problems of punishment they simply handed
over to the family, which now assumed this responsibility *in loco collegii*. Order and discipline now were imposed in ways that changed the intellectual
life of the student: scholarship became a competitive activity, and discipline
became internalized, a matter of self-control and family watchfulness. (10)

These new arrangements were not devised in reaction against the real violence of student life in the early nineteenth century. Nor did they originate from within the family itself; they were not produced by some new sensibility that led parents to express a greater concern for the welfare and safety of children. Rather, they came as responses to interruptions in old routines and customs. All efforts to enforce ancient routines and to preserve an old disciplinary system appropriate to a secluded collegiate community simply collapsed under the weight of violations that stemmed from the necessities of an impoverished student population. And it is important to remember that the new system of discipline—together with the disintegration of the collegiate community—took place in institutions that were still very small. By no means were these changes the results of size or of sudden growth; they appeared in institutions long before the scale of university size had been reached. Rather, they were products of social change in New England: of the invasion of the poor.

NOTES

1. In slightly more than half a century, eight new colleges were founded in New England, closer to the hill towns and the rural poor than Harvard or Yale, transforming the institutional setting of higher education in New England. Those eight new institutions founded by 1822 were Brown, Dartmouth, Williams, Middlebury, Vermont, Bowdoin, Waterville (Colby), and Amherst. See Donald Tewksbury, *The Founding of American Colleges and Universities Before the Civil War* (New York, 1932), pp. 32–54.

2. Herman Humphrey, *Valedictory Address, Delivered at Amherst College* (Amherst, Mass., 1845), pp. 16–17. Humphrey placed the exact number of charity students at 501; my own counts indicate that Amherst enrolled about thirteen hundred students in this period, including nongraduates. My estimate for the rest of New England institutions is based on scattered and fragmentary figures for the number of students who kept school, received tuition grants, or received aid from the education societies. This evidence has been compiled from various sources in published college histories and college archives. A close study of the social origins of all students from Southampton, Massachusetts, suggests that the one-quarter estimate is a fair minimum.

3. "View of the American Colleges, 1831," *American Quarterly Register* 3 (May 1831): 294–95; "View of the American Colleges, 1833," *American Quarterly Register* 5 (May 1833): 332–33.

4. Historians have produced a large body of literature on this crowding, poverty, and exodus. See Lois Kimball Mathews, *The Expansion of New England* (New York, 1962; originally published 1909); Percy W. Bidwell, "The Agricultural Revolution in New England," *American Historical Review* 26 (July 1921): 683–702; Bidwell, "Population Growth in Southern New England, 1810–1860," *Quarterly Publications of the American Statistical Association,* n.s. 15 (December 1917): 813–39; Bidwell, "Rural Economy in New England at the Beginning of the Nineteenth Century," *Transactions of the Connecticut Academy of Arts and Sciences* 20 (April 1916):

241-399. Kenneth Lockridge has focused on the revolutionary implications of crowding and poverty in "Land, Population and the Evolution of New England Society, 1630-1790," *Past and Present,* no. 39 (April 1968), pp. 62-80; see also Lockridge, *A New England Town: The First Hundred Years* (New York, 1970), pp. 181-86. See also Lester Earl Klimm, *The Relation Between Certain Population Changes and the Physical Environment in Hampden, Hampshire, and Franklin Counties, Massachusetts, 1790-1925* (Philadelphia, 1933), pp. 5-10, 41-67, 106-9.

5. On the size of the student population, see [Francis Wayland], *Report of the Corporation of Brown University on Changes in the System of Collegiate Education* (Providence, 1850), pp. 29-30. Wayland's figures, based on statistics in the *American Alamanac,* compare closely with my own counts based on published biographical registers of the colleges.

6. David F. Allmendinger, Jr., "Indigent Students and Their Institutions, 1800-1860" (Ph.D. diss., University of Wisconsin, 1968), pp. 73-102; and Beverly McAnear, "College Founding in the American Colonies, 1745-1775," *Mississippi Valley Historical Review* 42 (June 1955): 24-44.

7. This estimate is based on determinations of the ages at graduation of students at Brown, Dartmouth, Williams, Middlebury, Vermont, Bowdoin, Waterville, and Amherst. The sources were the published biographical registers of students at each institution.

8. This paragraph and the four that follow are based largely on evidence in Allmendinger, "Indigent Students," pp. 73-164.

9. The colleges did continue to provide housing for most students even after the newer alternatives developed, though traditional arrangements of the residential college could not be maintained. By the 1840s some college officials were urging the abandonment of all efforts to house students within the institutions.

10. Evidence for these statements comes from published college histories and from the manuscript faculty minutes and records of Amherst, Harvard, Yale, Bowdoin, Vermont, and Middlebury. These records are deposited in the archives or special collections of each institution.

6

Harvard Students, the Boston Elite, and the New England Preparatory System, 1800–1876

Ronald Story

THE HARVARD COLLEGE student body, like the university as a whole, changed markedly in the ante-bellum era, but it changed less in size than in composition. (1) Though the number of yearly graduates remained stable at about 60 from 1810 to 1850, the students came increasingly from Boston's "rich and fashionable families." (2) More precisely, they came from the new business and professional families who provided the funds for Harvard's rapid growth and came by degrees to control its governing bodies. The Harvard "experience" became an important part of the process of elite social, economic, and cultural consolidation in these years, and contributed to the cohesiveness, cultivation, and hauteur of the distinctive Brahmin upper class that was to flourish after the Civil War. (3) Analysis of the way in which Harvard came to be monopolized by the Boston elite should throw light not only on the development of the class but also on the evolving educational network which formed a portion of its institutional underpinnings.

There was considerable discussion in the ante-bellum years of Harvard's "aristocratic" exclusiveness, particularly after 1820 when the pattern became both acutely visible and pronounced. (4) University officers explained this new condition by reference to the religious bigotry which made Orthodox Congregationalists keep their sons away from Harvard, then controlled predominantly by Unitarians. They noted, too, the establishment of other colleges in which young men now matriculated. (5) Neither of these explanations, however, satisfied Harvard's critics, who argued that its Unitarian ambience reflected the predominance of the Boston elite at the college. They also maintained that many boys attended other "seminaries" only because they could could not gain admission to Harvard, whose facilities and advantages

Ronald Story is associate professor of history at the University of Massachusetts—Amherst.

were far superior to those of its competitors, including Yale. The critics, who ranged in label from Orthodox Congregationalists to Jacksonian Democrats to radical Free-Soilers to working-class Know-Nothings, singled out two simpler and more specific factors to explain the change in the college's student body: the rising cost of a Harvard education and the rising educational requirements for admission.

Surviving evidence confirms that costs were moving upward. As early as 1831 critics were complaining that "the expense of an education at Cambridge are greater than are necessary." (6)   In 1845 a leading Democrat charged: (7)

The expenses of tuition have been increased at least 50 per cent beyond what they formerly were; and for some of the classes 33 and a third per cent beyond what they were when I was a student [in 1817]. Yet the College has all the time been growing more opulent. The charge for tuition is greater in Cambridge than at those institutions where there are no endowments.

Tuition proper rose from $20 in 1807 to $75 in 1845 to $104 in 1860. Overall expenses (to which critics generally referred) also increased, although how much is not clear. University officials placed the minimum cost of a year for a Harvard undergraduate at $176 in 1825, $185 in 1835, and $249 in 1860, a rate of increase much faster than the rate of inflation, but still one that was relatively modest. (8)

The actual minimum costs were probably higher. In 1837 a youth wrote to industrialist Amos Lawrence: (9)

The expense of an education at Cambridge is much greater than is generally supposed; and far exceeds your estimate. Those who are concerned in the government of the University, have ever represented the *necessary* expenses as less than they really are. Mother has made many inquiries of students, and has taken great care to obtain correct information. But few indigent students have gone ... to Cambridge, most of them being obliged to enter at some college where they can live more cheaply.

In 1854 a student from New York wrote that tuition aside, "travelling expenses, furnishing the room, etc., though all extravagance was avoided, have required more than we anticipated." (10)   A knowledgeable English traveller observed in 1861: "The expense of education at Harvard College is not much lower than at our colleges.... The actual authorized expenditure in accordance with the rules is only 50 L per annum, i.e. 249 dollars; but this does not, by any means, include everything." (11)   The real minimum cost of a Harvard year, though impossible to estimate precisely, probably rose from about $150 in the early 1800s to about $400 by the outbreak of the Civil War.

"The cause of education, of good morals, of sound learning," wrote one of Harvard's critics in 1848, "demands that the expenses of obtaining a thorough education in our Commonwealth should be greatly reduced and brought as low as possible;—the highest, as well as those of inferior grade." (12)   In practice even the "well-born" sometimes had difficulty entering Harvard, as Theodore Parker pointed out a year later. (13)   Poor relations begged funds from their affluent cousins; sons of men in sudden financial straits turned elsewhere or simply did not enter college. In *The Barclays of Boston,* a society novel written by Mrs. Harrison Gray Otis in the mid-1850s, the son of heroine Emma Sanderson was "filled with an ardent desire to go to Cambridge." But the widowed Emma was "unable to meet the expenses attendant on a college life." (14)

Expense was as much a question of living standards as of survival, and the standard of living, of course, had been rising at Harvard since the turn of the century. Presidents John T. Kirkland (1810-1828) and Josiah Quincy (1829-1845) had tacitly, and indeed sometimes openly, encouraged social elegance at the college. A Virginian complained in 1813 "that your Principal and Professors take a pride in the extravagance of the students, and encourage it." (15)   Six years later a committee of University Overseers agreed that: (16)

the increase of the *private* expenses of the Students is a subject deserving of the most careful consideration. It is found that there is a perpetual inclination to indulge in expensive pleasures, & in useless & unnecessary extravagance of dress.

But the root of this tendency was less the administration than the students themselves, who brought elite tastes and resources with them: "Father wants cheap living; Son has his way: and has his way, because it is *not fashionable* to live cheap." (17)   A more sumptuous scale of living resulted, as noted in this report from the 1850s: (18)

A carpet on a college room . . . was 50 years ago, an unknown luxury; and 25 years ago, the want of one would not have been noticeable. Now all the rooms are carpeted; and a similar change has taken place in furniture, dress, and the supplies of the table.

Average expenses were, in fact, significantly higher than the minimum estimates and rose equally, if not more, rapidly. The following table provides a rough approximation of the increase of average as compared to other costs: (19)

	1810	*1835*	*1860*
tuition	$20	$55	$104
official minimum costs	na	185	249
real minimum costs (est.)	150	300	400
average costs	225	400	700

The average, significantly, did not rise so precipitously because of the inordinate extravagance of a few students, although expenditure of $2,000 a year were not uncommon by the 1860s. Rather, it rose because a greater proportion of the students—certainly a considerable majority—spent relatively large sums. The average, that is, was more than a mere average: it was also a standard.

By 1840 this fashionable lifestyle was affecting the composition of the student body. As a critic wrote in 1845 with regard to Harvard: (20)

The habits of economy at a place of education are affected by the character of the collective body of the pupils. As expenses increase, the sons of the less affluent begin to remain away, and the absence of their influence aggravates the tendency to expensive gratifications.

A faculty member noted soon after that "a standard of expense, in regard to dress, pocket-money, furniture, etc., has been established which renders it almost a hopeless matter for a young man of slender means to obtain an education there." (21)   For as an Overseer committee observed a few years later: (22)

Parents will not, as a general thing, expose their sons to the severe test of sending them to a place where they may possibly meet expenses which are absolutely necessary, but where they will be unable to conform to the common mode of living of the community with which they associate. Such a trial is beyond the strength of most young men of the age at which they usually enter college.

Scholarship aid, except of the kind extended by the wealthy to their impecunious kinsmen, was generally unavailable. Only two of thirty-four large-scale private bequests to Harvard from 1800 to 1850 were for undergraduate assistance, and the first of these did not accrue until 1839. Unrestricted funds invariably went for other purposes, as did tuition fees. Some scholarships did exist, including a few surviving fellowships for boys from designated towns and a small grant from the state. But in 1831 only thirty-four Harvard students received aid as opposed, for example, to 144 at Yale. In 1851 President Jared Sparks told an inquirer that a very good student might, at best, receive $50 a year outright and an equal sum on loan. After 1826, moreover, the university reduced the length of its winter vacation, making it more difficult for needy students to earn money teaching school. In the 1850s several scholarship funds were established in response both to extreme political pressure and to faculty complaints about the quality of academic life. By 1860 Harvard was offering 32 scholarships worth from $100 to $300 a year, plus grants and loans of $20 to $80 a year for about fifty students. (23)   Perhaps 15 per cent of the students received aid in the 1860s. But the fact remains that a growing proportion of those who attended ante-bellum Harvard paid their own way.

And the fact that they paid dearly helps explain the increasing monopolization of the college by the Boston elite.

Admissions requirements rose, apparently, even faster than costs. In 1818 President Kirkland wrote that improved schools were producing students better prepared in mathematics and the classics. As of 1826 a boy versed in the fundamentals of English and arithmetic needed perhaps a year's extra labor in the classics in order to pass the still casual admissions examination. In the early 1830s, however, candidates began to fail in significant numbers; many others were accepted "conditionally." By 1840 Harvard's admissions requirements were unquestionably the highest in New England, necessitating from three to four years of preparation. Moreover, the entrance examination continued to increase in difficulty. In 1845 the list of classical readings was much longer than in 1835; by 1855 it contained samplings of geography and history. In 1850 the qualifying examination was eight hours long; by 1865, when the requirements, though still traditional, were also still the stiffest in New England, the examination took three days to administer, and "no one could be certain of getting through." (24)

The stiffening requirements raised the average age of Harvard students from roughly fifteen and a half in 1810 to seventeen and a half in 1850. They also affected the social composition of the student body, causing a Democrat in 1845 to question the notion (25)

that higher qualifications should be the requirement of admission. Such additional requirements could easily be made a part of instruction in the excellent public school in Boston and in some few Academies and private schools. They could not be made general in the preparatory schools of the country; and they would, therefore, shut the doors of Harvard College still more effectually against almost all but the sons of residents in Boston and a few favored places.

An undergraduate of the mid-1830s observed that the stricter requirements favored boys from "the Public Latin Schools of Boston and Salem, the academies of Exeter and Andover, and the famous Round-Hill School at Northampton." (26) A rural student of the late 1840s recalled: (27)

A lad thus partially trained must enter college badly handicapped in a company of classmates thoroughly drilled in such schools as the Boston Latin, Andover, Exeter and the large private fitting schools of cities.

It is difficult to discover precisely which schools prepared Harvard students because the data is extremely fragmentary for the entire ante-bellum period, especially for the years before 1830. In general, however, the pattern that emerges from presidential reports, class books, school histories, contemporary descriptions, and latter-day biographies is roughly as shown in the following table on the percentage of students entering Harvard from certain schools and types of schools in three successive periods: (28)

	1801-20	*1821-45*	*1846-70*
Boston Latin School	15%	12%	14%
Phillips Academies	15	14	20
Boston private day schools	10	15	21
other academies	20	21	10
private boarding schools	20	18	2
private tutors	20	18	17
other public schools	0	2	17

Even at first glance the figures tend to support the main allegations of contemporary observers. Early in the era the Boston Latin, Phillips Exeter, and Phillips Andover supplied between a quarter and a third of Harvard students; by midcentury they supplied slightly more than a third. The Boston day schools raised their total from approximately a tenth to approximately a fifth over the same period. These three sources provided approximately two-fifths of the students in the early years; they provided well over half later on. Meanwhile, the number of students from rural academies other than Andover and Exeter fell by half; the private (or proprietary) boarding schools declined even more. Public high schools outside Boston, on the other hand, came from nowhere to occupy a supply role comparable to the Boston Latin itself.

The gross categories obscure some aspects of the overall trend. For instance, the proportion of Harvardians from private boarding schools—institutions providing preparatory instruction to boarders for profit—was about the same in the twenty years after 1820 as in the twenty years before. In the earlier decades, however, these schools, often in western Massachusetts, were mainly conducted by ministers who boarded a few boys in order to supplement their ministerial and farming income. The school of the Reverend Samuel Ripley and his wife in Waltham and Concord was a singularly successful, long-lived version of this type of ministerial schooling. Pedagogically gifted, the Ripleys attracted enough patronage from prominent families to become one of the four main private boarding schools preparing students for Harvard in the second quarter of the century. Of the other three, the one conducted by Stephen Minot Weld in Jamaica Plain from the 1820s till about 1850 was perhaps closest in spirit and form to the older type, charging fees to a comparatively small number of boys in return for unadorned classical training. But Weld, who had graduated from Harvard in 1826, was an educator rather than a minister, and he staffed his school with well-paid aspiring teachers from the new Harvard. Weld himself was also from a prominent family and drew from a broader, more prominent clientele than his predecessors.

More important yet were the Round Hill School in Northampton and the Wells School in Cambridge, each of which sent almost 50 boys to Harvard between the mid-1820s and the mid-1830s. Round Hill, the most famous American school of its time, was conducted by a group of men who had attended Exeter and Harvard, traveled in Europe, and obtained a loan from no less than Harvard itself to establish an institution for the sons of "the best families" of Boston, New York, and the South. Modeled in part after the German gymnasium, Round Hill offered an excellent but very expensive education and at the same time provided an elegant lifestyle with servants, stables, and tours of the estates of prominent Bostonians. Its rolls bore the names of dozens of Boston's elite families. (30) The school of Williams Wells, a former Boston publisher and bookseller, operated according to the traditional English rules of strict discipline and plain living. But Wells too offered sound training, utilizing Harvard graduates as instructors. His school "had a wide-spread influence and reputation." (31) By 1830 it was "regarded as being—with the possible exception of the Boston Latin School— the best place in which to fit for Harvard College, and was therefore much sought by the best Boston families." (32) Wells likewise attracted the sons of Harvard faculty members and other Cambridge literati, some of whom were day students. The Wells and Round Hill Schools both disbanded in the 1830s, but while they lasted they were the most exclusive preparatory establishments in the country, prefiguring by a quarter of a century the Episcopalian boarding schools of St. Paul's and St. Mark's which eventually succeeded them—a far cry from the parlor of the rural minister.

The private day schools of Boston took up a part of the slack caused by the eclipse of the private boarding school. Again the broad category obscures important developments. In the early years of the century a third of Boston's 1,500 school children attended private schools, several of which provided classical education on a comparatively exclusive basis. The following regulation was typical: (33)

In order that the School may always be a select one, it is distinctly understood, that the consent of at least two-thirds of the original parties to this instrument must be obtained before any other persons are admitted.

Sometimes the preceptors were socially prominent and operated according to British patterns. The three leading schools—those of William Jenks, J. S. J. Gardiner, and Elisha Clap—were all conducted by ministers. Even the best of these schools, however, seldom lasted a decade.

Over the next thirty years six important private day schools operated in the Boston area. Five were run along conventional lines by professional educators with Harvard degrees. The schools of Daniel G. Ingraham, Thomas G. Bradford, and William H. Brooks sent boys to Harvard on a sporadic basis from 1820 till the 1850s. That of Frederic Leverett, who served briefly as headmaster of the Boston Latin, lasted from 1822 to 1835, when it was replaced, in a sense, by the school of Samuel Eliot, who taught from 1840 to 1855 before leaving for Trinity College. The sixth school was the Chauncy Hall School founded in 1828 by Gideon Thayer, who previously had run a smaller Boston school. Chauncy Hall mainly provided "English" (or non-classical) education to boys not bound for college; it therefore resembled both the public Boston English High School which had opened in 1821 and the many rural academies with their "practical" curricula. Thayer's facilities were supposedly "unsurpassed" as of 1830, and his "classical department" supplied modest numbers of Harvard students far beyond 1855, when Thayer himself retired to head an insurance company owned by Chauncy Hall graduates. (34)

Phase three of the Boston private day school system began in 1851 when Epes Sargent Dixwell, an 1827 Harvard graduate who still lived in Cambridge, resigned the headmastership of Boston Latin to open his own school. A wealthy man with legal training, Dixwell was the brother of a prominent banker and the husband of a Bowditch. He was also "a most accomplished man, an elegant scholar, a gentleman of the world." Not surprisingly, his school quickly became "the best fitting-school for Harvard," the resort of boys from Brookline and other suburbs as well as Beacon Hill. (35) Most of the growing share of Harvard students from Boston private day schools in the middle years of the century may be accounted for by the opening of Dixwell's, whose clientele was no less well-educated, prominent and exclusive than that of Round Hill. Dixwell's school explains, at least in part, the following figures on Boston private education: (36)

	1849-50	1859-60	% change
number of schools	61	58	-5
number of pupils	1,800	2,100	17
annual budget	$133,000	$185,000	39
budget per school	$2,100	$3,190	46

While the number of schools (primary as well as advanced) declined, the number of pupils rose, as did annual expenditures. The budget per school increased most of all, with each school becoming (like Dixwell's) more affluent. By the early 1860s the Hopkinson and Noble schools, modeled after Dixwell's, were in operation. The three institutions together virtually inaugurated the high-quality upper-class day school system of the late nineteenth century.

The New England academies were quasi-public post-common school institutions that sprang up mostly in the period immediately following the Revolution. Of the 400 or so in existence in Massachusetts as of 1860, perhaps a third had state charters and possibly a tenth had public or private endowments. All but one or two charged tuition, and all without exception had self-perpetuating private boards of trustees. Located mostly in rural areas, they usually offered an "English" curriculum and catered principally to local residents, some of whom boarded. Many also offered a classical program for future collegians, but comparatively few offered mainly or exclusively college preparatory work or catered to a clientele outside the immediate vicinity. (37) The academies fed a steady stream of boys to Harvard (and other colleges) in the ante-bellum era, supplying slightly more than a third of the incoming students at Cambridge before 1820 and slightly less than a third after 1845.

Here, too, additional analysis is in order. Harvard-oriented academies always were incorporated, for example, and always taught the classics. Usually old, well-endowed, and better known and equipped than their imitators, they were the best of the lot. Only about twenty of these New England academies sent boys to Harvard even in the first third of the century, and only a dozen or so after about 1840. Among these were the Roxbury Latin School and the Milton Academy near Boston and the Dummer, Lawrence, and Leicester Academies of Byfield, Groton, and Worcester, respectively. Before 1840 the Beverly, Westford, and Lancaster Academies, the Derby Academy of Hingham, and the Bristol Academy of Taunton sent a sprinkling of boys to Cambridge; after 1841, the Hopkins School of Cambridge and the Williston Seminary of Easthampton sent a few. (38)

Most important were the Phillips Academies of Andover, Massachusetts, and Exeter, New Hampshire, which were old and well-endowed, concentrated mainly on mathematics and the classics, and attracted widespread elite patronage virtually from their founding about 1780. Together they accounted for some two-fifths of the academy-prepared Harvardians before 1820, slightly fewer until about 1845, and then two-thirds thereafter, when they increased their flow as other academies faded. But even this figure is misleading, for Andover's contribution had declined for religious and other reasons. While an occasional Andoverite still appeared at Cambridge, by 1855 the academy was offering only half the Greek and Latin required by Harvard; her gradates went mostly to Yale. Phillips Exeter, by contrast, matched its curriculum closely to Harvard's requirements; by 1845 fitting for "college" at Exeter "of course meant Harvard." (39) After 1850, in fact, Exeter supplied over one-half the academy boys at Harvard, an average of perhaps fifteen a year, or almost a fifth of all entering New Englanders. In the late 1860s the Exeter total was 23 a year, highest by far for any single school. (40)

Private tutors, the next to last majority category, sent boys to Harvard throughout the period, their number declining proportionately only slightly if at all. Yet even here there was a change. Before 1820 the tutor was often a local minister who instructed a boy as a favor to a rural family or kinsman; in many cases the tutee was the minister's son. Thereafter, however, tutors were more commonly young Harvard graduates who lived in the household of wealthy Boston-area families, especially during the summer season in Brookline, Nahant, or some other elite suburb. (41) Occasionally the tutor also served as European travelling companion, chaperoning as well as teaching. More and more, in fact, private tutelage occurred in Europe under Europeans, sometimes in connection with a school in England, France, Germany, or Switzerland. By mid-century private tutees as a whole were a slightly less important component of incoming Harvard classes. Those who did arrive came less often from the rural minister's study and more frequently from the family townhouse or suburban estate; a significant number—among them three Coolidges, two Lowells, and an Appleton—came freshly prepared from Europe.

Finally, there were the public schools: tax-supported, tuition-free, controlled by elected officials. Of these the most important by far was the ancient Boston Latin School. Even in the early nineteenth century, when the Boston Latin was in comparatively shabby and disreputable state, it managed to supply a tenth of all Harvard students and was in fact the only public school to supply any at all. After 1815 headmaster Benjamin Apthorp Gould, a wealthy and well-connected protege of President Kirkland of Harvard, introduced several innovations—the misdemeanor mark, the weekly declamation, the school library, regular report cards—which attracted students (or parents) and enabled the school to keep pace with Harvard requirements. During the headmastership of Epes Dixwell from 1836 to 1851, the school moved to new quarters and a private Boston Latin School Association emerged to provide political support and financial aid. Despite stiff competition, the Boston Latin was supplying by mid-century about as large a share of incoming Harvard classes as it had 50 years before. A Boston Latin graduate of the 1850s recalled the "sprinkling" of Beacon Hill boys as "small." Nonetheless, it was still "a select school, principally . . . for the rich and exclusive." (42) Boys from the Boston Latin, like those from Exeter and Dixwell's, "seemed to touch the appreciation of the Harvard examining board a little more deftly than an applicant from any other place." (43)

Until the 1820s Boston Latin was the only public school contributing to Harvard. By 1830 the Salem and Cambridge Latin Schools had revived from their eighteenth-century doldrums and were fitting a few boys. Twenty years later the modern high school movement was well underway. In Salem and Cambridge new high schools absorbed the older Latin schools, which became classical departments. Elsewhere classical departments developed with the school. Every sizeable Massachusetts town had a high school—over a hundred as of the Civil War—offering a basic English curriculum. (44) But not every public high school could boast a college preparatory program, and those that did often had curricula that were inadequate for Harvard. Outside Boston, only Salem and Cambridge sent many boys to Cambridge; next came Brookline, Dorchester, and Charlestown in roughly that order. Only about fifteen of the Massachusetts public schools sent boys to Harvard even after 1850, and a mere half-dozen—all in the Boston vicinity—provided 80 percent of these. The residue came from Lowell, Lynn, Worcester, and other industrial towns, whose new high schools helped further to eliminate the rural academy as a significant component in the preparatory network.

Refined by analysis, the table of Harvard preparatory education appears as follows:

	1801-20	1821-45	1846-70
public schools:			
Boston Latin School	15%	12%	14%
North Shore/suburban	0	2	12
other	0	0	12
academies:			
Exeter	8	9	16
Andover	7	5	4
other	20	21	10
private boarding schools:			
ministerial	15	5	1
other	5	13	1
private tutors:			
ministerial	10	8	5
other	10	10	12
Boston private day schools:			
Dixwell/Noble	0	0	12
other	10	15	9

The dozen most important schools for Harvard between 1800 and 1870 were approximately as follows:

	active years	number of students sent to Harvard (approx.)
Boston Latin School	1801-70	750
Phillips Exeter Academy	1801-70	550
Phillips Andover Academy	1801-70	250
Cambridge High School	1820-70	100
Salem High School	1820-70	75
Dixwell School	1851-70	75

Round Hill School	1823-34	50
Wells School	1824-35	50
Milton Academy	1807-60	50
Lawrence Academy	1801-70	50
Ingraham School	1820-50	50
Noble School	1860-70	50

As of mid-century three schools—Exeter, the Boston Latin, and Dixwell's in that order—supplied almost 40 percent of incoming Harvard classes. Andover, Chauncy Hall, and the Cambridge and Salem High Schools (plus Roxbury Latin, Charlestown High, and Noble's after 1860) supplied another quarter or more. Students from the other rural academies and private boarding schools were largely gone from the Harvard scene; those from the new public high schools and Episcopal boarding schools for the most part had yet to arrive.

The cost of preparatory education varied enormously from one decade or type of school to the next. Public schools were tuition-free, of course, as was the private Roxbury Latin School. Among the private boarding schools tuition at Round Hill came to $300 a year; Wells, Weld, and Ripley's charged from one-third to one-half of that amount, and the ministerial schools probably $50 a year or less. As of 1865 St. Paul's and St. Marks's charged $500. A ministerial tutor in 1810 might charge little or nothing, whereas a Boston tutor by 1850 sometimes asked as much as $500. The cheapest of the private Boston day schools, Chauncy Hall, cost $80 for the classical track in 1835, $100 in 1855, and $155 in 1865; other day schools ranged from about a hundred dollars in 1815 to about $250 in 1855. Among the academies the Phillips schools, which assessed a boarder about $60 as of 1820, were often cheaper in the early years than other academies, which generally required a boarder to pay from $80 to $100; at these rates many boys from poor families could and did attend. But by the 1850s the Phillips schools cost a minimum of about $150, while the other academies were charging in the vicinity of $125. (45)

As schools evolved from the transient, the amateur, and the modest to the more permanent, professional, and luxurious, they also moved from the relatively cheap to the relatively dear. The literature of the period is full of examples of boys unable to pay for preparatory education or able to obtain it only with great sacrifice. The public high schools constituted a countervailing current to this trend. In the mid-nineteenth century, however, these schools, although free, were mainly for the progeny of the community elites. This was especially true in the Boston area, from which most high-school-fitted boys came. (46)   The best high schools were in fact mostly in the eastern part of the state. The following table suggests the general pattern:

% *Harvard students from:*	*1801-15*	*1820-45*	*1850-65*
Boston area schools	40%	55%	65%
schools charging $150 per year or more	0	10	45
schools from Boston area or charging $150 per year or both	40	60	75

The figures corroborate the judgments of observers that the stiffer Harvard admissions requirements favored Boston-area students. But by the 1820s cost, too, was a factor: as the years needed to pass the entrance exam increased, so did the cost per year.

In 1846 Theodore Parker wrote: (47)

The poor man's son, however well-born, struggling for a superior education, obtains his culture at a monstrous cost; with the sacrifice of pleasure, comfort, the joys of youth, often of eyesight and health. . . . The rich man's son needs not that terrible trial. He learns from his circumstances, not his soul. The air about him contains a diffused element of thought. He learns without knowing it. . . . All the outward means of educating, refining, elevating a child, are to be had for money, and money alone.

Parker was overstating his case a bit. The high schools and remaining academies as well as the ministerial tutors produced a small stream of impecunious but deserving boys, who subsequently benefitted from scholarship assistance at Cambridge. For the 70 percent who were neither public school graduates nor charity students, the cost of a Harvard degree—three years of preparation and four of residence—was about $2,000, a figure near the top of the middle-class income range, equivalent in 1970 terms to about $30,000. "To be the son of rich parents," said Brahmin James Cabot in 1867, "considerably increases the chances of being sent to college." (48)

Did Harvard deliberately adopt policies, as critics sometimes insinuated, which excluded the provincial and the poor? Over the years the administration spent tuition and endowment funds to beautify Harvard Yard, expand and modernize its plant, and pay better salaries to more instructors. It also raised entrance requirements to improve the quality of incoming students. High tuition and high requirements both had the unexceptionable aim of enhancing the quality of student life and instruction. In practice, it improved the situation of a small number of students who came, as critics and defenders alike acknowledged, increasingly from the Boston elite. The fact that costs and requirements began to rise just as Boston lawyers and businessmen gained administrative power at Harvard doubtless made matters seem vaguely collusive. University patrons and officials, for example, endowed or supervised many parts of the preparatory network—the Boston Latin, Cambridge High, Exeter, Dixwell's, Roxbury Latin, Milton, Lawrence, Dummer, Round Hill, and Wells, among others. Having made arrangements for their own sons and those of other members of the elite, they could raise requirements with relative personal impunity. They could then shape school offerings to match new university requirements, which they also determined.

The consequences of these developments were in any case profound. The hero of *Fair Harvard,* an anonymous novel of the 1860s, said to the father of a prospective Harvard student: (49)

One cannot over-estimate the advantage to your son of becoming a member of Harvard College. Not only will he thereby become master of all ancient and modern languages, sciences, and arts; not only will society of the highest fashion and fortune open their doors to welcome him: but he will secure for himself the sure means of future preferment and honor, in any profession he may choose to follow.

Though comically exaggerated, the passage was close to the truth, as a few figures suggest. By the 1870s, Harvard graduates comprised two-fifths of the chief officers of the large New England textile firms and half the directors of the leading Boston banks and insurance companies. Prominence in law, medicine, politics, and scholarship was at least equally great. And as of 1892 approximately 34 percent of the millionaires of Boston had Harvard degrees. (50) By the 1870s Harvard was essentially what Santayana said it was, "the seminary and academy for the inner circle of Bostonians." (51)

Also important was the two-fold way in which this trend influenced New England educational developments. In Massachusetts, a cluster of liberal arts colleges was founded by two groups which Harvard largely ignored: the older provincial elite (Williams, Amherst) and the newer metropolitan middle class (Tufts, Boston University, Boston College). By 1870 these colleges were joined by the Massachusetts Institute of Technology and the Massachusetts Agricultural College, also catering mainly to the middle class. A system of educational "tracking" consequently emerged in the state to parallel the new class structure.

But the influence of the new Harvard also extended to secondary education, for the rising admissions requirements helped produce a system of elite private schooling in which each pupil enjoyed not only comparatively outstanding facilities but a rate of annual expenditure many times that provided to a public school pupil. The preparatory school system was more casual and open than it would later become, but it was there, nonetheless. Recent scholars have worked fruitfully in ante-bellum public education without, perhaps, recognizing the degree to which secondary education was being permanently tracked along upper and middle (and lower) class lines even in the age of reform. It would appear, further, that tracking at both secondary and higher levels relates more or less directly to, among other things, the emergence of the Boston upper class.

Notes

1. For changes at ante-bellum Harvard, see e.g. Samuel Eliot Morison, *Three Centuries of Harvard* (Cambridge, Mass., 1965), pp. 195-301; David B. Tyack, *George Ticknor and the Boston Brahmins* (Cambridge, Mass., 1967), pp. 85-128.

2. Andrew P. Peabody, "The Condition and Wants of Harvard College," *North American Review* 60 (January 1845): 39. For the list of Harvard graduates by years, see *Harvard University Quinquennial Catalogue of the Officers and Graduates, 1636-1930* (Cambridge, Mass., 1930), pp. 208-281.

3. For the emergence of elite funding, control and monopolization, see Ronald Story, "Harvard and the Boston Brahmins," *Journal of Social History* 8 (March 1975). For the Boston upper class in general, see e.g. Robert K. Lamb, "The Entrepreneur and the Community," in William Miller, ed., *Men in Business* (New York and Evanston, 1962): 94-119, 350; Frederick Cople Jaher, "The Boston Brahmins in the Age of Industrial Capitalism," in F. C. Jaher, ed., *The Age of Industrialism in America* (New York and London, 1968), pp. 190-193; Richard Eddy Sykes, "Massachusetts Unitarianism and Social Change, 1780-1870," (unpub. diss., University of Minnesota, 1967); Ronald Story, "Class and Culture in Boston," *American Quarterly* 27 (1975).

4. Morison, *Three Centuries,* 216-218; Frederick Robinson, "A Letter to the Hon. Rufus Choate," in Charles Haar, ed., *The Golden Age of American Law* (New York, 1965), p. 91.

5. Josiah Quincy, *Speech of February 25, 1845, on the Minority Report of Mr. Bancroft* (Boston, 1845); Jared Sparks et al, *Memorial on Harvard College* (Boston, 1850).

6. George T. Curtis, *A Memoir of Benjamin Robbins Curtis* (Boston, 1879), p. 49.

7. George Bancroft-Board of Overseers, January 1845, Harvard Overseer Reports, v. 7, Harvard University Archives (HUA).

8. See the *Harvard University Catalogue* for 1825, 1835, 1845, and 1860; and William R. Thayer, "The Tuition Fee," *Harvard Graduates Magazine* 23 (December 1914): 228.

9. ?-Amos Lawrence, December 22, 1837, Amos Lawrence Papers, Massachusetts Historical Society (MHS).

10. Sarah H. Emerson, *Life of Abby Hopper Gibbons* (New York and London, 1897) I: 177.

11. Anthony Trollope, *North America* (Baltimore, 1968), p. 143.

12. Samuel H. Walley, Jr., January 20, 1848, Harvard Overseer Reports, v. 8, HUA.

13. Theodore Parker, "A Sermon of Merchants," November 22, 1846, in *The Works of Theodore Parker,* ed. Frances Cobbe (London, 1876) VII: 9.

14. Mrs. Harrison Gray Otis, *The Barclays of Boston* (Boston, 1854), p. 46.

15. Edmund Quincy, *Life of Josiah Quincy* (Boston, 1868), p. 341.

16. April 27, 1819, Harvard Overseer Reports, v. 1, HUA.

17. William G. Stearns-Amos A. Lawrence, July 4, 1860, Amos A. Lawrence Papers, MHS.

18. E. R. Hoar, J. W. Churchill, L. N. Thayer, January 28, 1858, Harvard Overseers Miscellaneous Reports, v. 1, HUA.
19. See e.g. Ruth H. Sessions, "A Harvard Man's Budget in 1790," *Harvard Graduates Magazine* 42 (December 1933): 141; Andrew P. Peabody, *Harvard Graduates Whom I Have Known* (Boston and New York, 1890), p. 82; Isabel Anderson, ed., *The Letters and Journals of General Nicholas Longworth Anderson* (New York, London, Edinburgh, 1942), pp. 129-131; William Everett, "Harvard in 1855." *The Harvard Monthly* 3 (November 1886): 46; George L. Locke-Amos A. Lawrence, July 14, 1858, Amos A. Lawrence Papers; George Torrey, *A Lawyer's Recollections* (Boston, 1910); Robert Grant, *Fourscore* (Boston and New York, 1934), p. 90.
20. George Bancroft-Board of Overseers, January 1845, Harvard Overseer Reports, v. 7, HUA.
21. Francis Bowen, "Eliot's Sketch of Harvard College," *North American Review* 68 (January 1849): 118.
22. E. R. Hoar, J. W. Churchill, L. N. Thayer, January 28, 1858, Harvard Overseer Miscellaneous Reports, v. 1, HUA.
23. *Harvard University Catalogue for 1860-61.*
24. John A. Garraty, *Henry Cabot Lodge* (New York, 1953), p. 21. For admissions requirements and examinations, see the catalogues for 1825, 1835, 1845, 1855, and 1865; the annals of the Harvard classes of 1835 and 1852; "Harvard University," *Monthly Chronicle* 2 (February 1841): 64; John T. Kirkland, "Literary Institutions," *North American Review* 7 (July 1818): 270-271; Francis Bowen, "Classical Studies at Cambridge," ibid. 54 (January 1842): 48; Horatio J. Perry, "Harvard and Vacation Fifty Years Ago," *New England Magazine* 9 (October 1893): 208; Samuel G. Ward-Thomas W. Ward, September 9, 1839, Thomas W. Ward Papers, MHS; Ethel Fisk, ed., *The Letters of John Fiske* (New York, 1940), p. 27.
25. George Bancroft-Board of Overseers, January 1845, Harvard Overseer Reports, v. 7, HUA.
26. Thomas Cushing, "Undergraduate Life Sixty Years Ago," *Harvard Graduates Magazine* 1 (July 1893): 553.
27. James C. White, "An Undergraduate's Diary, I," *Harvard Graduates Magazine* 21 (March 1913): 423.
28. In arriving at these proportions I have relied most heavily on the classbooks and annals of the Harvard classes of 1811, 1814, 1817, 1822, 1828, 1830, 1835, 1841, 1844, 1852, 1856, 1857, and 1860. None provides complete information for all members of the class, especially before 1830. Two useful supplementary sources are Samuel A. Eliot, ed., *Heralds of a Liberal Faith* (4 vols., Boston, 1910), a biographical compilation covering dozens of early Unitarian ministers, most of whom attended Harvard; and *Harvard Memorial Biographies* (2 vols., Cambridge, 1866), which sketches members of Harvard classes from 1828 to 1865 who died in the Civil War. Charles W. Eliot's *Forty-Ninth Report of the President of Harvard, 1873-1874* (Cambridge, 1875), 82-84, produces an invaluable table on which schools prepared how many entering students from 1867 through 1874. Useful school histories are cited below, as are some of the hundreds of relevant articles and biographical studies of the period. The percentages, needless to say,

are estimates only. In deriving them I have generally excluded‾the southern students, who bulked fairly large in several ante-bellum years.

29. See e.g. George F. Hoar, *Autobiography of Seventy Years* (New York, 1903) I: 86.

30. John S. Bassett, "The Round Hill School," *American Antiquarian Society of Proceedings* n.s. 27 (April 1917): 18-35; J. G. Cogswell, *Outline of the Round Hill School* (Boston 1831); George Bancroft-Ebenezer Francis, March 19, 1827, College Papers, ser. 2, v. 1, HUA.

31. Samuel A. Atkins, *A History of Cambridge, Massachusetts* (Cambridge, Mass., 1913), p. 103; Samuel Eliot Morison, *The Class Lives of Samuel Eliot and Nathaniel Holmes Morison* (Boston, 1926), p. 3.

32. Thomas Wentworth Higginson, *Old Cambridge* (New York and London, 1900), p. 154. Other important private boarding schools between 1830 and 1850 were those of J. A. Weiss in Roxbury and W. P. Greene in Jamaica Plain.

33. William Jenks, "Plan of a School," c. 1815, ms., Boston Public Library (BPL).

34. *Annual Catalogue of the Teachers and Pupils of Chauncy-Hall School* (Boston, 1835); Thomas Cushing, *Memoir of Gideon Thayer* (n.p., 1865).

35. William Lawrence, *Memories of a Happy Life* (Boston and New York, 1926), p. 12; Octavius B. Frothingham, *Recollections and Impressions, 1822-1890* (New York, 1891), p. 20. See also Charles W. Eliot, *A Late Harvest* (Boston, 1924), pp. 19-20.

36. Computed from the reports of the secretary of the Massachusetts Board of Education for 1849-50 and 1859-60.

37. Theodore Sizer, "The Academies: An Interpretation," in Theodore Sizer, ed., *The Age of the Academies* (New York, 1964): 1-48.

38. *Report of the Roxbury School Committee, 1840*; *Report of the Roxbury Perambulating Committee, 1866*; A. K. Teele, *History of Milton Academy, Mass., 1798-1879* (Boston, 1879); John Ragle, *Governor Dummer Academy History, 1763-1963* (S. Byfield, Mass., 1963); *A History of the Dummer Academy* (Newburyport, 1914); *A General Catalogue of the Trustees, Teachers, and Students of Lawrence Academy, Groton, Massachusetts, 1793-1893* (Groton, 1893); *The Jubilee of the Lawrence Academy* (New York, 1855); *The Centenary of Leicester Academy* (Worcester, 1884); Joseph Sawyer, *A History of Williston Seminary* (Norwood, Mass., 1917); "Hopkins Classical School," flyer, Cambridge, October, 1840; "Hopkins Fund Records, 1726-1854," typescript, HUA; G. B. Emerson, *Reminiscences of an Old Teacher* (Boston, 1878): 24-64. Other relevant academies in the early years were the Atkinson Academy, N. H., and the Framingham Academy, Mass.

39. Samuel F. Batchelder, *Bits of Harvard History* (Cambridge, 1923), p. 308.

40. *Biographical Catalogue of the Trustees, Teachers and Students of Phillips Academy, Andover, 1798-1830* (Andover, 1903); Claude M. Fuess, *An Old New England School: A History of Phillips Academy, Andover* (Boston and New York, 1917); *Catalogue of the Officers and Students of Phillips Exeter Academy, 1783-1883* (Boston, 1883); Edward Echols, *The Phillips Exeter Academy* (Exeter, 1970); L. M. Crosbie, *The Phillips Exeter Academy* (Exeter, 1923).

41. See e.g. Thomas Mumford, *Memoir of Samuel Joseph May* (Boston, 1873), pp. 25-26, 59.

42. Grant, *Fourscore*, p. 31; Henry Jenks, *Catalogue of the Boston Public Latin School, with an Historical Sketch* (Boston, 1886), p. 71. See also Joseph Powers and Lee Dunn, "Brief History of the Boston Latin School," typescript, Boston Latin Papers, BPL; "Records of Subscribers to Association Funds," Boston Latin School Ms. #186, BPL.

32. Mark D. Howe, *Justice Oliver Wendell Holmes: The Shaping Years, 1841-1870* (Cambridge, Mass., 1957), pp. 6-7; Amos French, ed., *Exeter and Harvard Eighty Years Ago: Journals and Letters of F. O. French, '57* (Chester, N.H., 1932), p. 68.

44. Alexander Inglis, *The Rise of the High School in Massachusetts* (New York, 1911); George Wright, "The Schools of Cambridge, 1800-1870," *Cambridge Historical Society Publication* 13 (June 1918): 89-112.

45. On the early day schools, see e.g. Henry B. Fearon, *Sketches of America.* (2nd ed., London, 1818), pp. 112-113; on the academies, Rufus Ellis, "The Academies and Public High Schools of Massachusetts," *Christian Examiner* 50 (January 1851): 27.

46. Michael B. Katz, *The Irony of Early School Reform* (Boston, 1970), pp. 19-112.

47. "A Sermon of Merchants," November 22, 1846, in *Works of Theodore Parker* VII: 9.

48. James E. Cabot, "Bigelow's Classical and Utilitarian Studies," *North American Review* 104 (April 1867): 616.

49. *Fair Harvard* (New York and London, 1869), p. 99.

50. Percentage of Harvard millionaires computed by comparing the composite graduates list in *Harvard University Quinquennial Catalogue,* 1213-1461, with the list of Boston names in Sidney Ratner, ed., *New Light on the History of Great American Fortunes* (New York, 1953), pp. 9-22. The financial institutions analyzed include the Massachusetts, State, and Suffolk Banks, the Bank of Commerce, the Provident Institution for Savings, the Massachusetts Mutual Life Insurance Company, and the Boston Manufacturers Mutual Fire Insurance Company. For textile firms, see Frances Gregory and Irene Neu, "The American Industrial Elite in the 1870's," in Miller, *Men in Business*, p. 203.

51. George Santayana, *Character and Opinion in the United States* (New York, 1920), p. 40.

7

The Origins of Public Education: A Reassessment

Michael B. Katz

DURING the last fifteen years a modest revolution took place in the historiography of education. Historians rejected both the metaphor and the method which had characterized the record of the educational past. The method had divorced inquiry into the development of educational practices and institutions from the mainstream of historical scholarship and left it narrow, antiquated, and uninteresting. The metaphor portrayed education as a flower of democracy planted in a rich and liberating loam which its seeds continually replenished.

The contemporary rejection of metaphor and method has attempted to incorporate the study of education into current scholarship and, even more, to expand notions of social, cultural, intellectual, and political development through exploring and highlighting the role of education in modern history. The work on education at its best, however, has not been simply the reflex of social or intellectual history, plugging schooling into the framework erected by scholars in more academically established specialties, but, rather, a catalyst which itself has forced the expansion of interpretations and the re-opening of historical issues.

Too often the men and women who have worked to reshape educational history are lumped together loosely and called revisionists. Criticisms of their work too often portray their interpretations as if they had created a coherent image which distorted the educational past and maligned the educational present. That image itself comprises a more serious distortion than nearly anything these men and women have written. For it glosses over basic differences in method and sharp, sometimes fundamental distinctions in interpretation.

A good measure of the criticism directed at what has been called revisionism is implicitly political. It perceives in the interpretations it challenges a clear antagonism to existing social and educational structures and to the version of the past through which they are justified.

Michael B. Katz is professor of history and director, Urban Studies Program, at the University of Pennsylvania. "The Origins of Public Education: A Reassessment" was Katz's presidential address to the History of Education Society in 1976. A substantially revised version appears in his book, Reconstructing American Education, *published by Harvard University Press in 1987. The revised version adds the development of a distinctive form of democratic politics in America to the delineation of the contextual factors associated with the origins of public education, and it omits the discussion of hegemony, which Katz now believes was too crudely developed in the original version.*

That perception is accurate. For the historians labelled revisionist—despite their basic differences—do reject both the method and metaphor of educational history that preceded their work. Their critics, I would argue, want to accept the former, the critique of method, but to adopt only a muted and ultimately denatured rejection of metaphor. The analyses to which the critics object almost without exception represent critical history. To some extent all its practitioners share the view ascribed by Hayden White to the "exponents of historical realism," namely, that "the task of the historian" is "less to remind men of their obligation to the past than to force upon them an awareness of how the past could be used to effect an ethically responsible transition from present to future." (1) By contrast the old metaphor and its supporters serve to "remind men of their obligation to the past" rather than to attempt to liberate them for a new educational future.

Even their critics agree that historians of education of the last decade have dealt a devastating blow to the form in which the old metaphor had been cast. A simple narrative of the triumph of benevolence and democracy no longer can be offered seriously by any scholar even marginally aware of educational historiography during the last fifteen years.

Nonetheless, the extent of disagreement among the practitioners of educational history and the segmental nature of much of their work—the important concentration upon detailed case studies, for instance—has made difficult the emergence of a new and satisfying synthesis.

Here I cannot review and synthesize in detail the significant work in the field during the last fifteen years. Rather, I can offer you the outline—a sketch—of what, at this point, appears to me the most balanced and useful account in light of what our colleagues in the field have written and my own research shows.

If I were to treat the origins of public education fully, I should have to address at least three questions: why did people establish systems of public education; how did they go about that task; and what results did their efforts have? Given the limits of space, I shall confine myself, for the most part, to the first question and try to convey to you my sense of the purposes which people of the time hoped public school systems would serve.

For a variety of reasons, my own work during the last several years has focused not on the history of education but on the history of social structure and family organization during industrialization. That research has centered on a case study of the city of Hamilton, Ontario, during the last part of the nineteenth century. I have undertaken a basically quantitative reconstruction of the entire population of the city at various intervals from the manuscript census, assessment rolls, and a variety of other sources. (2) My colleagues and I currently are extending the work to include a comparison of Hamilton with Buffalo, New York, and rural Erie County in the same period.

The results of this line of research have been enormously exciting for me; for the numbers have become patterns which represent the lives of an entire population in a time of momentous social change. Indeed, my colleagues and I have been able to examine questions which hitherto have seemed unanswerable and, even more interesting, to find questions we never would have thought to ask.

Eventually, my goal is to unite this empirical work on the composition of society and families with the study of social institutions. For I believe the kind of research in which I am now engaged has profound implications for the questions about the history of education which I set out to answer more than a decade ago. (3) The interpretation which I shall offer you here draws on some of this recent work and circles backwards, trying to integrate what I believe happened to social structure and to the family with the development of systems of public education.

I

At the outset it is well to make clear exactly what I wish to try to explain: namely, the emergence of *systems* of public education. Here the word systems is crucial. For in neither Canada nor the United States were schools unusual or novel creations in the nineteenth century, and in neither place was it unusual for them to receive some sort of public support, though, as I shall mention again, in most places the line between public and private was not drawn with precision until well into the nineteenth century. Though schools existed and frequently received some public support, the haphazard arrangements of the seventeenth, eighteenth, and early nineteenth centuries cannot be considered true progenitors of the school systems we know today. For by the latter part of the nineteenth century the organization, scope and role of schooling had been fundamentally transformed. In place of a few casual schools dotted about town and country there existed in most cities true educational systems: carefully articulated, age graded, hierarchically structured groupings of schools, primarily free and often compulsory, administered by full-time experts and progressively taught by specially trained staff. No longer casual adjuncts to the home or apprenticeship, schools were highly formal institutions designed to play a critical role in the socialization of the young, the maintenance of social order, and the promotion of economic development. Within the space of 40 or 50 years a new social institution had been invented, and it is this startling and momentous development that we must seek to understand. (4)

The origins of public educational systems cannot be understood apart from their context. For they formed part of four critical developments that reshaped North American society during the first three-quarters of the nineteenth century. Those developments were: first, industrialization and urbanization; second, the assumption by the state of direct responsibility for some aspects of social welfare; third, the invention of institutionalization as a solution to social problems; and fourth, the redefinition of the family.

In the remainder of this discussion I shall comment on the relation of public educational systems to these four developments; highlight five particular problems which schools were designed to alleviate; comment briefly upon the process through which public educational systems actually emerged; and conclude with a few observations about the relation of the educational past to the educational present.

During the early and mid-nineteenth century industrialization, urbanization, and immigration reshaped the economic and social order of North America. The pace and timing of social development varied of course, from region to region. However, everywhere a close temporal connection existed between social development and the creation of public educational systems. In the United States, for example, the date at which the first high school opened provides a rough but convenient index of educational development which, across the country, retained a strong association with social and economic complexity. (5) Our understanding of the relationships between the introduction of industrial capitalism, the transformation of the technology of production, the redistribution of the population into cities, and the creation of systems of public education remains far from precise, and I shall speculate on the connection between them later on in this discussion. At the outset, however, it is important to observe and remember the *temporal* connection between the economy, the social order, and the schools.

The development of systems of public education did not comprise the sole thrust of governments into the area of social welfare during the early and mid-nineteenth century. For in England, the United States and Canada it was in this period that governments generally began to exchange their haphazard and minimal concern with social problems for a systematic approach to questions of welfare. At the start of the period problems of poverty, public health, crime, insanity, disease, and the condition of labor remained more or less untended, subject to ancient legislation, custom, sporadic regulation, and public and private charity. By the end of the third quarter of the nineteenth century each had become the subject of public debate, legislative activity, and the supervision of newly created state administrative bodies with full-time, expert staffs. It may be anachronistic to look on the first half of the nineteenth century in Britain, as one historian does, as the period of the "origins of the welfare state" because few people at the time had in mind the creation of an apparatus with the size and scope which we know today. Still, the results of their activities created the framework within which subsequent state activity in the realm of social welfare commenced its growth; and their actions provided the first precedents for more contemporary innovations. (6)

The state did not enter into the area of public welfare without serious opposition. Its activity commenced at a time when the very distinction between public and private had not emerged with any sort of clarity, and in this situation the definition of public responsibility became an especially elusive task. In most cases voluntary activity preceded state action. Philanthropic associations, composed often primarily of women and usually associated with the spread of evangelical religion, first undertook the alleviation of social distress. In part their activity reflected the lack of any public apparatus to cope with the increased misery that people discovered in the growing cities of the late eighteenth and early nineteenth centuries; in part, too, it reflected the belief that social distress represented a temporary, if recurring, problem which charitable activity could alleviate. The activities of voluntary associations, however, usually convinced their members that problems were both far more widespread and intractable than they had believed, and they turned, consequently, to the public for assistance, first usually in the form of grants, later in the assumption of formal and permanent responsibility. (7)

No very clear models for action, however, existed, and people concerned with social policy at the time debated not only the legitimacy of public activity but its organizational form. As I have argued elsewhere in the case of education, their disagreements over the nature of public organizations reflected fundamental value conflicts and alternative visions of social development. If the shape that modern society eventually assumed appears inevitable to us today, it did not appear at all clear to the people of the time, which is an observation we must remember if we are to understand the passion aroused by debates about social institutions and policies in the nineteenth century.

In fact, in the United States four distinct models for the organization of formal education coexisted and competed in the early and mid-nineteenth century, and at the time the outcome of their conflict did not appear at all self-evident to many sane and responsible people. The alternative that triumphed might be called, as I have suggested, incipient bureaucracy. Though its advocates generally supported the extension of a competitive and laissez-faire approach to economic issues, they encouraged a strong regulatory role for the state in the area of social welfare and morality. Their model organizations were controlled by bodies responsible to legislatures, financed directly through taxation, administered by experts, and relatively large in size. They were, in short, public *institutions*, in a novel and dramatic sense. (8)

Thus, the victory of incipient bureaucracy reflected a new faith in the power of formal institutions to alleviate social and individual distress. The novelty of this commitment to institutions must be appreciated, for it represented a radical departure in social policy. Prior to the nineteenth century institutions played a far smaller and much less significant social role: the mentally ill, by and large, lived with other members of the community or in an undifferentiated poorhouse; criminals remained for relatively brief periods in jails awaiting trial and punishment by fine, whipping, or execution; the poor were given outdoor relief or, if they were a nuisance, driven from the community. By the middle or third quarter of the nineteenth century all of this had changed. In place of the few, undifferentiated almshouses, jails, and schools there now existed in most cities, states and provinces a series of new inventions: mental hospitals, penitentiaries, reformatories, and public schools. Shapers of social policy had embodied in concrete form the notion that rehabilitation, therapy, medical treatment and education should take place within large, formal, and often residential institutions. The explanation of how that idea swiftly permeated public practice comprises one of the most fascinating, frightening and significant stories in modern history. For it is the account of the origins of the institutional state which governs and regulates our lives today. (9)

Lest it should seem inevitable that modern society should be an institutional state, it is worth pointing out that responsible people at the time did see alternatives. In New York, for instance, Charles Loring Brace proposed the shipment of city urchins to the West as an alternative to their institutionalization, and elsewhere opponents and skeptics at the time critically, perceptively, and with, in retrospect, an eerily modern ring, pointed to the dangers and limitations of institutions. (10)

One of their common arguments centered on the family. Both proponents and critics of institutions agreed that the ideal family provided a paradigm for social policy. Rather than supply an alternative to the family, to their supporters institutions would become, quite literally, as Alison Prentice and Susan Houston have argued, surrogate families for the mentally ill, the criminal, the delinquent, and the schoolchild. In fact, it was precisely through their embodiment of a familial environment that new institutions, according to their sponsors, would perform their rehabilitative, therapeutic, or educational work. The difficulty, as critics astutely pointed out, was that no institution could imitate a real family. (11)

Nonetheless, in the early and mid-nineteenth century both critics and supporters of institutions shared a widespread sense that the family was in some sort of trouble, though about the exact nature of that difficulty they remained somewhat vague. In fact, they probably mistook change for deterioration because the fragments of historical evidence about the family in this period indicate not breakdown but an important shift in domestic structure and relations.

Commonly, social theorists have believed that the nuclear replaced the extended family during industrialization. The work of Peter Laslett and other historians has shown quite conclusively that, as it is usually argued, this proposition is clearly wrong for British, American or Canadian Society, and probably for Western Society in general. The majority of families—or, in Laslett's terminology, co-resident domestic groups—at any point in time appears to have been nuclear in structure. That is not to say, however, that their role and other aspects of their organization did not change, for they did. And it is these more subtle, but real and consequential alterations that historians are just beginning to appreciate. (12)

The most dramatic change that occurred during industrialization has been pointed out frequently. It is, of course, the separation of home and workplace. Not only within rural but also within urban areas this gradual division of place of residence and place of work fundamentally altered the day-to-day pattern of family existence, the relationships between family members and (sociologists would argue) the very influence of the family itself. (13)

The separation of home and workplace formed one part of the process by which the boundaries between the family and community became more sharply drawn. As part of the increasing specialization of institutions, the family shed its productive function as well as its role in the treatment of deviance. Rather than diminish in importance, however, the family gained stature through its heightened role in the socialization of its children, which earlier had been shared more widely with the community. This tightening and emotional intensification of the family fundamentally reshaped the process of growing up.

My argument here is tenuous, and you should realize that it rests on speculation made on the basis of data from my study of Hamilton and the bits of evidence I have been able to assemble from other studies. If I am right, for centuries it had been customary for parents of various social ranks to send their children away from home to live as surrogate members of another household for a number of years between puberty and marriage. Young people in this stage of their lives, which I call semi-autonomy, exchanged the complete control of their parents for a supervised yet relatively more autonomous situation in another household. It would take me too far from my topic here to elaborate upon the evidence for this stage or upon its meaning. Rather, I wish simply to point to semi-autonomy as a phase in the life cycle that virtually disappeared during the development of modern capitalist society. By the mid-nineteenth century, or shortly thereafter, depending upon the pace of economic development, young people began to remain within their parents' home after they had found work, staying there roughly until marriage, far longer than ever had been the case before. At the same time, many remained in school for prolonged periods of time, and young men began to enter their fathers' occupations far less frequently. Certainly, I am deliberately foreshortening a complex process in order to provide support for the main point I wish to make about the family: namely, that it acquired an increasingly important and specialized role in the socialization of its children as part of a general tightening of the boundaries between social institutions and between the family and community. (14)

The heightened attention that people gave to their children is at least suggested by trends in fertility. In the United States marital fertility among native whites fell during the first half of the nineteenth century. In Ontario, it decreased sharply after 1870. At some point between the second and third quarters of the nineteenth century, it appears, very substantial numbers of people began to make a conscious decision to limit the size of their families. The reason is unclear. As some scholars have argued, the decision could reflect the decline in infant and child-hood mortality. Women needed to bear fewer children to assure that a reasonable number would survive. At the same time decreased early childhood mortality provided parents with a heightened incentive to invest emotionally in each of their offspring. On the other hand, it is possible to point to the difficulty that parents had providing for their children. As it became necessary to keep children at home and in school, a large family may well have become an intolerable economic burden to people of middling means. Whatever the exact explanation for the decline in fertility, and it remains one of the most hotly argued and contentious issues in historical demography, it does point, again, to a sharpened concern with shaping and controlling the family, and it does imply an intensification of the emotional bonds between parent and child. (15)

Popular ideas about domesticity and the role of women reflected the redefinition of the family. The "cult of true womanhood," as it has been called, urged women to create within the home a haven against the harsh world of commerce and a nest in which children could be reared with attention and affection. From one perspective the ideal of domesticity has justified a not especially subtle attempt to keep wom-en within the home subservient to their husbands. However, it also elevated the importance of women as the moral guardians and spiritual saviours of an increasingly corrupt and irreligious society. Despite this tension in its meaning, popular ideology reinforced the structural changes within the family. In both social thought and reality, the family —and I suspect in time the working as well as the middle class family—

became an increasingly private, intense, and sharply defined agency for the nurture of the young. (16)

One aspect of the history of women illustrates especially clearly the complex interconnections between educational change and the ideological, demographic, institutional, and technological factors that we have observed. I refer to the feminization of teaching, which occurred with remarkable swiftness around the middle of the nineteenth century in the eastern United States and a bit later in Canada. In both places, by and large, women took over from men the education of young children in primary schools. As the ideology of domesticity to which I have referred would lead us to expect, the moral and spiritual role assigned to women not only justified but made imperative their entrance into classrooms as surrogate mothers. If the school, like other mid-nineteenth-century institutions, was to resemble a home, it should be presided over by a wise and loving mother. In this sense the shift from men to women in the schoolroom paralleled the shift in primary moral responsibility from husbands to wives in the ideal middle-class home. As men increasingly left home to work, they left the schoolroom as well. (17)

However, cultural imperatives did not comprise the only forces at work in the feminization of teaching. As the state assumed increasing responsibility for the public provision of schools, it became necessary for communities to expand the proportion of school places available. At the same time urbanization and, especially, massive immigration enlarged the absolute number of eligible school children enormously. Obviously, the combination of a desire to expand schooling and a substantial population increase placed a severe strain upon local financial resources. In this situation, women provided a ready solution to a potential problem. For they were paid but half as much as men, who, in an era of expanding commercial and industrial opportunity, increasingly had before them job prospects more attractive than teaching. Thus, through the feminization of its teaching force a town could find a sufficient number of teachers to double its school places while holding its expenditures for salary roughly constant.

Although the payment of women a wage half that given to men was exploitative, it obviously did not deter women at the time from entering teaching. Wherever I have found accounts of hiring, many women applicants always competed for every job. The reason is not hard to understand. In the period when teaching opened to them women had essentially only four other occupational alternatives: domestic service, dressmaking, work in a mill, or prostitution. To many young women at the time, teaching, despite its low wages, must have appeared a welcome and genteel opportunity. (18)

Thus, we are left with an intricate problem: what caused the feminization of teaching? Rather than attempt to weave together the strands, I should like, simply, to leave the feminization of teaching with you as at once a problem to ponder and, even more, as an illustration of the way in which the contextual elements I have isolated intertwined with the origins of systems of public education in the nineteenth century.

However, though educational development can be viewed as part of a larger series of changes in North American society, it must become the focus of our attention in its own right. For school promoters argued that the introduction of public educational systems would alleviate a number of specific and substantial problems within contemporary society.

II

For the most part, in the remainder of this discussion I shall outline briefly the connection people of the time perceived between the origins of public educational systems and the alleviation of a number of critical problems. However, my emphasis to some extent minimizes the most interesting and complex task. For when it stops you should have a sense of the broader developments of which public educational systems formed a part and the specific tasks they were to undertake. You will have, however, only a glimmer of the coherent explanation, for which the simple listing of factors cannot substitute. What you will require, even if you do not disagree seriously with the main propositions in this analysis, is an explanation which shows exactly how the developments and problems listed here interacted with each other to produce systems of public education. That explanation is an important and subtle task, drawing as it must not only on historical events but on a theory of social development and on a sociology of knowledge and motivation. Though I cannot undertake that task in any adequate way in a brief discussion, I should indicate at least the general shape which the explanation, in my view, should assume.

Most interpretations of the relationship between institutional development and social change in the nineteenth century remain unsatisfying because they reflect the inadequate conceptual framework through which early North American history usually is viewed. Most histories of the period from Colonial times to, roughly, 1875 rest on a simple two-stage paradigm: a shift from a pre-industrial to an industrial society, or from a rural to an urban one. (19) This paradigm makes difficult the systematic relation between institutions and social change. For, though the transformation of economic structures and the creation of institutions did take place at roughly the same period, the chronological fit between industrialism and institutions is imperfect, and attempts to construct causal models or to develop tight and coherent explanations usually appear too mechanistic or vague.

When a three stage paradigm replaces the two-stage one, the fit between social change and institutional creation becomes tighter. In the three stage paradigm, North America shifted from a peculiar variety of a mercantile-peasant economy to a mercantile capitalist to an industrial capitalist society. Though the pace of change varied from region to region and stages overlapped each other, the most important aspect of the late eighteenth and early nineteenth centuries was not industrialization or urbanization but, rather, the spread of capitalism, defined, in Dobb's words, as "not simply a system of production for the market . . . but a system under which labour-power had 'itself become a commodity' and was bought and sold on the market like any other object of exchange." Theoretically, in this point of view capitalism is the necessary, though conceptually distinct, antecedent of industrialization. (20)

Consider the chronology of institutional development. In New York State dissatisfaction with the existing system of poor relief led to the passage of a law creating specialized county poorhouses in 1825; the first special institution for juvenile vagrants and delinquents opened in 1827; the New York Public School Society emerged out of the Free School Society in 1824. In Massachusetts the first state hospital for the mentally ill opened in 1833; poor relief underwent fundamental shifts in the 1820s; agitation for educational reform really began in the same decade. The point of these examples is to show that the drive towards institutional innovation *preceded* the industrial take-off in the Northeast. (21)

On the other hand, the similarity in the timing of movements toward innovation in public policy did not happen by accident. The policies that created institutions arose in response to shifting social conditions: most directly from pressures felt within cities and regions experiencing a shift to a capitalist mode of production.

The most characteristic and important feature of capitalism for the development of institutions, including public school systems, was its utilization of wage-labor and the consequent need for a mobile, unbound labor force. The shift in the nature of social organization consequent upon the emergence of a class of wage-laborers, rather than industrialization or urbanization, fueled the development of public institutions.

This interpretation must remain partly speculative because we lack hard data on a variety of critical, specific issues, especially the proportion of the work-force engaged in wage-labor at various points in time. However, enough clues do exist to make the three-stage paradigm at least plausible—consistent with social reality, that is, as well as with social theory. For instance, the most striking change in New York

City's occupational structure between 1796 and 1855, using Carl Kaestle's figures, was the increase in the proportion of men who listed themselves simply as laborers, a rise from 5.5% to 27.4%. We know, too, that apprenticeship, whose emphasis on bound labor is incompatible with capitalism, had ceased to function with anything like its traditional character well before industrialization. From a different point of view, one historian recently has pointed to an unmistakable increase in the wandering of the poor from place to place in late eighteenth-century Massachusetts. Of course, the expansion of commerce in this period has been documented extensively, and we already have observed the abandonment of mercantilist economic regulations by the state in the same period. (22)

Capitalism as a concept assists in the interpretation of institutional development for two reasons: first, institutions reflected the drive toward order, rationality, discipline, and specialization inherent in capitalism. There is a parallel between the way in which a capitalist society processes its business and its problems. The problems themselves communities had coped with disaster, distress, and deviance.

Consider these circumstances: The seasonality and irregularity of work in early capitalist society posed problems as great as the meagre subsistence wages paid to laborers. At the same time that chronic underemployment became a permanent situation, the creation of a mobile labor force and increasing transiency sundered the ties of individuals to communities. In crises or periods of difficulty, people decreasingly found themselves within a community of familiar neighbors and kin to whom they could turn for help. In this situation, state and local authorities had to innovate in order to cope with the dislocation, distress, and destitution of landless wage workers. (23)

Early and mid-nineteenth century school promoters argued that public educational systems could attack five major problems, which, with hindsight, appear products of early capitalist development. Although observers at the time were more definite about symptoms than causes, they surely would agree with the identity and urgency of this list: (1) urban crime and poverty; (2) increased cultural heterogeneity; (3) the necessity to train and discipline an urban and industrial workforce; (4) the crisis of youth in the nineteenth-century city; and (5) the anxiety among the middle classes about their adolescent children.

According to nineteenth-century social commentators, a massive increase in both crime and poverty accompanied the growth of cities and the development of modern industry. Though the actual dimensions of the problem remain unclear—that is, whether crime and poverty increased disproportionately or merely kept pace with population growth—what matters for our purposes is the widespread belief among the "respectable" classes in an epidemic of lawlessness and pauperism threatening the foundations of morality and the maintenance of social order. In the formulations of the time, it is important to observe, crime and poverty did not comprise two distinct problems. Rather, the terms criminal and pauper overlapped and merged into synonyms for deviant and anti-social behaviour that stemmed from individual, moral failure. (24)

The process or causal mechanism through which urbanization worked its mischief remained vague in mid-nineteenth-century social commentaries. Nonetheless, neither crime nor poverty appeared, as they once had been, the accidental results of misfortune or deviance among an otherwise stable and reliable population. To the contrary, the emergence of fundamentally new classes of people, it was argued, had accompanied social transformation. Criminals and paupers were not merely individuals but representatives of the criminal and pauper class, and it was the implications of the iceberg rather than its tip that frightened respectable people.

Although people concerned with the explanation of crime and poverty often relied on environmental rather than genetic explanations, their arguments still reflected the lack of any very deep understanding of the relationship between social structure and social deviance. For in the last analysis blame fell upon the lower classes. Crime and poverty became moral problems, which arose because the lower-class urban family failed to implant earnestness and restraint within the character of its children. Raised in an atmosphere of intemperance, indulgence, and neglect, the lower-class urban child began life predisposed to criminality and unprepared for honest work. By definition, in this argument, the lower-class family became the breeding place of paupers and criminals.

Given these premises, schooling held an obvious attraction. Exposure to public education, it was widely believed, would provide the lower-class child with an alternative environment and a superior set of adult models. Through its effect upon the still pliable and emergent personalities of its clientele, a school system would prove a cheap and superior substitute for the jail and the poorhouse. As some of the more acute commentators at the time observed, the school was to become a form of police. Thus, though expenditures on public schooling might seem high, they would in fact ultimately lessen the burden imposed upon society by adult crime and poverty.

Mid-nineteenth-century social policy blurred more than the distinction between poverty and criminality; it equated cultural diversity with immorality and deviance as well. Thus, the ethnic composition of expanding cities became a source of special anxiety. At first it was the massive immigration into North America of the famine Irish that made the problem acute. To the "respectable classes" of North America poor Irish Catholics appeared alien, uncouth, and menacing. Once again we must confront the relationship between reality and the perception of people at the time. For most contemporary research indicates that the Irish were not intemperate, shiftless, and ignorant as the nativists portrayed them. To the contrary: the immigrants, it now is reasonable to suppose, may have represented a select, especially highly motivated, and unusually literate portion of Irish society. And whatever instability their lives in North America might have revealed probably stemmed—as Theodore Hershberg and his associates have discovered in the case of ex-slaves—from the harsh and discriminatory urban social structure which they encountered rather than from any moral slackness within their culture. (25)

Nonetheless, as in the case of crime and poverty, social commentators proved unable or unwilling to connect the problem they thought they saw around them with its structural basis, and they consequently, once again, retreated to an explanation which traced the source of a social problem to a moral weakness, in this case embedded in a set of foreign and inferior cultural traditions. As with most cases of nativist behavior the shrill exaggeration with which observers dwelled on the subversive potential of the immigrants' alleged sensual indulgence reveals more about the critics themselves than about the objects of their attack. It is tempting to argue that nativists projected onto the Irish the sensuality that they consciously repressed within their own lives and hated them for acting out the fantasies which they denied themselves. Certainly, the key phrases in contemporary prescriptions of the good life were restraint and the substitution of higher for lower pleasures, attributes precisely the opposite of those which many thought they saw in the lives of the Irish immigrant poor. (26) Whatever the truth of this speculation may be, it is quite clear that the brittle and hostile response to Irish immigrants revealed an underlying fear and distrust of cultural diversity.

Once more the implications of a widespread social problem for the role of schooling are transparent. Although the cultural predisposition of adult immigrants might prove intractable, the impending rot of Anglo-American civilization could be averted through a concerted effort to shape the still pliable characters of their children into a native mold. This massive task of assimilation required weakening the connection between the immigrant child and its family, which in turn, required the capture of the child by an outpost of native culture. In short, the anxiety about cultural heterogeneity propelled the establishment of systems of public education; from the very beginning public schools became agents of cultural standardization.

The need to discipline an urban workforce interacted with the fear of crime and poverty and the anxiety about cultural diversity to hasten the establishment of public educational systems. Although the problem still persists in developing societies today, it perhaps first arose in its modern form during the early industrialization of Britain, as E. P. Thompson has eloquently described. The difficulty emerged from the incongruity between customary rhythms of life and the requirements of urban and industrial work settings. In contrast to the punctuality, regularity, docility, and deferral of gratification demanded in a modern workforce, populations, both peasant and urban, usually had governed their activities more by the sun than by the clock, more by the season and customary festivities than by an externally set production schedule, more by the relationships established within small work groups than by the regimentation of the factory. (27)

At the same time, rewards had been distributed more on the basis of ascribed than achieved qualities. Social position devolved upon successive generations mainly as a result of heredity, and it would be considered not corrupt but correct to favor a kinsman over a more qualified stranger in the award of jobs or favors. The contrast in this respect between traditional and modern custom certainly remains less than absolute in practice. Nonetheless, the ideal that governs behavior has nearly reversed itself. For democratic ideology, with its emphasis upon merit and concepts such as equality of educational opportunity, advocates the substitution of achievement for ascription as the ideal basis for the distribution of rewards in contemporary society.

Their promoters expected public school systems to bring about precisely this substitution of achievement for ascription combined with the inculcation of modern habits of punctuality, regularity, docility, and the postponement of gratification. It is no accident that the mass production of clocks and watches began at about the same time as the mass production of public schools. (28)

These disciplinary goals became especially obvious in the reports of local school committees across the continent. Everywhere the major obsessions—and difficulties—were punctuality and regularity of attendance, while the villains were parents uneducated to the importance of schooling who allowed or encouraged their children to remain at home for what, to school promoters, appeared whimsical reasons or who took the side of their child against the teacher. At a higher level, state and provincial authorities continually complained about the refusal of local school committees to introduce universalistic criteria into the hiring of teachers who, too often, were simply kin or friends. In this way the school system as a whole became an object lesson in the organization of modern society, a force, as its promoters were fond of pointing out, which would radiate its influence outward through entire communities.

Through the establishment, organization, and ' correct operation of school systems the habits of a population would be transformed to match the emerging and radically new social and economic order. (29)

Among their litany of complaints about urban populations, social commentators repeatedly included a denunciation of the masses of idle and vagrant youth roaming city streets. Once I was tempted to treat their observations on this score as middle-class moralizing. Now, though they are moralistic to be sure, the evidence points to their firm anchor in social reality, for school promoters saw about them a very real crisis of youth in the nineteenth-century city. In pre-capitalist Western society long-standing customs defined the expectations and duties of people throughout their life cycle with reasonable precision. Young people left home, perhaps around the age of 14, to work as servants or apprentices, almost always dwelling in another household. During no span of years was it unclear where young people should live or how they should spend their time. Thus idleness, on any large scale, was an unimaginable social problem. (30)

However, during the rapid growth of cities in the eighteenth and nineteenth centuries the population of young people increased enormously while apprenticeship gradually decayed as an effective social institution. Indeed, the demise of a prolonged, highly regulated apprenticeship accompanied the first phase of capitalist development and preceded industrialization by some decades. And the practice of keeping male servants apparently had declined well before apprenticeship. Whether young women found fewer opportunities for work as domestic servants remains unclear; however, there is evidence that large numbers of young women were neither in school nor employed outside their family. (31)

Traditional practices declined not only prior to industrialization but also before the creation of any network of institutions to contain and manage young people. Young people who once would have worked as apprentices or servants now had literally almost nothing to do, for in a pre-industrial urban economy, contrary to what is often believed, there existed little work for young men. Their labour, in fact, was scarcely more necessary than that of adolescents today. Without schools or jobs, large numbers of youths undoubtedly remained in an unwilling state of idleness until, in the case of young men, they became old enough to find work or, in the case of young women, until they married. The existence of these idle young people is the situation which I call the crisis of youth in the nineteenth-century city.

In Hamilton, for example, during the decade that population growth made the problem of youth most acute, about half of the young people over the age of 13 or 14 were neither in work nor at school and exactly how they spent their time remains a puzzle. Not a puzzle, though, is the timing of the creation of a school system, which took place, precisely, in the decade following the sudden appearance of large numbers of idle youth on the city's streets. The establishment of a school system with special provisions for young people over the age of 11 or 12 almost immediately and dramatically reduced the proportion of idle youth. However, it is apparent that many young people entered school simply because they could not find work, for when jobs in factories first became available during the next decade, large numbers of working-class young men left the schools while their more affluent contemporaries— and young women—remained behind. (32)

Affluent parents had promoted the establishment of school systems partly on account of their own problems, which might be called middle-class anxiety. I use the term middle class with trepidation. If nothing else, my study of social structure during the last several years has taught me the elusiveness and ambiguity of class labels. By middle class I mean not only professionals, entrepreneurs, and others in non-manual occupations but also the more prosperous and independent artisans. For the greatest dividing line in the nineteenth-century commerical city did not separate white and blue collar in our modern sense. Indeed, the independent artisan was at once a proprietor and a producer. Rather, the great gulf divided the skilled from the unskilled workman. Paid badly, working irregularly, the unskilled formed what might be called a laboring class. My point is not that laborers cared less about their families but, simply, that they could not share one of the two fundamental concerns that made the others anxious. For one of those concerns was downward social mobility, and the laboring class already had hit the bottom.

The anxiety about slipping down the social ladder which permeates both nineteenth-century social commentary and fiction relates in a complex manner to actual experience. Nineteenth-century cities revealed at once a curious combination of rigidity and fluidity. Within them sharply entrenched patterns of inequality persisted, while the experience of individual people and the very identity of the population itself changed with dazzling rapidity. Nineteenth-century cities can perhaps best be thought of as railroad stations with waiting rooms for different classes. Although the population of the station constantly changed, those who departed were replaced by people with remarkably similar characteristics. And, though their populations constantly increased, the proportions in the various waiting rooms remained about the same. Studies of individual social mobility within nineteenth-century cities reveal this combination of stability and transience. On the one hand they show a high rate of status transmission from father to son; the popular image of a continent of opportunity wide open to talent simply cannot be sustained, though many men made modest gains that undoubtedly appeared critical to their lives. Few laborers, that is, replicated the rags to riches version of success, but many managed eventually to buy a small house. At the same time, entrepreneurs failed in business with extraordinary frequency. Indeed, entrepreneurial activity entailed enormous risks, which made the threat of catastrophe ever present. For example, almost half of one small sample of entrepreneurs whose histories I followed around the middle of the century failed in their businesses. (33)

For different reasons, the position of artisans became increasingly insecure as technological development eroded the association of skill and reward that had been the hallmark of many crafts. In the 1850's, for instance, the introduction of the sewing machine suddenly brought about a deterioration in the position of shoemakers and tailors as manufacturers flooded the market with cheap goods. In this situation, artisans no longer could assure the comfort and prosperity of their sons through passing on to them their skills. Indeed, it is poignant to observe the extent to which sons of shoemakers ceased to follow their fathers' crafts within the course of one decade. In practical terms, in order for the artisan to assure his son a position commensurate to his own he had to assist his entry into different occupations, particularly commerce or the expanding public bureaucracies. (34)

A generalized uneasiness about adolescence itself accompanied this widespread anxiety about the transmission of status. This was particularly evident in the controversies between the proponents of high schools and private academies. That debate revealed a growing reluctance to send youths away from home. The complementary arguments that no school could replicate a family and that actual residence within the family for a prolonged period had become a critical aspect of socialization reflected the shift in the life cycle that I observed earlier: young people increasingly spent more of the years between puberty and marriage in the home of their parents. (35)

The source of the heightened anxiety about post-pubescent young people in the nineteenth century reflected, at least partially, their newly ambiguous and uneasy position in the family and community. Partially, too, uncertainty about their economic prospects formed one strand of the anxiety. The *intensity* with which people began to worry about what we since have come to call adolescence, however, is what I wish to highlight for the moment because one of its outcomes, quite naturally, was a search for a form of schooling that would allow young people to live at home while they acquired the education necessary to retain their parents' status in an uncertain and shifting economic order. Despite a good deal of egalitarian rhetoric to the contrary, I suspect that the anxiety of the middle-classes about their children formed the driving force behind the establishment of public secondary schools and, in fact, solidified the commitment of the middle-classes to public education itself.

You will observe that my discussion of the purposes of public schooling has omitted one area of concern: the transmission of cognitive skills. Very simply, the cultivation of skills and intellectual abilities as ends in themselves did not have nearly as much importance in the view of early school promoters as the problems which I have outlined. Public school systems existed to shape behavior and attitudes, alleviate social problems, and reinforce a social structure under stress. In this context, the character of pupils remained of far greater concern than their minds.

III

The process through which school promoters translated their aspirations into institutions forms a topic of nearly equal importance to the purposes which they hoped to achieve, though one which I can only mention today. For the style of educational development, as I have argued elsewhere, had lasting consequences for the relationship between school systems and the communities which they served and for the nature of the educational experience itself. Though the documents are there, historians have been slow to examine the question of process systematically. From one point of view, we need more studies which try to account for the way in which institutions embodying a passionate commitment to social reform turned relatively quickly into large, rigid, and unresponsive bureaucracies. From another perspective, we should encourage more of the kind of work David Tyack has done on the way in which ethnicity, class, and politics intertwined in the processes through which school systems were fashioned and refashioned. Finally, historians must confront head-on the question which I raised some years ago about the class relationships represented by the style of educational promotion in the mid-nineteenth century. To what extent can public educational systems be said to have been imposed upon the poor? The answer to that question, I think, must involve considerably more sophisticated models of class and class relations than historians of education hitherto have brought to bear upon the problem. It is, moreover, a question of considerable importance because its answer, I suspect, will enable us to understand the vexing issue of why the ideology of public education came to be an axiom of popular belief accepted throughout the social structure. For the results of public education have remained quite at variance with its promise, especially to the poor and to minorities.

The resolution of that puzzle requires an analysis that extends far beyond the scope of this discussion. However, it may be useful to point to one direction which its exploration should take. To begin, a distinction in the use of the concept of imposition must underlie the discussion. In Antonio Gramsci's terms, "the apparatus of state coercive power which 'legally' enforces discipline on those groups who do not 'consent' either actively or passively. . . ." must be contrasted with "the 'spontaneous' consent given by the great masses of the population to the general direction imposed on social life by the dominant fundamental group." (36)

In the case of public educational systems we at best marginally confront imposition in the first sense. Education became compulsory only after attendance had become nearly universal. The initial popular reaction to public educational systems sometimes reflected apathy, resentment, or hostility but, given its radical intrusion into the life-cycle and the relations between parents and children, the ease with which public education entered social life stands out as truly remarkable. Most people, by and large, did not need to be coerced to send their children to school. (37)

Thus, the question becomes spontaneous consent. The introduction of public educational systems, initiated, sponsored, and governed by well-to-do and locally powerful people, represented, to repeat Gramsci's phrase, a "direction imposed on social life by the dominant fundamental group." Imposition, in this sense, it is critical to understand, does not imply conspiracy or malevolence. The relationship between ideologically sustained imposition and group consciousness is immensely complex. This complexity—and the underlying distinction between individual motivation and ideology—has been expressed especially clearly by David Brion Davis in his discussion of the ideology of anti-slavery. "Ideological hegemony," writes Davis, "is not the product of conscious choice and seldom involves insincerity or deliberate deception. . . . Ideology is a mode of consciousness, rooted in but not reducible to the needs of a social group. . . . At issue, then, are not conscious intentions but the social functions of ideology; not individual motives but shifting patterns of thought and value which focused attention on new problems, which camouflaged others, and which defined new conceptions of social reality." (38)

Note that Davis speaks of "ideological hegemony." By this he means the second use of imposition, "the predominance, obtained by consent rather than force, of one class or group over other classes," or "the 'spontaneous' loyalty that any dominant social group obtains from the masses by virtue of its social and intellectual prestige and its supposedly superior function in the world of production." The popular acceptance of public education represented ideological hegemony: the unselfconscious and willing acceptance of a direction imposed on social life by the dominant fundamental group. (39)

The question is why? It is easiest to understand the social functions of the ideology of public education for the dominant fundamental group; I have dealt at some length with them in this discussion. However, the popular acceptance of an institution whose results from the start differed sharply from its ideological justification requires a more complex explanation.

Public education received popular assent at least partly because it did not differ from the dominant ideology of democratic capitalism in nineteenth-century North America. Public educational systems crystalized key components of social ideology into an institutional form and assured its transmission. The school system became a miniature version of the social order. Within both school and society, according to the ideal which underlay their organization, universalistic and individualistic criteria replaced the handicaps of birth, and achievement became available on the basis of ability. Within the public schools, as within society at large, the able should rise simply by virtue of their own talents. As Stephan Thernstrom has written:

> The function of the ideology of mobility was to supply the citizens of nineteenth century America with a scheme for comprehending and accommodating themselves to a new social and economic order. According to this doctrine, a distinctively open social system had appeared in the United States. The defining characteristic of this open society was its perfect competitiveness, which guaranteed a complete correspondence between social status and merit. (40)

In time the connection between achievement in school and achievement within the social order made even more intimate the ties between schooling and life.

The underside of the meritocracy, of course, is failure. It is an axiom of the same ideological theorem that failure, within democratic capitalism and its schools does not reflect artificial barriers. By definition, all vestiges of unfairness have disappeared. Failure, therefore, reflects individual responsibility, a lack of energy or ability. The distribution of inequality thus mirrors the distribution of talents in a system which meters rewards in terms of the achievement of public tasks.

Popular acceptance of the ideology of public education reflected popular acceptance of the ideology of democratic capitalism. Schools reflected, legitimized, and sustained the social order. Consequently, any attempt to explain the successful imposition—in the definition used here—of public education must be part of a larger inquiry into the hegemony of democratic capitalism in North America.

The exposition of the mechanisms of hegemony could provide work enough for a generation of scholars. Here I only want to make three observations about that task: first, it may be a bridge between the advocates of consensus and conflict as keys to the American past. The consensus version of American history did have a point: the assent of the people to the institutional order and its ideological justification has been a remarkable feature of American history. Yet, as proponents of a conflict version rightly have pointed out, an emphasis on censensus can both mask the glaring inequality that has been a steady feature of North American society and miss the continued undercurrent of opposition. Perhaps, however, episodes of opposition, in the understandable search for a dissenting tradition, sometimes appear more significant than they actually were. They may reveal not a radical or revolutionary strain in North American history but, rather, the initial, generally ineffective resistance to innovations that occurred at the moments of transition when, albeit momentarily, policy options did appear open, or they may signify periodic outbursts of frustration, eruptions of a pervasive, long standing but relatively diffuse malaise, among people who generally have accepted the legitimacy of the social order that generates the inequalities which scar their lives. (41)

The second point about the mechanisms of hegemony takes its lead from the work of the British historian John Foster who describes the role of small scale success systems in accommodating people to a larger structure of inequality in which access to real power or wealth remains largely blocked. Capitalism, in this conception, works through subdividing the population into distinct groups within which small but visible ladders of success exist. The role of occupational specialization and the creation of limited careers within manual working-class jobs stand out as particularly important in this respect as, for white collar workers, does the creation of graded if limited ladders of advancement within bureaucracies. In a similar way, the realistic and widespread aspiration to homeownership, even among men who remained laborers, un-doubtedly, as Stephan Thernstrom contends, served an analogous pur-pose. The grouping of the population into ethnic communities which, in their internal structure, are vertically ordered, can serve the same end. Clearly, historians are just beginning to unravel the nature and meaning of small-scale success systems in North America, and their elu-cidation forms a major topic to which research should be directed. (42)

The third observation I wish to make about hegemony concerns education. Whatever its initial source, school systems became key agents in its perpetuation and transmission. As Robert Dreeben has shown, with even their internal organization a reflection of social ideology, schools have taught the legitimacy of the social order. Insofar as most people spontaneously have accepted the structure of inequality which circumscribes their lives, schooling in North America has been a mag-nificent success. (43)

Measured against the ideology of their early promoters, on the other hand, school systems have not succeeded very well. Of course, historical research is still far too primitive to enable us to assess the consequences of schooling for various social groups in anything like the manner attempted by Christopher Jencks' *Inequality*. Nonetheless, it does appear clear from the record that school systems have reflected social class differences from their inception. Statistics of school attendance show marked social class differences in the mid-nineteenth century. At first the differences existed throughout the school system; children of the poor simply went to school much less than children of the affluent, and early secondary schools were very largely middle-class institutions. During the course of the last century, as lower levels of schooling became universal, more affluent young people have stayed at school for increasingly long periods. In this way, despite an overall rise in school attendance, the class differential in educational attainment has been preserved. Thus, despite the argument of early school promoters that education would reduce inequality, it is most likely that public school systems have reflected and reinforced existing social structures. (44)

In light of their early purposes, of course, schools have failed most vividly as agencies of social reform. They have not eradicated crime, poverty, and immorality. And they could not realistically have been expected to do so. Indeed, the imposition upon schools of the burden of ameliorating social disease has been an evasion for which we all have paid dearly.

The relationship—or more accurately lack of relationship—between the schools and social reform brings me at last to the moral of educational history. Of course, history has no moral in any straightforward sense. At best it provides a coherent and reliable set of evidence about which people may legitimately draw various conclusions. Thus, you must realize that what I see clearly as four lessons of the story represent only my judgements upon the record which I have sketched for you.

First, we should at long last stop relying on the schools for social reform. Crime, poverty, inequality, alienation, and other social problems are rooted in social and economic structure. They will be solved, if solved at all, through an attack on their origins, which will mean a redistribution of power and resources. They will not be eliminated, or seriously alleviated, in the schools, which cannot be expected to do more than reflect the social structure in which they exist.

Second, we should ponder the implication of the fact that public schools always have been more concerned with morals than with minds. In reality, moral and intellectual outcomes never can be severed. Still, it would constitute a minor educational revolution if the emphasis, or primary goal, of public schooling shifted from the development of character to the cultivation of intellect.

Third, we must remember that institutions are a modern invention.

None of the large social institutions which dominate our lives today existed in anything more than embryonic form one hundred and fifty years ago, and at the time of their creation sane, intelligent people believed in alternatives. Those who cannot see beyond the asylum or the bureaucracy have a foreshortened view of history. The timidity of our efforts at reform reflects the narrowness of our imagination, not the limits of the possible.

Fourth, young people grew up differently in times past. Adolescence, as we know it, did not always exist. The prolonged institutionalized dependency to which we subject the young today is neither a product of their biology nor their psychology; it is a product of culture and of history. Yet we reform schools as if the life cycle were immutable. We question the setting in which prolonged, institutionalized dependency takes place; we do not question nearly often enough our definition of adolescence itself. Perhaps if we could decide how to alter the experience of growing up in North America, we would find how to fix the schools along the way.

Notes

1. Hayden V. White, "The Burden of History," *History and Theory*, 5 (1966): 111-134, 132. The works especially important in starting the rejuvenation of the history of education are: Paul H. Buck, Clarence Faust, Richard Hofstadter, Arthur Schlesinger, Jr., and Richard Storr, *The Role of Education in American History* (New York, 1957); Bernard Bailyn, *Education in the Forming of American Society: Needs and Opportunities for Study* (Chapel Hill, N.C., 1960); Lawrence A. Cremin, *The Transformation of the School* (New York, 1961).
2. On the first phase of the work see, Michael B. Katz, *The People of Hamilton, Canada West: Family and Class in a Mid-Nineteenth Century City* (Cambridge, 1975). On developments since then see Social History Project, York University, *First Research Report* (1975), *Second Research Report*(November, 1976).
3. For earlier formulations see, Michael B. Katz, *The Irony of Early School Reform: Educational Innovation in Mid Nineteenth Century Massachusetts* (Cambridge, 1968); Michael B. Katz, *Class, Bureaucracy and Schools: The Illusion of Educational Change in America* (New York, 1971), expanded edition, 1973).
4. David Tyack, *The One Best System* (Cambridge, 1974); Carl F. Kaestle, *The Evolution of an Urban School System: New York City 1750-1850* (Cambridge, 1974); Stanley K. Schultz, *The Culture Factory: Boston Public Schools, 1789-1860* (New York, 1973); Selwyn Troen, *The Public and the Schools: Shaping the St. Louis System, 1838-1920* (Columbia, 1975).
5. Michael B. Katz, "Secondary Education to 1870," *The Encyclopedia of Education* (New York, 1971) 8: 159-165.
6. David Roberts, *Victorian Origins of the British Welfare State* (New Haven, 1960); Oscar Handlin and Mary Flug Handlin, *Commonwealth: A Study of the Role of Government in the American Economy: Massachusetts 1774-1861*

(New York and London, 1947); Karl Polanyi, *The Great Transformation: The Political and Economic Origins of Our Time* (Boston, 1957; first published, 1944).

7. Carroll Smith-Rosenberg, *Religion and the Rise of the American City* (Ithaca, 1971); Raymond Mohl, *Poverty in New York 1783-1825* (New York, 1974); Susan E. Houston "The Impetus to Reform" (Ph.D. dissertation, University of Toronto, 1974).

8. Katz, *Class Bureaucracy and Schools*, ch. 1.

9. David J. Rothman, *The Discovery of the Asylum: Social Order and Disorder in the New Republic* (Boston, 1971); Gerald N. Grob, *The State and the Mentally Ill: A History of Worcester State Hospital in Massachusetts 1830-1920* (Chapel Hill, N.C., 1966); Gerald N. Grob, *Mental Institutions in America: Social Policy to 1875* (New York, 1973); W. David Lewis, *From Newgate to Dannemora: The Rise of the Penitentiary in New York, 1796-1848* (Ithaca N.Y., 1965); Robert M. Mennel, *Thorns and Thistles: Juvenile Delinquents in the United States 1825-1940* (New Hampshire, 1973).

10. Charles Loring-Brace, *The Dangerous Classes of New York and Twenty Years' Work Among Them* (New York, 1872); Katz, *Irony*, Part 3.

11. Houston, "Impetus"; Alison Prentice, "Education and the Metaphor of the Family: The Upper Canadian Example," *History of Education Quarterly*, 12 (Fall 1972): 281-303.

12. Peter Laslett, ed., *Household and Family in Past Time* (Cambridge, Eng., 1972), pp. 1-148; Katz, *People of Hamilton*, ch. 5.

13. Robert Dreeben, *On What is Learned in Schools* (Reading, Mass., 1968).

14. Katz, *People of Hamilton*, ch. 5; John R. Gillis, *Youth and History: Tradition and Change in European Age Relations, 1770-Present* (New York, 1974), pp. 1-3; Michael B. Katz and Ian Davey, "Youth and Early Industrialization" (forthcoming in a volume on the history of the family from the University of Chicago Press).

15. Yasuckichy Yasuba, *Birth Rates of the White Population in the United States 1800-1860* (Baltimore, 1962); Jacques Henripin, *Trends and Factors of Fertility in Canada* (Ottawa, 1972); Ansley J. Coale, "The Demographic Transition Reconsidered" (Liege, 1973); J. A. Banks, *Prosperity and Parenthood* (London, 1954); Colin Forster and G. S. L. Tucker, *Economic Opportunity and White Fertility Ratios* (New Haven, 1972).

16. Barbara Welter, "The Cult of True Womanhood: 1820-1860" *American Quarterly*, 18 (Summer 1966): 151-174; Kathryn Kish Sklar, *Catherine Beecher: A Study in American Domesticity* (New Haven, 1973).

17. Katz, *Irony*, pp. 56-58; Alison Prentice, "The Feminization of Teaching in British North America and Canada 1845-1875," *Histoire Sociale—Social History*, 8 (May 1975): 5-20. Dee Garrison, "The Tender Technicians: The Feminization of Public Librarianship, 1876-1905" *Journal of Social History*, 6 (Winter 1972-73): 131-159.

18. Joan W. Scott and Louise Tilly, "Women's Work and the Family in Nineteenth Century Europe", in *The Family in History*, Charles E. Rosenberg, ed., (Philadelphia, 1975), pp. 145-178; Patricia Branca, "A New Perspective on Women's Work: A Comparative Typology," *Journal of Social History*, 9 (Winter 1975): 129-153; Theresa McBride, *The Domestic Revolution: The Modernization of*

Household Service in England and France 1820-1920 (London, Ltd., 1976); Michael B. Katz, "Women and Early Industrialization", *First Research Report* (York University, 1975).

19. As an example see, Herbert C. Gutman, "Work Culture and Society in Industrializing America", *American Historical Review*, 78 (1973): 540.

20. Maurice Dobb, *Studies in the Development of Capitalism* (New York revised edition, 1963), p. 7; Karl Marx, *Capital* (Moscow, 1954; first English edition, 1887), pp. 318-347.

21. Martha Branscombe, *The Courts and the Poor Laws in New York State, 1784-1929* (Chicago, 1943); David M. Schneider, *The History of Public Welfare in New York State 1609-1866* (Chicago, 1938).

22. Carl F. Kaestle, *The Evolution of an Urban School System*, p. 102; Douglas Lamar Jones, "The Strolling Poor: Transiency in Eighteenth Century Massachusetts", *Journal of Social History* (Spring 1975): 28-55; Oscar Handlin and Mary Flug Handlin, *Commonwealth*.

23. Ian E. Davey, "Educational Reform and the Working Class: School Attendance in Hamilton Ontario, 1851-1891" (Ph. D. dissertation, University of Toronto, 1975); Stephan Thernstrom and Peter Knights, "Men in Motion: Some Data and Speculations about Urban Populations in Nineteenth Century America" in Tamara K. Hareven, ed., *Anonymous Americans: Explorations in Nineteenth Century Social History* (Englewood Cliffs, N.J., 1971) pp. 17-47; Katz, *People of Hamilton*, ch. 3.

24. Houston, "Impetus"; Harold Schwartz, *Samuel Gridley Howe: Social Reformer, 1801-1876* (Cambridge, 1956); Katz, *Irony*; Raymond Mohl, *Poverty in New York, 1873-1925* (New York, 1974).

25. Kaestle, *Evolution*; Harvey J. Graff, "Literacy and Social Structure in the Nineteenth Century City" (Ph. D. dissertation, University of Toronto, 1975); Frank F. Furstenberg, Jr., Theodore Hershberg, and John Modell, "The Origins of the Female-Headed Black Family: The Impact of the Urban Experience," *Journal of Interdisciplinary History*, 6 (Autumn 1975): 211-234.

26. Katz, *Irony*, pp. 120-121.

27. E. P. Thompson, "Time, Work Discipline, and Industrial Capitalism", *Past & Present*, 38 (December, 1967): 56-97; Gutman, "Work Culture & Society . . ."

28. Leo Marx, *The Machine in the Garden, Technology and the Pastoral Ideal in America* (New York, 1964), p. 248.

29. Katz, *Class, Bureaucracy and Schools*, pp. 32-37; Katz, *Irony*, pp. 45-46.

30. Katz, *People of Hamilton*, ch. 5; Daniel Calhoun, *The Intelligence of a People* (Princeton, N.J., 1973).

31. See note 22.

32. Katz and Davey, "Youth and Early Industrialization".

33. Stephan Thernstrom, *Poverty and Progress: Social Mobility in a Nineteenth Century City* (Cambridge, 1964); Stephan Thernstrom, *The Other Bostonians: Poverty and Progress in the American Metropolis, 1880-1970* (Cambridge, 1973); Katz, *People of Hamilton*, chs. 2, 3, 4; Michael B. Katz, Michael Doucet, and Mark Stern, "The Restlessness of a People: Migration and the Social Order in Mid Nineteenth Century Erie County, New York" (forthcoming).

34. Alan Dawley, *Class and Community: The Industrial Revolution in Lynn* (Cambridge, 1976), ch. 3; Michael B. Katz, "Fathers and Sons: A Comparison of

Occupations, Hamilton, Ontario 1851 and 1871, Buffalo, New York, 1855," *Second Reserach Report* (New University, Fall 1976).

35. Katz, *Irony*, pp. 50-52; Alison Prentice, "Education and the Metaphor of the Family"; James McLachlan, *American Boarding Schools: A Historical Study* (New York, 1970), pp. 116-126; 176-182.

36. Antonio Gramsci, as quoted in David Brian Davis, *The Problem of Slavery in the Age of Revolution: 1770-1823* (Ithaca, N.Y., 1975), p. 349.

37. Davey, "Educational Reform".

38. Davis, pp. 349-350.

39. Davis, ibid; Aileen S. Kraditor, "American Radical Historians on their Heritage" *Past and Present*, no. 56 (August 1972): 141-142.

40. Thernstrom, *Poverty and Progress*, p. 58.

41. Kraditor, ibid; Gutman, "Work, Culture and Society".

42. John Foster, "Nineteenth Century Towns—A Class Dimension," in H. J. Dyos, ed. *The Study of Urban History* (London, 1968), pp. 281-300; Thernstrom, *Poverty and Progress*, p. 58.

43. Dreeben, *What is Learned*; Samuel Bowles and Herbert Gintis, *Schooling in Capitalist America* (New York, 1976).

44. Christopher Jencks *et. al.*, *Inequality: A Reassessment of the Effects of Family and Schooling in America* (New York, 1974); Bowles and Gintis, *Schooling*; Katz, *Irony*, pp. 39-40; Davey, "Educational Reform".

8

Popular Education in Nineteenth-Century St. Louis

Selwyn K. Troen

It is both encouraging and gratifying to the members of this Board to witness the unexampled success of our school system, and the great popularity of the schools. This is still the more gratifying, when we feel a consciousness that this popularity is deserved; and that the more our schools are tried and the closer their operations are examined, the greater will be their popularity, and the confidence reposed in them. (1)

So Isaiah Forbes concluded his annual report as president of the St. Louis Board of Public Schools in 1855. Mid-nineteenth century school directors, superintendents, and heads of departments universally echoed this confidence in the success of the schools and their continued growth. Moreover, they attempted to substantiate their claims with an impressive array of statistics that both summarized yearly operations and placed them in historical perspective. Beginning with Forbes' report, successive Boards published through the end of the century, in English and German, an average of five to seven thousand copies for local and national distribution to broadcast the triumphs of the public schools.

These *Annual Reports* dramatically delineate the expanding popularity of the public schools both in absolute and relative terms. Between 1840, or shortly after the first schools were established, and 1880, when they had evolved into a complex and diversified system ranging from kindergartens to evening, high and normal schools, the student body had grown from 266 pupils to 55,870. When correlated with the city's total population, these numbers show that between 1840-1850, its first full decade of operation, the system reached about one in fifty of the city's population. By 1880, one out of every six or seven persons came into contact with the schools, with the greatest proportion of this rise occurring in the post-Civil War period. (2) By this date, the schools had become one of the city's most important social institutions, touching the lives of more people on a daily and continuing basis than perhaps any other.

Selwyn Troen is Sam and Anna Lopin Professor of Modern History, Ben-Gurion University of the Negev, and director, Ben-gurion Research Institute and Archives, Sede Boger, Israel.

Nevertheless, while public education expanded, some of the system's basic features remained constant. Despite its increased complexity and size, it performed much the same kind of work in 1880 as it had in previous decades. In the 1850's, the period when good records become available, as well as during the next two decades, the average student was between nine and ten years of age. (3)   Furthermore, little change took place in the length of schooling since the burden of the system's work was devoted to instructing seven through twelve-year-olds who were in the first three grades. Thus, the Board continued to be primarily involved in teaching the fundamentals of reading, writing, arithmetic, some geography and group singing. (4)   These comprised the natural limits of public education for the majority of parents permitted their children to drop out despite the availability of free higher schooling. This paper is concerned with defining who continued, who left, and what factors influenced their decisions.

Of prime importance in exploring these questions are the cumulative tables in the *Annual Reports* that deal with such matters as enrollments, age and sex of pupils, occupations of parents, and the number in each grade. However, since it was uncertain how representative school records were of the patterns operating in society at large, and since the variables present in the tables are limited, a collective biography of more than fifteen thousand children, drawn from the manuscript census of 1880, was established. The biography yields a cross section of the community's economic, social and racial groups and is based on an analysis of about 45,000 persons or one eighth of the nation's fourth largest city, in twenty-six selected election precincts. (5)   Since the data revealed that race was a critical factor in educational and vocational opportunities and in the character of the family, only an analysis of the population of white children is presented here. Moreover, blacks were denied public schooling until 1866 and engaged in a limited boycott until 1876. The story of the black child, therefore, necessitates separate treatment and has been presented elsewhere. (6)

In addition to emphasizing the importance of elementary education, the *Annual Reports,* by themselves, suggest that the major difference between those who left school and those that remained was the level of the fathers' occupations. Although St. Louis educators prided themselves on an open and democratic system, clearly children in higher economic groups used the schools to better advantage. Table A shows that about 50 per cent of the system's students were children of unskilled or skilled workers with an approximately equal division of the two categories between 1860 and 1880. (7)

Despite their large representation in the system as a whole, Table A illustrates their disproportionately low distribution in the higher reaches of the system. For example, in 1880, they comprised about 21 per cent of the high school and but 18 per cent of normal school students.

TABLE A

Occupations of Parents of Students in Day Schools: 1860, 1870, 1880[a]
by Percentages

Occupation	1860				1870				1880			
	TS	DS	HS	NS	TS	DS	HS	NS	TS	DS	HS	NS
Unskilled Labor	22	24	13	1	27	27	5	4	27	27	3	7
Skilled Labor	31	32	9	19	24	24	18	21	26	26	18	11
Clerk & Minor White Collar	8	8	12	4	9	8	17	9	11	11	18	15
Businessmen & Managers	20	19	36	23	26	26	30	20	24	25	28	24
Professionals	4	4	6	13	4	3	13	8	4	3	13	5
Unclassified	14	13	24	39	11	11	16	38	8	8	20	38
Total Number	10,908				24,347				51,251			

[a]TS indicates total number of students; DS, those in the district schools; HS, those in the high school; and NS, those in normal school. Annual Report, 1860, p. 55, Annual Report, 1870, pp. lxxii–lxxiii, and Annual Report, 1880, p. cxii.

The relationship between class and education becomes even more striking when the category of unskilled labor is isolated and examined. In 1880, for example, they comprised 27 percent of day students, that is, pupils in the district, high and normal schools, but supplied only three percent to the high and seven percent to the normal school. Breaking this category down into its constituent parts, it becomes clearer how few advanced beyond elementary instruction. There were 8,262 children of "laborers", the major component in the unskilled classification, in the district schools, but there were only 23 in the high and two in the normal school. Similarly only one child of a "laundress" was found in the high school and none was preparing for teaching but 1,711 were in the district schools. Yet another component, "draymen and teamsters", made the same kind of showing, sending 1,984 to district schools, four to the high and two to the normal school. On the other hand, "professionals", with a number approximate to that of "laundresses" and to "draymen and teamsters" sent 113 to the high school, nine to the normal school, and 1,866 to the district schools. This pattern of unequal distribution by class, established with the first high school class in 1857, remained one of the constants in the social structure of the schools. (8)

Sex is another area of maldistribution. While there is no way in which differentiation can be made by grades, it is possible to delineate differences between levels. In the day schools as a whole, there was approximately equal distribution of males and females, with males predominating by one per cent in 1860 but with one to two per cent more females during the 1870's. In the high school there were somewhat more males than females in the early years, but after 1865 an increasing proportion of girls enrolled. Between 1855 and 1860 it was 46 per cent female, but between 1875 and 1880 it was 59 per cent. (9) The normal school, however, was from its beginnings in 1857 almost completely a female institution. This data suggests that commencing in the post war period, girls were receiving more schooling in the teen years. Such a conclusion may be unwarranted since it does not take into account the opportunities available for males at non-public institutions found in the city and elsewhere. Indeed, for a refinement and elaboration of all the dynamics described above—ages of attendance, the significance of class and sex for educational advancement—as well as additional factors influencing attendance, it is necessary to turn to the manuscript census.

An important advantage to the census data is that it relates school to other experiences, allowing for a profile of the stages in the development of children. Table B shows that after five years at home, schooling began at six for 56 per cent; the peak years of education were from eight through eleven when about 90 per cent enrolled; then, beginning at twelve, ever larger numbers of youngsters left school. The exodus became so massive that less than half of the fourteen-year-olds and less than a fifth of those sixteen continued to take advantage of St. Louis' diverse schools. Based on the patterns of education and employment in Table B, children can be divided into four age groups: one through five; six through twelve; thirteen through sixteen; and seventeen through twenty. Only the second group was involved with schooling *en masse*, confirming the data drawn from the *Annual Reports.* Thereafter, most children either became unknowns, probably returning home, or graduated into the world of work. (10)

TABLE B

Education and Employment from Age 5 Through 20

Age	5	6	7	8	9	10	11	12
Attending School	19.5	56.2	80.6	89.0	90.1	90.9	89.3	82.0
Employed	0.0	0.0	0.2	0.4	0.6	2.1	3.6	9.4
Unknown	80.5	43.8	19.2	10.6	9.3	7.0	7.1	8.6
Total Number	625	657	573	546	494	573	524	545

Age	13	14	15	16	17	18	19	20
Attending School	70.7	48.9	35.1	19.3	11.6	5.4	3.7	1.7
Employed	17.5	33.0	43.1	60.0	64.2	68.7	71.1	76.1
Unknown	11.8	18.1	21.8	20.7	24.2	25.9	25.2	22.2
Total Number	532	585	536	576	541	710	678	769

The kind of job a child was able to obtain when he dropped out was related to the age at which he left school. Since girls tended to go to school longer than boys and found different kinds of employment, Table C separates the sexes in order to define more precisely what children did between the ages of ten and twenty. Throughout this period there is an expansion of the work force in all the categories and movement into jobs of greater status and complexity with the advance of years. For example, whereas 20 per cent of the twelve-year-old boys had left school, only 58 per cent of these had jobs, and most of them, 88 per cent, were employed in semi-skilled or un-skilled occupations. By sixteen, 15 per cent remained in school. Of their peers who left, 86 per cent were employed: 47 per cent were semi-skilled and unskilled workers; 15 per cent were now in skilled categories; 21 per cent held white collar jobs as various kinds of clerks; and 3 per cent were even in the higher occupations. At eighteen and twenty, at least 50 per cent of all males were skilled workers or better.

TABLE C

Occupations of White Males and Females, Ages 10 Through 20

Age	10		12		14		16		18		20	
Sex	M	F	M	F	M	F	M	F	M	F	M	F
Attending School	90.4	91.5	79.6	84.7	46.0	51.7	14.8	23.6	4.6	5.9	2.4	1.1
Higher Occupations	0.0	0.0	0.4	0.0	0.7	0.3	2.8	2.1	5.3	2.4	5.8	3.0
White Collar	0.0	0.0	0.0	0.4	2.1	0.3	18.0	1.7	21.4	2.8	22.7	1.4
Skilled Workers	0.4	0.0	1.1	0.0	7.0	2.0	12.7	3.4	23.5	3.8	23.3	3.9
Semi-Skilled Workers	0.7	0.0	4.6	0.4	11.6	0.0	14.1	0.3	13.3	1.6	13.9	1.4
Unskilled Workers	2.9	0.3	6.0	5.7	21.8	20.7	26.1	39.4	21.1	47.5	24.5	55.8
Unknown	5.7	8.2	8.5	8.8	10.9	25.0	11.6	29.5	10.9	36.0	7.3	33.5
Totals	280	293	284	261	285	300	284	292	285	425	330	439

While a few girls also began to work at age twelve, a greater proportion of twelve to sixteen-year-olds stayed in school. At ages twelve, fourteen, and sixteen there are 5, 6, and 9 per cent more girls in school than boys. By eighteen and twenty, there is a return to parity as education becomes increasingly less significant for both sexes. When females left school, however, it was for experiences fundamentally different from those of males. Fewer girls worked. At age twelve, 6 per cent less were employed; at fourteen, 20 per cent; at sixteen, 27 per cent; at eighteen and twenty, 25 per cent. Moreover, those employed generally worked as maids, seamstresses, laundresses, or kept house for their own families. Only about one out of ten girls, by the late teens, had left the home, whether her own or someone else's, for the factory, shop, and office. (11)   After several years in school, large numbers simply returned home. At sixteen, 30 per cent were unemployed and in the family. Between seventeen and twenty, the average rose to 36 per cent. By contrast, only about 9 per cent of the boys were similarly disengaged from both work and school.

One wonders why more girls, faced with the prospect of returning home and not contributing to the family income, did not take greater advantage of the city's schools. The fact that they did not, even though they received, on average, more schooling than males probably means that education was not considered of particular value for girls and reflects indulgence and minimal parental economic expectations as they awaited their real vocation. While for boys school was a prelude to a lifetime of work, for most girls it served as a hiatus between the freedoms of early childhood and the responsibilities of marriage. Thus, despite this distinction, the most significant trend for children of both sexes was their abandonment of education in their early teens.

The relationship of a child to his household is another factor which affected the length and quality of his school experience. Children who lived with both or even one of their parents were at a decided advantage. Those living in institutions, in households headed by a relative other than a parent, or as boarders, went to work earlier. In their case, too, the beginning of adolescence marks a convenient demarcation point. While children in families in the six to twelve group had a somewhat greater opportunity for going to school, Table D shows that their chances increased to almost two to one through the teen years.

Not only does the educational gap between children within and without the family grow wider through the teen years, but those children who reside outside the family attend school under less favorable circumstances. For example, in the thirteen to sixteen group, less than 1 per cent of family children who went to school also held jobs as compared with 28 per cent of those who were not in the family. In the seventeen through twenty group, the proportions become 4 per cent as opposed to 29 per cent. Clearly the

TABLE D

Family Status of White Children 6–12, 13–16, 17–20

Ages	In Family	% In School	Not In Family	% In School
6–12	3,765	82.4	107	73.8
13–16	1,795	47.5	379	28.2
17–20	1,491	7.3	1,125	3.4

family provided a protective umbrella for the child in its midst, giving him an opportunity for prolonged schooling, and for an education without the distractions of work.

In addition, children who lived at home were not required to work as soon or in the same numbers as those who were on their own. In the seventeen to twenty group, 11 per cent of the males and 55 per cent of the females living with their families were unemployed as opposed to only 3 per cent of those who were outside the family. The family, then, also provided some young men and especially the ycung ladies with a base of support where they might await the creation of their own households. It therefore may have made possible for some females such avocations as reform and charity work. (12)

For children living at home, the school and job experience was further influenced by the father's occupation. Its influence was minimal for youngsters between six and twelve. At this stage with an average of 82 per cent in school, there was a large measure of equality of experience. For example, children of unskilled and skilled workers had attendance rates of 83 and 80 per cent, while children of professionals and petty officials and businessmen had rates of 88 and 87 per cent. Moreover, if a child were not in school he was at home. Age, not economics, was important.

The earnings and status of the father were of greater importance in the thirteen through sixteen-year-old, for as participation in education diminished, significant variations based on class occur. Table E indicates how distinctions between subgroups widened as the average attendance dropped from 81 per cent for six to twelve-year-olds to 43 per cent for thirteen to sixteen-year-olds. We find at one extreme, children of professionals with 80 per cent in attendance, and at the other children of unskilled workers with 32 per cent. While from six through twelve there was a difference of 5 per cent between children in these categories, for the four-year span after twelve the gap had widened about ten-fold to 48 per cent. It made little difference whether the father of a child eight or twelve was a physician or a boatman; for most children it made all the difference a few years later.

TABLE E

Crosstabulation of Father's Occupations by Sons' Occupations,
Ages 13 Through 16

Father's Occupation	Sons' Occupations							Row Total
	At School	Higher Employment	White Collar	Skilled	Semi-skilled	Unskilled	Unknown	
Professional High Official	80.0	2.9	11.4	0.0	0.0	2.9	2.9	3.8 (35)
or Businessman	70.0	0.0	12.5	1.3	5.0	2.5	8.8	8.6 (80)
White Collar	64.1	2.6	9.0	5.1	6.4	7.7	5.1	8.4 (78)
Petty Official or Businessman	55.9	2.2	7.5	5.4	3.2	6.5	19.4	10.0 (93)
Skilled	32.0	0.0	10.0	12.1	12.1	25.1	8.7	24.9 (231)
Semi-skilled	35.9	0.0	6.4	3.8	16.7	21.8	15.4	8.4 (78)
Unskilled	31.7	0.8	4.0	8.7	6.3	37.3	11.1	13.6 (126)
Unknown	36.2	2.4	7.7	6.8	15.0	22.2	9.7	22.3 (207)
Column	43.4	1.2	8.3	7.1	9.9	19.7	10.3	100.0
Totals	(403)	(11)	(77)	(66)	(92)	(183)	(96)	(928)

Based on a hierarchy of parental occupations, Table E also delineates a critical factor for the nineteenth century drop-out. The community of drop-outs was initially and largely drawn from the male children of skilled, semi-skilled, and unskilled workers. These sons had attendance rates ranging from 32 per cent to 36 per cent with a median of 33 per cent. Sons of fathers with higher occupational levels had a median of 65 per cent with a range of 56 per cent for petty officials and businessmen to 80 per cent for professionals. The clear point of division was whether one's father wore a white or a blue collar.

While unemployment rates were nearly identical with sons of blue and white collar workers at about 11 per cent, significantly more working-class children were employed. Although sons of blue collar workers had more than doubled the employment rate, 57 per cent to 25 per cent, and entered the labor force at an earlier age, they held inferior jobs, with the majority in unskilled areas, and diminishing numbers in more highly skilled positions. Although some sons of white collar workers also took unskilled jobs when they left school, many more of them worked as clerks or held other white collar jobs. For example, sons of unskilled workers had eight times as much chance to be themselves unskilled as to hold a white collar job, while children of high officials and businessmen had a five-to-one chance to escape unskilled positions and find white collar jobs. In sum, sons of households with higher occupational levels could not only stay in school longer, but could also begin at a better job than children from working class homes.

The disparity between children of different classes was most marked among the seventeen through twenty group. The higher the father's position, the greater the son's chance for schooling, the better his job, and the smaller the chance of unemployment. As an illustration of the critical importance of father's occupation, sons of blue collar workers had one-third the chance to become clerks and twice the likelihood of holding unskilled jobs as those sons who came from white collar families. The same inequalities affected the experiences of the daughters. Females from blue collar families were more likely to leave school and enter domestic service, while daughters of white collar workers remained in school longer, or stayed at home. Class distinctions impinged on the experiences of children of both sexes.

As was anticipated, the social structure of education as revealed in the census data complements the information in the *Annual Reports*. It is now clear that schooling was nearly universal during mid-century, with about 90 per cent of all children between eight and eleven in school and the great majority in public schools. The efforts expended by public and non-public institutions to reach the mass of the city's children and to create generations of literate individuals were successful.

As both the census and school records also indicate, several factors were responsible for a significant divergence in experience and opportunity for children beyond age twelve. Sex played a minor role as girls become a small majority in the public schools, although this may not have been true of the non-public academies. Also, presence in a family headed by a parent was significant, probably because it provided the kind of security necessary to delay entry into the labor market. The importance of economic security is underscored by the critical impact of the fathers' occupations. While some working class children went beyond the district school, prolonged education was more likely to occur in white collar families. Thus, while the system was open and free, children of different classes did not make equal use of it. Equipped with a basic education, particularly working-class children embarked in large numbers during the early teens into an increasingly industrialized and complex society. The stratification of the public system necessarily mirrored society at large. Class became the most important parameter and, in effect, controlled the length of childhood and the nature of the options available to the young.

That many children from the lower classes failed to attain more schooling is not surprising. Large numbers had to work to assist their families. There is no data available on children's earnings or on family income, but numerous writers have commented on the phenomenon of nineteenth century urban families which required the income of their offspring. Before the widespread adoption of cash registers, telephones, and child labor laws, there was ample opportunity for unskilled work as cash boys, messengers, and light manual laborers. (13)

While drawing attention to the importance of economics, the census data suggested that other factors also contributed to extended schooling. Working-class children may have entered the work force earlier through press of circumstances, but many children of businessmen and especially white collar workers also left. They departed in smaller numbers and perhaps a year or two later, but the fact is that most ended their education in the early teens instead of taking advantage of the public high school and similar institutions. Of all the groups, it is the sons of professionals, who had themselves experienced extensive training, that have the highest and most persistent attendance records. Not only income but attitude probably kept the lawyer's son in school and sent the businessman's or clerk's son out to work. (14) The extraordinary percentages of professionals' children in school may reflect the value their households placed on learning.

On the other hand, if children outside the working class were not required to augment the family income, their employment suggests that the experience of working in factories, offices, and stores was deemed by their parents as being more worthwhile than the classical or modern curriculum of the high school. Professionalization, or the concept of attaining the skills required for modern industrial society through formal education, was only just forming in late nineteenth century America. (15) It is possible that employment for these sons was viewed as a quasi-apprenticeship system. Thus, while elementary instruction was widely appreciated by both parents and schoolmen alike, clearly the value of more education was far less understood. Perhaps it is because of this perception that the *Annual Reports* express no dismay over the fact that there were ten times as many children enrolled in the first three grades of the district school as in the three years of high school. (16)

Indeed, the patterns of school attendance and employment which emerge from the St. Louis census and school records in 1880, when placed together with data from other studies, suggest a broad continuum of practice and attitudes. While research beginning with the census of 1840 is underway to test this hypothesis, there is some evidence from other sources that offer support. As late as 1908 the Dillingham Commission on Immigration reported that the St. Louis public schools contained about 65 per cent of their students in the fourth grade and below. (17) Attendance levels began to advance only with the popularization of the high school and of vocational and commercial courses around the turn of the century. (18) It is possible, therefore, that from the middle of the nineteenth century, when St. Louis developed extensive public and parochial systems, through the first decade of the twentieth century, the patterns of school attendance remained the same—a few years of schooling in the pre-teen period. (19) Thus, 1880 may be a mid-point for a condition that spanned several generations. Certainly educational practices in the first ten years of this century were more similar to those current in mid-nineteenth century than to our own.

The continuity of educational practice may be further inferred from Joseph Kett's recent analysis of children in rural New England from 1800 to 1840. Among his conclusions are that children attended school between eight and twelve, after which sons passed into apprenticeship or employment. Sons of ministers and other wealthy parents, who correspond to professionals' children in this study, tended to stay in school longer than children of mill owners and manufacturers, demonstrating the importance of parental values. (20) The continuum of behavior in these aspects of growing up between rural New England in the first part of the nineteenth century and St. Louis in the latter part, suggests that for the history of childhood and education there are limits to the significance of a rural-urban dichotomy and to a chronology that would divide the nineteenth century. Rather, traditions firmly rooted in American culture persisted throughout the period.

Certainly St. Louis educators accepted as natural and perhaps even desirable the practice of initiating children into the work force after a few years of formal learning. Superintendent William Torrey Harris (1868-1880) was the most systematic and well-known spokesman for this view. (21) Perceiving that society had entered a period of extensive and continuing transformations, he rejected vocational training on the grounds that specialization could result in exposing workers to the dangers of obsolescence. He preferred that the schools equip children to be adaptive and flexible in a dynamic society. On this basis, Harris could be viewed as a proponent of liberal education. More to the point, however, he held a very traditional notion concerning the individual's responsibility for his own destiny. Arguing, for example, that the fundamental purpose of the public school curriculum was "providing the pupil with the mental discipline, and an equipment of tools and intelligence, so that he may help himself," he expected that the individual would continue his education outside the school. "With the proper discipline," Harris observed, "the pupil becomes an industrious investigator; let him loose in the library and he will become learned." The result would be that the "public school and the library render possible a perpetual education in the community." Harris reiterated this belief on numerous occasions, explaining that the nation's educational system was based on "the American idea of self-help." (22)

Thus, while Harris and his contemporaries were convinced of the possibility of individual and social betterment through education, it is not difficult to understand their expectation that a relatively short period of formal schooling was sufficient to insure it. Inequalities of attendance in the higher reaches of the system aroused little concern in a society which did not especially demand formal and specialized instruction. Since the schools were representative during the important few years of nearly universal education, the fact that the higher grades were undemocratic in character and rather poorly attended troubled neither professional educators nor the public. Significantly, St. Louisans in the 1860's and 1870's complained that the system offered too much rather than too little education, charging that the high school's curriculum was aristocratic, not that its student body was unrepresentative. (23) In a society where schooling consumed such a small portion of childhood, and where its relation to work was still imprecise, inequities did not command serious attention.

The lack of concern for educational equality is related to a fundamental difference in attitudes over the role of schooling between the nineteenth century and the present. Pointing to the relationship of educational attainment and job-level, the sociologists Lipset and Bendix have written concerning mid-twentieth century that "education was the principal avenue for upward mobility in most industrialized countries." Furthermore, they suggest that an open society is supported by the openness of the educational system through which even the poor can advance. (24) In this society, the deprivation or obstruction of individual or group access to schooling of quality has important and measurable economic and social consequences. Similarly, failure to exploit opportunities can be disastrous. With the widespread recognition that so much is at stake, the assessment of the educational system and of its relationship to society becomes an issue of paramount importance. In addition, as the child and society come to expect so much from the child, the schools come to demand a great deal from the child, exacting a seemingly ever-increasing commitment of time and energy.

While much was also expected of education in the nineteenth century, the popular investment in schooling was far less. There were two related factors accounting for this. First, educators had confidence in the ability of a good teacher to teach and in the capacity of children to learn. Among the many examples of this belief two may be offered here. Harris introduced the kindergarten to the public system with the conviction that even one year of exposure to educational "games" would benefit the young child for the rest of his life, endowing him with the capacity to engage successfully in a wide variety of employments from the needle trades to the foundry, to the preparation of foods in the home. (25) In addition, St. Louis educators justified evening schools on the basis that they would render adult newcomers to the city and those natives who had missed the district school, literate, capable of self-improvement, and qualified participants in a democratic society. All this was to be accomplished by teaching an abbreviated elementary school curriculum for two hours on sixty-four nights during the year. (26) In the context of this confidence, it was reasonable to hope for a great deal from the three, four, and perhaps five years spent in the system.

Moreover, the mass of society, from unskilled workers to businessmen, shared this belief. They gave it expression by insisting that their children go to school and then by withdrawing them by the early teens in the expectation that they were now adequately equipped to begin their careers. Except for males headed for the professions, for females destined to be teachers, and for those few whose families valued higher learning, the encounter with education was relatively brief. Its brevity testifies to how little direct impact school made on one's career. Among the most telling evidence for the lack of a measurable connection between school and vocation is the fact that girls stayed in school, on the average, longer than boys. Parents were generally reluctant to delay the entry of sons into the world of work.

Thus, in mid-nineteenth century, young children attended as popular and democratic an educational system as the nation ever possessed. Divorced from the stigma of a charity venture, (27) the public schools were not yet marked by hierarchies of quality and specialization as their importance was not recognized. The result was a remarkable homogenization of experience that was enhanced as the graded curriculum was standardized. The ideal of a common school where children from all segments of society would have a common experience was approximated. It was this achievement that led St. Louis schoolmen to broadcast with such confidence the progress of their schools.

Notes

1. Isaiah Forbes, "President's Report," *Second Annual Report of the Superintendent of the St. Louis Public Schools for the Year Ending July 1, 1855* (St. Louis, 1855), p. 6.
2. *Annual Report, 1880,* pp. cxxviii-cxxix, and the *Tenth Census of the United States,* XIX, Pt. II, p. 567.
3. In 1860 the proportion under ten was 66 per cent; in 1865, 54 per cent; in 1870, 49 per cent; in 1875, 53 per cent; and in 1880, 56 per cent. *Annual Report, 1860,* p. 55, and *Annual Report, 1880,* p. 31.
4. The curriculum is broadly outlined in *Annual Report, 1879,* p. cvi.
5. The data was taken from the Second Enumeration of the manuscript census for 1880, and was processed in an SPSS file that is stored at the Computer Center of the University of Missouri/Columbia. Information was gathered on 15,312 children, with child defined as any person at any age who resided in the household of his mother and/or father, and any person twenty-one and younger who lived outside the family unit.
6. Selwyn K. Troen, "Measuring the Black Response to Public Education in Post Civil War St. Louis," a paper delivered at a symposium on "Urban Education and Black Americans in the Nineteenth Century," Division F, AERA Annual Meeting, April 5, 1972.
7. The table was constructed by aggregating the data on specific occupations which were recorded by the *Annual Reports.* For a discussion of the system of classification and tables illustrating the raw data, see Selwyn K. Troen, "Schools for the City: The Growth of Public Education in St. Louis 1838-1880," Ph.D. diss., University of Chicago, 1970), Appendix D.
8. *Annual Report, 1855,* pp.116-121. For a discussion of a parallel structure in Massachusetts, see Michael B. Katz, *The Irony of Early School Reform: Educational Innovation in Mid-Nineteenth Century Massachusetts* (Cambridge, Mass., 1968), pp. 39-40, and Appendix C.
9. *Annual Report, 1881,* p. 100.
10. Unknowns represent those for whom the census enumerators marked "at home" or left a blank. It is assumed that these omissions represent those who were neither employed nor at school and they are, therefore, calculated with those whom we know to be "at home." The assumption is based on three considerations. First, since the enumerator is account-

ing for nearly all children between nine and twelve, with an average unknown of about eight per cent, is appears unlikely that he was less accurate or less avid in determining occupations or school attendance at other ages. Secondly, the curve reflected by unknowns is so well-ordered as to suggest important meanings rather than chance. Thirdly, the pattern of employment and school attendance conforms to expectations. We know from school reports that children began dropping out in large numbers at about twelve when they gradually began to be absorbed into the work force.

11. Of 734 girls seventeen through twenty-one who were listed as unskilled laborers, 66 per cent (488) were servants and maids, 20 per cent (144) were keeping house, nine per cent (63) were seamstresses, and five per cent (39) were in various other occupations, including 15 prostitutes.

12. For a portrait of comfortable females who make reform their vocation, see Christopher Lasch, *The New Radicalism in America, 1889-1963: The Intellectual as a Social Type* (New York, 1965), chapters 1, 2, and 4.

13. A classic progressive accounting of poverty is Robert Hunter, *Poverty: Social Conscience in the Progressive Era*, ed. by Peter d'A. Jones (New York, 1965). An example of contemporary scholarship is Stephan Thernstrom, *Poverty and Progress: Social Mobility in a Nineteenth-Century City* (Cambridge, Mass., 1964).

14. Although the census does not include information on income, it is possible to establish occupational hierarchies that reflect both status and wealth. The occupational matrix for the prosopography is an adaptation of the one developed by Stephan Thernstrom and Peter Knights in their studies of occupational mobility in Boston, and has been modified to include children's and women's vocations. A copy can be sent on request. For an abbreviated version of the matrix see Peter R. Knights, *The Plain People of Boston 1830-1860* (New York, 1971), Appendix E.

15. On professionalization see Robert H. Wiebe, *The Search for Order, 1877-1920* (New York, 1967), pp. 111-132. Also, the teen years were not yet defined as a distinct period in the life-cycle and special attention in the form of institutional care had not yet developed. Hence, the shift from the fourth or fifth year of school into the factory or office was considered natural. On attitudes towards teens, see John Demos and Virginia Demos, "Adolescence in Historical Perspective," *Journal of Marriage and the Family*, (November, 1969), 632-638.

16. *Annual Report, 1880*, pp. cxviii-cxix. There were 22,954 in grades one through three but only 2,233 in grades seven through nine.

17. Report of the Immigration Commission, *The Children of Immigrants in Schools* (Washington, 1911), pp. V, 213-219.

18. For a discussion of the expansion and the popular appreciation of the

high school around the turn of the century, see Edward A. Krug, *The Shaping of the American High School* (New York, 1964), pp. 169-189.

19. There are no precise figures available for parochial schools on a regular basis. Catholic parish schools comprised the largest group and they were not yet organized into a system. Based on Catholic directories and newspaper descriptions of students and curricula in the *Western Watchman*, which was sponsored by the St. Louis archdiocese, at least 80 per cent of the students were receiving elementary instruction and the ages of the students ranged from seven to sixteen. *Sadler's Catholic Directory, Almanac, and Order for the Year of our Lord, 1880* (New York: 1880), pp. 155-158; "The Catholic Schools," *Western Watchman*, August 20, 1870; "Examination of St. Patrick's Parochial Schools," *Western Watchman*, May 20, 1871; "The 'Globe' on the Public Schools," *Western Watchman*, May 3, 1873.

20. Joseph F. Kett, "Growing Up in Rural New England, 1800-1840," in *Anonymous Americans: Explorations in Nineteenth Century Social History*, ed. by Tamara K. Hareven (Englewood Cliffs, N.J., 1971), pp. 1-16.

21. A major source for Harris' ideas are the *Annual Reports* from 1867 through 1880. Other sources include Merle Curti, *The Social Ideas of American Educators* (Paterson, N.J., 1959), pp. 310-347; John S. Roberts, *William T. Harris: His Educational and Related Philosophical Views* (Washington, 1924), and Kurt Leidecker, *Yankee Teacher* (New York, 1946).

22. *Annual Report, 1867*, p. 71; *Annual Report, 1871*, p. 165, and *Annual Report, 1872*, p. 150. Harris never tired of this refrain. In 1900 as United States Commissioner of Education, he wrote: "In the United States the citizen must learn to help himself in this matter of gaining information, and for this reason he must use his school time to acquire the art of digging knowledge out of books." William T. Harris, "Elementary Education," in *Education in the United States*, ed. by Nicholas Murray Butler (Albany, N.Y., 1900), p. 11.

23. Indicative of popular feelings are the letters to the editor in the month preceding the April elections for school directors. For example, see *St. Louis Globe-Democrat*, March 14, 15, 18, and 29, 1878. For the Catholic viewpoint, see "Our Common Schools," *Western Watchman*, September 22, 1883.

24. Seymour Martin Lipset and Reinhard Bendix, *Social Mobility in Industrial Society* (Berkeley, Calif., 1964), pp. 91-101.

25. *Annual Report, 1879*, pp. 131-133.

26. *Annual Report, 1856*, pp. 46-47, and *Annual Report, 1879*, pp. 142-144.

27. Paul Monroe, *Founding of the American Public School System* (New

York, 1940), I, pp. 295 ff. For the problem of the charity stigma in a neighboring state, see John Pulliam, "Changing Attitudes toward the Public Schools in Illinois, 1825-1860," *History of Education Quarterly,* VII (Summer, 1967), 191-208.

9

The Ever-Widening Circle: The Diffusion of Feminist Values from the Troy Female Seminary, 1822-1872

Anne Firor Scott

"SHOULD WOMEN LEARN THE ALPHABET?" asked a nineteenth century feminist, intending irony, and suggesting what we all know, that education can lead to unforeseen and unintended consequences, social and personal. If schools accomplished only their announced purposes, if pupils learned only what they came to learn, the work of the historian of education would be easier than it is.

The Troy Female Seminary, officially opened in 1821 but tracing its roots to 1814, was the first permanent institution offering American women a curriculum similar to that of the contemporary men's colleges. The founder stated her purposes clearly: to educate women for responsible motherhood and train some of them to be teachers. It is only in retrospect that the school can be seen to have been an important source of feminism and the incubator of a new style of female personality.

The development and spread of nineteenth century feminism repre-sented a major value shift in American culture, the consequences of which reached into almost every aspect of personal and social life. The underlying reasons for this shift, and the mechanism by which new ideas about women's role spread, continue to puzzle and intrigue cultural historians. One reason—there were many others—was a dramatic in-crease in the number of well educated women. In order to examine the mechanism involved it is necessary first to suggest a way of looking at the distribution of traditional and feminist values in the population. (1)

Historians usually divide nineteenth century women into three groups: a tiny handfull of feminists, known to their contemporaries as "strong-minded women," another small group of anti-feminists who were artic-

Anne Firor Scott is W.K. Boyd Professor of History

ulate about what they saw as the threat to family life inherent in feminist values, and a large undifferentiated mass of women untouched by feminism at all.

Such a classification is too crude to be useful. Not only does it fail to account for a great many particular cases, it is also static, except insofar as it assumes that members of one group occasionally go over to another. A different kind of description comprehends a much larger amount of the evidence, provides a more accurate way of describing change, and is helpful in explaining some apparent paradoxes. Let us imagine a continuum that looks like this:

Feminist values

100	90	80	70	60	50	40	30	20	10	0
0	10	20	30	40	50	60	70	80	90	100

Traditional Values

Such a continuum has a place for everybody. At one end were the handful of radical feminists, who began early in their lives to question the whole conception of "woman's sphere," and the old definition of woman as a creature of emotion rather than reason, inherently self-abnegating, born to serve others, and defined by her sex. At the other end were the women who believed all these things, and who, comfortable in their assigned role, felt no need to question its underlying value structure. What is more important, this continuum has a place for the very large number of women who were not at either end, but somewhere in between, often holding some part of each set of values simultaneously. It also accomodates those who were in motion, moving toward the feminist end of the spectrum.

Large numbers in the middle or in motion should not surprise us, since changes in the key values of a society or a social group rarely occur as sharp and sudden breaks with the past. When the wind has been blowing from the West for a while the waves of the sea roll consistently from that direction. If the wind shifts to the south the ocean waves will continue to roll from the west for a time, but soon, cutting across them, will be waves coming from the south, criss-crossing, and slowly, the older wave system will diminish to be replaced by the new. So it is with broad social attitudes, the old and new often exist not only side by side, but cutting across each other. We know from observation that people have an astonishing capacity to hold ideas which reason and logic would call contradictory.

In retrospect, the thought and behavior of women who were still attached to the older values while they were experimenting with the new has sometimes seemed paradoxical, but they were simply exhibiting the ambivalence which is common when values are in the process of change. Indeed the most effective purveyors of new values were often those who had some attachment to the old, and therefore were not so frightening. There were also many active feminists who used the old values as a shield against criticism. In so doing they inadvertently misled historians who are only beginning to realise that while radical feminists were few, women who were to some degree affected by the "woman movement" were numerous. (2)

If the changing state of women's self-perceptions and value structures was not simply a matter of a few radicals, but rather one of the major phenomena shaping nineteenth century social history, it is important to examine the various ways the new values spread. (3) A good deal of attention has justly been paid to reform movements and voluntary associations as seed beds of feminism, but the early seminaries and pre-Civil War "colleges," insofar as they have been attended to at all, have been seen as bulwarks of tradition. A close look at the history of Troy Female Seminary and its alumnae in the framework I have just sketched, will suggest a different conclusion.

Like many individuals, Troy as an institution combined an allegiance to certain well-defined ideas about what was proper for women, with a subversive attention to women's intellectual development. Its founder and head, Emma Willard, provided a powerful example of a "new women" whose achievements were made possible because of her ability to integrate new values with the prevailing ones. Her life work, she always said, was to further "the progress of my sex," yet she adhered to the ideology of woman's domestic role (though with a very broad definition of "domestic") and to the idea of separate spheres and spoke highly of the patriarchal family. By carefully selecting from her own words it would be possible to paint her as a prime exemplar of "true womanhood," *or* as a thoroughgoing feminist. In fact, she was both, and in this fact lay much of her effectiveness.

Between 1821 and 1871 more than 12,000 women spent some time at Troy, and thanks to the efforts made by a group of alumnae in the 1890's, biographical data for more than 3500 of these women was gathered and preserved. From these and related materials it is possible to piece together the process by which Emma Willard made her very proper female seminary into an early source for and disseminator of certain feminist ideas. (4)

Her stated goals show how, almost from the beginning, she deftly combined an appeal to the prevailing view of woman with a revolutionary emphasis upon women's intellectual capacities and with an innovative proposal for broadening "woman's sphere" to include professional work. The educational program and the atmosphere of Troy were quite different from those of most female seminaries, and the process by which Willard spread her message and the ingenious ways in which she institutionalized this process of dissemination, are all part of a complex pattern.

The biographies of women who went there show how the Troy experience affected at least some indivduals who attended the school.

Emma Willard's Views and Methods

Emma Hart was born in 1787 in Berlin, Connecticut, next to the last of seventeen children. She was a precocious child who had good luck in her early teachers, and by the age of 17 was herself teaching in a village school. Her reputation spread, and at 20 she took charge of a female academy in Middlebury, Vermont, where the presence of a new college exacerbated her frustration at being denied higher education. While steadily developing her own affinity for the intellectual life, she began to feel a divine call to improve women's educational opportunities. (5)

In 1809 she married a much older man (who encouraged her ambitions), had a child and began to concoct a comprehensive plan for the improvement of women's education, which, when it was finished and polished, she presented to the Governor of New York asking him to submit it to the legislature. She proposed that the state provide money for a group of first-rate female seminaries, better than any then existing. Her argument ingeniously combined tradition and innovation; it ran like this:

1. It is the duty of government to provide for the present and future prosperity of the nation.
2. This prosperity depends upon the character of the citizens.
3. Character is formed by mothers.
4. Only thoroughly educated mothers are equipped to form characters of the quality necessary to insure the future of the republic.

After describing the structure and curriculum necessary for such superior schools, Willard went on to argue that the educated citizenry essential to the success of republicanism could only be created by universal primary education.

To provide *that,* women would have to be trained to be teachers since there were not enough men available to staff common schools for all the children.

Earlier republican experiments had failed, she said, because of "inadequate attention to the formation of the female character," and only educated women could prevent the inevitable "destruction of public virtue" when the country — as it was bound to do — grew large and rich.

By adopting her plan, she said, the legislature could bring into being a population of moral, hardworking women, whose taste for intellectual pleasures would prevent them from loving "show and frivolity." Such women, taught to seek "intrinsic merit," would be prepared, whether as mothers or as teachers, to raise children of good character. Further, able women who "yearned for preeminence" could achieve it as administrators of these publicly supported schools for their own sex.

The first nation to give women "by education that rank in the scale of being to which our importance entitles us," she wrote, would add to its national glory, "Who knows how great and good a race of men may yet arise from the forming hands of mothers, enlightened by the bounty of that beloved country, — to defend her liberties, to plan her future improvements and to raise her to unparalleled glory?" (6)

The argument that the preservation of the republic depended upon educated women had been around for decades, but she added three innovations: 1) that the state should spend public money to provide what amounted to colleges for women, something which did not at that time exist anywhere in the world; 2) that women were capable of intellectual excellence in any field; and 3) that women should be specifically trained for a profession. Willard's plans thus went far beyond anything previously proposed.

The idea of teacher training itself was relatively new. From the beginning the men's colleges had recognized a mission to prepare their graduates for the learned professions, the ministry, law, medicine or college teaching. Many young men taught school for a while before or after college, but usually as a stepping stone to another career. What Willard was proposing was to treat school teaching as a serious profession *and* to open it to women, who had hitherto gotten much the shorter end of the educational stick. (7)

Troy Takes Shape

Members of the New York legislature spoke in praise of the Plan, but did not appropriate any money. It remained for Emma Willard to create from private sources, and with the help of the city of Troy, a school where she could endeavor to approximate her ideal.

For tactical reasons she had distinguished between colleges (which were for men) and a seminary planned especially for women. In fact, however, Troy bore a remarkable resemblance to the contemporary men's colleges. Mrs. Willard, like her male counterparts, the presidents of Brown, Amherst, Williams, Dartmouth and Union, used a domestic metaphor, speaking of her pupils as "daughters" as they did of "sons." Like them she emphasized the building of character as the chief aim of education, dwelt upon the importance of the Christian religion, and gave weekly lectures aimed at instilling moral values. Like them she taught the senior course in Mental and Moral Philosophy, using Lord Kames, Paley, and later Wayland as her texts. She was, says her first biographer, "one of the first modern educators to dwell on bringing out the latent powers of the mind . . . and this was the great revolution she made in female education." (8)

The curriculum included mathematics, science, modern languages, Latin, history, philosophy, geography, and literature. An early enthusiast for the teaching of science, Willard had the good fortune to become a friend of Amos Eaton (a key figure in the founding of the Rensselaer Polytechnic Institute, also in Troy) who welcomed young women to his classes and helped develop a science program for the Seminary. He took Almira Lincoln, Emma Willard's sister and protegé, as a sort of graduate assistant, and together they set pupils to doing their own experiments, perhaps the first teachers in the country to do so. All three were interested in the psychology of learning and were stimulated by the ideas of Pestalozzi. (9)

Although it was difficult for young women to find schools to prepare them for an advanced curriculum, the difference between the Troy students and their male counterparts either in preparation or in the quality of their educational accomplishment was not very great. (10) Indeed it might be argued that in some ways Troy was leading where the colleges would later follow, in its reliance upon a pedagogy which demanded that pupils think for themselves, in its science program and in the teaching of modern languages. There can be no doubt of its innovative spirit with respect to women; nowhere else in the country in the 1820's were young women told that they could learn any academic subject, including those hitherto reserved to men, that they should prepare themselves for self-support and not seek marriage as an end in itself. To underline this last point, Willard provided "instruction on credit" for any woman who would agree to become a teacher, the debt to be repaid from her later earnings. Mrs. Willard could, of course, find her a job. The school was hardly under way before she was running a flourishing teacher placement agency, and the demand soon outran the supply. Someone commented that Emma Willard's signature on a letter of recommendation was the first form of teacher certification in this country.

In addition to the shaping force of an intellectually demanding curriculum and high expectations, there was the imposing personality of Mrs. Willard herself. (11) Where else in the 1820's and 30's could young women daily see one of their own sex, married and a mother, yet founder and administrator of what they all knew to be the best known school for women in the country, author of best-selling textbooks, advisor to politicians, formulator of scientific theories, a woman unafraid of any challenge, who had, as Elizabeth Cady Stanton remembered when she looked back to her school days at Troy, "profound self-respect (a rare quality in woman) which gave her a dignity truly regal . . ." (12)

In certain settings Emma Willard was forthright about her feminism. "Justice will yet be done. Women will have her rights. I see it in the course of events," she wrote five years before Sarah Grimké's *Letters on the Equality of the Sexes* and fifteen years before Seneca Falls. (13)

Yet this same woman often presented herself as a model of female respectability who gave voice to traditional values. She wrote Catharine Beecher:

> In reflecting on political subjects my thoughts are apt to take this direction: the only natural government on earth is that of the family—the only natural sovereign the husband and father. (14)

The early rules of the Seminary included the following:

> Above all preserve feminine delicacy. Let no consideration induce any young lady to depart from this primary and indispensable virtue . . . Each pupil must be strictly careful to avoid the least indelicacy of language or behavior such as too much exposure of the person in dress . . . (15)

In her the "true woman" and the feminist co-existed, and however much ambivalence this may have caused her from time to time, it was one source of her influence.

The Uses of a Network

Pupils who began to leave the Seminary as early as 1822 to marry or teach, or both, were agents of cultural diffusion, spreading Willard's ideas about women's capacities and about the need for women's education, and often setting an example by their interest in study and learning. George Combe, the phrenologist and friend of Horace Mann, observed what was going on at Troy and labeled Emma Willard "the most powerful individual at present acting upon the condition of the American people in the next generation." She herself hoped that "educated women who are rising up" would prove capable of "investigating our rights and proving our claims . . . it is to the future lives of my pupils, taken as a body, that we must look, as the test of our success." (16) A poem she wrote for a pupil about to take charge of a Female Academy summed up her philosophy: ". . . Go, in the name of God/Prosper, and prove a pillar in the cause/ of Woman. Lend thy aid to waken her/ from the long trance of ages. Make her feel/ She too hath God's own image. . . "

By regular correspondence and visits she bound the alumnae to her, and provided support and reinforcement for what, in many parts of the country, were seen as advanced or dangerous views about women's education. Bit by bit she created a network of former pupils spreading to the northwest, the southeast and then to the southwest, a network held together by a common belief in women's capabilities and by personal relationships. By 1837 when she made part of this network formal by organizing the Willard Association for the Mutual Improvement of Teachers, it had been in the making for sixteen years. In a pamphlet written for members of this group she spoke of guiding them in the execution of their "important duties, that not only yourselves may obtain benefit, but the thousands of the rising generation who are under your instruction . . ." (17)

Several examples show how the network developed. Julia Pierpont, a Willard pupil in Middlebury, had been sent by her mentor to Sparta, Georgia in 1819. There she opened a school, married and had a child. Both husband and child soon died, and in 1824 Julia Warne, as she then was, came to Troy for further study. Afterward she returned South, and married Elias Marks, author of a proposal to the South Carolina legislature along the lines of Willard's *Plan*. Together they took charge of the South Carolina Collegiate Institute at Barhamville and endeavored to build a southern version of Troy. They remained part of Willard's closest inner circle. (18) In the 1930's a South Carolina scholar, intrigued by the pervasive influence of Troy in his state, identified more than a hundred South Carolina women who had had some connection with the Seminary and concluded that directly, and through the agency of Barhamville, Troy's influence had been a major factor in the shaping of southern culture in the years it was spreading to the southwest. (19)

Before Julia Warne left Sparta a replacement arrived in the shape of Elizabeth Sherrill. Sherrill, whose mother had been Emma Willard's Middlebury housekeeper, had served an apprenticeship as an assistant teacher at Troy. In Georgia she married an army officer whom she induced to resign from the Army and join in her educational career. The two went on to take charge of an academy in Augusta and continued part of the network for many years.

Urania Sheldon finished Troy in 1824, taught first as a governess, then set up her own school in Washington County, New York and was invited to move it to Schenectady. After seven years there her reputation was such that the trustees of Utica Female Academy built a house to induce her to take charge of their school. This she did and administered it until 1842 when she became the third wife of Eliphalet Nott, the almost legendary president of Union College.

Example after example might be described. Caroline Livy, who studied at Troy from 1837 to 1841, married a minister and set out for Alabama. En route, they were persuaded to settle in Rome, Georgia. Her husband found a church which suited him, and she became principal of the local Female Academy. Rome was then a small frontier community which had been part of Cherokee Georgia until Andrew Jackson's Indian Removal opened it to white settlement. More than 5000 girls were said to have studied under Mrs. Livy's direction (and that of her husband, who later joined her in the enterprise.) She had five children along the way. It was her son's perhaps somewhat biased judgment that "her influence in moulding the after-life of her pupils and thus refining and elevating the community cannot be over-estimated."

Other outposts of Troy appeared in many parts of the country. Almira

Lincoln Phelps, younger sister and protegé of Emma Willard, became head of the Patapsco Female Institute in Maryland and largely modelled her program upon that at Troy. Sarah Foster, described as having "conceived the greatest admiration for Mrs. Willard and yielded herself implicitly to her care and direction . . . ," headed schools first in Ohio and then in Pennsylvania. Admiring pupils thought she "infused new life and vigor into the school which was felt throughout the surrounding country."

Jane Ingersoll established a seminary in Cortland, N.Y. "on the Troy plan" and braved community opinion to follow Mrs. Willard's example by offering a course in physiology. (20) By the mid-thirties across the country Troy graduates, reinforced by pupils and protegés of Catharine Beecher and Mary Lyon, were busy creating a profession which, from its inception, was open to women.

Of course, the professionalization of school teaching was going on in many places in both western Europe and North America in the early nineteenth century. By the late 1830's Horace Mann, Henry Barnard and a group of like-minded men were working for the establishment of teacher training institutions of various kinds, first in Massachusetts, Connecticut, New York and then elsewhere. It is not surprising to find many Troy graduates taking an active part in the common school movement when it began to burgeon in the 1830's. (21)

Henry Barnard persuaded Emma Willard herself to run for the office of supervisor of schools in Kensington, Connecticut; the male voters elected her. With the help of one former pupil she developed a demonstration school for training teachers, and with another she organized a Woman's Association for the Common Schools, the purpose of which was to bring the mothers of the community into active responsibility for the school system. It was up to the mothers, she said, to improve working conditions and pay so that the "best women" would be willing to become teachers. She also suggested that they make sure that all the children in the district had proper clothing and books, and that classes be invited to meet in homes so that the women themselves could examine the children. "Such a plan would keep the mothers along with the improvements of the time . . . it would set you to review old studies, or look over new ones. And if you would but try it, you would find your mature minds would with a little labor master subjects that require pains to teach the young . . . " (22)

In a letter to Henry Barnard written at the same time she said that the more she reflected on "the condition of our country" the more need she felt for the influence of women to set things right.

The Kensington experiment and the work of the association of mothers were reported in the educational press, and Emma Willard was soon being invited all over New York state to conduct teacher institutes, to lecture on pedagogy, and to organize mothers as she had done in Kensington. A former pupil who worked with her recorded that when asked to speak she insisted upon sitting down, since she did not believe it proper for women to speak in public. By remaining in her chair she could consider her speech to be merely conversation, and therefore appropriately feminine. (23)

In 1846 she extended her efforts through the rest of the country, travelling 8,000 miles "by stage coach, packet boat and private carriage" into every state south and west of New York except Florida and Texas, visiting former pupils, lecturing on women's education, conducting teacher institutes and organizing associations.

By all these means, and by the work of her former pupils, which she continually watched over and encouraged, the "Troy idea" spread through the country. In time there were said to be 200 schools modelled upon the original, each one disseminating by precept and example Willard's view of women's capacities and their appropriate responsibilities.

By the time the census takers came round in 1870 they counted 200,515 teachers of public elementary and secondary schools, more than half of them women. Thirty years of normal school work had had a great deal to do with this change in the composition of the teaching profession as had the fact that women persisted in being willing to work for lower wages than men. But for the sources of the changing social attitudes which contributed to the professionalization of school teaching, and for the willingness of women to enter that profession, we must begin with Troy. (24)

A New Personality?

From a slightly different angle of vision, what did the Troy experience mean to individual women? How did it contribute to changing their self-perceptions and the way they ultimately lived their lives? Such questions present difficult methodological problems and, given the nature of the data, invite speculation rather than solid assertion. Yet this question is both intriguing and important.

In these first generations of educated women it is possible to discern the emergence of a new type of personality and some new patterns of adult life. The personality was one which, precisely as Emma Willard had forecast in 1819, included an intellectual component, a certain kind of seriousness of purpose beyond the domestic and religious spheres, and a degree of personal aspiration which precluded that tendency to "show and frivolity" the proponents of women's higher education always deplored. The ideal was described in a memorial address given by Emma Willard's daughter-in-law and successor as principal at Troy when she said that her predecessor had shown "that young ladies are capable of learning those intellectual subjects which discipline their minds, train their reasoning powers, strengthen and elevate their characters, and make them more permanently attractive than when educated by light and trivial studies." (25)

A handful of Troy pupils left some record of what they thought the long term influence of the institution and its founder upon them had been. A number who replied to the questionnaires sent out in the 1890's responded with long letters, and others, even in brief answers, threw some light on how they recalled the experience. Still others, simply by describing their lives, inadvertently bore witness to the kind of strength of character which Troy reinforced. What stands out in most of these records is the great importance of Willard's own personality in providing her pupils with a new image of what woman could be.

One, for example, had travelled with her on a steamboat in 1842 and described the experience: Willard had inquired "what object in life I had in mind. . . " "She inspired me with a self-respect and dignity new to me." (26)

The editor of *Mrs. Emma Willard and Her Pupils* was surprised at the outpouring of information about events which had occurred so many years before. ". . . Mrs. Emma Willard's influence is immortal. I am surprised to note even in my sequestered life that I am continually coming upon new clues that lead out to a scholar of the old Seminary . . . " (27) The same woman remarked that she had been "mentally reinvigorated in this daily intercourse with teachers and girls who were once such important factors in my life." (28) Teachers described their schools which had been modelled on Troy and indicated that they had tried to follow Emma Willard's example as closely as possible.

The nephew of a long-dead woman wrote that his aunt had frequently spoken of the "influence exerted on her life and the lives of other pupils by the training they had received under Mrs. Willard's supervision." (29) Several correspondents spoke of being rejuvenated by the call to write about their school days, others referred to the deep impression made upon them by the Saturday morning talks which had been given by Mrs. Willard, Mrs. Lincoln, and later by Lucretia Hudson Willard, who succeeded her mother-in-law as principal of Troy. "My whole after life (to a certain extent) has been influenced by them," wrote one octogenarian; and another wrote: "indeed she was the grandest woman America ever produced." (30)

One of the longest letters came from a woman who had spoken at the Chicago World's Fair in 1893 on "Emma Willard and the Troy Female Seminary." She wrote not only of the influence of the school upon herself but of her perception of its far reaching social consequences: first, spreading the idea of intelligent study of geography; second, because of its emphasis upon "the importance of women in their own right;" third because of the pioneering teacher training and systematic study of pedagogy available there; fourth because of the great influence of Willard and her pupils on the development of the common school movement and finally because she felt that Willard's textbook, *The Republic of America,* did much "toward uniting people into a nation." (31)   The daughter of another pupil from the 1820's reported that the Willard name had been a "household word" in her family. Another recalled a picture hanging in her home of "that much loved and honored teacher." (32)

A pupil who had been in the first class, writing in a clear firm hand, noted that "Mrs. Willard was my ideal of perfection, she was the embodiment of everything that was lovely in both mind and body." "She taught with the enthusiasm of an originator, thus enkindling the enthusiasm of her pupils," said her daughter-in-law.

The alumnae of Troy who survived into middle age and beyond include many examples of what the late nineteenth century called "new women." There was Carolyn Stickney, who, hearing that her brother was on trial for murder in Colorado Territory, came from England and "by personal intervention gained his acquital" and took him back to England for safe-keeping. Mary Newbury Adams founded a society for the study of the arts and sciences in Iowa with the aim of educating the whole midwest, women and children in particular. Lucretia Willard Treat founded normal schools in Michigan, while Rebecca Stoneman cultivated her own orange grove in California. Adeline Morse Osborne, self-made geologist, gave her papers to the American Association for the Advancement of Science, and Jane Andrus Jones, widow, ran a large farm "in a very successful way." Miranda Aldis, trained in the law by her father, was her husband's legal assistant, Elizabeth Marshall managed a factory, Cornelia Whipple, wife of the Bishop of Minnesota, gave all her time to the cause of the Indians. Elizabeth Mather Hughes helped her husband run the Minnesota *Chronicle*, and Jane Bancroft Robinson took a Ph.D. in Zurich. Clare Cornelia Harrison wrote a well known history of French painting, Lucy Marsh dealt in real estate, Dr. Elizabeth Bates delivered 2400 babies without losing one mother "at the time of delivery," but she added, in the interest of accuracy, she had "lost some cases from diseases incidental to the lying-in-period." Charlotte Henry worked to improve conditions for the freed slaves; Harriet Maria Pettit House translated books into the Siamese language; Sara Seward, seventeen years out of school, undertook medical training so she could become a medical missionary; Sophie L. Hobson taught English to Spanish speaking youngsters in California. The testimony runs on and on, often in the copperplate handwriting Emma Willard had insisted they learn in the interest of effective communication. Each one in her turn was an example to the young.

The fact that the biographical committee, working twenty years after the most recent boarding pupil had left the school and seeking to find others whose school days were anywhere from seventy to thirty years behind them, was able to secure more than 3500 responses was itself some evidence of the strength of the Troy tie. So was the fact that so many children and grandchildren, filling out questionnaires for long-dead alumnae, remembered the significance mothers and grandmothers had attached to their schooling. Many of these descendents spoke of the women's intellectual interests. "She [a deceased mother] was a woman of scholarly tastes who read Greek and Hebrew," or, another, "My mother was possessed of greater general information than anyone I almost ever knew." "She keeps herself in touch with the questions of the day and is fond of intellectual pursuits," wrote another. (33) A pupil of the 1850's was said to have read Caesar for recreation, and to have kept up her studies in art and modern languages till the last week of her life; another was recorded as "an authority on questions of history, geography and politics." Perhaps one of the most significant comments came from the daughter of an 1829 graduate: ". . . her pupils *and their daughters* scattered over the wide world revere her name . . ." (34) It may be that one of the delayed effects of the Troy experiment, if we could measure it, would be found in the educational expectations among the daughters of the early pupils.

Of course such evidence must be interpreted with care. Obviously, a woman who felt very much attracted to Troy would be likely to write a detailed response to the questionnaire; children who remembered such attachment would be likely to take the trouble to reply. There was certainly a process of self-selection on the part of the women who chose to go to Troy. These fragments do bear witness, however, to the beginning of a new personality type, the educated woman who was not ashamed of learning and who would inevitably have a wider notion of what the world had to offer than her sisters who had not been encouraged to read widely or to think for themselves. (35)

Another way of examining the effects of the Troy experience is through some statistical analysis of the biographical material collected in the 1890's. This analysis is still in a preliminary stage but the early findings are suggestive. (36)

Figure I represents a rough systematization of some of the data into what I have called a Life Cycle Table. Several rather striking things emerge from this table: the rather high proportion of the women who remained single, particularly among those who were at school after 1840. For comparison we may look at the figures for all American women born between 1835 and 1855, of whom between 6% and 8% never married. (37) When this fact is added to the rather small families of Troy women, compared to those of the average of all U.S. women, a startling contrast emerges. Among Troy women who left school between 1852 and 1863, 21.2% had only one child, compared to 10.6% of New York women born between 1836 and 1840, and 7.8% of all U.S. women.

Figure 1

	Troy Women		Life Cycle Experience			
Decade left school	1821–32	1833–42	1843–52	1853–62	1863–72	Total
Number reporting	372	540	769	975	845	3,501
Never married	49 (13%)	97 (17%)	160 (20%)	210 (21%)	217 (25%)	733 (22%)
Married once	303	413	582	721	611	2,630
Married twice or three times	20	30	27	44	17	138
Married but no children recorded	104	141	200	226	183	844
Average # of children of those who had children	4.5	3.8	2.7	3.1	2.6	3.4
% of children dead by 1898	28%	27%	20%	17%	11%	21%
Worked for pay before marriage	39 (12%)	111 (25%)	124 (20%)	166 (21%)	75 (12%)	515 (14.7%)
Number and percentage of all single women who remained single and worked for pay	6 (12.2%)	34 (35%)	57 (35%)	89 (42%)	54 (24%)	240 (38%)
Number of married women who worked after marriage; percentage of all married women	15 (5%)	35 (8%)	29 (5%)	58 (8%)	29 (5%)	166 (6%)
# who joined any voluntary association	55 (14%)	90 (16%)	162 (21%)	315 (32%)	224 (26%)	845 (24%)
Founded or administered a school	16	44	36	36	14	146
Created some non-school institution	2	5	2	12	3	24
Coded "unusual": subjective judgement based on the biographical data	34 (9%)	59 (10%)	37 (4%)	65 (7%)	27 (3%)	222 (6%)

At the other end of the spectrum, while 19.1% of all women were having 5 or 6 children, only 13.7% of Troy women were bearing such large families. If we look at those who had 7–9 children, Troy figures drop to 4.7% while for the whole country the figure is 21.7%. (38)

While one of Emma Willard's avowed goals was to make better wives and mothers, her pupils were less likely to marry than women in general and, if married, they bore fewer children than their contemporaries.

Figure 2

The Revolving Scholarship 1839–1863 (based on Annual Reports)

	Instruction on Credit (for those intending to teach)	Number Sent Out To Teach
1839	100	43
1840	100	54
1841	36	38
1842	24	28
1843	(not given)	25
1844	30	25
1845	14	12
1846	14	25
1847	14	14
1848	17	17
1849	29 (+4 partial)	31
1850	29 (+9)	24
1851	34 (+6)	27
1852	18 (+5)	35
1853	42 (+3)	36
1854	22	50
1855	22	27
1856	24	34
1857	17	(not listed)
1858	30	12
1859	22 (+5)	12
1860	12 (+1)	12
1861	11	7
1862	3 (+3)	9
1863	5 (+3)	–
TOTALS	669 (+39)	597

Annual reports begin in 1839, after Troy was chartered by the New York legislature and thus made eligible for a small subsidy from the Literary Fund, the subsidy being based on the number of pupils receiving full time instruction. It is possible that instruction on credit was at its peak in 1839. It may also be significant that a normal school opened in that year, and others soon followed, so that women wishing to be trained as teachers had other options. However, note that the largest single group of teachers left the school in 1854. If the average for the years before 1839 was approximately the same as the average for the years for which we have information, the total number of teachers would have exceeded a thousand.

Twentieth century experience is that the more education a woman has the more likely she is to work for pay, whether single or married. This effect may have occurred among Troy women as well, though comparisons are difficult since our data reveals the number of women who worked at any time in their lives—26%—while the census reports all the women who are working at the particular moment the census taker appears. Even so, since most "working women" in the nineteenth century were domestic servants, factory workers and agricultural workers, the fact that 26% of this group of middle class women spent some time in the labor force may be significant.

Even more interesting is the proportion of married women who worked while they were married (about 6%), the proportion of widows who supported themselves in widowhood (more than 10%), and the proportion of the teachers who made teaching into a serious career (we estimate about 40%.) The number of Troy graduates who founded or administered schools is also significant.

In addition to the married women who worked for pay after marriage there were 202 women who said they shared their husband's work. Most of these were wives of ministers, missionaries, and teachers, but some were wives of lawyers, who reported learning to write briefs and otherwise acting as aides, or scholars, exemplified by the woman who learned Swedish in order to be her husband's research assistant, or another "more fond of books than housekeeping" who—with her husband—translated German tales.

Figure 3

Changing Patterns of Childbearing Of Those Who Had Children, Percentage Who Had What Number of Children, By Decade n = 1924

# of Children	1821–32	33–42	43–52	53–62	63–72
1	13.7	16	18.6	21.2	22.2
2	12.3	16	23.2	22.3	27.6
3	16.4	21.8	18.3	20.8	21.1
4	16	13.1	15.6	16.3	12.6
5	10	10.9	9.5	9.1	8.5
6	7.3	10.3	5.4	4.6	2.7
7	8.2	3.5	2.9	1.9	2.7
8	3.7	2.9	3.2	1.9	1.3
9	5.9	1.3	2.0	0.9	0.4
10	3.2	2.6	0.5	0.4	0.4
11	1.4	1.0	0.0	0.6	0.2
12	0.9	0.3	0.5	0.0	0.0
13	0.9	0.3	0.2	0.2	0.0

It is not surprising to find that 38% took part in some kind of voluntary association, but it is surprising that among those who worked for pay the percentage was higher than for those who were not in the labor force. There is as yet no control group to show whether this rate of participation in voluntary associations is higher than among middle class women in general.

Even in its present primitive state, the statistical analysis strengthens the argument that Troy and by implication similar places, such as Mt. Holyoke, Hartford, Georgia Female College, or Wheaton, despite their emphasis upon the importance of woman's sphere, were important agents in that development of a new self-perception and spread of feminist values which contemporary observers described as the "great nineteenth century movement for the elevation of women." The process was repeated on a larger scale when the women's colleges got underway in the years after 1865 and initiated what might be called the second great wave of consciousness-raising. (39)

Conclusion

At the broadest level of generality, the evidence presented here suggests that higher education for women, as it began to develop at Troy and spread thereafter, played an important part in the diffusion of feminist values. This was true despite the fact that early and late leaders of educational institutions for women reiterated the traditional values of home and motherhood and accepted the idea that women were destined to spend their lives in a "sphere" separate from that of men. Feminist values not only coexisted with the more traditional ones but spread more easily when they were carefully attached to "correct" views of woman.

At a more specific level, it is clear that Emma Willard's role in the social history of the nineteenth century was more complex than has generally been understood. She not only was one of the first to offer young women higher education; along with it she offered a cluster of new values as she encouraged self-respect, self-support and assured her pupils that marriage was not essential to a useful life. She encouraged intellectual development and self-education and built a carefully cultivated network of women through the country whom she had trained and influenced and whom she expected to train and influence others. The result was that schools for women and associations of women to oversee the common schools spread across the land.

Willard was not only one of the first Americans to speak publicly about women's "rights," she was among the first to think seriously about the problems and methods of teacher training and to encourage the professionalization of school teaching, a process which opened a new range of opportunities to women. She also understood the virtues of what is now called "continuing education," or lifelong learning and put great stress upon it in training her pupils and encouraging the women in her Association of Teachers.

Together with some of her former pupils she played a major part in the common school movement, especially in New York and New England but to some extent across the middle west and even in the post-Civil War South — by way of Patapsco and Barhamville.

Although the term has been trivialized, she was certainly a powerful "role model" — so much so that twenty-five years after her death admiring former students were raising money to place her statue in a prominent place in Troy, and gathering themselves in an association bearing her name. There were few women available to be such role models in the early days of Troy. After the first two decades, however, Willard's pupils began to supply such models in many parts of the country. In this, too, the multiplier effect was at work.

Women, education, and the prevailing social values were all parts of a system in which there was constant interaction and feedback. Educated women became carriers of the newer values, and the spread of feminist ideas led more and more women to seek education. In each succeeding generation after 1820 there were a larger number of women enrolled, first in the seminaries, then in the colleges; and each succeeding generation contained more independent women. Education appears to have been a major force in the spread of feminism.

NOTES

1. Essential feminist values include: 1) the belief that women should be seen as individual human beings with a range of potentialities which they should be free to develop, 2) men and women should be equal before the law, 3) marriage should be a partnership between equals. There are many specific feminist attitudes, but these three are fundamental. For more detailed statements see Alice Rossi, *The Feminist Papers* (New York 1974).

   Traditional values included these: 1) the idea that woman, the weaker sex, was created to serve man, and her role and functions in life are defined by her sex, 2) the idea that women are feeling rather than reasoning beings, 3) the view that women should be pious, submissive, and obedient, putting the needs of husband and children ahead of her own. To these basic ideas which have persisted through centuries were added in the 19th century a cluster of beliefs which laid stress upon the existence of a separate sphere for women in which they were to exercise their moral responsibilities. For detailed statements of the 19th century version of the traditional values see Barbara Welter, "The Cult of True Womanhood," *American Quarterly*, 18 (1966): 151–175, and Nancy L. Cott, *The Bonds of Womanhood* (New Haven, 1977), pp. 1–2.

2. The existence of a large number of women who combined the old values with the new is amply documented in Karen Blair, "The Clubwoman as Feminist" (Unpublished doctoral dissertation, SUNY Buffalo, 1976). For a useful analysis of the concept of women's consciousness see Jessie Taft, *The Woman Movement from the Point of*

View of Social Consciousness (Chicago, 1915). Other works which have strengthened my conviction that we need to find a new way of describing the distribution of feminist and traditional values in the nineteenth century include, Cott, *Bonds of Womanhood,* already cited; Susan P. Conrad, *Perish the Thought* (New York, 1976); Daniel Scott Smith, "Family Limitation, Sexual Control and Domestic Feminism in Lois Banner and Mary Hartman (eds), *Clio's Consciousness Raised* (New York, 1974); Ellen Du-Bois, "The Radicalism of the Woman Suffrage Movement," *Feminist Studies,* 3 (Fall 1975), and *Feminism and Suffrage,* (Ithaca 1978). I am also indebted to Carl Degler for letting me see the manuscript containing his discussion of the anti-suffragists which will be part of his book on women and families, due out in 1979.

It may be relevant to recognize here that holding on to old values and experimenting with new ones is not necessarily a comfortable thing to do. Ambivalence was common among women in the middle of the scale, as is clear from many biographies. The founder of Troy Female Seminary herself once wrote that women who spoke up for women's rights were accused of having cast off their feminine sensitiveness "and often when such women are found moody and are thought capricious it is this which is the cause of their ill-humor and dejection. . . " See Emma Willard, *The Advancement of Female Education* (Troy, N.Y., 1833), p. 10.

3. Of course a larger question is where the new values come from in the first place, but for the purpose of this discussion I want simply to assume their existence, and pursue the question of how they spread and became gradually acceptable to ever larger numbers of women. As is always the case with a major attitudinal change the sources are apt to be complex. In this case they included the rapid population growth and economic development of the country, the changing pattern of production which took many of women's historic functions out of the home, the increasingly pervasive spirit of individualism and egalitarianism among men, the spread of evangelical religion and — possibly — the romantic movement in art and literature.

4. Mrs. A.W. Fairbanks (ed.), *Mrs. Emma Willard and Her Pupils or Fifty Years of the Troy Female Seminary 1822-1872* (New York, 1898). The material in this book was gathered by a committee of alumnae of the school who sent questionnaires to every former pupil they could find, and to friends, descendants and even postmasters of those who had died. The original manuscript questionnaires are in the Archives of Emma Willard School, Troy, New York.

5. See John Lord, *Mrs. Emma Willard* (New York, 1873); Henry Fowler, "Emma Willard," in Henry Barnard, (ed.), *Memoirs of Teachers* (New York, 1861); James Monroe Taylor, *Before Vassar Opened* (Boston, 1914); Alma Lutz, *Emma Willard: Daughter of Democracy* (Boston, 1929); Willystine Goodsell, *Pioneers of Women's Education* (New York, 1931). Ezra Brainerd, "Mrs. Emma Willard's Life and Work in Middlebury," read at Rutland, Vt. September 1893 and printed for private distribution by a member of the class of 1841 at Troy Female Seminary. See also A.F. Scott, "What Is This American: This New Woman," *Journal of American History,* 65 (December 1978).

6. Emma Willard, "An Address to the Public Particularly to the Members of the Legislature of New York proposing a Plan for Improving Female Education " (Albany, 1819). Linda Kerber, "Daughters of Columbia: Educating Women for the Republic 1787-1805" in Eric McKitrick, (ed.), *The Hofstader Aegis: A Memorial* (New York, 1976), pp. 36-59, found all these arguments being made in the years immediately after the ratification of the Constitution. Emma Willard drew them together in a

logical progression and tied them to specific proposals for state supported higher education for women and for teacher training. "Nothing in those early days compares in influence . . . with this noble appeal . . . it was far beyond anything then proposed or known." James Monroe Taylor, *Before Vassar Opened* (Boston, 1914), pp. 5-6. The Willards had 1000 copies of the *Plan* printed and bound for sale in bookstores.

As I read Willard's early writings, it seems to me likely that she had already begun to observe the general deterioriation of the female personality which occurs when prosperity lightens the load of necessary labor and education has not yet provided other things to think about. Novelists, from Jane Austen and George Eliot to Elizabeth Gundy, have dealt effectively with this phenomenon; historians have tiptoed around it, though it was a familiar theme among nineteenth century feminists of all degrees of radicalism. See Lord p. 110 for her advice to a pupil on the importance of self-education: "It will keep you from that desire of gadding about which is so fatal to the improvement of your sex."

7. Merle Borrowman, *The Liberal and the Technical in Teacher Education* (New York, 1956), p. 55 lists three schools which had set out to train teachers before 1821. He seems never to have heard of Troy, or Mount Holyoke, and therefore is under the misapprehension that serious teacher training began with the first normal school in Massachusetts in 1839. Many other historians of American education have been similarly uninformed.

8. Ezra Brainerd says that she deliberately chose the word seminary thinking that it would "not create a jealousy that we mean to intrude upon the provence of man." See "Mrs. Emma Willard's Life . . ." p. 16. Lord, *Willard*, p. 96.
   Henry Home Kames, *Essays on the Principles of Morality and Natural Religion* (Edinburgh, 1751); William Paley, *Paley's Moral Philosophy* (London, 1859); Francis Wayland, *The Elements of Moral Science* (Cambridge 1963), originally published 1835.

9. Emma Lydia Bolzau, *Almira Lincoln Phelps: Her Life and Work* (Philadelphia, 1936).

10. Before one makes too much of the ambitious college curriculum with its Livy, Tacitus and Xenophon as daily fare, it is worth listening to President Francis Wayland of Brown, reporting to the fellows of the college of 1841, asking for a tightening of entrance requirements because "students frequently enter college almost wholly unacquainted with English grammar and unable to write a tolerably legible hand." The fellows themselves, a year later, noted that "students are frequently admitted very ignorant of the grammars and are uanble to read but a very small portion of Latin and Greek at a lesson." See Walter C. Bronson, *The History of Brown University* (Providence, 1914), p. 217.

Willard's pedagogy, more than that prevailing in the colleges, emphasized the development of critical thinking, and while even Harvard still depended upon the deadly daily recitation as its chief pedagogical tool, she introduced the Pestalozzian dialogue, and assured her pupils that, until they had learned a subject well enough to teach it, they could not consider that they had mastered it.

The whole question of what constituted "higher education" in the nineteenth century is a slippery one. The quality or difficulty of a curriculum was not necessarily revealed by the label placed upon it, and a wide variety of institutions were engaged in providing some part of what would eventually come to be defined as a collegiate education. The variation in institutions was matched by the variation in students, who might be 15 or 50, who might be seeking intellectual culture or professional skills, and who, taken collectively, made up a heterogeneous mass of learners. See Douglas Sloan, "Harmony, Chaos and Consensus," *Teachers College Record* (1971). Opportunities for women to get serious academic instruction developed in bits and pieces from about 1787 to 1821. Then came Troy, and until the opening of Mt. Holyoke Seminary and the Georgia Female College in 1836, it provided the best academic opportunity available to women in this country. John Lord, himself a Dartmouth graduate, testified "Whatever name her school may go by, yet in all essential respects it was a college . . . " Lord, *Willard*, p. 51.

11. The head of the Clinton, Georgia, Female Seminary went in 1837 to see for himself what was going on at Troy. He found Emma Willard's personal appearance "Very different from what I had anticipated. She is considerably above ordinary size of females, quite corpulent, but dignified and commanding, easy and pleasant in her manners; in her conversation shrewd and intelligent, but fond of adulation and self-esteem. Her dress was more gaudy than my 'beau ideal' of a literary lady and instructress of youth. I witnessed the examination of her pupils — and was much gratified by their proficiency." He heard classes examined in arithmetic, French, philosophy, history and geometry. Diary of Thomas Bog Slade, Southern Historical Collection, University of North Carolina.

12. Lutz, *Emma Willard*, p. 173, taken from a speech Stanton made at the Chicago World's Fair in 1893.

    At about the same time a former pupil wrote to Emma Willard's granddaughter, "Your grandmother's great distinction seemed to me to be a supreme confidence in herself and, as a consequence, a stubborn faith in the capacity of her own sex . . ." Eliza Athrop to Mrs. Scudder, May 9, 1892. Archives of Emma Willard School. Willard herself compared her work in education to that of the Founding Fathers in creating the Constitution!

13. Emma Willard, *Advancement of Female Education* (Troy, 1833), p. 9.

14. Lutz, *Emma Willard*, p. 121.

15. Typescript in Archives of Emma Willard School.

16. Willard, *Advancement of Female Education*, p. 137. In 1826 she had written a member of the New York Assembly: "I never expect that complete justice will be done our sex until this old set [of legislators] are chiefly with their fathers. But I am confident that our cause is a righteous one. . . " E. W. to Mr. Granger, Granger Papers, Library of Congress.

17. "Letter to the Members of the Willard Association for the Mutual Improvement of Teachers" (Troy, 1838), p. 5.

18. See letter from Julia Marks' daughter: "Mrs. Willard, Mrs. Lincoln Phelps and my mother were three educators acting in union. . . ." Archives of the Emma Willard School.

19. Handwritten notes of Henry Campbell Davis, deposited in South Caroliniana Library, University of South Carolina. In the 1930's Davis was engaged in tracing the influence of Troy in the south and west and concluded that it was "an important fact in the history of culture of America." As far as I can find out, his research on this subject was not published.

20. Fairbanks, *Mrs. Emma Willard and Her Pupils*, pp. 70, 171-172, 201, and manuscript questionnaires for each of these women in the Archives of the Emma Willard School, Troy, N.Y.

21. The work of Mrs. Willard and her pupils in the common school movement is rarely

mentioned in the secondary sources dealing with that movement, which is odd since the richest primary sources *The Annals of American Education, The Massachusetts Common School Journal,* and Henry Barnard's *American Journal of Education* all paid close attention to Willard and her ideas. See Emma Willard to Henry Barnard November 18, 1945, Henry Barnard Papers, NYU for an example of the close relationship between them.

22. Emma Willard to Mrs. Hotchkiss 30 April 1841 and Emma Willard to Henry Barnard, in Henry Barnard Papers, New York Univesity Library. In a letter to Gov. William Marcy of New York in 1826 she had said ". . . my views for the advancement of female education are connected with those I entertain of the improvement of the common schools . . ." Lutz, *Emma Willard,* pp. 194-195.

23. Sketch of Sarah Fisher Hoxie, *Mrs. E. W. and Her Pupils,* p. 516. At about the same time that she was thus paying tribute to the power of the idea of "woman's sphere" she was writing an article for the *American Literary Magazine* in which she proposed that France which had recently experienced a revolution should set up a separate congress of women to deal with those matters for which women should be especially responsible, including education. See "Letter . . . on the Political Position of Women," *American Literary Magazine* (1848), II, pp. 246-54.

24. I do not mean to minimize the importance of the other two women whose contribution to the professionalization of teaching was as important as that of Emma Willard: Catherine Beecher and Mary Lyon. See Kathryn K. Sklar, *Catherine Beecher* (New Haven, 1974), and the "Following essay" of David Allmendinger on Mt. Holyoke Seminary. Their contributions come a little later.

25. Memorial of the late Mrs. Emma Willard, A Proceedings of the Seventh Anniversary of the University Convocation of the State of New York, Albany 1871, p. 79.

26. Margaret Stanley Cowles, "A brief sketch of an incident of travel with Mrs. Emma Willard," Archives of the Emma Willard School, Troy, New York.

27. Mary Fairbanks to Olivia Slocum Sage, Archives of the Emma Willard School.

28. Mary Fairbanks to Olivia S. Sage, 14 October 1895, Archives of Emma Willard School.

30. Nephew of Ziporah de Camp Jacques 1823-1826, Archives of Emma Willard School; Fairbanks, *Mrs. Emma Willard and Her Pupils,* p. 405.

30. Eunice Samantha Bascom Memoir, Archives of Emma Willard School.

31. Mary Newberry Adams of Dubuque, Iowa to Olivia S. Sage, November 4, 1893, Archives of Emma Willard School.

32. Daughter of Jane Pelletreau Ashley Bates, replying to questionnaire. Archives of Emma Willard School.

33. Daughters of Elsie Van Dyke, 1827, and Agnes Powell, 1829-32, Archives of Emma Willard School; Fairbanks, *Mrs. Emma Willard and Her Pupils* p. 399.

34. Daughter of Sarah Serbine Stewart, Archives of Emma Willard School.

35. Almira Lincoln Phelps, *The Female Student* (New York, 1836), contains weekly lectures given to Troy pupils. One continuous thread runs through these lectures: learn to use your mind. Mrs. Phelps also dwelt upon the need to be prepared for self-support.

36. My collaborator in this venture is Professor Patricia Hummer presently of the Department of History of Michigan State University. She has done a great part of the technical side of the computer assisted analysis and is planning to write specifically about the Troy women who became teachers.

37. Irene and Conrad Taeuber, *People of the U.S. in the Twentieth Century*, (Wash., D.C., 1971), p. 378.

38. Wilson Grabill, Clyde V. Kiser and P.K. Whelpton, *Fertility of American Women* (New York, 1958), p. 56.

39. In 1974 Keith Melder published "Masks of Oppression: The Female Seminary Movement in the United States" in *New York History*, 55 (July, 1974), in which he argued that because of their adherence to the idea of separate spheres, the female seminaries perpetuated the oppression of women. I am persuaded that at least with respect to Troy this is a misapprehension, and that many of Willard's pupils, like Willard herself, found it possible to combine the old values and the new in creative ways.

PART III

The Twentieth Century

Introduction

THE TWENTIETH CENTURY has proven to be one of the most fertile areas of research for American social historians. Scholars have continued their love affair with the Progressive era, that fascinating period of educational change that spanned the years of the Depression of 1893 and World War I. Articles and monographs on the early 1900s continue to flow without abatement. Moreover, our comprehension of modern educational development promises to increase continually, as historians turn their focus to the years of the Great Depression and beyond. If anything, social historians will undoubtedly produce even more scholarship that provides insight into how ordinary people experienced the process of growing up and being educated.

It is hardly surprising that most social historians of education who study the twentieth century have thus far concentrated on the Progressive era. Historians properly understand that the period witnessed the birth of our modern public school system, with all of its problems and possibilities, with all of the contradictions of the larger society of which it was an integral part. By the early 1900s, the school's importance in the lives of children and families far exceeded the dreams of educators only a half century before. Children spent more and more time in school, to the degree that high schools were constructed at the rate of one per day between 1890 and 1920!

In addition, school boards were centralized, vocational courses were added to the curriculum, psychological testing became common, superintendents assumed greater control over educational policy and, not surprisingly, in cities where these changes were first felt most powerfully, teachers in dramatic cases formed their first unions. In the midst of a society increasingly defined by the rise of a more industrial, urban population whose character was racially and ethnically diverse, schools found themselves surrounded by social forces that seemed to make traditional beliefs and practices obsolete.

The problem of organizing schools and defining their central purpose is never an easy one in a pluralistic society, whether in the Progressive era or in our own. Indeed, the articles by David B. Tyack and by David N. Plank and

Paul E. Peterson provide different perspectives on how and why school organization and control changed so dramatically early in this century. Explaining and identifying how schools change, who benefits from change, and how
priorities in shaping educational policy are determined was a complicated
process for those who lived in the past as well as for later historians who
attempt to recapture the dynamics and flavor of that past for scholars and
students.

Were schools more attentive to the needs of parents or experts, boys or
girls, children of immigrants or the native born as citizens encountered the
realities of a more secular society increasingly dominated by large scale bureaucracies and economic structures? Did centralized school boards provide
more opportunities for all children, who increasingly were removed from the
work place and attended school for more years of their lives as the twentieth
century progressed? Did the professionalization of the school administration
and teaching staff create intolerable chasms between lay people and experts?
These questions remain timely ones even today, as politicians and scholars
debate once again the proper role of parents, teachers, employers, and governmental agencies in the education and socialization of young people in a
democratic, pluralistic society.

By the early 1900s, as scholars have continually reminded us, a wide
variety of racial and ethnic groups drawn from diverse economic backgrounds helped form the heterogeneous populations who attended school.
This only complicates the problem of forming generalizations concerning the
social role of schools in children's lives, but it has also produced a growing
literature that highlights the richness of community and educational life at
the turn of the century. The articles by John L. Rury, Michael R. Olneck
and Marvin Lazerson, and James D. Anderson explore the realities of being
a student who happened to be a member of a particular ethnic or racial
group or was female. As schools were increasingly centralized and influenced by professional and corporate interests, did they provide more equal
education for these groups? Were schools simply mirror reflections of the
larger ethnic, racial, and gender divisions in the larger society? To what
degree did the schools fulfill the promise of the famous nineteenth-century
educator, Horace Mann, who believed that public education comprised
the great promise of American life, a solution to the dilemmas of poverty
and the continual threat of social disorder in a heterogeneous, competitive
society?

Social historians do not speak with a single voice in addressing these questions. And so debates will certainly continue over whether schools primarily
opened avenues of mobility and opportunity for these social groups, or
whether they generally reaffirmed existing inequalities, rooted in family
background and personal characteristics, that children brought with them to
school. On the one hand, it is clear that the promise of American life was
systematically denied to black Americans during the Progressive era; hous-

ing, health care, economic opportunities, and education all reflected the realities of comprising a segregated economic underclass. And yet the faith of black Americans in the potential of schooling was immense and would lead in the post World War II years to a larger struggle for integrated schools.

Ethnic groups of an amazing variety also flooded into schools early in the century, with Catholic immigrants sometimes even supporting a substantial network of parochial schools. Scholars will continue to appraise the effects that cultural background played in shaping school achievement, whether Americanization programs greatly influenced the consciousness of youth, and the degree to which and the reasons why certain groups succeeded or failed at school. Did immigrants on balance benefit from attending public schools? How well did vocational programs prepare young people for a changing world of work? As the article by Marcia G. Synnott indicates, even the admission practices of elite colleges were shaped through much of the twentieth century by the realities of ethnicity and religious diversity as higher education responded in selective ways to those who sought the good life through the higher learning.

One noteworthy development in the social history of American education is the growing appreciation of the experiences of women in different educational environments. Besides examining the influence of race, ethnicity, and social class, scholars now have a greater sensitivity to the interplay of these variables and to the influence of gender differences. Women's history has, of course, been heavily influenced by the feminist movements of our times as well as by the general effort of social historians to recapture the lives of ordinary citizens. Historians now realize that for too long too few women graced the pages of our history books. Yet women have been an integral part of our educational past, as students, teachers, and leaders. School curricula have been shaped with so-called women's needs in mind, and in every aspect of education, formal and informal, historians have begun to document the difference being male or female has made in this century. Have the schools reinforced middle-class male values in our culture? Have schools gradually improved their record in providing all children with a more equal education?

Like most of the articles presented on the twentieth century, those written by Guadalupe San Miguel, Jr., and by Mary Aicken Rothschild deal with the larger issues that have stimulated many social historians in recent years. Have schools and education in their various guises played a constructive role in attaining greater social justice for outcast groups? For most of the twentieth century, as schools have gained more power than the family at times in shaping children's education and socialization, a great many Americans have seen the schools as a central part of the American dream of individual mobility, social order, and civic advance. The theory if not the practice of equality of educational opportunity has become a sacred canon of the American belief system.

To understand how wide the road is between the promise and reality of American life has often been a main stimulus behind the new social history. In this context one needs to travel to disparate places in our educational past: through the Mexican-American communities of Texas, through the inner-city ghettos of immigrants and native blacks, through the depressed areas of rural Appalachia, and even through the small towns in Mississippi where Freedom Schools contributed to the civil rights crusade of the 1960s. Only by traveling to some of these places can one experience vicariously the struggles of those who came before us, who encountered the difficulties of realizing the promise of American life through basic educational institutions. In their own distinctive ways, all of the authors in the following pages help to recapture these visions and struggles, all of which shaped our immediate past and now are replayed in different form in the great educational debates of our own times.

10
Pilgrim's Progress: Toward a Social History of the School Superintendency, 1860–1960

David B. Tyack

"THE DEATHS of great men in national and political history are commemorated by song, story and memorial days," Aaron Gove told his fellow school superintendents in 1900. "Only in secluded family circles, and midst the personal friends, are the works and lives of heroic schoolmasters recorded and remembered." To this day, historians have largely neglected those who probably did more than any other individuals to shape the day-to-day operation of American public education—the superintendents of school districts. Not entirely neglected, of course: we have Raymond Callahan's important, path-breaking work; several scholars have enlightened us about changing metaphors of leadership and the ideologies of administrators; early historians have traced the administrative duties of school chiefs; and we have a number of narratives about individual superintendents. (1) But we are still just beginning to understand the character of educational leadership in the past. We need to focus especially on superintendents in the *local districts,* where the chief decision-making power resided for most of American history rather than at the state or federal level (a statistic illustrates this point: in 1890 the median size of state departments of education was *two* persons, including the superintendent.) (2)

Superintendents talked and wrote a good deal about their ideologies, their expectations, their practices, and their problems. We know a good deal about their social characteristics and career lines, at least in the

Many people have helped me with this essay. I would especially like to thank Eric Bredo, Edwin Bridges, Ronald Cohen, Larry Cuban, Robert Cummings, Suzanne Estler, Miriam Gallaher, Keith Goldhammer, Wayne Hobson, Clarence Karier, Marvin Lazerson, Susan Lloyd, James March, and John Meyer. I am also grateful for support from the Ford Foundation and from the Center for Advanced Study in the Behavioral Sciences.

David B. Tyack is Vida Jacks Professor of Education and professor of history at Stanford University.

twentieth century. We have a fair amount of perceptive observation of the occupational socialization of educators. The main problem the educational historian faces is to fit these disparate data—often presented in snapshot style, limited to particular time and place—into an interpretive framework. There are useful places to turn for help in this task. Historians have recently been analyzing a wide range of occupational groups—social workers, priests, engineers, lawyers—and sociologists of occupations and of organizations have contributed both theory and empirical knowledge useful in understanding work in complex settings. This is an opportune time, then, to draw on such scholarship in conceptualizing the social history of the school superintendency. (3)

In this essay I explore some ways to make sense of the complex tale of stability and change that emerges in the social history of the superintendency. In the first section I suggest that superintendents in the nineteenth century conceived of their task in part as an evangelical enterprise, a search for organizational means to realize the goal of creating a "redeemer nation." As aristocrats of character in their own idealized self-conception, they were certified not so much by professional training as by church membership and a shared earnestness. In short, they were quintessential Victorians: evangelical Protestant, British-American, bourgeois. Although this tradition became much attenuated by newer sources of ideology in the twentieth century, it nonetheless left behind a legacy of millenial optimism and an ideal of heroic leadership. (4)

In the second part of the essay I indicate the remarkable continuity of social characteristics among superintendents in the several periodic surveys conducted in the twentieth century. This consistency of attributes was not accidental, and therefore I attempt to interpret the functional significance of sex, age, years of school experience, community of origin, ethnicity, marital status, and social mobility. Why were they so predominately middle-aged, white, native-born, Protestant, married males from non-urban (mostly farm) backgrounds?

Next I move on to examine how occupational socialization may help to explain the behavior of superintendents—how their prior careers as pupils, teachers, and principals may have shaped their notions of schools and links with the communities. Here I distinguish between cities and towns. In modest-sized school systems, superintendents tended to internalize the moral and educational expectations of the people they served in face-to-face communities. In the larger cities the size and complexity of the school system, coupled with new political arrangements that buffered the bureaucracy from lay influence, resulted in rather different managerial functions. In other words, while superintendents generally may have experienced some common forms of occupational socialization as they moved up the career ladder, specific organizational and political settings often differentiated the tasks they did and how they conceived of their roles.

Finally, I explore the quest for new sources of authority during the twentieth century. Increasingly, superintendents began to see themselves as a distinct occupational group, certified by training and specified experience, linked into associations, sponsoring and being sponsored by fellow experts, developing occupational norms, elaborating legal and bureaucratic rules, and turning to science and business as sources of authority in an uncertain enterprise. Both *acting* as managers and *reacting* as public servants, they mirrored transformations in other socio-economic sectors as the nation became increasingly a complex society of large organizations and functional groups.

ARISTOCRACY OF CHARACTER: SELF–CONCEPTIONS OF SUPERINTENDENTS IN THE NINETEENTH CENTURY

Consciously or unconsciously, many superintendents who wrote auto-biographies echoed John Bunyan's *The Pilgrim's Progress*. After the Bible, Bunyan's tale was the second most popular book in the childhood homes of superintendents who grew up at the turn of the twentieth century. Like Christian tangling with Apollyon in the Valley of Humiliation, schoolmen wrote of contests with bully-boys in one-room schools. They told of the Pliables or Obstinates who lost faith when they encountered the pedagogical Slough of Despond. Mr. Worldly Wiseman often appeared in the guise of textbook salesman in the autobiographies. The city school board sometimes resembled the jury in Vanity Fair, with its Mr. Blind-man, Mr. No-good, Mr. Malice, and Mr. Hate-light. Fiery darts came from the wicked in every quarter, while deceptive by-paths distracted Schoolman from his quest for the Celestial City. Gove spoke of his fellow pioneers who had pursued their pilgrimage "thru devious ways, against tremendous obstacles, and over the trail, by the sacrifice of almost infinite trial with vigorous opposition, in contest and in conflict to the end. One and another languished, fell, died, and are buried by the side of the road." But the goal was clear, the dream of common schooling announced by the Evangelist Horace Mann. (5)

For many years the Department of Superintendence of the National Education Association printed "necrologies" or brief biographies of its departed pilgrims. Here one finds important clues to the self-image of nineteenth century school leaders. Again and again certain key words recur: "earnest," "Christian character," "pure," "missionary enterprise," "perseverance," "Puritan stock," "New England tradition," and "true scholar." A fitting inscription for most of them would have been Longfellow's "Psalm of Life": "Life is real! life is earnest!/ And the grave is not its goal!" Here was an aristocracy of *character*, its worth certified by church membership and social service. Rarely did biographers dwell on educational background or professional training, for the age of specialization and certification did not come until the twentieth century. Rather, leadership in public education was often seen as a *calling* similar to that of church missionary; indeed, in teachers' institutes superintendents were sometimes as interested in converting to religion as in evangelizing for schooling. Their belief in an "All-Seeing Eye"— that God witnessed all human behavior—invested even the commonplace with cosmic significance. (6)

As Timothy Smith and I have attempted to document, evangelical Protestants were in the forefront of the common school crusade, especially on successive frontiers. Missionaries, settled ministers, devout laymen and women—such people often provided the leadership both for setting up and running schools; they tended to take a proprietary interest in their creation, seeing public education as a pan-Protestant establishment. Paul Mattingly and others have shown how Protestant motivation informed the early efforts to professionalize teaching and administration. Speeches of educators in the NEA and other forums indicate how much their version of civic and moral instruction depended on religion as an ultimate sanction. Indeed, in Victorian America it is almost impossible to disentangle religion from politics or economic life. As Daniel Howe has said, the Victorian was characteristically British-American, bourgeois, and evangelical Protestant—and the superintendents of the time mostly fit these criteria. Victorian educators, like contemporary ministers, tended to believe that God had chosen America as *the* Christian nation. Since the true citizen was a moral individual rooted in a Christian community, the common school was an instrument of both divine and republican purpose. The *nation* was not so much the formal apparatus of government as it was a state of mind, something constructed within the hearts and minds of the individuals who comprised American society. The leader—in education as in political life—was an exemplar of that state of mind. Social institutions—whether family, church, or school—existed chiefly to nurture Christian, republican individuals. And all this coincided with and reinforced the rapid development of attitudes and attributes that sustained a bourgeois economic order: the notions that wealth was a God-given gift and poverty the result of individual weakness; the traits of thrift in time and money, future orientation, control over emotion, sobriety, and hard work. (7)

Because there was fairly broad consensus on these issues in the dominant Victorian culture, there was also broad agreement on the qualities of character required for the job of superintendent. Indeed, agreement on these broad social values—as represented, for example, in the 120,000,000 copies of the *McGuffey Readers* that were sold—may have provided coherence to public education at a time when superintendents were struggling to standardize highly heterogeneous systems of control, non-symmetrical structures, and hodge-podge curricula. In other words, one might argue that laymen of the nineteenth century were mostly agreed on *what* schools were supposed to do but not on *how* they were to do it, whereas today *structures* of education are well established but *goals* are increasingly unclear. As John Meyer and Brian Rowan have argued, the integration of an educational system exists not simply in organizational charts and in allocations of power and responsibility but also in the understandings in peoples' minds. (8)

The school boards that hired superintendents during the nineteenth century, especially in cities, were often not sure what the job should entail. Especially in the years before 1890, many superintendents shifted back and forth from education to other occupations, such as the ministry, law, business, or politics (the NEA necrologies indicate how fluid many careers were at that time). Within the schools, career ladders were often ill-defined and short, since job categories shifted and school systems often had only a four-tiered structure: student-teacher-principal-superintendent. The actual duties of superintendents usually depended on the expectations of school boards and the drive and personality of the school officials. Some were clerks in function as well as in name. Some were really head teachers, people who inspired and guided the staff and concentrated on classroom instruction. Others saw the job as comparable to that of drill sergeant or inspector general who certified rigid compliance with rules and regulations. Here and there superintendents compared their managerial duties with those of supervisors of factories, though the analogies were rarely more than superficial. An occasional scholar like William T. Harris of St. Louis thought of himself as an educational statesman, almost a philosopher king, whose duty it was to shape the educational thought and practice of city and nation.

But the conceptions and metaphors of leadership were essentially confused, as one educator confessed in 1899 in his talk on "What the Superintendent Is Not." "You are not supernumeraries," he declared, nor "super-critics," nor "supercargo." "You are the conductor" of the pedagogical train, he insisted. "Your watch is the only standard on that train. Your word alone is law; by the movement of your hand every official is guided." Under your leadership, he told superintendents, the school system "is to be conducted into the great union station of this imperial nation." Despite the mechanical imagery of the railroad, however, he retained the evangelical sense of purpose of the generation of Mann. It is false, he said, to compare educators with managers of mills or factories: "It is left to you to be the only true superintendents, superintenders of the moral well-being of the universe." This Bunyanesque sense of the cosmic importance of their task helped superintendents of the nineteenth century to cope with crochety or corrupt school boards, culturally different people who resented forced assimilation to Victorian norms, and ungrateful patrons. Few pilgrims expected applause. (9)

Towards the end of the nineteenth century the specifically Protestant character of the superintendents' rhetoric changed, and they increasingly invoked the language of science and business during the twentieth century to justify educational leadership. They did not consider "science" or "efficiency" antithetical to idealism, however. Faith in progress had undergirded the notion of America as a redeemer nation; now the notion of evolution seemed to give the authority of science to that optimism. The progressive era was enamored with a form of efficiency that nicely complemented evangelical earnestness. John Higham has observed that "the distinctive feature of the period from 1898 to 1918 is not the preeminence of democratic ideals or of bureaucratic techniques, but rather a fertile amalgamation of the two . . . For a time it seemed that a modernized Americanism and a social gospel could be the moving spirit of a technical society." Theirs was an expanding enterprise, and in the modernized school organizations their own roles were becoming more prestigious and sharply defined.

Indeed, I am struck by the powerful optimism so many superintendents displayed in the face of immense challenges in the early twentieth century, in city schools in particular. Although the New York school system lacked tens of thousands of seats for the children flocking to its doors, Superintendent William Maxwell pushed hard for effective compulsory schooling legislation. Even tragedy could not dim the basic faith. Frank Whitney had been Superintendent of schools in Collinwood, Ohio, in 1908 when a disastrous fire claimed the lives of 162 students and two teachers, yet he reflected that "just to be alive in that period and to have a sense of sharing even in some small way . . . in the great adventure called education was a privilege beyond all price." To educators, he wrote, schooling "seemed indeed to be at the very heart of all progress. It was the key to the future. It was the focus of all those wild and entrancing dreams of what seemed the coming golden age, no longer dim and remote but just around the corner." (10)

To fulfill such great expectations required heroic leadership. So the AASA kept reminding its members in yearbook after yearbook, well into the twentieth century: "Not every superintendent, possibly no superintendent, can be a second Lincoln, but every superintendent can be conscious of a goal toward which he is constantly working, and which guides his thinking, his doing, and his decisions along the way." The 1933 AASA Yearbook continued: Superintendents have no lesser task than "to mold human character and to ameliorate the whole intellectual, moral, social, civic, and economic status of their fellows." It then went on to present a grandiose self-rating form that might have caused their *beau ideal* Lincoln to sneak back to Springfield in dismay. The best leader, it said, "attacks problems with vigor and with definite objectives. Meets difficulties with full force of mind and body. Never lets go until progress has been made or the problem has been solved. Always has reserve strength to meet and overcome new developments." Even his leisure had to be "on a high level." As late as 1952 the heroic image was still alive and well in the yearbook: "Today's mid-century attacks upon the schools and school leaders are not more powerful nor more vicious than those of 100 years ago. The Horace Manns and Henry Barnards had to win school support by sheer missionary zeal and convincing logic." Now, as then, it concluded, "it is the superintendent of great heart and courageous spirit, possessed of sound judgment and deep understanding, who will carry the profession and the schools forward . . . . His world will be immeasurably enriched by his service and leadership." Nothing less would do than to attract to the superintendency "the wisest, the strongest, the bravest, and the most understanding of the truly great men and women our civilization produces." (11)

Of course, such incantations—like inspirational speeches at conventions—may simply have become background music for most school administrators. The rhetoric of charisma may not have matched the routinization of the work. But at least until the last generation, this sense of millenial hope and this ritualistic call for heroic leadership have constituted a vital part of the expressed ideology of the occupation. In looking later at the actual ways in which superintendents became socialized to their occupations during the twentieth century, I will examine actual experience against these heroic aims. Now I turn to an analysis of the social characteristics of the persons who became superintendents.

SOCIAL CHARACTERISTICS, 1899-1960

For more than fifty years students of educational administration have conducted extensive surveys of the social characteristics, education, and career lines of school superintendents. Thus we have useful snapshots at different points in time. Most of these studies have significant defects: of sampling, rate of return of questionnaires, temptations to exaggerate in self-reports (as in numbers of books read), and interpretations long on exhortation and short on analysis. Nonetheless, the surveys are an invaluable source of data on the historical development of the occupation.

Appendix 1 summarizes evidence on superintendents in 1899 compiled by Robert Cummings from an issue of the *Journal of Education*. Please attend the cautions he outlines in the headnote. Appendix 2 compresses some of the statistics on social characteristics from AASA yearbooks on the superintendency; some of the problems in the data are discussed by Stephen Knezevich in his most recent survey. (12) While these data are approximate at best, one fact stands out: the remarkable consistency in the portrait of superintendents since 1899. While the governance and goals and internal operation of American schools have changed substantially in the last hundred years, the social attributes of superintendents have apparently remained relatively constant. Why?

City superintendents have almost all been married white males; characteristically middle-aged, Protestant, upwardly mobile, from favored ethnic groups, native-born, of rural origins. Typically, they had long experience in education, beginning their careers as young teachers, going on to principalships, and then becoming superintendents (in larger communities they often became assistant superintendents along the way). In disproportionate percentages they have been older sons in larger than average families. Mostly they remained in the same state for their entire careers as superintendents. They have been joiners, participating actively in civic and professional groups. Most of them picked up their advanced education while they practiced their profession, with long gaps of time between their academic degrees. They have been disproportionately Republican and have generally been moderate to conservative in their social philosophies. (13)

The data suggest interesting anomalies. Superintendents were almost all married males whereas teachers were 85 percent female in 1920 and typically single people at that time; almost all native-born, and mostly Anglo-Saxon, when the United States was a nation of immigrants from dozens of lands (in 1910, 40 percent of Americans were first or second generation immigrants); overwhelmingly Protestant in a religiously pluralistic nation and in a public service in which the separation of church and state made religious distinctions constitutionally irrelevant; raised in rural areas when the nation was undergoing rapid urbanization; and middle-aged in a sea of youngsters and mostly young teachers. (14)

Probably none of these characteristics is surprising. Surely they are not accidental. If such characteristics as sex, age, and race did not count in a systematic way, one would have found a more random distribution. In most respects superintendents matched leaders in comparable occupations (though, as we shall see, they were more upwardly mobile than most other leaders and more rural in origins). Superintendents also tended to match the characteristics of the school boards that hired them—again not accidentally. Numerous studies of school boards, beginning early in the century, have shown that school board members were white, middle-aged, predominantly male Protestants who came disproportionately from the upper reaches of the occupational and social structures of their communities. Of course communities differed markedly in their social composition, and both school board members and superintendents probably varied accordingly, for schools were more locally-controlled and locally-oriented than most other complex organizations.

The very ambiguity and diffuseness of the goals of schooling, and the consequent difficulty of measuring "success" or "failure," probably reinforced the significance of maleness, mature age, "proper" ethnicity, acceptable church membership, and appearance (not surprisingly, superintendents were taller than the average, giving people someone to look up to). For a superintendent to be a member of a respectable church and to have a stable marriage gave moral certification, a comforting sign of reputability. Like the banker's conservative dress, such social characteristics were an outward sign of safe leadership in an ambiguous enterprise. (15)

Hardly any superintendents were people of color until the 1960s. Before then some blacks had reached high administrative ranks, though not the superintendency, in dual school systems in the segregated South and in border cities, but in the North few blacks had even become principals. Perhaps the most striking version of powerlessness has been evident in the Bureau of Indian Affairs. B.I.A. schools scattered in reservations across the nation have been far more responsive to white bureaucrats in Washington, D.C., than to the communities they served. Mexican-Americans and Puerto Ricans were an infinitesimal percentage of school leaders even in communities where their children furnished a majority of pupils. (16)

Maleness, like whiteness, was almost everywhere essential to selection as superintendent. Teachers were predominantly female, and there was a high dropout rate of teachers of both sexes. Thus persistence in the schools gave an important edge to male aspirants to the superintendency. A few women won low-status jobs as county superintendents, driving their Model Ts along dusty roads from one rural school to another, but in practically every well-paid superintendency, men held sway. Hierarchy within the school system relied heavily on the dominance of men in the outside society: the male boss symbolized authority. Sponsorship and encouragement of younger men by older male administrators and professors was a potent means of recruitment and placement in the superintendency, a network of "old boys" in symbiotic relationship. The education honorary society Phi Delta Kappa was exclusively male. The inner councils and the conventions of the National Education Association were long dominated almost exclusively by men; not until 1910, and then only through a feminist revolt in the ranks, was a woman elected President of the NEA. (17)

But it was not only within the schools that maleness was an asset. Study after study showed that by actively participating in prestigious civic and fraternal organizations superintendents linked schools to the power structure of their communities. In a number of these community organizations no women were permitted to become members. Even in mixed organizations they would have found it awkward to develop the sort of informal business contacts and official camaraderie that elite men established with one another, so powerful were sex-typing and social inhibitions. If the male superintendent was, in some respects, still an outsider, a stranger in the halls of the mighty, a woman superintendent would have been all the more so. Yet close contact with local business and professional elites often was crucial to superintendents. The head of the Madison, Wisconsin, school system wrote that the administrator "who devotes some time to the Rotary Club, the Kiwanis Club, and other organizations for men will find the professional incrustation within which he has insulated himself violently perforated." He told of a western superintendent who admired the "empire builders" in the local Chamber of Commerce and who "hunted with them, fished with them, and became their friend and companion. When the time came to direct the schools into some new and untried venture, these men threw their mighty enthusiasm into the project not because they were advocates of the educational principle upon which the experiment was based, but because they wanted their friend to win." (18)

Being Protestant, and an active church member, has often been an important unofficial requirement for selection as superintendent, especially in small or medium-sized communities. Among 796 superintendents who reported their religion in Frederick Bair's study in 1934, only six were Roman Catholic, none Jewish, and none agnostic; 93 percent reported that they attended church. Neal Gross found in the mid-1950s that not only did superintendents and school boards in Massachusetts overwhelmingly prefer hiring white males but that they also tended to favor Protestants over Catholics or Jews (28 percent of superintendents, for example, thought their successor should be Protestant; 35 percent thought he should not be Jewish; 20 percent did not approve selection of a Catholic). (19)

Superintendents grew up predominantly in rural areas and small communities. The AASA study of superintendents in 1933 reported that 69 percent went to high school where the population was under 5000. Bair reported an even larger percent of rural backgrounds in his study; about half of the superintendents' fathers were farmers. Almost two-thirds of his sample worked on farms as children. Superintendents who wrote autobiographies often commented about their distaste for hoeing and harvesting but were proud of their lifelong habits of early rising and hard work. Commonly their homes offered little intellectual stimulation; 25 percent of superintendents told Bair that there were *no* books in the home that were important to them as children. Carlson has shown by a reanalysis of 1958 data on superintendents that they differed from the general population in that they grew up far less frequently in large cities and much more than average in places with populations between 2500 and 10,000. In this respect they also contrasted with leaders in government, business, and the military, who came more frequently from large cities. (20)

Thus the public schools have for a long time drawn teachers and administrators heavily from rural areas and small communities. Perhaps one reason is that school employees in such neighborhoods were among the very few role models of white collar workers for young persons who wished to escape the plow and the farm kitchen. As Carlson observed, big cities offered more diverse and visible opportunities for ambitious youth. Ellwood P. Cubberley warned the aspiring administrator that to be a small town principal was only to be a big frog in a little professional pond and that the principal might gain a false sense of his own importance. In a small community, he wrote, a principalship gives a man "at once a special standing . . . . The people naturally look up to him as a man of more than ordinary training and importance. On the streets the men call him 'Professor,' and pretty grade teachers and women with marriageable daughters seek him out, and flatter his vanity. His daily work in superintending women and children, who usually accept his pronouncements as law, perhaps gives him an added importance in his own eyes." (21)

Although superintendents often sought to escape the drab routine of farm lives they knew as children, many also tended to accept the values they learned in their small communities and to glorify socialization in the countryside. Indeed, they often saw the city as a source and center of social problems (although professionally it offered far greater opportunity and autonomy in personal life). It is likely that the rural-raised superintendent would have gained little first-hand knowledge of the out-of-school life of the city child and would have seen the role of the school, as did many trainers of administrators, as compensatory. Ironically, the further his ambition propelled him—to the big city—the further he traveled from the source of virtue, small-town America. In 1933 37 percent of superintendents in cities over 10,000 attended high schools in places whose population was under 2500; another 23 percent came from communities 2500-5000; and only 12 percent from cities of 100,000+. Overwhelmingly native-born, Anglo-Saxon, Protestant, raised in the provincialism of the homogeneous small town, the school superintendent was likely to regard his own values and patterns of belief as self-evidently "American" and thus correct (and so he was assured when he met in convention with his peers or took courses with administration professors, most of whom were of similar backgrounds). After all, those values had worked for him in his upward ascent. (22)

Most superintendents appear to have been somewhat more upwardly mobile than leaders in other occupations. In Bair's sample, for example, two-thirds of the parents had gone no further than grade school; half were farmers; and a few of the rest were executives or professionals (except for a liberal sprinkling of ministers and teachers). Carlson discovered similar evidence in a later period. One reason, probably, why superintendents tended to be socially mobile is that generally they had to enter their work through the relatively low-status occupation of teacher. In comparison with lawyers, doctors, most executives in business and government, and typical military officers, they started lower in the ranks and remained there longer. In some respects their career pattern was similar to that of a Catholic bishop, who had normally to serve a long stint as curate (or assistant to a pastor), then as pastor, and then, finally, win his episcopacy. Another parallel might have been the career of a police chief, who began as a patrolman, worked up as sergeant and lieutenant, and finally moved to the top office. For superintendent, bishop, or police chief, long experience counted heavily in advancement. It is the possible effects of this long work experience in schools as student, teacher, and administrator on the superintendent's role conception and performance that I shall now explore. (23)

OCCUPATIONAL SCOCIALIZATION: THE PATH TO THE SUPERINTENDENCY IN THE TWENTIETH CENTURY

"Teaching makes the teacher," Willard Waller wrote in 1932 in his insightful book *The Sociology of Teaching.* Whatever teaching does for students, "teaching does something to those who teach." In a similar way, one might say that school work makes the superintendent. As shown in Appendix 2, the typical superintendent in the twentieth century was a career educator for over twenty years. He almost always started as teacher (often serving both in elementary school and high school), then worked as principal (more often in high school than elementary), and in city schools frequently as assistant superintendent (in 1960 in cities from 100,000-500,000 population, 48 percent had been assistant superintendents, while the percent increased to 71 in cities over 500,000). Thus the career ladder differed somewhat according to the size of the school system, but in both small and large districts the school chiefs had almost all been teachers and principals. In this section I will explore some of the mechanisms and results of occupational socialization generally, look at some of the ways in which the interaction of school and community shaped the behavior of teachers in small districts, examine how administrators functioned in those small systems, and finally discuss occupational socialization in the larger cities. (24)

As research in occupational socialization has shown, jobs have a variety of powerful effects on those who work in them. The nature of the work one does helps to fix one's place in the larger social structure, for the pay and prestige of occupations differ substantially. One's job has become a vital element of self-conception. The public images of different kinds of work tend to attract different kinds of people to occupations as diverse as librarian, rock musician, and test pilot. But occupations themselves tend to have an important effect on the behavior and attitudes of those who work in them. Those who stay in complex occupations over long periods of time, as do superintendents or U.S. Senators or doctors, sometimes form significant inner fraternities to set standards and sponsor mobility in accord with the values and habits they have acquired in their own socialization at work. These "hidden hierarchies" help provide important continuity and institutional memory. (25)

Many occupations not only have distinct niches in the social system and provide peer socialization in the work group but also develop ideologies to advance the group and justify its standard operating procedures. "The world of occupational organizations is one in which a Veblenesque vision of gigantic conmanship is almost a methodological imperative," writes Peter Berger. The attempt to "professionalize" jobs, to acquire or manufacture the characteristics presumed typical of high-status occupations, often results in what looks to the demystifying sociologist like "fantastic bamboozling." Not only may such efforts be functional for the group, but proponents may be quite sincere, if one accepts David Riesman's definition of the "sincere person" as one who believes his own propaganda. (26)

Even if there is not a fully articulated ideology, which usually develops when an occupation becomes self-conscious and seeks higher status, most occupational groups have norms to which the worker is expected to conform. "When the teacher has internalized the rules which bind him," Waller observes, "he has become truly a teacher . . . . a person is not free in any occupation until he has made conformity a part of himself. When conformity is the most natural thing for him, and he conforms without thought, the teacher is free, for freedom is only an optical illusion that results from our inability to see the restrictions that surround us." Even if one dissents from Waller's bleak sociological determinism, his point nonetheless contains much truth. (27)

Comparison of occupational groups sometimes highlights the socialization process. The occupational development of priests and bishops offers some useful analogies to that of teachers and superintendents. Both groups have tended to come from pious, middle-class families whose fathers have less than a high school education. Both spend the greater proportion of their lives under the aegis of a single institution, the church or the public schools. Both churchmen and superintendents are much in the public eye both at work and abroad in their communities and are expected to display conspicuous virtue rather than to take risks. Both move up through subordinate positions in regular sequence starting at the bottom of the organization. In each case seniority and persistence in the organization count heavily in advancement, in part because of the difficulty of measuring "success" in what Waller calls "museums of virtue." Conformity to rules and loyalty to superiors are typical and valued qualities in both institutions. Access to informal networks of sponsors and sponsorees, such as that gained by advanced training at favored institutions (Teachers College or the North American College at Rome), often hastens advancement. An important difference in the two groups, however, is that the priesthood normally requires early vocational commitment, whereas superintendents (in the past at least) often drifted into administration over a long period of time. Another significant difference is that advancement to the top

position of the Church depends on clerical superiors in a complex
bureaucracy; superintendents are elected by local lay boards. (28)

The superintendent normally begins his career in public education
as student in kindergarten or first grade. Thus its standard operating
procedures become familiar at age five or six and are reinforced by
almost unbroken familiarity until retirement, as Larry Cuban has pointed
out. It is often hardest to question that which is most obvious. While
educators, like most Americans, tend to place an exaggerated value on
"innovation"—and admen even invent the NEW Old Dutch Cleanser—
basic strategies and structures of schooling usually show great continuity
over time, in part, perhaps, because of the self-evidence of these routines to school people who have known them since childhood. Although educators ordinarily change their perspectives on schooling as
they shift from student to teachers, or from teachers to administrators,
they do not normally need to undergo the powerful resocialization
through training that transforms, for example, civilian recruits into
army lieutenants. This is not to deny that "teaching makes teachers"—
in other words, that the occupation shapes their attitudes and behavior
—but simply to say that the process of occupational socialization builds
on a base of prior knowledge of schooling, including substantial prior
familiarity with teachers' and administrators' roles (although these roles
tend to appear different from diverse vantage-points in the system). (29)

1. Patterns of Socialization in Small Communities

Willard Waller and others have given us a vivid sociological portrait of
teachers who served—as did so many superintendents—in small districts.
In the communities studied by Waller in the early 1930s the beginning
teacher was expected to meet the converging expectations of students,
peers, principals, and parents about conservative dress, firm demeanor,
and other forms of behavior thought proper for teachers. Evaluation
forms used by principals and superintendents commonly rated the loyalty (or "cooperation") of the teacher, his or her neatness, punctuality,
efficient processing of forms, tact, and above all, his or her effectiveness
in discipline. Evaluating the results of instruction might be difficult, but
anyone could see if the classroom window shades were drawn at half
mast or if the room were quiet. "One suspects," wrote Waller, "that
'professional ethics,' a creation of executives for the guidance of subordinates, is really loyalty under another name." Loyalty and tact, the
preeminent virtues of the domestic servant, were also prized in teachers
as public servants. Toward the pupils, however, the teacher was encouraged to develop social distance. And the peer culture of teachers, like
that of police, reinforced the norm of "not making waves." (30)

Was it paradoxical that the teacher in a small community was expected to conform to the proper morals and mores of the town but was
often regarded as something of an outsider, not quite integrated into

the social life of the community? Evidence abounds that townspeople kept a vigilant eye on the out-of-class behavior of educators and that moral "lapses" resulted in firings far more often than did incompetence in teaching. Many communities assumed that teachers would become ex-officio Sunday School instructors. Yet teachers often complained that they were kept at arm's length socially, that women teachers were America's vestal virgins, and that men teachers were treated by other men rather like ministers and other quasi-townsmen.

The paradox begins to dissolve, however, when one realizes that often the public school served as a place where children learn that honesty is always the best policy, that the United States had statesmen of stainless steel, that proper diction and upright character go hand-in-hand. "Among these ideals are those moral principles which the majority of adults more or less frankly disavow for themselves but want others to practice," wrote Waller; "they are ideals for the helpless, ideals for the children and for teachers." As "a paid agent of cultural diffusion" of these ideals the teacher must be shielded from the untoward realities of saloons and cigars, seduction and salacious talk. "It is part of the American credo that school teachers reproduce by budding." Over time most teachers who remained in the profession internalized the community's stereotyped expectations; one teacher who resisted such stereotypes, a poet, called her poignant book *Teachers Are People.* (31)

Generalized moral expectations of the community shaped the behavior of teachers both in and outside the classroom, but so did the need to maintain order in the school—what Waller called a "despotism in a state of perilous equilibrium." Richard Carlson has observed that the public school, like the prison and the state mental hospital, occupies a special niche in the ecology of institutions: it has involuntary clients and cannot select among them. Some students want to be in school and are rewarding to teach; others resist, actively or passively, and pose special problems of social control. The beginning teacher often found the latter predominating in her or his classroom, since a common perquisite of seniority was to teach the willing student. Even experienced teachers had nightmares of class disruption or disastrous visits from supervisors. The task of getting and keeping order, and of imparting instruction to unwilling pupils, shaped the political structure of both classroom and school. (32)

Entering the white-collar occupation of teaching from lower-middle class backgrounds, most teachers did not hold notably liberal attitudes (although studies of teachers' attitudes were somewhat inconsistent). Even if their pedagogical training stressed progressive methods—on which there is again mixed evidence—the "reality shock" of initial teaching probably did most to determine their behavior. Just as beginning policemen learned from veterans to forget the police academy and to learn from peers about the real world of the beat, the most important sociali-

zation to teaching came from the craft wisdom of the teachers' sub-
culture and the social character of the classroom. Like the veteran
policeman advising the recruit to be firm, the older teacher sometimes
told the younger, "don't smile till Christmas." One study of attitudes
of novices before and after the initial teaching experience concluded,
for example, that experienced "teachers became less concerned with
pupil freedom and more concerned with establishing a stable, orderly
classroom, in which academic standards received a prominent position.
The change was accompanied by a decline in the tendency to attribute
pupil misbehavior or academic difficulty to the teacher or the school
. . . ." (33)

Learning to adapt to the moral and educational demands of the community and to preserve the tenuous authority of the classroom, then,
were important parts of the socialization of the small town teacher. The
majority of teachers—both male and female—left the classroom after a
brief stint. Of those who remained in education, the women teachers
found that their mobility was mostly horizontal; they tended to move
to larger communities or to choicer spots in the same system. Only a
few women applied to and gained administrative jobs, normally the
lower-status ones. Since few men persisted in public school careers over
a lifetime, they had relatively high chances for advancement. For the
men who wanted more pay, authority, and scope for altruistic hopes,
the ladder of ambition within education led through the principalship
to the superintendency. On the way they learned how to win the favor
of community influentials and to run an orderly school. (34)

In a small community the jumps from the classroom to the principal's
office to the superintendency were often not very large. In 1929 Fred
Ayer published a study of what principals and superintendents actually
did. His sample included mostly small districts. Ayer's findings are revealing: superintendents and principals performed many of the same
tasks with about the same frequency; both commonly taught classes
(71 percent of his superintendents taught in the high school of their
district); the work of both superintendents and principals was very
heterogeneous and often quasi-clerical or janitorial; and community
liaison was a vital and time-consuming part of the job, for superintendents interacted frequently with parents, ministers, medical workers,
salesmen, lay board members, and leaders from local associations. The
job required a good deal of social energy.

Ayer did not simply list dignified "professional" categories—like
supervision, financial management, curriculum, or pupil services—but
rather specified tasks, the percentages of superintendents who performed
them, and their frequency (*i.e.*, daily or weekly). Thus it is possible to
construct a picture of how they spent their time. For example:

86 percent went to the post office daily to get school mail;

93 percent inspected toilets weekly;

large percentages typed their own work, operated the mimeograph machine, checked to see if teachers arrived on time, inspected the janitor's work, and personally saw to building maintenance and construction;

smaller percentages wound the clocks and wrote memory gems on the blackboard daily.

Although 71 percent of them still taught classes, and almost all had risen to the superintendency through the ranks, their relationship with other teachers (mostly female) tended to be paternalistic. It was common for them to meet teachers at the railroad station, find them places to board in town, and advise them "on social and moral conduct," including "appropriate and sanitary dress." Only 23 percent discussed their ratings of teachers with the persons evaluated.

It is clear that these superintendents saw themselves—and were seen by the communities they served—as the guardians of decorum and morality. Indeed, as John Meyer has observed, it was in part these community understandings that gave symbolic structure and organizational coherence to schooling. Because the actual outcomes of public education were hard to measure, it was all the more important to preserve ritual and decorum. Community contacts and ceremonies such as assemblies took up much of the superintendent's day. Eighty-nine percent of Ayer's sample attended church regularly and 56 percent taught Sunday School. When asked what they did to improve themselves professionally, 73 percent said that they read religious literature weekly (this was number eight in frequency in a list of 28 items, of which number nine was participation in national professional organizations.) (35)

"Is the small town superintendency a glorified janitorship?" asked a writer in *School Executives Magazine* in 1931. The answer, not surprisingly, was yes. He must be "official chaperone for all teachers," quick to censure the woman who puts her feet on the landlady's davenport or attends a dance on a school night. He teaches a class; visits all classrooms regularly; monitors pupils at recess; "is the final court of appeal in all disciplinary matters; handles all business from the hiring of teachers to the purchase of stamps; keeps office hours for parents who are frank to question the soundness of his educational principles; arranges extracurricular activities, out-of-town contests, and so ad infinitum." In discipline he is expected to show "the wisdom of Solomon with the humility of Uriah Heep and the tact of an ambassador." On duty at all times, he may be called "at midnight to shoo amorous couples from the schoolhouse steps," buttonholed at a social meeting to discuss "school drain pipes" or "the sheerness of the seventh grade teacher's hose." All his traits are open to public scrutiny, his opinions dissected, his family a favorite topic of conversation. The superintendent's wife suffered all kinds of constraints on her actions. In other articles disenchanted superintendents spoke out—sometimes anonymously—about the trials of local politics, local pride and religious prejudice that made the superintendent an anxious servant of a fickle public. (36)

Given the fishbowl character of the job in small communities, it is not surprising that some administrators protested their lot. What is perhaps most significant is that so few did so. Indeed, in two studies of outside interest group pressures on superintendents, over half the school chiefs replied that they had experienced none. It is likely that through long and continuous socialization as student, teacher, and principal most superintendents came to internalize the values of the communities they served and that they accepted role prescriptions not as restrictions but as normal expectations—in short that they became "free" in Waller's sense through unconscious conformity. A large proportion of superintendents never left their own states during their entire careers; a study of mid-western administrators showed that only 13 percent of administrative moves were out-of-state. It was possible for many superintendents to find communities in which their values matched those of most of the patrons so that dissonance was minimized. Such administrators might feel it no more unreasonable to expect schools to be "museums of virtue" than for their churches to set high ethical standards. The high goals of an educational "celestial city" might give resonance even to menial tasks. They were "locals," attuned to the ethos of particular places and times, not "cosmopolitans" like their more mobile brethren, many of whom fled the small town for the city. (37)

Superintendents in small communities vastly outnumbered those in larger districts. In 1931 there were 980 superintendents in cities over 10,000 population as compared with 2,353 in cities from 2,500 to 10,000 and 3,620 "rural" (or county) superintendents. Typically they grew up in the communities they served or in ones much like them. As they passed through a path of socialization from student to teacher to principal to superintendent they experienced a broader perspective and growing authority until ultimately they became the most important link between community and school system. No doubt some of them acquired new ideas about education in their training and in their professional associations and became carriers of an adapted cosmopolitanism. Some, also, came in conflict with community factions or influentials. But their general socialization, as I have suggested, probably inclined them to reinforce the traditional values of the community and to perpetuate the structures and styles of pedagogy that they had known and their patrons preferred. (38)

2. Urban Patterns: Up the Organization

There were important differences, as well as similarities, in the experience of educators in large cities as compared with small communities. Career ladders contained the same initial rungs—teacher and principal—

but normally there were additional rungs before the top on the differentiated and multi-tiered urban systems. Partly as a result of these intermediate steps, the median age of superintendents in large cities was about seven to ten years higher than that of small city school chiefs in the years from 1923 to 1960. Increasingly the doctorate became required for the job in large cities (over 50 percent of those in cities over 100,000 had doctor's degrees in 1952 as compared with only 6 percent in cities from 2,500 to 10,000). Big city superintendents tended to move from small communities of origin into the city rather than remaining in familiar surroundings; as late as 1960, only 13 percent of superintendents in cities from 100,000-500,000 population, for example, had attended high schools in cities over 100,000. (39)

Big city school systems of the twentieth century were structurally far more complex than small districts, and their managers operated in a quite different manner. If the small school system was, in effect, a quasi-church (pan-Protestant) in which it was appropriate for the superintendent to say that he improved himself professionally by reading religious literature, the large urban district resembled in some respects a business corporation (and as Raymond Callahan has documented, educators of the early twentieth century carefully elaborated that analogy). Gone were the days of simple administration when the superintendent of the Los Angeles schools in the 1890s assembled all his teachers for a pep talk at the end of the month and handed each one a paper bag of cash as the month's salary. (40)

To some degree these changes in city schools paralleled transformations in business and industry. As the scale and complexity of corporate capitalism grew, whole new layers and functional divisions of management appeared. Railroad companies, for example, became differentiated into divisions of transportation, traffic, and finance. Large-scale industries producing a single product developed functional departments for extracting raw materials, manufacturing, and sales. As huge corporations diversified their products, they often created three-tiered structures consisting of central planning and administrative headquarters at the top, a second layer divided according to products produced, and a third echelon divided according to functional specialization within those product divisions. Increasingly, the central office developed techniques not only for evaluating past performance but also for forecasting and planning for the future. The budget became a central tool of management. (41)

Despite the desire of educational "executives" to emulate business organization, the adaptation of these new techniques of management came only piecemeal and in stages. Talk of "business efficiency" in education could not abolish three problems: the "output" of education was far more difficult to measure than profit and loss in General Motors; the goals of schooling were ambiguous; and the connection between the new organizational techniques and either goals or output was by no means clear. Nevertheless, under the corporate model of urban school governance, some rough parallels appeared between the structure of business enterprise and the organization of city schools: a large growth in the staff of the central office (where once only the superintendent and perhaps two or three assistants or clerks had held sway); diversification of the structure of the schools into functional divisions such as vocational schools, guidance departments, attendance services, building and maintenance, and special schools for the handicapped; and the creation of research and planning departments to provide evidence on operations and data for forecasting. Forms multiplied and files bulged. New corps of specialists appeared. Indeed, so complex became the sub-divisions that large cities sometimes required intermediate layers of supervisors of specialists so that the total number of administrators reporting to the superintendent would not be too great for effective span of control. (42)

A major goal of the movement to centralize control of city schools at the turn of the twentieth century had been to insulate the school system from community influences the reformers thought harmful: political machines intent on graft, ethnic factions on ward boards, and other lay interest groups. Under the centralized corporate model, the ideal was to vest power in a small board of "successful men" who would in turn delegate the actual running of the schools to the superintendent. Justified as "getting the schools out of politics," this was in effect a different form of political control, one which matched the ideology of business and professional elites. Under this model, promotion within the system depended on rational, meritocratic criteria: specialized educational training and credentials, favorably evaluated performance, and orderly progression up the hierarchial ladder or appointment from a similar background in another system. Numerous cities developed examination and promotion systems; New York's Board of Examiners was one of the most elaborate.

In practice the corporate model often did not work as the elites intended. Ethnic or religious criteria played no formal role in selection by merit, but informally they were significant in many cities, as different ethnic groups succeeded in moving up the hierarchies of school districts. In Boston, for example, Peter Schrag found that in the 1960s all members of the central administration "are graduates of Boston College, all have risen through the ranks and have been in the system for more than three decades, all are well over 50 years old, all are Catholics, and all, excepting only Superintendent William H. Ohrenberger with his German background, are Irishmen." In Chicago and elsewhere top administrators sometimes gave expensive cram courses designed to prepare aspiring educators for the "merit" examinations. "Getting the attention of superiors" became an art form for many teachers ambitious to rise in the system. Knowing the right people could sometimes turn a bureaucratic stone wall into a triumphal arch. In cities the "right people" might be one's superiors within the system—especially for those moving up the middle rungs on the ladder—or they might be school board members or other community influentials. (43)

Small districts and vast city systems provided rather different contexts, then, for occupational socialization. The big city offered escape to educators in their private lives from the vigilant eye of public opinion in the small town, and thus it served as a refuge for cosmopolitans who did not share small-town values. To a large degree centralization uncoupled schools from neighborhoods. The sheer size and diversity of the urban systems offered different routes upwards for persons of different talents. The corporate model of meritocracy shaped the *formal* screening process for advancement, yet *informally* such influences as ethnicity, religion, friendship, and old-fashioned graft did not disappear as significant factors in promotion. In any case, both in town and city an educator of the twentieth century who arrived at the superintendency at age 45 or 50 had normally spent almost all his life in the schools. That experience, like the selection process that resulted in leaders who had certain social characteristics, had much to do with the ways in which superintendents performed their roles.

THE SEARCH FOR AUTHORITY IN THE TWENTIETH CENTURY

As we have seen, superintendents have drawn on different kinds of authority in pursuing their careers in the schools. As pilgrims seeking Mann's celestial city, they relied on the authority of high moral purpose and were granted certification by nobility of character. Such authority was powerful when the common schools were, in effect, part of a Protestant *paideia*, education by a network of intersecting institutions of family, church, and school intent on moral and civic socialization of the young in accord with a general Protestant consensus on values. This vision has continued to be influential, especially in small districts, but its force has weakened as the nation has become more pluralistic in population and values. This ideal has tended to persist as a vaguely heroic conception of leadership. A second and largely implicit source of authority for superintendents has come from their social characteristics as white, middle-aged male Protestants of favored ethnic groups. Useful though such authority may have been in status interaction with women teachers, the young, and with less prestigious social groups, it hardly distinguished school administrators from members of school boards or other laymen before whom they wished to assert their expertise. A third kind of authority inhered in the way superintendents in homogeneous small communities personified and enforced the official morality of the village. All of these sources of authority, of course, could have combined in different ways to reinforce the legal and organizational authority of superintendents at the apex of school bueaucracies. (44)

But as superintendents began to see themselves as a specialized occupational group—especially in the large cities, with their vast school systems and heterogeneous citizenry—they increasingly regarded these earlier sources of authority as inadequate and sought new ones. Part of the problem lay in the ambiguous definition of "success" or "mistakes" or "failure." Superintendents saw fellow administrators unceremoniously fired by lay boards for what they regarded as courageous or wise acts; one educator's act of statesmanship might seem tomfoolery or arrogance to laymen. Everyone felt qualified, it seemed, to decide what teachers to hire or fire, what sort of spelling method to use, or to determine what kind of desks to buy. Because of the very diffuseness of the goals of schooling and the extravagant claims made for its efficacy, the sins of the young could be blamed on the schools, and ultimately on the superintendent. Like a police chief responsible for public law and order, the superintendent could easily be blamed for anything that went wrong, especially for the indiscretions of subordinates, but he was less frequently given credit for success. A schoolman's daily routine consisted —like that of a police chief's or surgeon's—in part of other people's emergencies, and the risks of mistake were great. But there was little effective way of sharing these risks within an understanding group of peers. So long as there was no agreed-upon canon of expertise in practice, and so long as laymen were the omnipresent judges, life for the superintendent could become an endless accusation of malpractice. (45)

School leaders responded to these problems of authority and vulnerability in a variety of ways. As we have seen, some turned to political reform of school boards and emulated the "non-political" corporate board of trustees. This strategy depended, however, on a conception of expertise in educational leadership that was still rudimentary at the turn of the century. The emerging new sources of expertise were twofold but related. One was adaptation of new patterns of management in business, a high-status sector of society that might reflect some of its glory back on educational leaders; this approach has been fully analyzed by Raymond Callahan. A similar route to expertise was to follow the dictates of "science" in education, to put into practice the new discoveries of the intelligence testers, the exponents of "social efficiency" in curriculum construction, and the endless new studies which sought to quantify wisdom about ventilation, evaluation of teachers, or methods of teaching reading. Both business and educational science contributed the jargon that seemed to be the hallmark of expertise, a convenient way of marking off boundaries around the initiated expert (though from the beginning, critics said that the new bafflegab of administrators was simply pretentious commonsense, thereby weakening its utility). (46)

Educational administrators turned to graduate education for degrees and to state departments of education for certification that would legitimize their authority. Specialized training in educational administration began in earnest in the first quarter of the twentieth century. The pioneers—men like Samuel Dutton, William Chancellor, Ellwood Cubberley, and George Strayer—had to invent a scholarly field. The existing literature was composed mostly of reminiscences of veterans, theoretical and philosophical works, and rudimentary monographs in educational history. The fact that these pioneer professors discovered subjects to teach, persuaded universities to give credit for their courses, and recruited students to pay tuition for them is no small tribute to their enterprise. The leading superintendents came to agree with their university colleagues that graduate work in educational administration would certify them as experts. Slowly, very slowly, such leaders persuaded state legislatures that certification by advanced study should be required for all superintendents. Although about half the states had at least minimal certification requirements by 1940, it was not until the 1950s that the practice became nearly universal. (47)

To what degree did graduate training actually enhance the authority and performance of school administrators? From one point of view, the history of the graduate education is encouraging; this table compiled from AASA surveys shows the rapid increase in the percentage of city superintendents with masters' and doctors' degrees:

HIGHEST DEGREE HELD
(All figures are percentages)

Trends, 1923–1960: Highest degree	Year				
	1923*	1933	1952	1960	
No degree	12.81	3.77	.2	2.0	
Bachelor's	54.64	36.22	5.5	2.4	
Master's	32.02	56.68	78.7	56.3	
Doctorate	2.92	2.97	15.5**	21.7	
Other	.37	.36	.1	17.6	(= "60 hours beyond bachelor's")

Source: see Appendix 2.
   *1923 survey did not ask for information on highest degree held, but asked for data on sum total of degrees. The percentages in this table for 1923 are *estimates* made by compilers of 1933 survey. Note, too, the total slightly and inexplicably exceeds 100 percent.
   **Includes 1.5 percent who reported honorary doctorates.

In such programs, students were exposed to many new standarized techniques of child accounting, sanitation, budgeting, public relations, curriculum development, and the design and maintenance of buildings. Influential professors also played an important role as sponsors in placing favored graduates in successive superintendencies. But it is easy to attribute too much influence to specialized training—how much effect did it actually have on the typical superintendent in comparison with the cumulative effect of the influences we have thus far analyzed? (48)

There are certain ways in which training programs for different occupations might be expected to have considerable impact on the subsequent careers and performance of their graduates. One is the transmission of particular skills or knowledge clearly needed in a distinct occupation—for example, in electrical engineering. Another way professional programs might have had an effect is by rationing entry into an occupation, as medical schools do by their restrictive admissions and limited output in a tightly controlled field. A third is to make professional training an intense, long-term socialization to the distinct norms of a group—for example, West Point for army officers or a seminary for Jesuits. (49)

Graduate training in educational administration in the years from 1900 to 1960 fit none of these models of influence very closely. There was little agreement in theory or in practice about what skills or knowledge superintendents needed. Unlike medical schools, programs in educational administration have generally not been selective in admissions nor has certification seriously narrowed the pool of eligible candidates for positions, at least until the last generation. And the way in which most administrators have pursued their professional training—sporadically, in summer or evening courses over a number of years—made it unlikely that graduate work by itself provided the kind of intense socialization that might have produced major changes in occupational behavior. Rather, for most students in administration courses graduate training was a low-risk, low-gain enterprise that probably reinforced prior patterns where it had an important impact at all. What fit experience was imprinted. Professional training probably enhanced the authority of superintendents, but it is dubious that it changed their behavior very much. (50)

Typically, superintendents earned their degrees by taking courses while they were employed in the schools. A comprehensive survey of superintendents in 1923 showed that only one-quarter had pursued graduate study full-time for one year; in 1960 AASA lamented the fact that 85 percent of training programs reported that they had fewer than 25 full-time students. When Harold Hand studied the professional lives of superintendents in eight states at the end of the 1920s, he found that 80 percent did not earn a B.A. until they had taught for five or more years, began their master's degree at age 29, and completed it at age 34 or 35. Aspiring teachers or principals could prepare for the possibility of higher position without losing a paycheck. In effect, they could drift gradually into administration rather than making an early commitment (indeed, the AASA report in 1923 actually advised educators not to make too early a career choice by attending graduate school at a young age). In 1931 a leading professor of educational administration concluded that since school boards generally hired superintendents the way they had in the past, before specialized training, there was "little hope for the immediate success of any educational plan that might contemplate educating young men and women for superintendencies in the belief that persons so educated may hope for an immediate appointment to an executive position of any consequence." For the average superintendent advanced training was not a narrow and essential passageway into high status, as it was for the physician, but rather a minor detour that might give him a shortcut on the main highway of promotion through experience and through being at the right place at the right time with the right friends and the right social attributes. (51)

Numerous experts called for more rigorous selection of students in administrative training programs. In 1941, after widely publicized over-supply of educators in the great depression, two observers visited graduate schools and expressed their dismay at the "indifference which national organizations of school administrators on the one hand, and professional schools offering training programs on the other hand, have displayed in the establishment of entrance requirements." In most institutions all that was required, they said, was a B.A. and cash to pay tuition. As Richard Carlson has noted, standards in admissions continued to be a serious problem thirty years later. (52)

Testimony and evidence on the quality of training of educational administrators was often depressing. In 1921 a study of the leading graduate departments of education reported that 74 percent had fewer than ten faculty members and that in half of these schools fewer than 50 percent of the professors had doctorates. Many did not even have a master's degree. The normal teaching load exceeded twelve hours per week. And these programs were the cream of the crop. In 1931 Fred Engelhardt lamented that almost every college or university that trained teachers felt itself capable of preparing superintendents of schools. The 1960 Yearbook of the AASA vigorously criticized the methods and content of graduate work: "Where the student should be 'scared' by exposure to the facts of administrative life, he is instead bored by the tame fare of second-hand success stories. Where the student should be fattened by a rich diet of multidisciplinary fare, he is starved by the lean offerings of provincial chow." (53)

Intellectual disarray, low admission standards, sporadic course-taking, and the marginal importance of professional training to most school boards, then, probably meant that specialized training in administration did not do a great deal to legitimize the authority.

It is likely, however, that under certain circumstances graduate study did have a significant influence in the lives of some administrators. Quite apart from what a student learned in the rest of his program of graduate study, often a particular professor who acted as sponsor in job placement did shape his career. Aspiring administrators sometimes acquired authority by association with such power brokers. The influence of such "barons"—usually professors of administration but sometimes other superintendents or even the ubiquitous textbook salesmen—has long been a common theme in the "higher gossip" among people familiar with schools. Autobiographies of superintendents sometimes talked about "the educational trust" and the hegemony of Teachers College. Numerous scholars have examined the "inner fraternity" of influentials who advanced the careers of younger men and women in such fields as law, medicine, labor unions, and business. But it was not until Robert Rose's perceptive dissertation in 1969 that sponsorship in the superintendency has been carefully documented. (54)

According to Rose, in many graduate programs of educational administration certain professors identified some of their students as able, ambitious, personable and loyal future leaders. They taught and counseled them while in the program, often employing them in teaching or consulting. Frequently sponsors were hired as members of screening committees and were asked for recommendations of candidates for superintendencies. In this capacity, professors tended to fall into one of two groups: the *locals* who had a strong sphere of influence in their region (these were normally professors in state universities); and the *nationals*, persons who spoke and consulted across the nation, were active in the councils of AASA, and were frequently consulted about filling superintendencies in the most prestigious and largest districts (these have traditionally been professors in a few major, usually private, universities, of which Teachers College has been the outstanding example). Such professor-sponsors were powerful role-models for their sponsorees, often referring to them as "my boys." They took vicarious pride in their successes and kept in close touch with them throughout their careers. (55)

The relation between sponsor and alumnus was often symbiotic. In return for assistance in moving ahead on the chessboard of superintendencies, the sponsoree helped the professor recruit students, invited the sponsor to consult for or survey his district, notified him of vacancies, helped place graduates, and kept him in touch with the field. The graduate turned to the sponsor for advice and help in getting ahead. His advancement often depended on the sponsor's continuing good will even more than it did on pleasing the local school board (of course, the two factors were connected).

The system employed by professors at Teachers College illustrated this symbiosis in its fullest development under George Strayer, Paul Mort, and Nicolaus Engelhardt. "All of them," said one of Rose's informants, "had the knack of conveying the feeling that they were definitely aware of you as a person, had an affinity for you, and were concerned with being helpful to you in your future career. . . . [They] took pride in talking about 'their boys'." The Columbia "barons" were persons "known to many board chairmen; they were known to practically all superintendents of schools." In the 1939 roster of the AASA, 287 superintendents held Teachers College M.A.'s and 32 had doctorates, a far greater proportion than that represented by any other university. (56)

Other institutions had similar networks of sponsors and students, though none so strong as Teachers College in the 1920s and 1930s. At the University of Chicago William C. Reavis sponsored students and inspired a Reavis Club. One informant told Rose that Ellwood P. Cubberley of Stanford "was kind of the sponsor and the mentor for practically all of the administrators in California in the early days." Another said that during a weekend with Cubberley in Palo Alto in 1926 he "discovered that Cubberley had an educational Tammany Hall that made the Strayer-Engelhardt Tammany Hall in New York look very weak." In some institutions—e.g. Ohio State University—there were sponsors who knew practically all the superintendents of the state by their first names and had great influence with school boards in their region. It was partially the spread to other universities of professors who had been trained by the Columbia barons that broke the hegemony of Teachers College, for canny graduates emulated their sponsors. One alumnus of Columbia recalled that "once when Strayer and Engelhardt came out to _____ for a meeting . . . they expressed disappointment that they were not getting some consulting work in this state. I told them I couldn't see why I shouldn't be making that money as well as they." Another reason for the declining influence of the barons from a single university has been the increasing use of a panel of consultants from several regions and institutions to screen superintendents. (57)

The influence of the sponsors and of the graduate programs they represented depended in part on political configurations in the local school districts. The sponsor was a power broker only if the school board recognized his authority. The corporate model of school governance was predicated on the expertise of the school executive and relied on governance by elites. Not surprisingly, local board members who fit the corporate model of "successful men" often turned to the universities for guidance, frequently in the form of school surveys. While paying some attention to peculiarities in the local situation, the surveyors basically came prepared to recommend a standard package of approved school practices—in administration, curriculum, attendance services, and personnel policies. Thus the survey strengthened the hand of university-trained superintendents in reforming the schools, for it seemed to carry the authoritative sanction of "science" with its quantitative standards for everything from the number of toilet bowls to the proper number of students per counselor. Even Frank Cody, an avowedly "political" superintendent, made much of "research" and "science" during his long and successful tenure in Detroit. Such authoritative precision helped allay criticism from school boards. In like fashion, James Bryant Conant's clear prescriptions for improving high schools during the Sputnik era served superintendents well. There was safety in objectivity. (58)

The professional association for superintendents—first the Department of Superintendence of the NEA and then the AASA, its successor—was another source of authority, especially for the rank and file of superintendents who lacked powerful sponsors or prestigious degrees. The Department of Superintendence had always been an inner sanctum of the powerful within the NEA, but in 1880 it created a still more august body called the "National Council of Education," composed of 51 persons who were supposed to decide disputed pedagogical questions, assess the merit of reforms, and serve as an educational supreme court ready to discipline the members of the profession prone to "heated partisanship" and "undignified intrigue" in their advocacy of pet panaceas. As Edgar Wesley observed, the Council "was founded to a considerable degree upon a belief in authority and also upon a widespread and persistent faith in eternal verities. The prevailing assumption was that there were such entities as good taste, truth, correct thinking" and that it was the task of the members with their Prince Albert coats and impressive beards to declare those proper principles to the country. One of the most important studies commissioned by the Council, the report of the Committee of Ten on the high school (1893), was welcomed by one superintendent as "the cloud by day and the pillar of fire by night that is to lead us into the promised land." Then, changing the metaphor significantly, he called the report "the superintendents' armor, offensive and defensive." But as Prince Albert coats and patrician pontifications went out of style, the Council endured slow decay and finally death in 1943. (59)

The AASA, however, became an important reference group and source of authoritative consensus and approved evasion for superintendents. Year after year the Association made resolutions on professionalization of administration and teaching, curriculum, school plants, and finance. Generally the resolutions were phrased in general and non-controversial language—understandable in view of the vulnerability of superintendents. On some public issues which they sensed were safe, at least vis-a-vis their school boards, they were lucid: "We believe that members of the Communist Party of the United States should not be employed as teachers." But on touchy issues like integration their language left considerable room for interpretation. They urged citizens to approach desegregation "with a spirit of fair play and good will. . . .

In this, majorities and minorities have both responsibility and opportunity." In 1960 the AASA still straddled the desegregation fence and worried about the example of Prince Edward County in Virginia, in which the public schools had been closed over an integration dispute: "The Association firmly believes that no social, economic or governmental problem is so grave, so deep-seated or so difficult as to justify the destruction or serious impairment of the institution of free public education in any state." (60)

Divisive public issues were not exactly the forte of AASA. Indeed, when superintendents left the tensions of the home office to go to professional meetings, blandness and good fellowship were as therapeutic as milk to an ulcer. "How many school administrators relish eagerly . . . opportunities for deep intellectual development offered by the annual convention?" asked the AASA Yearbook in 1960. "Let us admit, rather, that . . . the convention offers a chance to renew old acquaintances, a casual chat with a placement officer or two (either in behalf of the folks back home or oneself), good food, drink, and lodging for a man whose timetable affords these pleasures but rarely. . . . Let us observe that one does not have to go to Atlantic City and sit on a radiator in a smoke-filled room, squeezed between a poker game and a book salesman, to find a companionable bull session on education." (61)

Indeed, none of the outside sources of authority could change the fact that superintendents were still subject to the vagaries of lay control in their own districts. This fact was not lost on the 4,469 superintendents who answered a questionnaire in 1933 asking what personal qualities were necessary for success in their jobs. Number one was *tact*, mentioned by 1,056; *courage* came sixteenth, with 270 mentions. Bunyan's inner-directed pilgrim was becoming other-directed.

Increasing size of school districts also focused new attention on procedural rules and paperwork. Since mistakes of subordinates could get the leader in trouble, as with a police chief and his patrolmen, it was essential to develop the armor of standardized procedures and elaborate records. In part this stemmed from a concern for due process, but unfortunately, "professionalism" for educators, as for doctors, sometimes meant in practice a willingness to cover for the mistakes of others. Bulging files signified one kind of authority, that of the record-keeper. (62)

EPILOGUE

Despite the many constraints on superintendents and the ambiguity of the sources of authority, the educational leaders of the mid-twentieth century had come a long way in the century from 1860 to 1960. They had helped to shape a vast and well-supported system of schools that educated more people for more years of their lives than in any other nation in history. They had established educational administration as a distinct and important occupation with its own associations, its own extended training programs, its recognized responsibilities and rewards. They had won a degree of autonomy that would have pleased the pioneers. Many still retained some of the millennial hopes of the evangelical founders, even though their language of justification became more bureaucratic and scientific. Writers on administration in the 1950s were rather more likely to argue that schools were too much under the control of "the community" than too unresponsive. Even in 1960, few observers questioned the processes of selection that had resulted in a near monopoly of top positions by white males; this was largely taken for granted. The familiar patterns of occupational socialization seemed to work fairly well, giving continuity and consensus. (63)

Since 1960, of course, much of this has changed, and with it many of the old props of confidence and certainty. Advocates of affirmative action have attacked the selection processes that discriminated against people of color and women; they did not, they said, *invent* the importance of status characteristics like sex or race in allocating good jobs, but rather they were drawing attention to the social injustice of the traditional patterns. Scholars and activists have claimed that the older kinds of occupational socialization failed to prepare superintendents to cope with the new stresses and crushing challenges of the 1960s. Even "science," that former buttress of administrative status and moderate organizational adaptation, now seemed to turn foe, as new studies came from the presses documenting the "failures" of the educational system and its leaders. New entrants into the politics of schools—teachers' unions, militant minorities, lawyers pressing cases on civil rights and civil liberties, even students—now changed the work of superintendents so drastically that some observers said that the job was becoming impossible to do well. (64)

Perhaps. The contrast between waves of hope in the early 1960s and subsequent disillusionment has deepened the present pessimism. Dropping enrollments and deflated public esteem seem to make the older heroic ideology outmoded and quaint. Some speak of schooling as a declining industry. The older modes of leadership were largely designed for creation, constant expansion, and consolidation of public education. Those pioneer superintendents who identified with Bunyan's pilgrim had a view of reality that gave them trust but few illusions of ease, faith in their work but little applause. Superintendents at the turn of this century faced the enormous challenge of teaching millions of immigrant children who filled urban classrooms to the bursting point, yet their commitment to a new science of education, their trust in administrative reforms, and their belief in the power of schooling gave them an almost evangelical hope.

These traditions may contain value still, but today new conditions and challenges call for a rethinking of educational leadership. Instead of rushing to find new teachers and classrooms, superintendents today often face cutbacks and the task of improving education in a time of scarcity. Instead of focusing on centralization and "taking education out of politics," many administrators now seek to decentralize decision-making within the system and to make schooling more responsive to pluralistic constituencies. Conflict over the goals and outcomes of schooling reflects a broader breakdown of a majoritarian consensus as well as political realignments both within and outside education. The attempted social changes of the last generation were threatening to those who benefited from the existing distribution of wealth, power, and position, yet the reforms went hardly far enough in improving the lives of those at the bottom of the system. Now that part-time warriors on poverty have retreated, now that many whites seem to have forgotten about racial equity, now that many politicians seem to fear even the word "liberal," the full-time administrators and teachers still face every day the job of making schools work to promote social justice. The task is not an easy one, but it never was. (65)

Notes

1. Aaron Gove, "The Trail of the City Superintendent," *NEA Addresses and Proceedings* (1900), p. 215. In many ways the most useful general study remains Merle Curti, *The Social Ideas of American Educators* (Paterson, N.J., 1959). An insightful book from the same period is Jesse Newlon, *Educational Administration as Social Policy* (New York, 1934), a work which summarizes many studies of superintendents and treats the impact of business ideology. Raymond Callahan has carefully dissected the application of scientific management to education in *Education and the Cult of Efficiency* (Chicago, 1962) and has extended that analysis to other periods in *The Superintendent of Schools: An Historical Analysis* (Bethesda, Md., 1967). Two studies give detailed information on the evolution of administrative duties of superintendents: Theodore Lee Reller, *The Development of the City Superintendency of Schools in the United States* (Philadelphia, 1935), and Thomas M. Gilland, *The Origins and Development of the Powers and Duties of the City-School Superintendent* (Chicago, 1935). Among the more useful analyses of individual superintendents are John T. McManis, *Ella Flagg Young and a Half-Century of the Chicago Public Schools* (Chicago, 1916), and Selma C. Berrol, "William Henry Maxwell and a New Educational New York," *History of Education Quarterly*, 8 (Summer 1968): 215-28. Although it does not focus only on superintendents, Paul Mattingly, *The Classless Profession: American Schoolmen in the Nineteenth Century* (New York, 1975) provides an excellent interpretation of the religious and other sources of ideology; it provides an interdisciplinary analysis of the early stages of professionalization by concentrating on the American Institute of Instruction. Larry Cuban, "Schools Chiefs under Fire: A Study of Three Big-City Superintendents under Outside Pressure," unpub. Ph.D. diss., Stanford University, 1974, places the changes in school administration during the last twenty years in illuminating historical perspective: Cuban's study is scheduled

for publication by the University of Chicago Press. For other studies, including dissertations, that deal with the superintendency, see the bibliography of my *The One Best System: A History of American Urban Education* (Cambridge, 1974). In my conceptualization of the changes in the twentieth century I am indebted to Samuel Hays, "The New Organizational Society," in Jerry Israel, ed. *Building the Organizational Society: Essays on Associational Activities in Modern America* (New York, 1972).

2. NEA, Department of Superintendence, *Educational Leadership: Programs and Possibilities* (llth Yearbook, Washington, D.C., 1933), 246.

3. A sample of historical studies of occupational groups includes Roy Lubove, *The Professional Altruist: The Emergence of Social Work as a Career* (Cambridge, Mass., 1965); Donna Merwick, *Boston Priests, 1848-1910: A Study of Social and Intellectual Change* (Cambridge, Mass., 1973); Daniel Calhoun, *The American Civil Engineer: Origins and Conflicts* (Cambridge, Mass., 1960); William G. Rothstein, *American Physicians in the Nineteenth Century* (Baltimore, 1972); Wayne K. Hobson, "Lawyers in the Progressive Era," dissertation in progress, Stanford University. Some studies in the sociological literature about work and occupations are cited below in notes 25 and 26.

4. In my conception of Victorian culture in America, I have been much influenced by Daniel Walker Howe, "American Victorianism as a Culture," *American Quarterly*, 27 (Dec. 1975): 507-32.

5. Gove, "Trail of the City Superintendent," p. 215; Frederick Haigh Bair, *The Social Understandings of the Superintendent of Schools* (New York, 1934), pp. 156-60; John Bunyan, *The Pilgrim's Progress* (Harmondsworth, 1965). The following biographies and autobiographies of administrators are samples of a large literature: Samuel P. Abelow, *Dr. William H. Maxwell, the First Superintendent of Schools of the City of New York* (Brooklyn, 1934); Berrol, "Maxwell"; Frank K. Burrin, *Edward Charles Elliott, Educator* (Lafayette, Ind., 1970); Detroit Public School Staff, *Frank Cody: A Realist in Education* (New York, 1943); Willard B. Gatewood, Jr., *Eugene Clyde Brooks: Educator and Public Servant* (Durham, N.C., 1960); Solomon P. Jaeckel, "Edward Hyatt, 1858-1919: California Educator," *Southern California Quarterly*, 52 (Mar., June, Sept. 1970): 33-5, 122-54, 248-74; Francis Wayland Parker, "An Autobiographical Sketch," in William M. Giffin, *School Days in the Fifties* (Chicago, n.d.); Claude Anderson Phillips, *Fifty Years of Public School Teaching: From Rural School Teacher to University Professor* (Columbia, Mo., n.d.); Jesse B. Sears and Adin D. Henderson, *Cubberley of Stanford and His Contribution to American Education* (Stanford, Ca., 1957); Edward Austin Sheldon, *Autobiography*, ed. Mary Sheldon Barnes (New York, 1911); David Snedden, *Recollections of Over Half a Century Spent in Educational Work* (Palo Alto, Ca., 1949); Frank E. Spaulding, *School Superintendent in Action in Five Cities* (Rindge, N.H, 1955); John Swett, *Public Education in California: Its Origin and Development, with Personal Reminiscences of Half A Century* (New York, 1911); Joseph Crittenden Templeton, *Chronicles of a Pedagogue* (Sebastopol, Ca., 1948); Lester L. Tracy, Jr., *Life and Educational Contributions of Joseph D. Elliff* (University of Missouri Press, 1953); Frank P. Whitney, *School and I: The Autobiography of an Ohio Schoolmaster* (Yellow Spring, Ohio, 1957); also see bibliography by Warren Button in Francisco Cordasco and William W. Brick-

men, eds., *A Bibliography of American Educational History* (New York, 1975), pp. 228-248.

6. For a sampling of "necrologies," see *NEA Addresses and Proceedings* (1885), 13-18; (1886), 246-58; (1887), 664-66; (1888), 677-84; (1889),44-51; (1890), 42-46; (1892), 598-605; (1894), 222-251; (1896), 218-29; (1898), 282-93; (1899), 232-49; (1900), 712-15; (1901), 387-90;(1903), 369-74;(1904), 361-65; (1905), 329-35; (1907), 297-326; (1908), 492-98.

7. Timothy L. Smith, "Protestant Schooling and American Nationality, 1800-1850," *Journal of American History*, 53 (Mar. 1967): 679-95; David B. Tyack, "The Kingdom of God and the Common School: Protestant Ministers and the Educational Awakening in the West," *Harvard Educational Review*, 36 (Fall, 1966): 447-69; David B. Tyack, "Onward Christian Soldiers: Religion in the American Common School," in Paul Nash, ed., *History and Education: The Educational Uses of the Past* (New York, 1970), pp. 212-55; Mattingly, *Classless Profession*, chs. ii-iv; Howe, "American Victorianism as a Culture."

8. John W. Meyer and Brian Rowan, "Notes on the Structure of Educational Organizations: Revised Version," paper presented at meeting of American Sociological Association, August 1975.

9. A. E. Winship, "What the Superintendent Is Not," *NEA Addresses and Proceedings* (1899), pp. 308-309; Cuban, "School Chiefs Under Fire," ch. v; Henry Warren Button, "A History of Supervision in the Public Schools, 1870-1950," unpub. Ph.D. diss., Washington University, 1961; John T. Prince, "Evolution of School Supervision," *Educational Review*, 22 (Sept. 1901): 148-61; Jonathan Messerli, *Horace Mann: A Biography* (New York, 1972); David B. Tyack, ed., *Turning Points in American Educational History* (Waltham, Mass., 1967), p. 125; Stanley K. Schultz, *The Culture Factory: Boston Public Schools, 1789-1860* (New York, 1973), pp. 103-104, 116, 130-33; Charles Francis Adams, Jr., "Scientific Common-School Education," *Harper's New Monthly Magazine*, 61 (Nov. 1880): 937.

10. John Higham, "Hanging Together: Divergent Unities in American History," *Journal of American History*, 61 (June 1974): 24; Berrol, "William Henry Maxwell"; Whitney, *School and I*, pp. 28, 30-31; on the importance of an optimistic kind of evolutionary thinking in school administration. see Sears and Henderson, *Cubberley*, chs. ii, vii.

11. NEA, Department of Superintendence, *Educational Leadership*, pp. 159, 278, 325-30, 335, 334; American Association of School Adminstrators, *The American School Superintendency* (30th Yearbook; Washington, D.C., 1952), pp. 63, 437, 444.

12. Stephen J. Knezevich, ed., *The American School Superintendent* (Washington, D.C., 1971), p. 17.

13. Bair, *Social Understandings of Superintendent*, pp. 148-75; NEA, Department of Superintendence, *The Status of the Superintendent* (1st Yearbook; Washington, D.C., 1923); NEA, Department of Superintendence, *Educational Leadership*, ch. vi; AASA, *American School Superintendency*, ch. xi; AASA and NEA Research Division, *Profile of the School Superintendent* (Washington, D.C., 1960).

14. E. P. Hutchinson, *Immigrants and Their Children, 1850-1950* (New York, 1956), p. 3; Sol Cohen, "The Industrial Education Movement, 1906-17,"

American Quarterly, 20 (Spring 1968): 95-110; Tyack, *One Best System*, pp. 59-65, 255-68.

15. Lotus D. Coffman, "The American School Superintendent," *Educational Administration and Supervision*, 1 (Jan. 1915): 17; W. W. Charters, Jr., "Social Class Analysis and the Control of Public Education," *Harvard Educational Review*, 23 (Fall 1953): 268-83; on the importance of ambiguity in organizational goals, see Michael D. Cohen and James March, *Leadership and Ambiguity: The American College President* (New York, 1974).

16. Horace Mann Bond, *The Education of the Negro in the American Social Order* (Englewood Cliffs, N.J., 1934), ch. xix; Margaret Szasz, *Education and the American Indian: The Road to Self Determination, 1928-1973* (Albuquerque, 1974); Tyack, *One Best System*, pp. 109-25, 217-29.

17. Suzanne Estler, "Women as Leaders in Public Education," *Signs*, 1 (Winter 1975): 363-86; Grace C. Strachan, *Equal Pay for Equal Work: The Story of the Struggle for Justice Being Made by the Women Teachers of the City of New York* (New York, 1910); Robert L. Reid, "The Professionalization of Public School Teachers: The Chicago Experience, 1895-1920," unpub. Ph.D. diss., Northwestern University, 1968, pp. 212-33; Ralph D. Schmid, "A Study of the Organizational Structure of the National Education Association, 1884-1921," unpub. Ed.D. diss., Washington University, 1963.

18. Charles S. Meek, "How Shall the Superintendent Spend His Time?" *NEA Addresses and Proceedings* (1921), 730-31; "How Do Women Rate?" *Nation's Schools*, 37 (Mar. 1946): 45.

19. Bair, *Social Understandings of Superintendent*, pp. 89, 161; Neal Gross, et al., *Explorations in Role Analysis: Studies of the School Superintendency Role* (New York, 1958), pp. 336, 338; Richard O. Carlson, *School Superintendents: Careers and Performance* (Columbus, Ohio, 1972), pp. 29-34.

20. NEA, Department of Superintendence, *Educational Leadership*, p. 346; Bair, *Social Understandings of Superintendent*, pp. 85-88; Carlson, *School Superintendents*, pp. 15-19.

21. Ellwood P. Cubberley, *Public School Administration: A Statement of the Fundamental Principles Underlying the Organization and Administration of Public Education* (Boston, 1916), pp. 136-37; Carlson, *School Superintendents*, pp. 18-19.

22. NEA, Department of Superintendence, *Educational Leadership*, p. 346; Albert P. Marble, "City School Administration," *Educational Review*, 8 (Sept. 1894): 165-66; William A. Mowry, *Recollections of a New England Educator, 1838-1908* (New York, 1908), p. 9; Marvin Lazerson, *Origins of the Urban School: Public Education in Massachusetts, 1870-1915* (Cambridge, 1971), ch. i; R. Richard Wohl, "The 'Country Boy' Myth and Its Place in American Urban Culture: The Nineteenth Century Contribution," *Perspectives in American History*, 3 (1969): 77-156; Dana F. White, "Education in the Turn-of-the-Century School," *Urban Education*, 1 (Spring 1969): 169-82.

23. Bair, *Social Understandings of Superintendent*, pp. 148-53; Carlson, *School Superintendents*, p. 21; Douglas T. Hall and Benjamin Schneider, *Organizational Climates and Careers: The Work Lives of Priests* (New York, 1973), ch. ii; John D. Donovan, "The American Catholic Hierarchy: A Social Profile," *American Catholic Sociological Review*, 19 (June 1958): 98-112; James Q.

Wilson, *Varieties of Police Behavior: The Management of Law and Order in Eight Communities* (Cambridge, 1968), ch. iii.

24. Willard Waller, *The Sociology of Teaching* (New York, 1965), p. 375; AASA and NEA Research Division, *Profile of School Superintendent*, p. 107.

25. Everett C. Hughes, *Men and Their Work* (Glencoe, Ill., 1958), ch. ix; Howard S. Becker, et al., *Boys in White: Student Culture in Medical School* (Chicago, 1961), pp. 3-16, 419-43; Robert Merton, et al., *The Student-Physician: Introductory Studies in the Sociology of Medical Education* (Cambridge, 1957), pp. 40-42, 54-79; David J. Rothman, *Politics and Power: The United States Senate, 1869-1901* (Cambridge, 1966), ch. iv; W. W. Charters, Jr., "The Social Background of Teaching," in N. L. Gage, ed., *Handbook of Research on Teaching* (Chicago, 1963), pp. 741-44; Corrine Lathrop Gilb, *Hidden Hierarchies: The Professions and Government* (New York, 1966).

26. Peter L. Berger, "Some General Observations on the Problem of Work," in Peter L. Berger, ed., *The Human Shape of Work* (New York, 1964), pp. 230, 234-38; Peter L. Berger, *Invitation to Sociology: A Humanistic Perspective* (Garden City, N.Y., 1963), p. 41.

27. Waller, *Sociology of Teaching*, p. 420.

28. Hall and Schneider, *Organizational Climates and Careers;* Donovan, "American Catholic Hierarchy"; John Tracy Ellis, "On Selecting Catholic Bishops for the United States," *Critic*, 27 (June-July 1969): 47; John Tracy Ellis, "On Selecting American Bishops," *Commonweal*, 85 (Mar. 10, 1967): 643-49; Henry J. Browne, "Father, Statesman, Administrator," *Continuum*, 2 (Winter 1965): 605-11; Robert Dwyer, "Conformism and the American Hierarchy," ibid., pp. 611-18; Jay P. Dolan, "A Critical Period in American Catholicism," *Review of Politics*, 35 (Oct. 1973): 523-36; Donna Merwick, *Boston Priests, 1848-1910: A Study of Social and Intellectual Change* (Cambridge, 1973); Joseph H. Fichter, S.J., *Religion as an Occupation: A Study in the Sociology of Professions* (South Bend, Ind., 1961), pp. 34-128, 134-37, 153-71, 176-84.

29. Cuban, "School Chiefs Under Fire," ch. v; John Van Maanen, "Observations on the Making of Policemen," *Human Organization*, 32 (Winter 1973): 407-17.

30. Waller, *Sociology of Teaching*, pp. 424-25; Marian A. Dogherty, *'Scusa Me Teacher* (Francestown, N.H., 1943); Frances R. Donovan, *The Schoolma'am* (New York, 1938); Button, "History of Supervision," ch. vii; Van Maanen, "Making of Policemen." My authority on the proper traits of servants is Mr. Hudson in "Upstairs, Downstairs."

31. Waller, *Sociology of Teaching*, pp. 34, 40, 45, ch. iv; Agatha Brown (pseud.), *Teachers Are People* (3rd. ed.; Hollywood, Ca., 1925); on invasions of teachers' civil liberties, see Howard K. Beale, *Are American Teachers Free? An Analysis of Restraints upon the Freedom of Teaching in American Schools* (New York, 1936).

32. Richard O. Carlson, "Environmental Constraints and Organizational Consequences: The Public School and Its Clients," in Daniel E. Griffiths, ed., *Behavioral Science and Educational Administration* (63rd Yearbook of National Society for the Study of Education; Chicago, 1964), pp. 263-76; Waller, *Sociology of Teaching*, pp. 10, 401-405; Charles E. Bidwell, "The School as a Formal Organization," in James G. March, ed., *Handbook of Organizations* (Chicago, 1965), pp. 972-1022.

33. Charters, "Social Background of Teaching," pp. 746-52; Harmon Zeigler, *The Political Life of American Teachers* (Englewood Cliffs, N.J., 1967); Van Maanen, "Making of Policemen."

34. Howard S. Becker, "The Career of the Chicago Public Schoolteacher," *American Journal of Sociology*, 57 (Mar. 1952): 470-77; Daniel Griffiths, "Teacher Mobility in New York City," *Educational Administration Quarterly*, 1 (Winter 1965): 15-31; William D. Greenfield, "Socialization Processes Among Administrative Candidates in Public Schools," unpub. paper, Syracuse University, 1975.

35. Fred C. Ayer, "The Duties of Public School Administrators," *American School Board Journal*, 78 (Feb. 1929): 39-41 ff.; 80 (May 1930): 43-44; 78 (Apr. 1929): 39: 78 (May 1929): 52-53; 79 (Oct. 1929): 33-34, 136; 78 (June 1929): 60; William McAndrew, "The Plague of Personality," *School Review*, 22 (May 1914): 315-25; NEA, Department of Superintendence, *Educational Leadership*, p. 176.

36. Esther Selke, "Is the Small Town Superintendency a Glorified Janitorship?" *School Executives Magazine*, 50 (May 1931): 412; Anon., "Why Superintendents Lost Their Jobs," *American School Board Journal*, 52 (May 1916): 18-19; Anon., "Why I Do Not Want to Be a Small Town Superintendent Again," ibid., 73 (Oct. 1926): 52-53; J. H. Beveridge, "Hazards of the Superintendency and the Next Forward Steps in Reducing Them," *NEA Addresses and Proceedings* (1924), 864-69; H. E. Buchholz, "The Worst Job in the World," *American Mercury*, 27 (Nov. 1932): 315-22; George H. Henry, "Alas, the Poor School Superintendent," *Harper's*, 193 (Nov. 1946): 434-41; G. H. Marshall, Clara W. Marshall, and W. W. Carpenter, *The Administrator's Wife* (Boston, 1941).

37. Bair, *Social Understandings of Superintendent*, p. 50; Neal Gross, *Who Runs Our Schools?* (New York, 1958); Clyde Morris, "The Careers of 554 Public School Superintendents in Eleven Midwest States," unpub. Ph.D. diss., University of Wisconsin, 1957, p. 99; Robert K. Merton, *Social Theory and Social Structure* (rev. and enlarged ed.; Glencoe, Ill., 1957), ch. x.

38. NEA. Department of Superintendence, *Educational Leadership*, pp. 176, 192.

39. AASA, *American School Superintendency*, p. 449; AASA and NEA Research Division, *Profile of School Superintendent*, p. 74.

40. Callahan, *Education and Cult of Efficiency;* M. C. Bettinger, "Twenty-Five Years in the Schools of Los Angeles," *Publications of Historical Society of California*, 8 (1910): 68-69; Tyack, *One Best System*, pp. 184-85.

41. Alfred D. Chandler, Jr., and Fritz Redlich, "Recent Developments in American Business Administration and Their Conceptualization," *Business History Review*, 35 (Spring 1961): 1-31; William Walter Theisen, *The City Superintendent and the Board of Education* (New York, 1917).

42. Ellwood P. Cubberley, "Public School Administration," in I. L. Kandel, ed., *Twenty-Five Years of American Education: Collected Essays* (New York, 1924), pp. 177-95; Joel H. Spring, *Education and the Rise of the Corporate State* (Boston, 1972); Tyack, *One Best System*, part v.

43. Tyack, *One Best System*, part iv; Carlson, *School Superintendents*, chs. iv-vi; Joseph M. Cronin, *The Control of Urban Schools: Perspective on the Power of Educational Reformers* (New York, 1973); Arthur J. Vidich and Charles McReynolds, "Rhetoric versus Reality: A Study of New York City High School Principals," in Murray Wax, et al., *Anthropological Perspectives on Education*

(New York, 1971), pp. 195-207; James Stephen Hazlett, "Crisis in School Government: An Administrative History of the Chicago Public Schools, 1933-1947," unpub. Ph.D. diss., University of Chicago, 1968; Peter Schrag, *Village School Downtown* (Boston, 1967), p. 55.

44. Smith, "Protestant Schooling and American Nationally"; Mattingly, *Classless Profession*, ch. viii.

45. Callahan, *Education and Cult of Efficiency;* Wilson, *Police Behavior*, ch. iii; Willard B. Spalding, *The Superintendency of Public Schools—An Anxious Profession* (Cambridge, 1954); Arthur P. Coladarci, "Administrative-Success Criteria," *Phi Delta Kappan*, 37 (Apr. 1956): 283-85; Hughes, *Men and Their Work*, ch. vii; Newlon, *Educational Administration as Social Policy*, pp. 39-52.

46. Callahan, *Education and Cult of Efficiency;* Tyack, *One Best System*, pp. 198-217; Jesse Brundage Sears, *An Autobiography* (Palo Alto, Ca., 1959), chs. vii-ix.

47. Sears and Henderson, *Cubberley*, chs. v-x; Daniel E. Griffiths, *The School Superintendent* (New York, 1966), ch. ii; John Lund, *Education of School Administrators* (U.S. Office of Education, Bulletin No. 6, 1941; Washington, D. C., 1942), p. 85; AASA, *Standards for Superintendents of Schools: Preliminary Report of the Committee on Certification of Superintendents of Schools* (Washington, D.C., 1939).

48. Cubberley, "Public School Administration."

49. Another model, fascinating in itself but not quite germane to superintendents, is the upper-class English public school—see Lawrence Stone, "Literacy and Education in England, 1640-1900," *Past & Present*, No. 42 (Feb. 1969): 72-73.

50. John W. Meyer, "The Charter: Conditions of Diffuse Socialization in the Schools," in W. R. Scott, ed., *Social Processes and Social Structures* (New York, 1970), pp. 564-78.

51. NEA, Department of Superintendence, *Status of Superintendent*, pp. 25, 29; AASA, *Professional Administrators for America's Schools* (38th Yearbook; Washington, D.C., 1960), p. 84; Fred Engelhardt, "The Professional Education Program for School Executives," *American School Board Journal*, 83 (Nov. 1931): 49-51; Harold C. Hand, "Vocational Histories of City-School Superintendents," *ibid.*, 82 (Apr. 1931): 47-48, 132.

52. Lund, *Education of School Administrators*, p. 22; Carlson, *School Superintendents*, pp. 23-25.

53. Leonard V. Koos, *Standards in Graduate Work in Education* (U.S. Bureau of Education, Bulletin No. 38, 1921; Washington, D.C., 1922), pp. 17-18; Engelhardt, "Professional Education Program," p. 51; AASA, *Professional Administrators*, pp. 83-84; Michael B. Katz, "From Theory to Survey in Graduate Schools of Education," *Journal of Higher Education*, 37 (1966): 325-34.

54. Robert L. Rose, "Career Sponsorship in the School Superintendency," unpub. Ph.D. diss., University of Oregon, 1969; Detroit Public School Staff, *Frank Cody*, pp. 204, 221, 233, 464; Spaulding said that a board member in Minneapolis "came to me somewhat puzzled over the extent to which members of the faculty of Columbia's Teachers College figured in the recommendations of Superintendents" (Spaulding, *Superintendent in Five Cities*, p. 418). Because of their wide acquaintance with superintendents and board members, text-

book salesmen sometimes helped the careers of talented young administrators (I am indebted to Roald Campbell for this observation).

55. Rose, "Career Sponsorship," chs. ii-iii.
56. Ibid., pp. 71-73, 75-76, 81; statistics compiled by Robert Cummings from the roster of members of the AASA in its Yearbook for 1939.
57. Rose, "Career Sponsorship," pp. 82-83, 43-44, 85, 87-88.
58. Jesse B. Sears, *The School Survey: A Textbook on the Use of School Surveying in the Administration of Public Schooling* (New York, 1925); Hollis L. Caswell, *City School Surveys: An Interpretation and Appraisal* (New York, 1929); Detroit Public School Staff, *Frank Cody*, pp. 260-62.
59. *NEA Addresses and Proceedings* (1882), 86, 77-87; Edgar B. Wesley, *NEA, the First Hundred Years: The Building of the Teaching Profession* (New York, 1957), p. 265; Tyack, ed., *Turning Points*, p. 358; "Is There an N.E.A. Ring?" *Journal of Education*, 51 (June 14, 1900): 376; Schmid, "Organizational Structure of NEA."
60. William R. Johnston, "Trends in the Concerns of School Superintendents as Evidenced by a Review of the Resolutions Enacted by the American Association of School Administrators in the Twentieth Century," unpub. Ed.D. diss., University of Toledo, 1965, pp. 113, 146-47; NEA, Department of Superintendence, *Educational Leadership*, pp. 53-56.
61. AASA, *Professional Administrators*, p. 89.
62. NEA, Department of Superintendence, *Educational Leadership*, p. 339; Wilson, *Police Behavior*, ch. iii; for a view of opportunistic school ethics in the form of fatherly advice, see William H. Patterson (pseud. for George F. Miller), *Letters to Principal Patterson* (Washington, D.C., 1934), pp. 109-27.
63. AASA, *Professional Administrators;* Myron Lieberman, *The Future of Public Education* (Chicago, 1960), pp. 34-36; Gross, *Who Runs Our Schools?;* Tyack, *One Best System*, pp. 269-91.
64. Jacqueline Clement, *Sex Bias in Educational Leadership* (Evanston, 1975); Cuban, "School Chiefs Under Fire," ch. vi; Frederick M. Wirt, "Contemporary School Turbulence and Administrative Authority," paper presented at the David W. Minar Memorial Conference, Northwestern University, 1974; "The School Superintendency: An Impossible Job," *Education U.S.A.* (Mar. 4, 1974): 145.
65. James G. March, "Higher Education and the Pursuit of Optimism," paper delivered at Conference of National Association of Student Personnel Administrators, San Francisco, 1975; James G. March, "Commitment and Competence in Educational Administration," in Lewis B. Mayhew, et al., *Educational Leadership and Declining Enrollments* (Berkeley, 1974), pp. 131-41.

APPENDIX I

THE AMERICAN URBAN SCHOOL SUPERINTENDENT IN 1899: SOME STATISTICAL DATA

ROBERT CUMMINGS

These statistics were compiled from information contained in the *Journal of Education*, 50 (Dec. 7, 1899), 374-80. To celebrate the twenty-fifth anniversary of the *Journal*, its editor, A.E. Winship, gathered together a potpourri of information about education in the United States during the late nineteenth century. Included in this survey are biographical sketches of persons occupying the position of school superintendent in 113 cities in 1899. The range of information provided for each individual varies widely: some include only name and length of service in current job, while others offer fairly complete information on education and career patterns. We do not know the precise reasons why Winship included these particular 113 superintendents, nor do we know how the information was gathered, although it appears likely the editor asked the individuals to supply it.

The data on which these statistics are based are deficient in several ways. The size of the sample is fairly small, and for many of the subject areas, it is even smaller because of gaps in the reporting of information. (For this reason, we have included the size of N for each subject area.) It does not approach being a random sample, since the cases were included on the basis of editor Winship's judgment. And we do not know his criteria of selection. Big city superintendents, as the first table shows, are highly overrepresented. These data tell us next to nothing about superintendents in cities of under 10,000 population, a group which comprised the vast majority of school chiefs in 1899. The overrepresentation of big city superintendents makes comparisons of this sample with later twentieth-century surveys problematic, since these surveys were based on samples containing larger numbers of small cities (although even in these, big cities are overrepresented). This drawback can be partially compensated for, however, by restricting comparisons to specific city-size categories.

We know very little about the social characteristics and career patterns of nineteenth-century school superintendents, and generalizations about the "typical" school chief tend to be based on impressionistic evidence about a few eminent leaders. Despite the serious deficiencies in the statistics reported below, they do cast a wider net than earlier studies and thereby perhaps lessen our ignorance.

Appendix 1

THE URBAN SCHOOL SUPERINTENDENT IN 1899

Distribution of Cities in the Sample*

100+	50–100	30–50	20–30	10–20	5–10	5–	Total
			*City size (thousands)*				
28	24	25	20	13	2	1	113

*based on figures in *Federal Census of 1900.*

Age
(All figures are medians)

City size of current superintendency (thousands)

100+	50–100	30–50	20–30	10–20	5–10	5–	Total
58	50.5	40	46	41			43
N = 2	6	9	7	6	0	0	30

Sex

Male	112
Female	1 (Bangor, Maine—population: 21,850)

Highest Degree Held
(All figures are percentages)

City size of current superintendency (thousands)

Highest degree	100+	50–100	30–50	20–30	10–20	5–10	5–	Total
None		14.3	4.8					3.8
Bachelor's	66.7	50.0	57.1	56.3	66.7			58.2
Master's		21.4	14.3	18.8	16.7			13.9
Doctorate	13.3	14.3	14.3	6.3	8.3	100		12.7
Normal school	13.3		9.5	12.5	8.3			8.9
Other	6.7			6.3				2.5
N =	15	14	21	16	12	1	0	79

Years in Educational work
(All figures are medians)

City size of current superintendency (thousands)

100+	50–100	30–50	20–30	10–20	5–10	5–	Total
21.5	21.5	21.5	16	19			20
N = 6	10	14	7	7	0	0	44

Appendix 1 *(Continued)*

Position from Which Individual Entered First Superintendency
(All figures are percentages)

City size of current superintendency (thousands)

Prior job	100+	50–100	30–50	20–30	10–20	5–10	5–	Total
Principal of								
Master of:								
High school	18.8	16.7	31.8	6.7	16.7			19.3
Academy		11.1		6.7	8.3			4.8
Grammar	6.3	22.2	9.1	13.3				10.8
Not specified	18.8	5.6	22.7	6.7	33.3			16.9
Teacher in:								
College		5.6	4.6		8.3			3.6
Normal school			4.6		8.3			2.4
High school		5.6	18.2	20.0				9.6
Grammar		5.6						1.2
Rural			4.6		8.3			2.4
Not specified	25.0	16.7		13.3				10.8
County/district superintendent		5.6	4.6	6.7	8.3			4.8
Urban ass't sup't	18.8							3.6
Deputy state sup't				6.7				1.2
School board secretary					8.3			1.2
Right from college	12.5	5.6		20.0				7.2
N =	16	18	22	15	12	0	0	83

Years in Superintendency
(All figures are medians)

City size of current superintendency (thousands)

100+	50–100	30–50	20–30	10–20	5–10	5–	Total
7.5	8	8	10	8.5			8
N = 16	14	22	13	10			75

Years in Current Job
(All figures are medians)

City size of current superintendency (thousands)

100+	50–100	30–50	20–30	10–20	5–10	5–	Total
5	6	4	6	4	9.5	1	5
N = 28	24	25	20	13	2	1	113

Appendix 2

THE AMERICAN URBAN SCHOOL SUPERINTENDENT, 1923-1960:
STATISTICAL DATA*

Sex

1923	Subject is not discussed.	
1933	Subject is not discussed.	
1952	Male	99.4 percent
	Female	.6 percent
1960	"All the superintendents who responded were men; this means that the study missed the few women in superintendencies."	

Age
(All figures are medians)

1923	43.15
1933	44.
1950	49.
1960	51.8

*The statistics were gathered from four national surveys of the urban superintendency conducted by the Department of Superintendence of the NEA and its successor, the American Association of School Administrators:

NEA, Department of Superintendence, and Bennett Douglass. *The Status of the Superintendent.* First Yearbook. Washington, D.C., 1923. (Data collected in 1920-21)

NEA, Department of Superintendence. *Educational Leadership.* Eleventh Yearbook. Washington, D.C. 1933. (Data collected in 1931-32)

American Association of School Administrators. *The American School Superintendency.* Thirtieth Yearbook. Washington, D.C., 1952. (Data collected in 1950)

American Association of School Administrators and NEA Research Division. *Profile of the School Superintendent.* Washington, D.C., 1960.(Data collected in 1958-59)

Size of Community Where Sup't Was Graduated From High School
(= "hometown"?)
(All figures are percentages)

	Year	
High school community	*1933*	*1960*
Under 2,500	40.25	41.2
2,500–5,000	28.52	16.8
5,000–10,000	13.15	14.3
10,000–30,000	8.08	13.8
30,000–100,000	6.01	7.2
100,000+	3.84	6.7

Appendix 2 *(Continued)*

Highest Degree Held
(All figures are percentages)

Highest degree	1923*	1933	1952	1960
		Year		
No degree	12.81	3.77	.2	2.0
Bachelor's	54.64	36.22	5.5	2.4
Master's	32.02	56.68	78.7	56.3
Doctorate	2.92	2.97	15.5**	21.7
Other	.37	.36	.1	17.6 (= "60 hours beyond bachelor's")

  *1923 survey did not ask for information on highest degree held, but asked for data on sum total of degrees. The percentages in this table for 1923 are *estimates* made by compilers of 1933 survey. Note, too, the total slightly and inexplicably exceeds 100 percent.
 **Includes 1.5 percent who reported honorary doctorates.

Years in Educational Work
(All figures are medians)

1923	19.95
1933	21
1952	26.8
1960	not available

Superintendents Who Worked in Various Educational Positions
(All figures are percentages)

Position	1923	1952	1960
Principal			
High school	66.11	73.9	48.4
Jr. High school			11.3
Elementary	44.38	34.5	22.8
H. S.-elem. combined		31.5	
Level not specified			13.5
Teacher			
High School	37.51	85.2	74.9
Elementary	15.99	46.2	22.0
Rural school	42.08		12.5
College			5.5
Asst. superintendent		6.9 (city schools)	15.6

Appendix 2 *(Continued)*

Years in Superintendency
(All figures are medians)

1923	9.78
1933	10
1952	11.9
1960*	16.2

*Data for 1960 were computed by subtracting median data for "age at time of first superintendency" from median data for "current age."

Years in Current Job
(All figures are medians)

1923	4
1933	6
1952	6.1
1960	7.7

11

Does Urban Reform Imply Class Conflict? The Case of Atlanta's Schools

David N. Plank and Paul E. Peterson

THOUGH THE PRESSURES FOR CHANGE had been building for some time, reform came suddenly to the Atlanta public school system. On May 28, 1897, in a City Council meeting ostensibly called to consider some routine matters pertaining to the city's water works, Alderman James G. Woodward introduced a resolution which replaced the sitting seventeen-member school board with a new board comprising one member from each of the city's seven wards. Despite a recent escalation in the level of conflict between the school board and Mayor Charles Collier, the move came as a complete surprise to virtually everyone in Atlanta, including all of the members of the school board.[1] The entire operation took only a few minutes. As the Atlanta Constitution observed the next day:

> A Texas hanging couldn't have gone off with the precision and nicety of the sudden execution. . . . The ax revolved and the heads were basketed.[2]

The action of the City Council raised an immediate public outcry in Atlanta. A mass meeting held the following day denounced the move as "illegal, revolutionary, despotic, and dangerous." The city's newspapers gave the unfolding story front-page coverage and banner headlines for several days.[3] Within a week of the "astounding coup," however, the new board had organized itself and won the endorsement of both city newspapers. The new members set themselves to the tasks of educational reform in the city's public school system.[4]

In this paper we assess the adequacy of the prevailing class-conflict model of progressive educational reform for understanding the 1897 reform of the Atlanta schools. We show that many of the classic school reforms were carried out in Atlanta in that year: the school board was reduced in size, the

David N. Plank is associate professor of administrative and policy studies at the University of Pittsburgh. Paul E. Peterson is Benjamin H. Griswold III Professor of Public Policy at Johns Hopkins University.

administrative powers of the superintendent were increased, economy measures were implemented, and progressive curricular innovations were introduced. We also show, however, that the political process which led to reform in Atlanta was quite different from the "typical" process described by the proponents of the class-conflict model. While the reformers in Atlanta were members of the middle and upper classes, as the class-conflict model would suggest, the Atlanta school reforms were carried out not over the objections of working class politicians but rather at the expense of the city's most prestigious civic leaders. In contrast to the efforts of urban elites to "get the schools out of politics" described by the proponents of the class-conflict model, the political connections of Atlanta's reformers were so blatant that their opponents justifiably accused them of introducing politics into the public school system. In addition, we show that the political consequences of school reform in Atlanta were the direct opposite of those predicted by the class-conflict model. On the basis of these findings, we conclude that class conflict is not a necessary condition for urban reform, and that the sources of progressive reform were more complex than the class-conflict model has often implied.

THE CLASS CONFLICT MODEL OF URBAN REFORM

Urban reform in general and school reform in particular have frequently been interpreted in bi-polar class conflict categories. The forces behind the reform drive are said to have been social and economic elites, who had become disturbed by the rising power of working class, immigrant politicians and organizations. The ideology of efficiency and democracy which justified the reforms has been identified as an ideology protective of elite interests and consistent with elite values. Attacks on corruption and patronage, calls for efficient administration and scientific management, and demands for good government and citizen participation have been seen as more or less well disguised campaigns to dismember institutional bastions of working class power.[5]

Specific institutional changes are seen as consistent with the reformers' larger political objectives. Reformers introduced at-large elections because ward-based campaigns emphasized the neighborhood attachments and ethnic connections important to working class politicians. They called for non-partisanship, because the patronage-fed, political parties were "machines" which not only mobilized working class votes but, in return, distributed special favors to workers and immigrants when they needed help. Reformers called for the initiative, referendum, and recall because these more participatory mechanisms of citizen involvement were more likely to be used by middle and upper class voters. Scientific administration required the professional expertise which only the educated middle class could provide.[6]

Recent interpretations of school reform have also been based on a bi-polar, class-conflict model.[7] Katz has described educational reform movements in the Progressive Era as a "class effort . . . largely controlled by old stock first citizens," and motivated by "an anti-immigrant and anti-working class attitude."[8] Following Hays, Tyack has asserted that "the chief support for reform 'did not come from the lower or middle classes, but from the upper class'," and that "the reformers wished 'not simply to replace bad men with good (but) to change the occupational and class origins of decision makers'."[9] The major changes in urban school governance—smaller school boards, fewer board committees, at-large elections, professional superintendents directing a large central office staff, blue-ribbon advisory committees—have been described as devices by which upper class elites sought to break working class influence over school policy. The curricular and other innovations introduced by the reformers—compulsory schooling, manual training, school testing—are said to have embodied a similar bias.

Most of these analyses of urban reform have been carried out in northern cities. When attention has been paid to the South, the racist twists to populist and reform efforts have received the greatest emphasis. Yet the southern experience with reform requires broader consideration. Southern cities differed dramatically from their northern counterparts in a variety of ways at the turn of the century. Foreign immigrants represented a negligible fraction of the population in most southern cities, while blacks were nearly as numerous as whites. Industrialization was barely underway in the region, and the urban working class was racially divided and politically weak. Economic and political power remained firmly in the grip of the traditional, white, "Bourbon" elite.

Initially we asked whether the divergent political and economic characteristics of northern and southern cities spawned reform movements which differed significantly from one another. Did those differences come either in the political process through which reform was carried out or in the content of the reforms which were implemented? We regarded the Atlanta experience with reform as an especially promising test case. Atlanta has always been the southern city most attuned to developments in the North; it has styled itself as the "Gate City" and the capital of the progressive "New South." If the class-conflict model of urban reform is appropriate for analyzing reform movements in any part of the South, it would presumably account for developments in Atlanta. We found that the content of the reforms instituted in the Atlanta public school system in 1897 was similar to the content of contemporaneous reforms elsewhere. In addition, we discovered that the political process through which reform was carried out in Atlanta was decisively different from that described by the proponents of the class-conflict model. This interpretation suggests that the class-conflict model inadequately accounts for reform politics outside the major cities of the industrialized North. On the basis of this evidence we conclude that the primary sources of urban school reform are not to be found in bi-polar class conflict but rather in the new administrative requirements created by increasingly large and multi-faceted educational organizations, and in the rising political strength of middle-class professionals who were as suspicious of traditional social elites as they were of working-class politicians.

EDUCATIONAL REFORM IN ATLANTA

At the end of the nineteenth century, Atlanta was a relatively small but rapidly growing city. The city had barely 20,000 residents in 1872, when it began the public school system. By 1900 the population had more than quadrupled to nearly 90,000, and growth continued apace in the succeeding decade. The black population of Atlanta grew at a slower rate than the white population. At the turn of the century nearly 40 percent of the city's residents were black. The representation of immigrants in Atlanta's population declined from 6.5 percent in 1870 to an insignificant 2.8 percent in 1900. The city's economy was also growing and changing in these years. Between 1880 and 1890 the aggregate product of Atlanta's industries nearly tripled, as the locally-oriented, food processing and construction industries were surpassed by industries producing for regional and national markets. Though aggregate economic growth was slowed by the national depression between 1890 and 1900, technological and organizational changes in this decade greatly increased the productive efficiency of Atlanta's industries, and the amount of value added in the production process by each employee grew by more than 60 percent.

The demographic and economic development of Atlanta was reflected in the growth of the city's dual public school system. Table 1 shows that grammar school enrollments more than doubled between 1878 and 1890, and nearly doubled again in the following decade. At the secondary level there were no facilities provided for black children; white enrollments increased less rapidly and less steadily than at the primary level. Between 1878 and 1900 enrollments in the system as a whole grew by nearly 300 percent, and at the turn of the century more than half of the eligible children in the city were enrolled in school. The rapid growth of the city and its public school systems set the stage for educational reform in Atlanta in 1897.

A. *The Content of School Reform*

In some ways the Atlanta school reform fits rather well with the class-conflict model. The instigators of the reform movement were Mayor Charles Collier and newspaperman, Hoke Smith, both of whom were well-established members of the city's economic and political elite. Collier was a noted proponent of Henry Grady's "New South" ideology and an active advocate of Atlanta's economic growth and civic improvement. In this connection he had served as president of the corporation which had staged the Cotton States and International Exposition in Atlanta in 1895, an event intended to attract

TABLE 1
ATLANTA PUBLIC SCHOOL ENROLLMENTS, 1878-1910

Year	Black Primary Enrollment	Black Students per Teacher	White Primary Enrollment	White Students per Teacher	Secondary Enrollment (White)	Secondary Students per Teacher	Total[a]	Percentage[b] of Cohort in School
1878	1,269	90.6	2,081	63.1	317	45.3	3,667	
1882	1,111	69.4	2,813	63.9	332	41.5	4,256	
1885	1,533	N.A.	3,659	N.A.	379	42.1	5,571	
1890	2,373	N.A.	5,402	N.A.	638	49.1	8,413	39.2
1895	4,705	117.6	9,042	64.6	901	50.1	14,767	
1896	3,566	89.2	9,330	76.5	860	47.8	13,937	
1897	3,484	87.1	9,558	64.6	941	49.5	14,328	
1900	4,069	92.5	9,047	55.2	922	41.9	14,236	51.4
1905	4,164	74.4	10,066	46.4	810	31.2	15,359	
1910	5,346	75.3	14,146	40.8	1,271	28.2	21,418	50.1

SOURCES: Atlanta Board of Education, *Annual Reports*, 1878–1910.
1890, 11th Census of the U.S., Population, Vol. 1, pt. 2, p. 114.
1900, 12th Census of the U.S., Population, Vol. 1, pt. 2, p. 122.
1910, 13th Census of the U.S., Population, Vol. 1, p. 450.

[a]Includes night students, all of whom were white.
[b]School age cohort, 5–19.

entrepreneurs and northern capital to the Gate City and open up the city and the region for increased development and industrialization.[10] Smith was the editor of the *Atlanta Journal* and an increasingly important political figure known for his "progressive" sympathies. He had served as Grover Cleveland's Secretary of the Interior in the early 1890's, and he was to be elected Governor of Georgia in 1906. Like Collier, Smith was a vigorous proponent of southern development and industrialization; he maintained a lifelong interest in educational reform and especially vocational education.[11]

Collier had been elected in 1896 at the head of the Chamber of Commerce-dominated ticket of the J. W. English faction in city politics, and he came into office determined to administer the city according to "sound business principles."[12] Among his earliest legislative accomplishments was the passage of a substantial property tax cut, which reduced the expected revenues of the city by nearly $200,000.[13] The lingering effects of the national depression required cutbacks in the level of city services and the salaries of municipal employees, and Collier, like the leaders of reform movements in other cities, was quick to demand that Atlanta's public school system be operated more economically and efficiently. Expressing his unhappiness with the school board, the Mayor observed:

> I have been surprised and mortified to find that this department was the only one disposed to hamper us in our efforts to put the city government on a business basis.[14]

In a further parallel with educational reform movements elsewhere, the general concern for economy and efficiency within the Atlanta public school system expressed by Mayor Collier was coupled with a specific demand for reductions in school system expenditures. Shortly after his inauguration, Collier persuaded the school board to pass a 9 percent pay cut for all of the city's teachers. In addition, he pushed an ordinance through the city council which prohibited the school board from purchasing any supplies for the schools without the express authorization of the Mayor and the council.[15]

These efforts to enforce economy in the public school system were resisted by both the old school board and by Atlanta's teachers. In his annual report to the Mayor and council, the board president asserted the rights of the school board against those of the city's elected leaders:

> I ask for the schools the best financial support that the condition of the treasury will admit of, and that the Board be permitted to exercise its judgement not only as to what shall be taught and who shall teach, but also what shall be paid, keeping within such appropriation as you shall make for the schools.[16]

Though the board partially acquiesced to the Mayor and modestly reduced teacher salaries, its president chose to resign from the board rather than submit to all of Collier's demands.[17] Understandably concerned about the effects which the Mayor's economy measures would have on their standard of living, Atlanta's teachers supported the school board in its resistance to the

Mayor. A petition signed by every teacher in the school system asked the board president to withdraw his resignation and return to office.[18]

The drive for economy in the administration of the school system intensified after the abolition of the original school board. The newly-appointed board responded to the Mayor's demands for reduced expenditures by firing several teachers (including a number of principals), cutting the length of the school year by a week, and imposing additional salary cuts on the teachers in 1897 and 1898.[19] The approach of the new board was summed up by its president, Hoke Smith:

> As a rule the teachers are doing good work. The Board found it necessary to give up the services of some, and it may be necessary to give up the services of others.[20]

As Table 2 makes clear, the economy measures implemented by Mayor Collier and the new board of education had a profound impact on the public school system of Atlanta. Instructional expenditures were reduced absolutely in 1897, and they remained below the level reached in 1896 until after the turn of the century. The level of total expenditures, including building and other capital expenses, was affected even more dramatically. Total expenditures were reduced more than 25 percent between 1896 and 1897, and in constant dollars they did not regain their former level until 1905. These reductions in the level of appropriations to the school system occurred in a period in which the population of Atlanta was increasing rapidly, and the cuts in educational expenditures thus resulted in increased class sizes and the exclusion of substantial numbers of would-be students from the schools for lack of space. Per pupil expenditures were reduced almost 10 percent between 1896 and 1897, and further reductions were made in succeeding years.[21]

The content of the Atlanta school reforms corresponds closely to the content of reforms described by the class-conflict model in other respects as well. The change in board membership resulted in a shift of administrative power away from the school board to the professional staff of the school system. The reduction in the number of members on the school board from seventeen to seven and the reduction in the number of board committees from ten to two served to limit the extent to which board members could personally involve themselves in the day-to-day administration of the system. This shift in power was further encouraged by the addition of a full-time Assistant Superintendent to the administrative staff and by an extension of the rights and responsibilities of the Superintendent. He and his assistant were permitted to participate fully in the meetings of the school board for the first time, and a variety of administrative tasks which had previously been handled by board committees, including the adjudication of disputes between parents and teachers and the ordering of supplies, were placed under his authority.[22] As was often the case in other cities, the Atlanta school reform thus resulted in an increase in the power of the administrative staff of the school system at the expense of the school board itself.

TABLE 2
ATLANTA SCHOOL EXPENDITURES (IN DOLLARS), 1878-1910

Year	Instructional Expenditures		Total Expenditures		Instructional Expenditures per Pupil	
	Current	Constant[a]	Current	Constant[a]	Current	Constant[a]
	(000's)		(000's)			
1878	38,082	47,604	38,082	47,604	10.39	12.98
1882	44,780	52,070	55,265	64,262	10.52	12.23
1885	57,638	75,841	76,305	100,401	10.35	13.61
1890	89,309	114,500	137,530	176,321	10.62	13.60
1895	136,173	186,538	138,581	189,837	9.22	12.63
1896	151,834	205,181	198,747	268,578	10.89	14.72
1897	141,999	189,332	141,999	189,332	9.91	13.58
1900	143,960	179,951	168,698	210,873	10.11	12.64
1905	215,345	247,523	249,018	286,228	14.02	16.11
1910	343,710	358,031	475,763	495,586	16.05	16.72

SOURCE: Atlanta, Board of Education, Superintendent's Reports, 1878-1910.
[a]1913 = 100. Federal Reserve Bank of New York Cost of Living Index.

One further parallel between the reforms in Atlanta and those in other cities deserves mention. The members of the new board came into office committed to the introduction of manual training courses into the curriculum of all the public schools. In his first annual report to the Mayor and council, board president Hoke Smith expressed his desire "to see industrial work introduced all through our schools, and the minds of the children so trained as to fit them for the practical utilization of what they learn."[23] This wish was reiterated in the two succeeding years, and in 1900 a director of manual training was employed and a workshop was constructed in the Boys' High School. According to Smith, this was "simply the beginning of manual training. We hope to see it gradually develop until manual training for boys and girls will help to prepare the children of our schools for practical work."[24]

In sum, Atlanta's school reform removed the sitting board of education from office, strengthened the Superintendent and his staff at the expense of the board, imposed economy measures on the schools and salary reductions on the teachers, and added manual training courses to the curriculum of the school system. The list makes the Atlanta experience sound very much like the tales of reform movements in northern cities, where an increasingly powerful elite has been said to have seized control over the public school system, centralized power in the office of the Superintendent, and rationalized procedures throughout the system over the protests of the poor and working classes. A closer look at school reform in Atlanta, however, shows that, while the content of Atlanta school reforms was similar in many respects to the content of reforms of other cities, the process of educational reform in Atlanta differed decisively from that described by the prevailing class-conflict model. B. *The*

B. *Politics of School Reform*

1. Pre-Reform Politics

Politics in Atlanta prior to the reform of the school system were hardly working class politics. Power in the city was virtually monopolized by elite members of the business, commercial, and professional community. Atlanta's black citizens were not represented in city government after 1870, and they were deprived of what little political influence remained to them by the institution of the "white primary" in the early 1890s.[25] The white working class was significantly underrepresented in office as well, though the rival factions of Atlanta's elite required the support of the city's workers for electoral success and therefore competed for working-class votes.[26]

The pre-eminence of the city's elites in municipal politics was facilitated by the absence of party competition in Atlanta, where the Democratic Party was the only recognized political organization, and their influence was reflected in the putative, ideological consensus which governed political discourse in Atlanta. The consensus, which precluded the emergence of sharp divisions in the white electorate, was maintained in large part because of the ostensible need to keep Atlanta's black citizens out of power.[27] The consequence was a political system based on the distribution of graft and patronage and divided along factional lines.[28] As the *Atlanta Journal* explained:

> It is well-known that for several years past there have been two factions in the council. . . . They have alternated in the control of that body, and the faction that has a majority for the time being has everything its own way so completely that the minority might as well not be there so far as the choice of department officials is concerned.[29]

The two factions were led by J. W. English and W. H. Brotherton. Brotherton was a prosperous dry-goods merchant with strong ties to the local branch of the American Protective Association and Atlanta's organized working class, while English was one of the region's leading industrialists and a large scale employer of leased convict labor, with his political base in the Chamber of Commerce.[30] Brotherton was the leader of the powerful Prohibition Club in city politics, while English often worked with Atlanta's liquor interests.[31] At the same time, however, the composition of the two factions was subject to dramatic changes. In the municipal election of 1896, for example, a dispute between the labor and prohibition elements in the Brotherton faction caused the Atlanta Federation of Trades to break its customary political ties and endorse the English ticket.[32] Though union and other working-class support was eagerly pursued by the two factions, the split between them marked a division within the civic elite rather than a division along status or class lines, with the English faction tending to enlist the support of somewhat wealthier and more prestigious citizens and to present the more eminent candidates for office.[33]

A factor of importance in the factional division was the part played in the

struggle by Atlanta's two newspapers, the *Journal* and the *Constitution*.
Rivalry between the two was to emerge as the predominent feature of Georgia
politics in the 1900s, when the "progressive" faction led by Hoke Smith and
the *Journal* vied with the "conservative" faction led by Clark Howell and the
Constitution for political and economic control of the state. In the 1890s,
however, political competition between the two was largely confined to the
local arena. The *Journal* most often stood with the several elements of the
Brotherton faction, while the *Constitution* allied itself with the traditional
elites who dominated the English faction.[34]

A complicating factor in the municipal politics of Atlanta in these years was
the persistence of "friends and neighbors" ties, which eroded factional
divisions and occasionally transcended them altogether. The political ascen-
dancy of Clark Howell's brother, Albert, within the Brotherton faction in
1896, for example, caused the *Constitution* to sever whatever ties had
traditionally bound it to the English faction and to work vigorously for the
election of the Brotherton ticket.[35] This shift in itself would probably have
been enough to bring the *Journal* to endorse the English candidate, but the
nomination of C. A. Collier for mayor by the English faction ensured the new
alignment, for Hoke Smith had studied law in Collier's father's law firm, and
Collier himself had been a member of the original corporation organized by
Smith to purchase the *Journal* in the mid-1880s.[36]

The portrait of Atlanta's political system which emerges from this account
is thus one in which the principal function of municipal politics was the
distribution of economic and political favors and powers between competing
factions of the city's social and economic elite. Political conflicts were not
based on disputes over issues, with the possible exception of prohibition, but
rather over the control of city government and the economic and political
advantages which could be reaped from it. Blacks and the white working class
played virtually no role in city politics. They were unable to take part in the
definition of issues or to contest seriously for office, and their political
activities were largely restricted to efforts to trade votes to one faction or the
other in return for a share of the favors which were to be dispensed. Blacks
were deprived of even this power after the institution of the white primary, but
white workers continued to gain occasional concessions from the factions.
Though the factions were in some respects definable entities, their boundaries
remained relatively fluid, and dramatic shifts in membership could and did
occur. Personal antagonisms were frequently at the root of political rivalries,
and "friends and neighbors" relationships frequently determined the alignment of forces within the factional struggle.

Thus, in contrast to the picture of urban politics described in the literature
which develops the class-conflict model of urban reform, Atlanta politics in
this era were not controlled by working-class leaders or defined by conflict
between classes. The city's business and professional leaders were in firm
control of the economic and political institutions of the city, and such
political conflicts as did emerge in these years emerged within the city's elite.

2. Elites and Traditional School Politics

The school board, in particular, was a bastion of power for Atlanta's traditional civic elite. In contrast to the history of many northern cities, where the public school systems were stitched together over time from a motley assortment of village, borough, and proprietary schools, the Atlanta school system was created by an act of the city council in 1872, and was therefore unified from the start. The school board was uniformly composed of members of the city's business and professional elites, and included some of Atlanta's wealthiest and most eminent citizens. Among them were men like L. P. Grant, the president of the Atlanta and West Point Railroad; Logan E. Bleckley, Georgia's best-known lawyer and subsequently Chief Justice of the Georgia Supreme Court; E. E. Rawson, a pioneer industrialist who had made his fortune in real estate; S. M. Inman, a cotton merchant and reputedly the wealthiest man in Atlanta; and J. W. English.[37] Most important among the members of the school board, however, was Joseph E. Brown, who served as president of the board until his election to the U. S. Senate in 1888 and continued to dominate its deliberations until his death in 1894. Brown had served as the Confederate Governor of Georgia, and he reigned as a member of the state's "Bourbon triumvirate" after Reconstruction, serving terms in the United States Senate and as Chief Justice of the Georgia Supreme Court. He was also president of the Western and Atlantic Railroad, the Southern Railway and Steamship Company, the Walker Iron and Coal Company, and the Dade Coal Company, which made him one of the wealthiest and most powerful men in the southeast.[38]

Members of the school board were appointed for seven-year terms, and they were routinely re-appointed if they were willing to serve.[39] With the exception of authority over annual appropriations, which was retained by the city council, power over the school system was fully vested in the school board.[40] Exempted from political controversy by the wealth and status of its members, the nature of its charter, and the duration of its members' tenure, the pre-reform school board was essentially free to administer the schools according to its own conservative preferences, without regard for the exigencies of local electoral politics. Thus, in contrast to the situation commonly described in the literature on educational reform, in which pre-reform school politics are said to have been ward and neighborhood based, and under the control of working class politicians and their allies, in Atlanta the school system was unified under the direction of elite, "citywide" interests from its inception.

3. Issues in School Politics

The issues which precipitated the reform of the Atlanta schools also differ from those described by the advocates of the class-conflict model of reform. While the demands of Mayor Collier for economy and efficiency in the administration of the school system paralleled similar demands in northern cities, other issues in Atlanta were quite different from those which led to reform elsewhere. In the mid-1890s, public protest arose over the board's policies of textbook selection and the frequency with which new textbooks were assigned in the schools, because of the high textbook costs which parents were obliged to bear.[41] Controversy also arose over issues of curricular reform. Many Atlantans, including the Mayor and members of the city council, urged the introduction of such innovations as a departmental organization of the faculties in the Boys' and Girls' High Schools and the addition of manual training and vocational subjects to the curriculum of the primary and secondary schools. Although some slight modifications were made by the school board in response to these demands, efforts to modernize the curriculum proved largely fruitless in the years prior to 1897.[42]

By far the largest public dispute arose over the issue of corporal punishment in the schools. Protest over the thrashing of recalcitrant children increased dramatically after 1890, and demands that the practice of corporal punishment be forbidden in the public school system were directed to the school board by middle class parents, prominent citizens, and members of the city council with increasing frequency and impatience as the decade passed.[43] Altanta's teachers, however, argued that the right to resort to a hickory switch was essential to the maintenance of order in the city's classrooms. The school board sided with them.

Opposition to the school board found its champion with the inauguration of Mayor Collier in 1897. As was noted above, Collier was quick to protest against the prodigality of the school board in its administration of the public school system, and he joined in the public controversy over other issues as well. From his position as an ex officio member of the board, he tried unsuccessfully to encourage curricular and other reforms in the system, and he worked hard for the abolition of corporal punishment. Declaring that no living man or woman would ever whip one of his children, the Mayor explained that the retention of corporal punishment in the public school system had led him to enroll his own children in private schools.[44] Taking over the leadership of the forces opposing the practice in the city, he circulated a petition among the influential citizens of Atlanta which demanded that teachers in the public schools be prohibited from whipping children. When he had collected over one hundred signatures—from "persons whose names it was believed would have weight with the Board of Education"—he submitted the petition to the board.[45]

The public outcry against corporal punishment was heightened further by noisy press coverage of a sensational case involving a student at the Boys' High School who had been severely beaten by a teacher after allegedly drawing a knife in the classroom. The controversy between the boy's father and the teacher was heard by a committee of the school board over a period of weeks, and a number of columns appeared in the city's newspapers in which the opinions of prominent citizens on the "all-absorbing topic of the hour" were published.[46] The Grievance Committee of the school board nevertheless found in favor of the teacher, and a measure introduced by Mayor Collier to abolish corporal punishment throughout the school system was defeated by a board vote of twelve to four.[47] Speaking for the majority, D. A. Beattie asserted:

> This movement is all nonsense. They don't do half enough whipping in the schools now, and it's foolish to talk about stopping it altogether.[48]

The day after the vote was taken, the city council voted to abolish the school board. Among the first actions of the newly-appointed board were the prohibition of corporal punishment in the Boys' High School and the introduction of strict regulations governing its application in the city's elementary schools.

4. The Political Consequences of Reform

In further contrast with the class-conflict model of educational reform, the restructuring of the Atlanta school board was engineered not by a civic elite intent upon seizing control of the public school system from the working class and its political allies, but rather by a coalition of groups within the civic elite, including Mayor Collier, who sought to reform the educational system and by the Brotherton faction, which sought to exercise greater political control over the schools. The effect of school reform in Atlanta was thus to shift power over the educational system out of the hands of the traditional civic elite and into the hands of somewhat less prestigious men, including lawyers and other middle class professionals, small businessmen and men with political ties to the local labor movement.

The public response to the change in boards reflected its political character. The *Atlanta Journal*, formally allied with the English faction in city politics, greeted the change with equanimity despite the key role played by the Brotherton faction. The editor's "progressive" sympathies and his ties with Mayor Collier, who had instigated the reform movement, offset concern about the introduction of politics into the public school system. In contrast, the *Atlanta Constitution* expressed violent outrage at the council's action, despite its recent affiliation with the Brotherton faction, because its editors had had traditionally close ties with the conservative elites who had predominated on the "exterminated" board.[51] The *Constitution* devoted considerable attention to a mass meeting held on Saturday, May 29, which denounced the council's "illegal, revolutionary, despotic, and dangerous" action and attacked "the ring controlling our city government."

In response to the public uproar, three of the new board members who had had especially close ties to the old board and the city's traditional elite declined to serve, but replacements were quickly elected by the city council.[49] After a meeting with Mayor Collier the following Monday, the members of the new board were duly sworn into office, and they held their first meeting that afternoon. In the familiar cadence of reformers, they proclaimed,

We believe it to be true that the strongest thinkers upon the subject of municipal public schools advocate boards of education composed of a small number of members.[50]

To quiet apprehensions about political interference in the city's public school system, Mayor Collier proposed a successful amendment to the city charter which forbade future city councils from removing school board members from office before the expiration of their terms.[51]

The new members of the board differed but little from their immediate predecessors. A longer view, however, shows that the 1897 change in boards ushered in a new era in Atlanta school politics. After the change, the school board was no longer controlled by the city's traditional social and economic elites, but by men of substantially lesser prestige, as can be seen in Table 3. Members were appointed to shorter terms, and they remained on the board for shorter periods than their predecessors had done. The average term of board members prior to 1897 was nearly eight years; after 1897 the average term was just over four years. In addition, members were appointed by wards after 1897, and they were chosen more for their political connections and sensitivity to ward concerns than for their prominence in the city as a whole, as had been the case in the earlier period. While the old school board had been dominated by members of the civic elite, the new board was dominated by lawyers and minor politicians, and included representatives from a variety of interest groups, including organized labor.[52] Thus, in further contrast to the reform movements described in the literature informed by a bi-polar class-conflict model, the political changes which accompanied the reform of the Atlanta public

TABLE 3

SOCIAL COMPOSITION OF ATLANTA SCHOOL BOARD, 1872–1918
(Percent)

Occupation	1872–1897		1897–1918	
	Members	Board Years	Members	Board Years
Bank and corporation presidents .	20	31	—	—
Lawyers	29	24	36	43
Other professionals	16	15	7	7
Other bank and corporation officials	11	6	18	18
Realtors and insurance men	5	5	20	16
Proprietors	18	20	13	11
Employees	—	—	4	5
Unknown	—	—	2	1
N	(44)	(347)	(45)	(184)

SOURCE: Atlanta, City Directories, 1872–1918.

school system removed the city's traditional "downtown" elite from power over the school system and replaced them with men of lesser status and more particularistic, ward-based concerns, thereby increasing the political responsiveness of the educational system. Whereas in New York, St. Louis, and other cities reformers ostensibly worked to "get the schools out of politics," in Atlanta reformers accomplished the opposite result, and the schools became more closely integrated with the other institutions of city government.

C. *The Causes of Educational Reform in Atlanta*

While speculation as to the causes of the council's "astounding coup" was rampant in the midst of the controversy, two major viewpoints quickly emerged. Mayor Collier, as spokesman for the "combine" which had carried out the reform, asserted that the council had acted only in order to make the administration of the schools more efficient:

> There is no significance to the movement except that the board was too large and we thought to cut it down. None of the old members were re-elected because we did not want to offend half of them by leaving them off.[53]

This explanation satisfied the *Atlanta Journal*, though the paper also reminded its readers of the recent disputes over the questions of teacher salaries and corporal punishment, and even suggested that "the entire school system of the city may be revolutionized by this change of boards."[54] While the Mayor and his allies explained the changes largely in terms of improving the efficiency and accountability of Atlanta's schools, the *Constitution* took a much more narrowly political view of the council's action, asserting that the restructuring of the school board marked an end to the political independence of the public school system:

> The most vicious feature connected with it . . . is the fact that it throws our entire public school system into the very center of the whirlpool of political agitation. . . . At any hour of the day or night—especially night—it may become the victim of some political combination and suffer the deadliest results of secret deals, jobs, and manipulations.[55]

The competing explanations of the Atlanta school reform offered by the participants in the dispute were both partially correct. The narrowly political causes of the reform were the conflicts which had arisen between the city council and the school board in the mid-1890s. These were brought on by the unwillingness of the members of the school board to abolish corporal punishment, adopt curricular innovations, or modernize school administration, despite the demands of the Mayor and other politically influential citizens. In addition, the board's resistance to Mayor Collier's efforts to put the school system on a "sound business basis" through cuts in teacher salaries and other economy measures was intolerable to the Mayor and the city council, especially in light of the ongoing national depression and the recent reduction in the city's anticipated revenues. The intractability of the board and the persistence of these conflicts caused the Mayor to replace the sitting board members with men more closely attuned to his own political principles.

But if immediate political conflicts triggered the change, broader pressures for efficiency and modernization in education provided the context within which particular political circumstances could engender large-scale organizational consequences. Mayor Collier and other members of the "combine" which engineered the reform of the school system—especially Hoke Smith— were self-conscious advocates of a modern, industrialized, and prosperous "New South," with Atlanta as its regional capital, and they worked throughout their lives to bring their vision into reality. They were cognizant of contemporaneous reform movements in other cities, and aware of the ideas of educational experts and reformers elsewhere. Dedicated to the modernization of their region, they were alive to the contributions which a modern, reformed school system could make to the development of Atlanta and the South, and they chafed at the obstacle to development posed by the traditional, inefficient organization of the public school system and the domination of the system by the city's older civic elite. Recognizing the political opportunity presented by the conflict between the school board and the city council, the Mayor acted in 1897 to implement administrative and organizational changes which made the public school system more responsive to the changing economic and political circumstances of Atlanta and the South.

CONCLUSION

In this paper we have shown that the politics of Atlanta school reform differ from those implied by a bi-polar class-conflict model of urban reform. Despite the parallels between many of the Atlanta innovations and those carried out in other cities, we have shown that the changes in Atlanta were not carried out against the opposition of a locally-oriented working class, as is said to have been the case in some other cities. Instead, the Atlanta reforms were brought about by a younger faction of the city's elite which was dominated by professional men and concerned with the modernization and development of the city and the region, and the reforms were carried out at the expense of precisely the sort of economic and political elites whose interests were supposedly so well served by urban reformers. As opposed to the shift in power from ward politicians to city-wide elites and educational experts which occurred elsewhere, the Atlanta reforms resulted in a shift of power from the city's traditional civic elite to men of lesser status who were better attuned to the demands of ward and patronage politics. While the working class was not a visible participant in the reform movement, either in support or in opposition, the faction ordinarily supported by the city's labor movement was the one which engineered the reform.

Clearly, the political process through which educational reform was carried out in Atlanta in 1897 was distinctly different from the contemporaneous political processes which brought reform to the public school systems of New York, Philadelphia, St. Louis, and other cities; and many of the political consequences of the reform in Atlanta were precisely contrary to the consequences of reform elsewhere. The overwhelming political significance of the racial division in the southern population and the persistence in power of a conservative, paternalistic, "Bourbon" elite established a context in which urban politics in the South were very different from urban politics in the North, and southern movements for reform took dramatically different courses than did their northern counterparts.

At a minimum, this finding suggests that the utility of the class-conflict model of educational reform is limited to those large cities of the industrialized North which shared a number of economic and political attributes, including a sizable immigrant population and a large and politically-organized working class. The general applicability claimed by some of the bolder proponents of the class-conflict model of reform is thus shown to be unwarranted: the political process of educational reform was constrained by the political environment within which reform took place, and divergent political contexts generated dissimilar movements for reform.

At the same time, the similarities between the Atlanta school reform and reform movements in other cities are as significant as the differences between them. In spite of the marked contrasts between the political processes of reform in Atlanta and elsewhere, the content of the reforms which were implemented in various urban school systems was essentially the same. The size of the school board and the number of board committees were reduced, and administrative power over the school system was centralized in the office of the Superintendent and his staff. Measures reducing teacher salaries and other school system expenditures were instituted. The curriculum was modernized, and manual training and other vocationally-oriented courses were added to the offerings of elementary and secondary schools.

The fact that practically identical reforms were implemented in Atlanta and in a number of northern cities, despite dramatic differences in the political contexts in which reform movements were successful, represents an anomaly which the class-conflict model cannot explain. According to the model, conflicting class interests generate political controversy between two social classes, and the dominant social class secures a policy outcome favorable to its interests. But if the same policy consequences occur in *all* cities, whether reform is opposed by conservative elites or by organized workers, then in what sense can the policy reforms in any context be attributable to class-based political conflict? If progressive educational reform came about as a result of the victory of economic and social elites over working-class groups and organizations, then why did reform occur where no such class struggle was visible? If Y was a function of X in northern cities, then how could Y have occurred in Atlanta in the absence of X?

There are two complementary responses to this question. The first suggests that the political processes through which reform occurred in particular cities were essentially epiphenomenal. The changes which were implemented in school organization in the late nineteenth century were required by contemporaneous socio-economic changes in American society. The explosive growth of urban populations, the rapid expansion and diversification of urban economics, and the increasing complexity of urban social relationships, common to all regions at the turn of the century, imposed rapidly rising enrollments and a broader range of social responsibilities upon big-city school systems. As these systems grew larger and undertook to provide a new and diverse array of services, their management became increasingly complex. Organizations which once had been directed by a small group of part-time lay board members now required the full-time attention of a highly-trained professional staff. Urban school systems thus came to resemble one another not so much because of the particular political circumstances which shaped them as because of the attributes of function, complexity, and size which they had in common.

Although this functional argument is persuasive in many ways, it is theoretically problematic to identify the "causes" of a structural arrangement with its functions or "consequences." No matter how beneficent a social institution may be, the desirable consequences of its presence cannot constitute an explanation for the structure's coming into being.[56] Thus, the functional explanation only becomes plausible when linked to a second response to the query posed. This explanation, like that provided by a bi-polar class-conflict model, identifies a strong social group, an emerging professional class, with an interest in urban educational reform. Because it identifies a more complex pattern of social interactions than that suggested by the bipolarities of class conflict, however, it can resolve the apparent contradiction between the political process of reform in Atlanta and in the cities of the industrialized North.

The difficulty with a simple class-conflict model is that it reduces complex, multi-party political contests to simple two-sided disputes. Even in northern cities, where the model seems most appropriate, debates over urban reform involved Protestants, Catholics, teachers, administrators, professionals, and politicians, as well as workers and capitalists. While a full assessment of the broad range of political forces involved in reform controversies is beyond the consideration of this paper, recognition of the part played by one especially important social group can help to resolve the puzzle we have presented. The emerging autonomous role of middle class professionals in both northern and southern cities may have brought about urban educational reform without any close identification on the part of the reformers with the interests of either business leaders or workers. In class-conflict models the interests of middle class professionals are treated as almost synonymous with those of the business community, yet campaigns for urban reform pitted middle class professional groups against business elites as often as they divided the middle class from labor unions and other working class organizations.

As urbanization and industrialization progressed in the late nineteenth century, these processes generated an increasing demand for a wide variety of professional services, including those provided by lawyers, doctors, social scientists, journalists, social workers, teachers, and public administrators. Professional associations represented the interests of these and many other emerging occupations with increasing effectiveness. In addition, many professionals felt confident enough of their growing social esteem to argue that public policy was an arena for professional expertise, scientific administration, and the exercise of high levels of technical proficiency. While those offering class-conflict interpretations of urban reform have emphasized the differences between these middle class values and interests and those of working class, immigrant groups, few have appreciated the simultaneous challenge which these professionals offered to businessmen skeptical of any claim to expertise that was not market-tested, and wary of the likely costs of a new array of professionally-administered public services. The more politically sophisticated leaders of the emerging professional class understood their role to be located mid-way between the interests of capital and labor. If they felt unions were often too self-interested, they were at least equally alarmed at the increasing concentration of power in the business community. Their effort to reduce politics to administration was inspired in part by a desire to rationalize and subject to scientific scrutiny what had previously been decided by campaign rhetoric and political muscle.

Progressive educational reform is difficult to understand as a conflict between capital and labor simply because the innovations which were implemented had been designed by a social group which saw itself standing apart from class-based controversies. While the understanding of the reformers was in some ways myopic—in their public rhetoric, for example, they seldom mentioned the new jobs for professionals that would be required by their proposals, they nevertheless correctly understood that opposition to their suggestions came as often from business as from labor. In some northern cities working class politicians held sway over the nineteenth century school, and they and their allies formed the core of the opposition to educational reformers. In Atlanta the principal opposition came from traditional social and economic elites who, like the working class politicians in the North, wished to protect the institutional arrangements which ensured their power and privilege. If the political conflict over urban reform is understood as, at the very least, a three-party controversy, and not just as a bi-polar confrontation between business leaders and the working class, then the apparent differences between northern and southern reform movements can be readily reconciled.

There remains the question of the effect of reform on school expenditures in Atlanta. As in other cities during this same period, reform in Atlanta meant not just organizational and administrative modernization, but severe cutbacks in the level of school services provided to the children of the city. If other school reforms embodied no obvious class bias, it is more difficult to see how drastic budgetary cuts were anything other than hostile to the increasingly widespread popular demand for public schooling, which in Atlanta expressed itself in overcrowded classrooms and, in the black community, in continuous, organized efforts to gain better facilities. Was all the reformers' talk about efficiency simply a disguise for conservative, business-oriented concern with the rising costs of a labor-intensive public service?

The issue is in fact more complex than it at first appears. At the time of the reform, Atlanta and most other American cities were in the midst of a nationwide depression, which forced service reductions and economy measures in all sectors of soci ety, both public and private, and these measures were necessarily implemented in the public school system as well. To be sure, the depression may have created the political occasion which allowed reform movements in Atlanta and elsewhere to succeed, and once in power the reformers willingly accepted the responsibility for cutting public expenditures. Yet, in subsequent years of reform rule, as prosperity returned to the city and the nation, Atlanta's school expenditures regained and then surpassed previous levels.[57] Tables 1 and 2 show that for white students at least, and to a lesser extent for blacks, reform resulted in reduced class sizes and increased levels of expenditure per pupil after the turn of the century. The pecuniary consequences of reform thus proved to be among its least enduring features.

Advocates of the class-conflict model of urban educational reform have argued that the reform movements which transformed many big city school systems around the turn of the century not only reflected the values and interests of social and economic elites but were hostile to the values and interests of the poor and working classes. On the basis of our analysis of the Atlanta experience with educational reform, we have argued instead that many of the reforms which were implemented were functional requisites for the maintenance of rapidly growing, increasingly complex educational organizations, and were designed by middle-class professionals as antagonistic toward traditional business elites as they were toward working class groups.

NOTES

1. *Atlanta Journal* (28 May 1897); *Atlanta Constitution* (29 May 1897).
2. *Atlanta Constitution* (29 May 1897).
3. *Atlanta Constitution* (30 May 1897).
4. *Atlanta Journal* (31 May 1897); *Atlanta Constitution* (1 June 1897).
5. A classic statement of the class-conflict model together with a valuable summary of the literature can be found in E.C. Banfield and J.Q. Wilson, *City Politics* (Cambridge, 1963). Other important contributions include W.D. Burnham, *Critical Elections and the Mainsprings of American Democracy* (New York, 1970); M.G. Holli, *Reform in Detroit* (New York, 1969); E.C. Hayes, *Power Structure and*

Urban Policy: Who Rules Oakland? (New York, 1972); R.K. Merton, *Social Theory and Social Structure* (New York, 1957); W.D. Hawley, *Nonpartisan Elections and the Case for Party Politics* (New York, 1973); Richard Hofstadter, *The Age of Reform* (New York, 1955); G.E. Mowry, *The California Progressives* (Chicago, 1963); S.P. Hays, "The Politics of Reform in Municipal Government in the Progressive Era," *Pacific Northwest Quarterly*, 55 (1964): 157-169; R. Lineberry and E.P. Fowler, "Reformism and Public Policies in American Cities," *American Political Science Review*, 61 (1967): 701-716; Martin Shefter, "New York City's Financial Crisis: The Politics of Inflation and Retrenchment," *Public Interest*, 48 (1977): 98-127; Gabriel Kolko, *The Triumph of Conservatism* (Chicago, 1963); W.N. Chambers and W.D. Burnham, *The American Party System* (New York, 1967); R.H. Wiebe, *Businessmen and Reform: A Study of the Progressive Movement* (Cambridge, 1962); and R.H. Wiebe, *The Search for Order* (New York, 1967).

A critique of the class-conflict model and some compelling negative evidence are provided in R.E. Wolfinger and J.O. Field, "Political Ethos and the Structure of City Government," *American Political Science Review*, 60 (1966): 306-326.

6. With this general consensus on the sources and consequences of urban reform there is, of course, a good deal of variability in interpretation. For some analysts, including Hofstadter and Lazerson, reform movements represent a reactionary effort by a declining social elite to retrieve some of the presumed moral virtues and social harmony of a rural past. For other analysts, notably Wiebe, reform is an effort by a rising middle class to stabilize conflicts between big business and big labor. For still others, reform is the mechanism chosen by monopoly capitalists to depoliticize the working class, thereby making possible a level of capital accumulation necessary to finance ongoing industrialization. Nevertheless, all of these perspectives interpret urban reform in basically class-conflict categories: in nearly all the major accounts working class groups are perceived to be the "victims" of reform movements sponsored by middle and upper class groups.

7. Among the many studies which deal with school reform, the following are of particular interest: M.B. Katz, *Class, Bureaucracy, and Schools: The Illusion of Educational Change in America* (New York, 1971); M.B. Katz, *The Irony of Early School Reform: Educational Innovation in Mid-Nineteenth Century Massachusetts* (Cambridge, 1968); D.B. Tyack, *The One Best System* (Cambridge, 1974); J.M. Cronin, *The Control of Urban Schools* (New York, 1973); R.E. Salisbury, "Schools and Politics in the Big City," *The Politics of Education at the Local, State, and Federal Levels,* (ed.), M.W. Kirst (Berkeley, 1970), pp. 17-32; R.E. Callahan, *Education and the Cult of Efficiency* (Chicago, 1962); H.M. Zieger, M.K. Jennings, and W. Peak, *Governing American Schools* (North Scituate, Mass., 1974); Marvin Lazerson, *Origins of the Urban School: Public Education in Massachusetts, 1870-1915* (Cambridge, 1971); Colin Greer, *The Great School Legend* (New York, 1976); and Samuel Bowles and Herbert Gintis, *Schooling in Capitalist America* (New York, 1976).

8. Katz, *Class, Bureaucracy, and Schools*, pp. 115-16.

9. Tyack, *The One Best System*, p. 128. In a previous passage Tyack's argument is put somewhat more ambiguously: "Although school managers tried to create smooth-running, rational, conflict-free bureaucracies during the nineteenth century, often with the assistance of modernizing business elites, in most cities they encountered serious opposition. . . . In almost every city where the population was heterogeneous, contests erupted in educational politics. Although there were overtones of class assertion or resentment in such conflicts, the issues were not normally phrased in class terms but in the cross-cutting cultural categories of race, religion, ethnicity, neighborhood loyalties, and partisan politics. These concerns had great power to motivate political action, even though they may have blurred commonalities of class interest" (p. 78).

10. Walter Cooper, *Official Catalogue of the Cotton States and International Exposition and South, Illustrated* (Atlanta, 1896), *passim;* T.H. Martin, *Atlanta and Its Builders* (Atlanta, 1902), pp. 645-46; Southern Historical Association, *Memoirs of Georgia* (Atlanta, 1895), Vol. 1, p. 750; Walter Cooper, *Official History of Fulton County* (Atlanta, 1934), pp. 853-54.

11. Dewey Grantham, *Hoke Smith and the Politics of the New South* (Baton Rouge, 1958), pp. 25-26, 29-31; Wayne Urban, "Hoke Smith and the Politics of Vocational Education," Paper presented to the Annual Meetings, of the History of Education Society, 1978, pp. 4-7; Southern Historical Association, *Memoirs of Georgia*, p. 937; and Walter Cooper, *Official History of Fulton County*, pp. 44-46.

12. *Atlanta Journal* (28 August 1896).

13. *Atlanta Journal* (6 February 1897).

14. *Atlanta Journal* (28 January 1897).

15. Atlanta Board of Education, *Minutes* (15 February 1897).
16. Atlanta Board of Education, *Annual Report* (1897), p. 12.
17. *Atlanta Journal* (28 January 1897).
18. *Atlanta Journal* (1 February 1897).
19. Atlanta Board of Education, *Minutes* (15 February 1897); and Atlanta Board of Education, *Annual Report* (1899), p. 22.
20. Atlanta Board of Education, *Annual Report* (1898), p. 14.
21. Atlanta Board of Education, *Annual Reports* (1896-1910). The data are taken from the annual presentations of statistics on expenditures and enrollments.
22. Atlanta Board of Education, *Report* (1898), pp. 82-104. A full list of the new rules governing the public school system is presented in the 1898 School Board Report. Melvin Ecke, *From Ivy Street to Kennedy Center* (Atlanta, 1972), pp. 55-56, provides a summary of the most important changes made by the new board.
23. Atlanta Board of Education, *Annual Report* (1898), p. 14.
24. Atlanta Board of Education, *Annual Report* (1900), p. 21.
25. E.J. Watts, *The Social Bases of City Politics* (Westport, Conn., 1978), pp. 71-72, 74-76 and 160-164; and E.J. Watts, "Black Political Progress in Atlanta, 1868-1895," *Journal of Negro History*, 59 (1974): 282-85.
26. Watts, *The Social Bases of City Politics*, pp. 71-72, 74-76 and 160-164.
27. This consensus was maintained on very much the same terms into the middle of the twentieth century. See V.O. Key, *Southern Politics* (New York, 1949), Chapter 1 and especially pp. 5-9 for a discussion.
28. *Atlanta Journal* (1 March 1897).
29. *Atlanta Journal* (11 August 1896).
30. *Atlanta Journal* (2 February 1897 and 19 February 1897). See also E.J. Watts, "Atlanta's Police," *Journal of Southern History*, 39 (1973): 176-82; Herbert Jenkins, *Forty Years on the Force* (Atlanta, 1974), pp. 4-5; and especially Willie Bolden, "The Political Structure of Charter Reform Movements in Atlanta During the Progressive Era" (Ph.D. dissertation, Emory University, 1978), pp. 11-27 for an authoritative discussion of the factional split and its salience in Atlanta politics.
31. *Atlanta Journal* (3 February 1897).
32. *Atlanta Journal* (8-12 August 1896).
33. On the 1897 city council, for example, all five of the English partisans were mentioned in contemporary honorary biographies, while only one of the ten Brotherton representatives was mentioned.
34. Grantham, *Hoke Smith*, pp. 31-35 and 131-155; and Bolden, "Political Structure of Charter Reform," pp. 64-65 and Appendices B and C, pp. 268, 270, and 273.
35. *Atlanta Constitution* (29 August 1896).
36. Southern Historical Association, *Memoirs of Georgia*, p. 937; and Grantham, *Hoke Smith*, pp. 26-27. Bolden, "Political Structure of Charter Reform," p. 15 provides evidence of another tie between Smith and Collier.
37. For Grant, see Martin, *Atlanta and Its Builders*, pp. 655, 657; Southern Historical Association, *Memoirs of Georgia*, Vol. 1, pp. 793-95; and Cooper, *Official History*, pp. 858-59. For Bleckley, see Southern Historical Association, *Memoirs of Georgia*, Vol. 1, pp. 715-18. For Rawson, see Martin, *Atlanta and Its Builders*, pp. 693-94. For Inman, see Southern Historical Association, *Memoirs of Georgia*, pp. 833-34; and Cooper, *Official History*, pp. 846-48. For English, see Southern Historical Association, *Memoirs of Georgia*, Vol. 1, pp. 767-69; and Cooper, *Official History*, pp. 852-53.
38. Martin, *Atlanta and Its Builders*, pp. 633-37; Cooper, *Official History*, pp. 837-39; and C.V. Woodward, *Origins of the New South, 1872-1913* (Baton Rouge, 1971), pp. 13-14.
39. Charles Strickland, "The Rise of Public Schooling in the Gilded Age and the Attitude of Parents: The Case of Atlanta, 1872-1897" (Mimeographed, Emory University, 1980), p. 4.
40. P.N. Racine, "Atlanta Schools: A History of the Public School System, 1869-1955" (Ph.D. dissertation, Emory University, 1969), pp. 11-12.
41. Atlanta City Council, *Minutes* (19 April 1894).
42. Racine, "Atlanta Schools:" 81-91.
43. Strickland, "The Rise of Public Schooling," pp. 11-13.
44. *Atlanta Journal* (19 April 1897).
45. Ibid.
46. *Atlanta Journal* (5 April 1897).
47. *Atlanta Journal* (28 May 1897).
48. *Atlanta Journal* (22 April 1897).

49. Atlanta City Council, *Minutes* (29 May 1897). Among the three was expresident W.S. Thomson, the sole member of the old board to be reappointed by the Mayor.

50. Ibid.

51. *Atlanta Constitution* (1 June 1897); *Atlanta Journal* (30 May 1897); Georgia State Legislature, *Legislative Report* (10 December 1897).

52. Information on the occupations and addresses of board members was obtained from the annual editions of the Atlanta City Directory, 1872–1918.

53. *Atlanta Constitution* (29 May 1897).

54. *Atlanta Journal* (28 May 1897).

55. *Atlanta Constitution* (30 May 1897).

56. In biology it is possible to argue that the "survival of the fittest" ensures the emergence of eufunctional properties, but only an extreme Social Darwinist would argue that competition among organizational structures is so intense that random change can in a short period yield functional structural innovations.

57. Moreover, Atlanta school reforms in the 1910s and 1920s brought about major *increases* in per pupil expenditures. The impact of reform on educational finance seems to be largely a function of the economic context in which reform takes place. But that is a topic for another paper.

12

Vocationalism for Home and Work: Women's Education in the United States, 1880–1930

John L. Rury

BETWEEN 1880 AND 1930 millions of women poured into the American labor force. The rate of female labor force participation in this period increased from about fifteen to nearly twenty five percent, such that by 1930 almost one out of every four American workers was a woman. Taking jobs as typists, clerks, teachers and telephone operators, as well as traditionally female jobs in manufacturing and domestic service, women rapidly expanded the range of occupations then open to them. Not surprisingly, these changes raised troublesome questions about women's roles in society, and invited more than a little controversy. "For the past fifty years," wrote one observer in 1929, "there have been many 'scare' headlines and perturbed fathers, mothers, preachers, teachers and reformers, ready to tell of dire consequences to follow the entrance of women into new occupations". The movement of women out of the home and into the workforce was accompanied by a variety of changes in American social life. Not least among these was the development of a new range of educational experiences to prepare women for their rapidly changing world.[1]

Historians have long acknowledged the strong vocational orientation in American education during the opening decades of the twentieth century. They have carefully documented the process by which enthusiasm over manual education, justified initially by Calvin Woodward in educational rather than vocational terms, gave way to a groundswell of interest in industrial education. But few historians have included programs for women in their discussions of vocational education and its development. This was no small oversight. Most of the major changes in women's education in this period revolved around the new roles women had assumed in the labor force. Indeed, it was during these years that a distinct female curriculum evolved in American schools, largely in response to the growth of vocationalism. As more women moved into the workforce, schoolmen (and women educators too) wrestled with the problem of how best to equip them for their new roles.[2]

John L. Rury is assistant professor of education at The Ohio State University.

Many educators, of course, were ambivalent about training women for work. Home economics was introduced at this time to combat the movement of women out of their homes and into the labor market, and to elevate homemaking to the status of a respectable—though definitely female—occupation. On the other hand, the growth of commercial education, which affected the high school careers of tens of thousands of young women (particularly in large Northeastern cities), was a direct consequence of changes in the nature of women's work. Other programs were developed for female manual workers as well, ranging from courses in dressmaking in cities like New York and Boston to instruction in Agriculture for black women in the South. Educators everywhere decried the growing tendency of young women to leave school in order to work, yet they also established programs to make women better workers once they left the schools.

The arrival of vocationalism affected aspects of school life other than the curriculum as well. Coeducation, long a celebrated feature of pre-collegiate education in the U.S., gave way to a studied sexual differentiation in secondary schools, guided by educators' images of the roles men and women were supposed to play in the social order. Although the principle of coeducation was rarely renounced in practice, there is considerable evidence that boys and girls met in the same classrooms a good deal less after 1910 than they had earlier. As young men and women prepared for different careers the spirit of coeducation clearly shifted, even if formal policies of coeducation changed little.

These developments suggest that vocationalism was a major factor in the definition of women's education in the early twentieth century. Educational policy in this period often evolved in piecemeal fashion, and different programs for women developed independently of one another. This study will examine several of these discrete aspects of women's education. The high school curriculum that confronted teenage girls in 1930, after all, was the product of a long process of accommodation to competing educational purposes. In this respect women's education was hardly unique. But consideration of these varied aspects of women's schooling may help to underscore the importance of work and vocationalism in other dimensions of school reform during the opening decades of the century.

Homemaking as Vocation:
The Home Economics Movement and Women's Education

Home economics was the most important feature of the new high school curriculum for women which developed at the start of the twentieth century. Simply stated, home economics, or domestic science education as it was sometimes called, was the female equivalent of industrial education, which was generally thought of as a male feature of the curriculum.[3] This lineage was both the source of home economics' link to vocationalism, an association which helped home economics programs get support from Federal vocational education legislation in this period, and a source of considerable confusion about its purposes. While most educators agreed that homemaking was indeed a vocation (and one for which women were divinely suited), some insisted that it was also much more than that: it was a cornerstone of the modern social order. To these latter enthusiasts home economics was a reform movement, one of the general Progressive reforms of the time aimed at eradicating the overcrowding, poverty, disease and potential for social unrest associated with rapid industrialization and urbanization.

Home economics, like industrial education for boys, can be traced to the manual education movement which began to gain momentum in the 1880s. It was in the eighties that sewing and cooking first found their way into public school curricula, as the female component manual training for boys. Contrary to the impression given by advocates of home economics later, these early courses were not intended to give women training for the home. Instruction in the domestic arts was simply viewed as another context in which young women could learn manual dexterity and practical lessons about science. Indeed, unlike manual education for boys, there was virtually no mention of vocational aims for instruction in these skills.[4]

Leading proponents of manual education rarely discussed women's education in the years prior to 1900. Calvin Woodward, for instance, nearly always framed his discussions of the need for manual training in terms of educating young men, and his famous school at Washington University was for men only. Insofar as women's education was discussed at all, it was generally included as an afterthought. This was perhaps most striking in the context of discussions about ways in which manual education was to promote industrial growth. Training in manual dexterity for men, along with experience in industrial work gained in such training, was frequently cited as an aid to industrial development. But sewing and cooking classes were seldom seen in the same light. As a result, manual training for women in the late nineteenth century developed as a sort of women's auxiliary to the manual training movement. Like manual education for boys, its chief pedagogical aim lay in the new contexts for learning which manual activity afforded, but educators failed to identify any measurable social benefits from the results. In the eyes of some, sewing and cooking were simply things for women to do while their male counterparts were learning to be better industrial workers.[5]

As manual training gave way to industrial education in the late nineteenth and early twentieth centuries it became more vocationally oriented. This was partly the consequence of agitation from groups such as the National Association of Manufacturers and organized labor, along with other supporters of industrialization who gathered to form the Society for the Promotion of Industrial Education in 1906. Part of the impetus for this new organization came from a widespread impression that American youth lacked the skills required to promote further industrial growth in the U.S.

Schoolboys in the U.S., the argument went, needed training commensurate with the requirements of modern industry. Where manual training had urged a generalized education with emphasis on manual dexterity and the development of mechanical comprehension, industrial education sought to fit young men precisely to the needs of industry. This was a subtle shift insofar as males were concerned, for the manual traning movement had been permeated with undertones of industrial purposes from its inception. But the more explicit concern with vocational ends raised troublesome questions about what industrial education for women ought to entail.[6]

Perhaps the biggest problem facing educators pondering industrial education for women was determining just which occupations women needed training for. At its second meeting in 1908, the National Society for the Promotion of Industrial Education (NSPIE) called for the development of a comprehensive program of vocational education in American cities, linked to local industry and designed to equip young men to work immediately upon leaving school. But educators had difficulty with the prospect of preparing women for jobs in industry, particularly inasmuch as industrial jobs for women were limited to begin with. Some argued that schools could help prepare women for employment in the garment industry or as domestic servants and cooks. But the garment industry was relatively small outside a few large cities, in particular New York, Rochester and Chicago. And domestic service, although deemed important, hardly seemed worthy of an elaborate program of industrial training. Besides which, many educators—most of them male—were uncomfortable with the idea that women should be educated for any industrial role that would take them away from their families. To the extent that educators saw rising rates of female employment as a threat to the family, they hit upon a common solution to their dilemma: a woman's proper occupation was the care of her children and her home.[7]

This simple formulation became the cornerstone of a movement to make home economics the female equivalent of industrial education for males. In 1908, furthermore, it was an idea whose time had clearly arrived. That year witnessed the formal organization of the American Home Economics Association (AHEA) by a group of leading women educators in Saranac Lake, New York. Their purpose was to promote the study of home economics as a means to improving "the conditions of living in the home, the institutional household, and the community". Home economics, the term adopted by the new organization to describe the study of housekeeping, included the old female subjects of cooking and sewing and much more. In addition to the traditional concerns of the manual training curriculum, home economics included the study of family consumption (or household economics), nourishment, family relations (calling upon psychology and sociology), and personal hygiene. According to its proponents, the object of this avowedly broad approach to homemaking was to prepare women for their roles in sustaining the central institution of modern industrial society: the family.[8]

The organizers of the AHEA numbered among thousands of reform-minded middle class Americans in this period who linked the growth of industry, the rapid expansion of cities, and associated problems of poverty, overcrowded living conditions and ill health with a general decline in national morality. To these women the American family lay at the center of this maelstrom, and was threatened with "destruction" unless some substantial effort was made to save it. This, moreover, was hardly a philanthropic concern, for the family was also seen as the very means by which morality and order could be restored to the twentieth century. The family, after all, was the context in which all previous generations of Americans had acquired their sound values and respect for authority. And what better place could there be to combat disease and malnutrition? Many of the early enthusiasts of home economics even believed that poverty itself could be circumvented by proper management of household resources. The effort to promote the study of home economics, in that case, came to assume the dimensions of a general reform movement. In the words of one of the AHEA's early leaders, Ellen Richards, the "upheaval in educational ideals" associated with the introduction of home economics to secondary education was "nothing less than an effort to save our social fabric from what seems inevitable disintegration".[9]

The family, in that case, was determined to be the true aim of women's work, and homemaking the "natural" vocation for women in the new industrial order. From the very start, however, proponents of home economics were hard pressed to explain why women suddenly needed training for housework. While some educators and social reformers celebrated the rising numbers of women workers as yet another demonstration of the openness of American society, others expressed concern that women were losing touch with their roles as homemakers. These commentators pointed to the rising incidence of teenage employment, speculating that while these young women were at work they missed valuable exposure to the work habits and household skills of their mothers. The home, they argued, had historically been the context in which women learned the art and science of running a household and rearing a family. The danger in large numbers of women leaving the schools to work was the possibility that they would be unprepared for their true vocation as homemakers. Advocates of home economics pointed out that most women only worked four or five years before getting married. Hence the principal work of women's lives was housework, and the schools should assume responsibility for guaranteeing that they knew how to carry it out. After home economics courses had become widely accepted in principle, these arguments were also used to support the establishment of home economics continuation schools, aimed explicitly at working women. If women were unable to learn to be good mothers and wives at home, it was the duty of educators to see that they got the opportunity in school.[10]

Champions of home economics also argued that homemaking had become more complex with the development of modern civilization, and that learning housework at home, apart from the matter of female labor force participation, simply was not adequate to the task of training good modern mothers. This issue drew greater attention from educators than the problems of working women, in part no doubt because it attributed a sophistication to home economics which flattered its practitioners. The argument invariably began with identifying the family as a vital source of essential social activities. The most basic of these, the production of household goods and their consumption, drew the most attention from the AHEA through the first decade of its existence. Although early home economists recognized that industry had taken many household tasks out of the home, or had invented new machines to make housework easier and faster, they insisted that modern housewives needed even more training than their mothers had. Indeed, women's growing reliance on machinery and consumption goods produced outside the home was often cited as a circumstance requiring such instruction. "Tomorrow, if not today", declared Ellen Richards in 1911, "the woman who is to be really mistress of her house must be an engineer, so far as to be able to understand the use of machines, and to believe what she is told".[11]

Some reformers stressed the economic effects of improved homemaking. The seemingly small efficiencies gained from better management of household budgets, they argued, could contribute to more efficient use of society's resources if practiced on a massive scale. Some argued that if women could learn to prepare meals cheaply and trim household expenses, families could save money and help contribute to capital formation. Others suggested that such savings could be invested in a wide range of goods and services, ranging from houses to higher education. Frank Gilbreth, who along with Frederick Taylor pioneered the use of scientific management in industry, even suggested that women consider the use of time and motion studies to organize household tasks more productively. Discussions such as these helped to establish homemaking as a legitimate occupation for women, a productive role with genuine economic consequences.[12]

A wide range of other considerations accompanied the view that the family was the vocational sphere of women. One which received a great deal of attention in the *Journal of Home Economics* throughout this period was nutrition. If American industry was to benefit from strong and healthy workers, after all, proper nourishment at home and school was necessary. The same was true of personal hygiene and household cleanliness, as these were associated with combating disease. Other supporters of home economics stressed the importance of a proper family environment for raising children. They argued that women, in their roles as mothers, played a critical role in the regeneration of society. In this regard women were made responsible for the nation's human capital, with an eye to "the truer production of human energy, which . . . creates, organizes, combines and controls all other forces". Women were to develop both the skills and character in future generations necessary for continued social and economic development.[13]

Early home economists, of course, exhibited many of the prejudices of other Progressive reformers. One recurrent theme in the opening decades of the AHEA's existence was the problems of immigrant families. Advocates of "American standards" in matters of nutrition and cleanliness never tired of complaining that immigrant women did not appreciate the importance of proper sanitation. The issue, as they often saw it, was not one of poverty alone. Most supporters and practitioners of home economics believed that any family could improve its standard of living if only women were mindful of the need to do so, and followed the proper techniques of homemaking. The problem with immigrant women in particular was ignorance, possibly aggravated by an unwillingness to learn. Such was the sentiment of educators at a conference on the education of immigrants in New York in 1931.

> The immigrant woman is ignorant of the value of fresh air, and in our campaign of education we have to make the mother of a family realize that ventilation prevents sickness and that sickness means expense before she will attempt to ventilate her home. The educator has to create a horror of flies by drawing attention to the flies on the filth in the street, and then showing how they convey germs into the house. Such a thing as ventilating clothing or comforters or pillows is unknown, and the educator shows that unheard of things are possible by assisting at the first bed cleaning.[14]

This passage demonstrates the importance which home economics supporters assigned to personal hygiene and cleanliness, but it also reveals their steadfastly middle class prespective. Nowhere did they make reference to the social structure or the unequal distribution of income when discussing such problems as overcrowded and run-down housing, disease and malnourishment, or even the ignorance of proper means of ventilation. Their remedy for these problems focused resolutely on the woman's role as household worker: if she could be trained to guarantee proper nourishment, a clean and sanitary living environment and a context for the proper spiritual development of her children, the American family could be saved from the dangers posed by modern industrial society. Poverty, they felt, was not an insurmountable problem. If urbanization and the industrial economy had made society more complex, and life more difficult for many, women simply required training in ways to better cope with their new environment. What most advocates of home economics failed to recognize was that many—perhaps most—working class women lacked resources more basic to survival than instruction in domestic science.

If enrollment figures are a guide, promoters of home economics achieved mixed results in their efforts to make domestic science a universal element of women's education. As indicated in Table 1, large numbers of women were enrolled in these courses nationwide. By 1928 nearly one out of three women in public high schools was enrolled in some sort of home economics class, which meant that virtually all women took domestic science at some point in

TABLE 1   Percent Of All Public High School Female Students Enrolled In Domestic Science Courses, 1922 and 1928, Selected States & Regions

	1922	1928	*
Massachusetts	19%	33%	9%
New York	16%	14%	7%
Connecticut	20%	32%	15%
Rhode Island	13%	29%	9%
Ohio	26%	29%	23%
Illinois	25%	25%	13%
Michigan	26%	28%	16%
Wisconsin	20%	27%	22%
Mississippi	34%	38%	32%
North Carolina	21%	32%	28%
Alabama	26%	31%	27%
Louisiana	46%	47%	38%
Iowa	34%	35%	26%
Kansas	36%	39%	26%
Missouri	23%	24%	13%
South Dakota	23%	24%	17%
California	32%	37%	18%
Oregon	27%	26%	15%
Washington	39%	37%	21%
U.S. Total	26%	30%	19%

*1928, women enrolled in home economics courses only (the other figures included women in vocational sewing and cooking classes)
Source: Calculated from data in *Biennial Survey of Education,* 1924 and 1930

their high school careers. In this regard the home economics movement was clearly a success. But there were important regional disparities in the popularity of these courses. Enrollments were highest in the South and West, and lowest in the Northeast. In 1928, when overall enrollment levels in all domestic science courses were generally even, the number of women majoring in home economics in the Northeast was still substantially less than elsewhere. The Northeastern states, of course, contained most of the nation's urban population and its greatest concentration of working class—particularly immigrant—families. Most of the problems that home economics enthusiasts were committed to eradicating were concentrated in this part of the country. Yet it was in these urban, industrial contexts that home economics courses suffered their lowest popularity.

The failure of the home economics movement to gain a wide following in the industrial Northeast probably contributed to the decline of its reformist zeal in the 1920s. With time the reform impulse gave way to a more diffuse interest in improving middle class family life, and home economics eventually became one dimension of education as "preparation for life".[15] The movement's ability to hold the attention of large numbers of working class women was hampered by an underlying flaw in its vocational premises. As a matter of curricular reform home economics started from the notion that family life could be improved if housework were subjected to the same rules of production and management as other forms of work. The key difference between housekeeping and other types of work was one which advocates of home economics failed to emphasize, but which in the last analysis was probably most important to many working class families: women were never paid for keeping their own homes. Given this, it is small wonder that women from these areas showed little interest in home economics. Homemaking was one career that offered no direct returns to an investment in secondary schooling.

If many women (and perhaps most working women) in this period did not see homemaking as an occupation, in what way could home economics lay claim to vocational purposes? There was, of course, the issue of whether working women had opportunities to learn household skills. As indicated earlier, some of the sentiment in favor of domestic science instruction was derived from the growth of teenage employment and fears that women were entering matrimony unprepared for the responsibilities of motherhood. More important, however, was the commitment of educators to the idea that homemaking was the only appropriate vocation for most American women. The term vocation when employed in reference to home economics was meant to convey a sense of women's calling rather than the modern notion of a particular occupation. A woman's life work, supporters of home economics argued, was her family. This was not, of course, a new argument; but it contained new implications for educators in the opening decades of the twentieth century. If the industrial education movement was committed to preparing men for careers in paid employment, the schools ought to be equally committed to preparing women for unpaid labor.[16]

The chief social benefits most of its advocates claimed for home economics were, in fact, economic in nature, suggesting that its supporters did indeed see it as training for a variety of work. Their biggest problem, it seems, was a matter of convincing female high school students to share their vision. Some of the difficulties which these champions of women's "true" vocation encountered can be comprehended in light of other school programs concerned with women's work. Home economists were required to contend with a variety of other changes in the high school curriculum competing for young women's attention.

Commercial Education: A Vocational Groundswell

One of the most important and least understood elements of the high school curriculum at the start of the twentieth century was education for office work, widely referred to by contemporaries as commercial education. Historians have neglected to emphasize the importance of commercial education, perhaps because contemporaries devoted comparatively little attention to it. Home economics, industrial education and the issue of vocationalism all received a great deal more commentary than did the development of the commercial curriculum. Commercial subjects generally were not included under the rubric of vocational education, probably because they did not prepare students for specific occupations, although most clerical workers in this period were trained in such courses. Yet, when educators were led to discuss education for business, they usually began by acknowledging its phenomenal growth and its association with the labor market.

Commercial education was among the fastest growing areas of study in high schools across the country in this period. This was undoubtedly a concomitant of the rapid growth of the clerical labor force, a circumstance which can also be linked to the large numbers of women enrolled in school. Commercial education became an important aspect of female high school education in the opening decades of the twentieth century, and presents one of the clearest examples of the manner in which women's education responded to changes in the labor market.[17]

Commercial education was by no means a new aspect of the high school curriculum at the turn of the century. Courses in bookkeeping and other branches of accounting had been regular fare in nineteenth century high schools. These courses were considered to have intellectual as well as vocational purposes, although one underlying aim clearly was to prepare young men for careers in business. It was not until the last decade of the nineteenth century that other business courses began to be offered in high schools across the country: commercial geography, principles of business, and most important for women, typewriting and stenography. The latter two subjects developed in direct response to technical innovations then beginning to revolutionize office work, changes which presaged the movement of women into the clerical labor force. These developments paralleled a dramatic expansion of commercial education in the nation's public high schools.[18]

Prior to 1900 most vocationally oriented business education took place outside of the public schools. In the 1870s and eighties a network of private business schools grew up in American cities to provide training for men and women seeking to go into the world of business. These schools developed the first courses in typing and stenography when typewriters were still a novelty and clerical work was dominated by men. Unregulated and subject to no higher authority than their ability to draw students, these schools flourished in the period prior to the development of the commercial course in the public schools.[19]

The three decades following 1890 witnessed a rapid rise in public school enrollments in commercial courses. Between 1893 and 1910 the proportion of all public school students enrolled in such courses more than doubled, jumping from five to over eleven percent of the entire high school population. In the two decades following 1910 commercial course enrollments grew less dramatically, but the number of students taking these classes continued to increase substantially. By 1928 roughly one out of every six high school students in the United States was enrolled in business courses. The period between 1890 and 1930 was characterized by rapid overall growth in high school enrollments, of course, so the growing share of total enrollments commanded by commercial courses represented a rapidly expanding constituency for this branch of the curriculum. In the public schools the absolute number of students in business courses increased by nearly 2,000 percent between 1890 and 1920, from fewer than 15,000 to nearly 300,000. Impressed with this massive influx of students into commercial courses, at least one contemporary suggested that the growth of commercial enrollments contributed much to the overall expansion of the high school in this period.[20]

The growth of public high school commercial enrollments was doubtlessly affected by educators' claims that the public schools maintained higher standards than did private business schools, and thus prepared their students better for business careers. High school courses generally were longer than those in the business colleges, and high schools had the advantage of offering a wide range of other courses to consider as electives. Of course, they were free as well. This point was probably especially important to most students in this period. In time the business schools came to be seen as ancillary to the public schools, a direction to turn if a student wanted to drop out of school and pick up a few office skills quickly before entering the job market.[21] As more public high schools offered commercial courses it became increasingly difficult for private business schools to compete with them for the growing commercial course clientele. By 1920—and probably much earlier—the era of the private business school had clearly passed, and commercial education was firmly implanted in the highly differentiated high school curriculum.[22]

Given the rapid pattern of growth in commercial enrollments in this period, it is clear that the commercial curriculum developed largely in response to changes in the demand for white collar labor. Enrollments increased most rapidly at the very time that the clerical labor force mushroomed, and commercial educators concerned themselves with finding ways of better fitting their courses to local labor markets. As indicated in Table 2, enrollments in business courses were highest in the urban Northeastern states, where the demand for clerical workers was greatest in this period. Enrollments were lowest in those parts of the country where there were relatively few clerical workers: the South and plains states. Educators and businessmen alike complained that commercial courses needed to be better adapted to local business conditions, yet enrollments in these classes were highest in those areas where there was the greatest need for training in office work.[23]

Occasionally educators acknowledged the problems of keeping women interested in other classes in the face of rising enrollments in commercial

TABLE 2 Percent Of All Female Public High School Students Enrolled In Business Courses (Typing),* 1922 and 1928, Selected States & Regions

	1922	1928
Massachusetts	32%	31%
New York	23%	26%
Connecticut	26%	30%
Rhode Island	27%	34%
Ohio	13%	18%
Illinois	22%	26%
Michigan	20%	28%
Wisconsin	17%	22%
Mississippi	5%	5%
North Carolina	3%	4%
Alabama	4%	9%
Louisiana	12%	9%
Iowa	8%	16%
Kansas	10%	19%
Missouri	14%	16%
California	26%	30%
Oregon	19%	28%
Washington	19%	24%
U.S. Total	17%	21%

*Note: Typing classes generally included all women enrolled in commercial classes.

Source: Calculated from data in the *Biennial Survey of Education,* 1924 and 1930

courses. Home economics supporters, concerned about enrollment levels, were especially sensitive to such pressures. It was hardly coincidental that commercial course enrollments were highest in the Northeast, where home-making courses were least popular. In a revealing article published in 1921, a domestic science teacher in Philadelphia lamented that "homemaking courses do not hold the girls in school". Declaring that such courses were "entirely extraneous to commercial work and (were) only of mild interest to the girl who gets enough practical domestic science education at home", she concluded that the vast majority of girls in her school were most interested in getting a "nice respectable job" as soon as possible. The promise of paid employment, it appears, exerted a strong attraction for many young women, particularly in large cities where demand for clerical workers was high.[24]

Unlike their counterparts in home economics education, commercial educators virtually never campaigned for increased enrollment levels in their courses. The demand for commercial education was considered sufficient reason to offer such courses, and provided plenty of students. Rising enrollments were not the consequence of efforts by educators to expand their field, but a natural concomitant of increases in office employment. Business education, in that case, bore a unique relationship to the labor market. It developed as a response to a growing demand from educational consumers, from students and to a lesser extent from businessmen, for training which would enable them to pursue careers in office work. Business education offered what was probably the period's clearest example of the schools responding directly to the demands of the labor market.[25]

Women, of course, constituted the bulk of the new entrants to the clerical workforce at this time. They also substantially outnumbered men in commercial education classes. Although there were slightly more girls than boys enrolled in high schools across the country, in 1920 girls outnumbered boys by better than two to one in shorthand and typewriting and held a three to two advantage in bookkeeping. These were the largest and most widely offered commercial courses in the country at this time, and generally speaking, they were dominated by women. The same male/female ratio characterized these courses seven years later, the last point prior to 1930 at which the Commissioner of Education's statistics permitted these sorts of comparisons. If clerical labor was becoming women's work in the opening decades of the twentieth century, business education came to be dominated by women as well. This, of course, is additional evidence of the manner in which commercial education in this period developed in response to the demand for particular types of labor.[26]

If business educators were aware of the preponderance of women in their classes they rarely made reference to it. They did, however, comment repeatedly on the different career patterns men and women followed in business. And some argued that distinctive male and female curricula ought to be established to accommodate such differences. A survey of sixty-six high school principals in 1917 found that nearly two thirds believed businessmen wanted training for men and women to differ. Boys, it was felt, required preparation for careers in administration and management, while women needed training for relatively short term employment as secretaries and typists. Consequently, men were to be given a broad education commensurate with the responsibilites they were expected to assume, while the technical details of office procedure were considered sufficient for women, whose working careers were generally short. Surveys of the occupational status of men and women in business confirmed the accuracy of these expectations. One of the best known such surveys found in Cleveland that "regardless of the position in which boys and girls started in life, boys worked into administrative positions", while women remained secretaries or clerks until they left the office to get married. As a matter of better adapting commercial education to the needs of business, in that case, nearly all the major commentators on business education in the decade prior to 1920 called for separate commercial training for men and women.[27]

Despite the unanimity displayed by business education leaders on the question of separate commercial training for women, however, there is little evidence that such proposals were seriously considered by other educators. A survey of 112 schools with between 100 and 200 students enrolled in commercial courses in 1917 found that nearly ninety eight percent made no distinction in requirements for boys and girls. Detroit appears to have been one of the few cities in the country which experimented with establishing different sets of requirements for men and women in the commercial course. Other cities which separated men and women did so because their public high schools were sex-segregated to begin with. Boston, for example, sponsored a female commercial high school, which offered courses leading to jobs as saleswomen, telephone operators and a wide range of other tasks requiring some education. For most school systems, however, such segregation was both prohibitively expensive and contrary to popular tradition. Whether for reasons of economy or principle, men and women continued to pursue the same course of commercial study in high schools throughout this period. The impact of the marketplace upon the development of commercial education was substantial, but it was not strong enough to bring educators to differentiate formally the business course by sex.[28]

Commercial education was a unique development in American education at the close of the second decade of the twentieth century. Almost wholly the result of interest generated by the expansion of job opportunities in business, commercial education mushroomed into significance by the very force of its enrollments. What contemporaries failed to emphasize was that commercial education was also largely female. Stenography, the fastest growing of the commercial courses after 1910, was better than eighty-five percent female by 1927. The strict orientation of commercial courses to the needs of the business community, the prevailing theme of the business education literature of the period, meant that commercial education—insofar as it trained students for office work—was increasingly women's education. In the face of labor market pressures it appears that an explicit policy of sex segregation in business courses would have been redundant. Women were entering these courses more rapidly than were their male counterparts. Commercial education appears to have been one area of the high school curriculum where formal policy was in fact made needless by the association between school and work.[29]

Women and Industrial Education

If commercial training was an educational success story, the opposite was true of industrial education for women. At the heart of the industrial education movement was the matter of training teenagers for jobs in industry. In practice this meant training men for industrial jobs, largely because most women did not aspire to become industrial workers. As indicated earlier, educators were opposed to the idea of women working at factory jobs. Besides which, those women who did seek factory work usually left school too soon to benefit from specialized industrial training. This situation was further aggravated by the narrow range of industrial employments then open to women, and the generally unskilled nature of the jobs that women held in industry. But despite these obstacles, schools for the industrial education of women were established in several American cities at this time. Intended to provide incentive for working class women to remain in school, these institutions shared important social and moral purposes in addition to their technical function of training women for factory jobs. A chief measure of their success was their small enrollments and the tendency of most contemporaries to confuse female industrial education with home economics.[30]

Most comprehensive high schools did not train women for industrial employment. Rather, industrial education for women was usually conducted in separate schools designated for such purposes. Specialized industrial training for women in this period was limited to a few large cities capable of supporting highly differentiated school systems or to cities with large numbers of women employed in industry. In the second decade of the twentieth century many of these schools were organized to reach working women who had already left school. Often conducted in the afternoon or evening, these were called continuation schools and were intended to provide women workers with an opportunity to acquire job-related skills. School systems in industrial cities conducted surveys of local history to determine the types of training that ought to be offered in such schools. The Commissioner of Education's *Annual Report* in 1914 listed such surveys in Troy, N.Y., Grand Rapids, Philadelphia, and New York. In each of these cities special schools for training female industrial workers were established.[31]

Not surprisingly, industrial schools prepared women for relatively few jobs. The only significant urban industry that employed women on a large scale in this period was the garment trades. Hence most of the industrial component of women's industrial education was related in some way to sewing. Some schools offered courses in commercial cooking and painting as well. All this, of course, made the female industrial course quite similar to home economics, and helps account for why contemporaries often confused them. To the extent that female industrial schools also endeavored to offer instruction in home economics, the distinction between the two courses blurred.

This confusion pointed to one of the chief difficulties that programs for women's industrial education encountered in this period: the work that women performed in industry was virtually the same as the work they did at home. The principal differences lay in the conditions under which work was performed. Hence, most industrial courses stressed factory methods of production. Women were taught to sew on machines in New York's Manhattan Trade School, and how to stitch gloves together by industrial methods. The object of the course was to bring each girl's work up to prevailing trade standards and guarantee her placement in the industry. The chief difference between schools such as this and the home economics course, in that case, was the narrow vocational orientation of industrial training.[32]

For the most part, the women who received industrial training did not find employment as skilled workers. Of nearly a thousand requests for girls from employers submitted to the Manhattan Trade School in 1914, over two thirds were for unskilled or semi-skilled operatives in the various branches of the needle trades. Since fewer than five hundred girls graduated from the school each year, its alumnae constituted a tiny fraction of the more than thirty thousand women working in the New York garment industry. Most unskilled women workers in this period either did not want industrial training or could not afford the opportunity costs associated with prolonged school attendance. And industrial training of the sort offered by the trade schools clearly was not necessary to gain employment in industry. It is possible that schooling enabled women to hold on to jobs, or to advance to skilled positions. But studies conducted in 1914 found it impossible to trace graduates of the Manhattan Trade School through their industrial careers because so many were laid off at the end of each season. This alone suggests that formal training offered women little advantage in the struggle for stable work at a liveable wage. Given this, it is small wonder that relatively few women were drawn to the industrial course.[33]

Unlike their male counterparts, women in industrial schools were confronted with a narrow range of career opportunities. Few of them, moreover, intended to make industrial employment their life's work. Most women in industry at this time performed tasks which were learned relatively easily on the job. And there is little evidence that schooling added anything to the industrial careers of women. Perceived widely as being unnecessary, female industrial education attracted few students. Women who wanted to work in factories simply dropped out of school and went to work. Many undoubtedly felt that working in the garment industry, where sweated conditions prevailed, was bad enough alone, and certainly was not worth struggling through school. For those women who did enroll in these courses, schooling was most definitely related to work. But their small numbers were a revealing measure of the irrelevance of formal education to the needs of industrial workers in this period.[34]

The Changing Face of Coeducation

The development of distinctly female courses of study in the opening decades of the twentieth century affected all aspects of women's education. Coeducation had long been a celebrated feature of public schooling in the United States. In 1900 the *Report of the Commissioner of Education* declared the United States to be a world leader in the matter of providing education "without distinction of sex". Yet in the years that followed boys and girls moved through school in curricula which became more sexually differentiated with time. While high schools remained coeducational for the most part, vocational courses taken by large numbers of high school students demanded that the sexes be separated. One effect of the growing concern with vocationalism in the public schools was the development of a distinctly female curriculum for women.[35]

Coeducation was a matter of considerable controversy in the early years of the twentieth century. While educational leaders, including the U.S. Commissioner of Education and most state and city superintendents, remained strong supporters of coeducation in principle, an odd assortment of academics, religious leaders and educators spoke out against teaching boys and girls together in high schools. Several of the nation's largest cities maintained sex-segregated secondary school systems throughout this period, and most urban private schools (many of which were religious) were either for girls or boys. This suggests that there was considerable popular support for sex segregated schools in this period, and that the public was quite amenable to the sexual differentiation in the high school curriculum that accompanied vocationalism.[36]

In 1901 the U.S. Commissioner of Education declared coeducation, "or the education of youth of both sexes in the same schools and classes", to be a "marked characteristic" of American education. Two decades later the same claim could not be made, at least with regard to secondary education. Teenage men and women continued to attend the same schools in most American cities, but took courses which were increasingly dominated by one gender group or the other. By 1930, for instance, roughly one out of three high school girls was enrolled in home economics courses, and about twenty percent of all males took manual training. And these were only the most extreme cases of sexual differentiation in high school courses. In stenography, which was taught at more schools than manual training, women outnumbered men by better than three to one. In typing classes enrollments favored women by a two to one margin. And on the academic side boys outnumbered girls by about three to two in physics and held a slight edge in most branches of mathematics, despite the fact that more women than men were enrolled in high schools.[37]

If this sort of sexual differentiation in public high schools failed to abrogate coeducation altogether, it certainly altered its spirit. While the figures cited above reflect enrollments at a given point in time, they indicate that most men and women took courses limited to their own gender at one time or another. If nearly a third of all women enrolled in high schools in 1930 were in home economics classes, virtually all women must have taken home economics at some point in their high school career. The same undoubtedly was true of manual training for boys. The effect of this was to link girls and boys to different high school curricula, despite the fact that in many courses— perhaps most—they continued to sit in classes together.

The vocational nature of the segregated courses accounted for this change. Few observers could escape the conclusion that high school boys and girls were destined for different careers. It was not simply a few courses that distinguished their high school careers, in that case, but the manner in which educators viewed their education. Different academic courses were judged suitable for young men and women. Physics, after all, was a branch of science with few practical uses around the home. Some educators argued that men and women should have separate classes in such subjects to augment the different purposes they had in education. The high school in Marianette, Wisconsin, for example, offered separate courses in chemistry for men and women. According to the Superintendent of Schools, the girls' chemistry was "built up largely around the chemistry of the home, of cooking, food values, and adulterations in their detection, while that of the boys' classes is like that of physics, more technical and 'scientific', calculated to be of most service to them in higher institutions and in the arts and crafts". Although these sorts of suggestions were rarely followed—indeed they often prompted spirited opposition—they reflected a recognition that the education of men and women was different despite the rhetoric of coeducation.[38]

Several of the period's best known educators were in the forefront of the controversy over coeducation. And again the issue of women's work figured prominently in their thinking. G. Stanley Hall, a prominent educational psychologist and outspoken critic of coeducation, argued that distinctions between boys and girls ought to be pushed to "their uttermost" by the schools, in order to "make boys more manly and girls more womanly". Hall believed that the most important social role played by women was in the home, and shared the concern of other educators that schooling was discouraging women from embracing their domestic duties properly.

David Snedden was another prominent advocate of sexual differentiation in education. A well known sociologist who served for a time as Superintendent of Education in Massachusetts, Snedden felt that courses for women in high schools should be fitted to their vocational requirements. He suggested that special courses in "applied" chemistry and physics be developed to suit women's interests in housework. Other commentators urged that mathematics requirements for women be relaxed, simply because little training beyond arithmetic was deemed necessary for homemaking. In all instances the underlying rationale for devising a distinctive curriculum for women was the same: women were to be trained to be effective wives and mothers. Men, on the other hand, were to be prepared for a variety of roles in the wage economy, and hence required a different sort of education. If coeducation ceased to be a celebrated feature of American education in this period, it was largely because educators were increasingly concerned about the relationship of schooling to the labor market.[39]

In addition to leading educators like Hall and Snedden, local public school officials in some parts of the country voiced opposition to coeducation. The location of these exceptions to the norm of coeducational policies corresponded to no general regional pattern, and shared little in common in industrial or demographic characteristics, other than size. Most of them had long-standing policies of sex-segregation dating from the establishment of public education. But all continued to defend their policies of maintaining separate boys' and girls' schools well into the twentieth century. Boston was probably the period's best known sex-segregated school system, and John D. Philbrick, its Superintendent in the late nineteenth century, was one of the country's most prominent critics of coeducation. Other big city school districts on the east coast also maintained separate schools for boys and girls, notably New York and Philadelphia. Yet others were scattered across the country haphazardly: Louisville, Atlanta, Chicago, Cleveland and Charleston. There appears to have been little similarity in the reasons given for such policies in these places. Some emphasized morality, others the different vocational aims of boys and girls, and still others the beneficial effects of separate schools on male school performance. Although segregated public school districts were not large in number in this period, the very existence of such systems—particularly among some of the nation's largest school districts—helped further to undermine the officially sanctioned ideology equating coeducation with progress.[40]

While sex-segregated school systems were maintained out of concern for protecting the virtue of female high school students in some cities, particularly in the South, in others such differentiation was defended in vocational terms. The latter was true of larger cities in particular, as their school systems could afford the expense of new schools for boys and girls. With the rise of vocationalism such cities were able to establish specialized schools for women. Boston, again, was a leader in this regard. By the second decade of the twentieth century high school aged women in Boston could choose between a female Latin (or academic) school, a girls' commercial school, and a female trades school. The city also maintained boys' schools in each of these areas, and as indicated earlier, eventually established programs to teach women to work in stores and as telephone operators. The only other city which approached Boston's commitment to such specialization was New York. Educators in these cities argued that specialized schools served the scholastic and vocational needs of both men and women better than the coeducational comprehensive high school then coming into fashion elsewhere.[41]

While most educators continued to cling to the rhetoric of coeducation—and the presumed equality of opportunity it gave to women—throughout this period, between 1900 and 1920 there was a decided drift away from coeducation both in the outlook of leading education spokespersons and in educational policy. As other students of this process have argued, this was partly associated with concern for propriety and guaranteeing a proper moral environment in the schools (as well as providing a more masculine environment for young men in an age when most students were women). But the development of a distinctly female curriculum for women was an important factor as well. Even in most schools which claimed to be coeducational, men and women attended different classes and pursued fundamentally different educational goals. And it was only a short leap from differentiation within the school to differentiation on a system-wide basis, as existed in some cities in this period.

The differences which characterized men and women's vocational education in this period, moreover, helped to highlight other factors militating against coeducation. If boys performed better in all male schools, it was in part because courses could better be adapted to their goals and interests. The movement of women into the labor force and the recognition of household labor as a legitimate field of study changed the high school curriculum dramatically in the opening years of the twentieth century, and helped shake traditional American commitment to coeducation.[42]

Recapitulation: Vocationalism and Women's Education

With the rapid expansion of secondary school enrollments in the opening decades of the twentieth century, the question of what teenagers were to do with their high school training became irresistable. As the high school evolved from an elite to a popular institution it is little wonder that schoolmen and women became preoccupied with finding practical purposes for education. A new utilitarian outlook permeated nearly all aspects of secondary schooling in this period. And as indicated above, it had a clear impact on women's education. Home economics and female industrial education were new elements of the curriculum designed for unmistakably female occupations. Other programs, though coeducational by design, became sex-typed by the occupational roles they were associated with. This was clearly the case with commercial education. Indeed, educators everywhere began to question whether coeducation was the best framework for preparing women for decidedly female working careers. As educational leaders confronted the issue of vocationalism is women's education, traditional educational objectives—in this case a commitment to coeducation—were abandoned in order to prepare men and women better for their different roles in society.

NOTES

This research has been supported by the National Institute of Education, Contract No. 400-79-0019. The opinions expressed herein, however, are those of the author alone, and no endorsement of the contents of this paper by NIE is implied.

1. Figures on female labor force participation were drawn from W. Elliot and Mary Brownless, *Women in the American Economy: A Documentary History, 1675-1929* (New Haven, 1976) p. 9. The quotation is from Thomas Woody, *A History of Women's Education in the United States* (New York, Vol. 2 1929) p. 16.
2. Perhaps the best discussion of the development of vocationalism in American education can be found in Marvin Lazerson and W. Norton Grubb, *American Education and Vocationalism: A Documentary History, 1870-1970* (New York, 1974), "Introduction." For a more general discussion of this period in educational history, see Lawrence Cremin, *The Transformation of the School* (New York, 1961), and Edward Krug, *The*

Shaping of the American High School, 1880-1920 (New York, 1964). For alternative interpretations see Joel Spring, *Education and the Rise of the Corporate State* (Boston, 1972); David Tyack, *The One Best System* (Cambridge, 1974); and Marvin Lazerson, *The Origins of the Urban School: Public Education in Massachusetts, 1870-1915* (Cambridge, 1971).

3. For a discussion of this issue in the context of industrial education generally, see Krug, *The Shaping of the American High School*, p. 229; also see Cremin, *The Transformation of the School*, p. 56. There is no historical monograph on the development of the home economics movement or the home economics curriculum itself.

4. Proponents of home economics later traced the roots of their cause back as far as 1789. See "Dates in this History of Home Economics," *Journal of Home Economics* (October 1911):388 (hereafter referred to as *JHE*). Also see "The Educative Value of Cookery," *Report of the Commissioner of Education, 1888-1889*, Volume One, (Washington, 1890) p. 419.

5. For an overview of this process see Cremin, *The Transformation of the School*, p. 32. Cremin emphasized the role of organized labor and businessmen's associations in promoting manual labor. These organizations almost always saw manual education as male education, a point which underscores the different purposes which educators and laymen alike assigned to male and female training in this period. For a sample of Calvin Woodward's views regarding manual training, see his article "Manual, Industrial and Technical Education in the United States," in *Report of the Commissioner of Education, 1903*, Volume One (Washington, 1904) p. 1019, a piece excerpted from the Encyclopedia Americana. Also see Berenice Fisher, *Industrial Education* (Madison, 1967) p. 76. Another reflection of the greater interest expressed by educators and other proponents of manual education in boys was enrollments in these courses. Of sixty six industrial and manual training schools surveyed by the Commissioner of Education in 1896, only 35 offered courses in sewing and cooking. Many such schools excluded women altogether. Enrollments nationally in manual education courses that year paralleled this pattern: males outnumbered females by nearly two to one. By 1902 the number of manual training schools in the U.S. had multiplied dramatically, to over two hundred thirty, and a substantially larger portion of these schools were coeducational. This openness was reflected in the male/female ratio, which was about 3 to 2, including both elementary and secondary schools. But the ratio of men to women in secondary manual education classes, where the social purposes of the manual training movement were most evident, remained close to two to one. Manual training, particularly as it was associated with vocational concerns, was a male dominated curriculum throughout the opening decade of the twentieth century. See "Statistics of Manual and Industrial Training, Branches Taught," *Annual Report of the Commissioner of Education, 1896-97*, Volume Two (Washington, 1898) p. 2285; and "Manual and Industrial Training," *Annual Report of the Commissioner of Education, 1902*, Volume Two (Washington, 1903) p. 1964.

6. For an elaboration of these points, see Cremin, *Transformation of the School*, Chapter Two, "Education and Industry." One of the key features of this shift was the growing role of the National Association of Manufacturers, followed by the American Federation of Labor, both of which threw their weight behind *trade education*, or training in specific skills associated with certain occupational categories. Woodward and other early advocates of manual education were opposed to trade education because they believed it to be too skill-specific. In this regard, see Fisher, *Industrial Education*, p. 75. Cremin appears to have overlooked this issue, and treats manual education and trade education as synonomous.

7. An account of the proceedings of the NSPIE convention is given in the *Annual Report of the Commissioner of Education, 1909*, Volume One (Washington, 1910) p. 194. For an overview of the discussion of women, see Bulletin No. 6 of the NSPIE, "Industrial Education of Girls." Also see Krug, *Shaping of the American High School*, p. 226.

8. The quote is taken from the constitution of the AHEA, reprinted in the *Annual Report of the Commissioner of Education, 1909*, Volume One, p. 178. Also see "Home Economics" on page nine of the same volume for an overview of home economics as a new area of study.

9. Ellen H. Richards, "The Social Significance of the Home Economics Movement," *JHE* 3:2 (April 1911): 117, 122. Also see Bertha M. Terrill, "A Study of Household Expenditures," *JHE*, 1:4 (December 1909):399; James P. Warbasse, "The Education of Girls in Domestic Sociology and the Arts of Homemaking," *JHE*, 3:1 (February 1911):52; David Kinley and Frank A. Fetter, "Economics and Household Science," *JHE*, 3:3 (June 1911):259.

10. See, for instance, Katherine Eggleston, "What Ought to be Done to Make the Schools Useful to Our Daughters?," *Women's Home Companion*, 36:9 (September 1909):20; David Snedden, "Current Problems in Home Economics," *JHE*, 6:5 (December 1914):430; and Anna Zalor Burdick, "The Wage-Earning Girl and Home Economics," *JHE*, 11:8 (August 1919):327.

11. Richards, "The Social Significance of the Home Economics Movement," p. 122; Elizabeth C. Condit and L. D. Harvey, "A School for Homemakers," *Annual Report of the Commissioner of Education, 1911*,

p. 313. Also see Elizabeth C. Condit, "Teaching Home Economics as a Profession," *JHE*, 11:6 (December 1910):591, and "Progress in Vocational Education," *Report of the Commissioner of Education, 1913*, Volume One (Washington, 1914) p. 252.

12. Agnes Houston Craig, "Report and Recommendation on Domestic Art Education," *JHE* 4:3 (June 1912): 272; Frank Gilbreth, "Scientific Management in the Household," *JHE* 4:5 (November 1912):438; Bertha M. Terrill, "A Study of Household Expenditures," JHE 1:4 (December 1909):399; Ellen Richards, "The Outlook in Home Economics," *JHE* 2:1 (February 1910):17.

13. Ellen H. Richards, "Wanted: A Test for 'Man Power'," *JHE* 5:1 (February 1913):60.

14. Mrs. Annie L. Hansen, "The Work of the Domestic Educator," in *The Education of the Immigrant*, Bulletin No. 12. U.S. Bureau of Education, 1914, p. 7; Dr. Mather Sill, "Malnutrition of School Children in New York City," *JHE* 1:4 (December 1909):396; Mabel H. Kitteredge, "The Need of the Immigrant," *JHE* 5:4 (October 1913):315; and "Methods of Americanization" (Editorial), *JHE* 11:2 (February 1919):85.

15. For discussion of early efforts to adapt home economics to "education for life," see Lawrence Cremin's account of curricular reform in Denver in the twenties, in *Transformation of the School*, 301. For a broad discussion of the twenties as a period of conservatism generally, see John D. Hicks, *Republican Ascendency* (New York, 1960) passim.

16. See Kinley and Fetter, "Economics and Household Science," p. 225. They argued that housework ought to be socially recognized as work. Other discussions of housework as a peculiarly female vocation include *Education for the Home*, Bulletin No. 18, Bureau of Education, 1910, p. 7; "Homemaking as a Vocation for Girls" in *Cooking in the Vocational School*, Bulletin No. 1, U.S. Bureau of Education, 1915, p. 7. Interestingly, proponents of home economics stressed its vocational value less as time wore on. In the 1920s articles in the *JHE* increasingly stressed such themes as good family relations and the moral value of clean living. In 1919 a survey of school principals and superintendents across the country revealed that nearly 40 percent felt that home economics was included in the curriculum for cultural rather than vocational ends. The remainder felt that vocational purposes were most important. See "Manual Arts and Homemaking Subjects," *Annual Report of the Commissioner of Education, 1920*, Volume One (Washington, 1921) p. 23. For an example of the thinking that characterized supporters of home economics in the twenties see Emma A. Winslow, "An Experiment in Socializing Home Economics Education," *JHE* 12:1 (January 1920):26; Francis Zuill, "Objectives in Home Economics for the Seventh, Eighth and Nineth Grades," *JHE* 16:3 (March 1924):107; and Cora M. Winchell, "Home Economics at the Crossroads," JHE 18:10 (October 1926):553.

17. For a discussion of enrollment levels in these courses, see John L. Rury, "Women, Cities and Schools: Education and the Development of an Urban Female Labor Force, 1890-1930," (Unpublished Ph.D. dissertation, University of Wisconsin, 1982) p. 295.

18. For a discussion of early courses in commercial subjects in American schools, see Krug, *The Shaping of the American High School*, p. 6.

19. Public educators railed against what they considered to be the unscruplous recruiting methods employed by some of these schools: open solicitation of prospective students in the public schools, often with exaggerated accounts of the financial returns to attending a business school. And investigators charged with determining the quality of education offered in these institutions reported that some were run by men intent upon deliberately cheating people. Yet there were also established schools with deserved reputations for effective instruction in the various branches of commercial education. Apart from occasional flashes of information revealed in surveys conducted to uncover evidence of fraud in these schools, little is known about the educational opportunities they offered. Prior to 1890, fully eighty percent of all commercial instruction in the country was conducted by private business schools. For a discussion of the recruiting methods employed by private business schools, and educators' responses to them, see Leverett S. Lyon, *Education for Business* (Chicago, 1922) p. 284. Interestingly, Lyon suggests that recruiters for private business schools appealed more to female students than to males.

20. Leverett S. Lyon, *A Survey of Commercial Education in the Public High Schools of the United States* (Chicago, 1919) "Introduction." Also see Lyon, *Education for Business*, p. 5; and U.S. Bureau of Education, *Biennial Survey of Education, 1926-28*, (Washington, 1930) p. 1058. For discussion of the way in which educators viewed the expansion of clerical enrollments, see Janice Weiss, "Education for Clerical Work: A History of Clerical Work in the United States Since 1850," (Unpublished Ed.D. dissertation, Harvard University, 1978) p. 135. Weiss accepts the candid observations of contemporaries that commercial education was an enormous boost to overall enrollment levels. My own research, however, indicates that enrollments rose in all different types of urban settings, independently of the type of labor markets they confronted. The rapid growth of commercial enrollments may have led some educators to believe that demand for commercial education was a driving force behind the growth of secondary education in this

period, but enrollments clearly did not respond primarily to increased demand for clerical labor. See Rury, "Women, Cities and Schools," Chapter Five, "Education and Employment."

21. Lyon, *Education for Business*, p. 5. The power of private schools to draw disaffected students away from the high schools with the lure of quick entry into the relatively well-paying world of office work was a common complaint among educators in this period. Yet the fact that the business schools were relegated to dealing with high school dropouts suggests that the high school business curriculum was the first, and hence for whatever reason the preferred, choice for most teenage youth seeking business related skills.

22. Ibid., p. 284. In his survey of the commercial course in public high schools, Lyon found that only 14% of the high school courses were a year or less. Most private business school courses could be completed within five or six months. Lyon, *A Survey of Commercial Education*, p. 13, On the dropout problem also see F. V. Thompson, *Commercial Education in Public Secondary Schools* (Yonkers, N.Y., 1915) pp. 92-96, and Albert H. Leake, *The Vocational Education of Girls and Women*, p. 354.

23. When educators discussed commercial education they generally started by acknowledging its rapid expansion, and turned to a series of recommendations for improving the business curriculum. These recommendations were virtually the same in every case. Perhaps the most important reflected an interest in fitting business education more perfectly to the needs of local business communities. The Committee on Business Education of the Kingsley Commission, a major high school policy review board, suggested that surveys be conducted by local school authorities to determine the best combinations of courses to offer, along with the establishment of cooperative education programs involving local businessmen. Other studies of business education agreed. While most educators did not classify commercial education under the general rubric of vocational education, they did believe that it had to be fitted closely to the requirements of local labor markets. The Kingsley Commission report even went as far as to suggest that business courses be offered early in four year high school course, to give dropouts an opportunity to acquire business skills before leaving school. Despite their arguments that business education was valuable for both intellectual and practical purposes, educators suggested reforms principally designed to make it more practical and efficient as a form of job preparation. See *Business Education in the Secondary Schools*, U.S. Bureau of Education Bulletin No. 32, 1919, p. 19. This bulletin reprinted the report of the Business Education Committee of the Kingsley Commission. Also see Thompson, *Commercial Education in Public Secondary Schools*, p. 30, and Lyon, *Education for Business*, p. 170.

24. Evelyn W. Allen, "Home Economics in a Girl's Commercial High School," *JHE* 13:4 (April 1921):148.

25. See Lyon, *A Survey of Commercial Education*, "Introduction," and Leake, *Vocational Education for Girls and Women*, p. 334.

26. These figures have been derived from the *Biennial Survey of Education*, Department of Education, 1918-20 and 1928-30.

27. Lyon, *A Survey of Commercial Education*, p. 45; Idem, *Education for Business*, p. 124; Thompson, *Commercial Education in Public Secondary Schools*, p. 125; and *Business Education in Secondary Schools*, p. 14.

28. Lyon, *A Survey of Commercial Education*, p. 15; Thompson, *Commercial Education in Public Secondary Schools*, p. 82.

29. Lyon, *Education for Business*, p. 297; *Biennial Survey of Education*, "The Public High School," 1927-28, p. 1078.

30. Industrial courses for women were offered in cities across the country. Male enrollments in 1920 in industrial education courses were twenty times female enrollments. See "Public High Schools," *Biennial Survey of Education*, 1920-1922. In 1910, however, one-third of all pupils enrolled in manual training and industrial schools at the secondary level were female. See "Manual and Industrial Training," *Report of the Commissioner of Education*, 1910, p. 1242.

31. *Report of the Commissioner of Education*, 1914, "Progress in Vocational Education," p. 269. Also see "Types of Vocational Secondary Schools," in *Vocational Education*, Bulletin No. 12, U.S. Bureau of Education, 1912, p. 33.

32. See Leake, *The Vocational Education of Girls and Women*, pp. 230-231 and 291.

33. Ibid., pp. 287-88.

34. Women dropped out of industrial schools, it appears, as rapidly as they did the comprehensive schools. Only a third of the Manhattan Trade School's 1200 students in 1914 eventually graduated. Another third dropped out after less than a month. See Leake, *Vocational Education for Girls and Women*, pp. 290-291.

35. *Annual Report of the Commissioner of Education*, 1901, Volume Two, "Coeducation of the Sexes in the United States," p. 1217.

36. For an overview of the debate over coeducation in this period, see John C. Maxwell, "Should the Education of Boys and Girls Differ? A Half Century of Debate," Unpublished Ph.D. dissertation, University of Wisconsin, 1966.

37. *Annual Report of the Commissioner of Education*, 1901, Volume Two, "Coeducation of the Sexes in the United States," p. 1218; *Biennial Survey of Education* 1920-1922, Public High Schools," pp. 581-594. There is evidence that industrial education courses became more male dominated with time. In 1910 2.6% of all high school women were enrolled in such courses, along with 12% of all high school men. In 1920 only one percent of all high school girls were enrolled in these courses, as opposed to 21 percent of high school boys. Men clearly were moving into industrial education at a faster rate than women.

38. See, for instance, suggestions that women be excused from math courses in *Annual Report of the Commissioner of Education*, 1913, Volume One, pp. 81-82; and *Special Features in City School Systems*, U.S. Bureau of Education Bulletin No. 31, 1913, "Segregation of the Sexes," p. 52. Also see Maxwell, "Should the Education of Boys and Girls Differ?," p. 13 and 186.

39. Maxwell, "Should the Education of Boys and Girls Differ?," p. 63; David Snedden, "Should There be a Difference in the High School Training of Boys and Girls?," *Yearbook of the New York High School Teachers Association* (1907-8) p. 39.

40. See "Coeducation of the Sexes in the United States," 1901, pp. 1219-1228; and *Report of the Commissioner of Education*, 1908, Volume One, "Coeducation," p. 90.

41. For discussion of Boston's school system in this period, see Rury, "Women, Cities and Schools," Chapter Seven, "Varieties of Adaptation: Local Studies of Women's Education and Women's Work." Educators in other cities invoked the same principle, although few school systems matched the level of differentiation exhibited in Boston or New York. Both Cleveland and Chicago, for instance, experimented with establishing separate schools for men and women in this period. Smaller communities could ill afford the cost of erecting new schools to serve either men or women alone. Yet for larger school systems, faced with the prospects of expansion to begin with, establishing sex-segregated schools was less problematic. Differentiation, it appears, helped to undermine coeducation in several of the nation's leading school systems. Leake, *The Vocational Education of Girls and Women*, p. 273; Maxwell, "Should the Education of Boys and Girls Differ?," p. 177; Thompson, *Commercial Education in Public Secondary Schools*, p. 143.

42. Maxwell, "Should the Education of Boys and Girls Differ?," Conclusion.

13

The School Achievement of
Immigrant Children: 1900–1930

Michael R. Olneck and Marvin Lazerson

PUBLIC SCHOOLING has held a central place in the mythologies cele-
brating the assimilation of immigrants into American life. It is no surprise
then to find that the historiography of schooling and immigration has been
characterized by a good deal of polemic and a paucity of data. Depending
upon their political persuasions, scholars have either described the schools
as an immense success in providing opportunities, or as reactionary institutions designed to perpetuate the existing class order. (1)

Scholars have also tended to concentrate on "the immigrant experience,"
and to neglect differences between nationality groups. While the popular
imagination has been dominated by the idea of the melting pot, professional
scholarship has tended to focus on the themes of alienation and disorientation. (2) We feel that the tendencies to characterize the history of immigrants and schools in these monolithic fashions have seriously obscured complex and varied patterns of experience, and have prevented historians from
pursuing the kinds of comparative analyses which such patterns demand.
While we cannot offer a full treatment of all the questions which might be
asked about immigrants and schools, we hope that the data and analyses
presented here will direct attention to where it properly belongs: the dimensions, sources, and consequences of differential patterns of adaptation to American institutions. (3)

The issue which we treat is limited, but it is a beginning point of an effort
to understand the roles schools played in assimilating immigrants into American culture, and in offering them avenues toward economic mobility. We
are concerned here with the school achievement of immigrant children com-

*Michael R. Olneck is associate professor of educational policy studies and of sociology at the
University of Wisconsin—Madison. Marvin Lazerson is dean of the Graduate School of Education at the University of Pennsylvania.*

pared to the achievement of children of native, white Americans, and with variations in school achievement between different nationality groups. (4)

The data which we draw on come from a variety of sources, all of them inadequate in some serious respects. We are limited in the measures of achievement that are available, in the accuracy of reports on the school performance and the socioeconomic characteristics of specific groups, and in the susceptibility of the data to combination and analysis. These limitations must be borne in mind throughout. They mean that despite any appearances of exactitude, whatever calculations or manipulations we have made, the data give only approximations and orders of magnitude. We believe, however, that the data we report and try to explain, suggest important conclusions about patterns of immigrant adaptation which might otherwise be ignored in the absence of "hard" data.

What follows is first a comparison of the children of the foreign-born to the children of white, native-born parents on measures of school attendance and school continuance during the first thirty years of this century. Then the performance of specific nationality groups compared to one another and to the children of native whites is analyzed on the basis of continuance, completion, and retardation rates, and on the basis of sex ratios at the secondary level. The last sections consider in detail two specific nationality groups: Southern Italians and Russian Jews. An effort is made to account for the differences between these two groups in school performance by considering the effects of nationality differences in parental length of residence in the United States, home language, age at school entrance, standardized test scores, and occupational and income levels. The inadequacies of differences on these measures to fully account for Italian-Jewish differences on school performance lead us to suggest the continuing importance of varying cultural factors for shaping the responses of these immigrant groups to the schools. We turn to these factors in the final section.

Immigrant Children and Children of Native Whites

During the first three decades of the twentieth century, the younger children of immigrants were as likely to be in school as children of native-born whites. At older age levels, however, they neither attended nor completed school in the same proportions as children of native whites. Throughout the schooling process, they were more likely to be older than other children in the same grade and were more likely to drop out when legally permitted, though the trend after 1920 was for most children to stay in school longer. These findings suggest that while attendance in elementary school was roughly similar for immigrants and non-immigrants, rates of progress through school varied. Nevertheless, the differences between native-born and immigrant were not large, and they were especially small for immigrant children from English-speaking homes. Only at the point of high school entrance did substantial disparities become evident.

Table 1 shows the national attendance rates for children of native whites, native-born children of foreign or mixed parents, and for foreign-born children in 1910, 1920, and 1930.

TABLE 1

Percent of Children Attending School in U.S. by Age
and Parentage; 1910, 1920, 1930

Date	Background	Age-Group			
		7–13	*14–15*	*16–17*	*18–20*
1910	Native white of native white parents	88	80	51	20
	Native of foreign or mixed parents	93	74	37	12
	Foreign-born	87	59	18	5
1920	Native white of native white parents	92	84	49	18
	Native of foreign or mixed parents	94	78	35	19
	Foreign-born	84	67	24	7
1930	Native white of native white parents	96	90	61	24
	Native of foreign or mixed parents	98	91	54	12
	Foreign-born	98	93	52	16

Source: U.S. Bureau of the Census, *Abstract of the Fifteenth Census of the United States* (Washington, 1933), p. 261; see also T. J. Woofter, Jr., *Races and Ethnic Groups in American Life* (New York, 1933), p. 166.

Table 1 tells us what proportion of children of a given age were in school at a particular time. But since children of the same age were not necessarily in the same grade, Table 1 cannot be used to make quantitative comparisons about educational attainment, though it is a safe inference that as attendance became more equal so did eventual attainment. This issue of the relationship between age and grade figured prominently in the educational debates of the early twentieth century. In city after city, researchers and administrators found that large numbers of elementary pupils were not in the grade considered normal for their age level, a condition universally defined as "retardation." (5) Using as a measure children two or more years behind their normal grade level, the U.S. Commission on Immigration found high proportions of children retarded in twelve major cities in 1908. But the Commission also found only five percent more of the children of immigrants were behind than children of native whites. Immigrant children from English language nationalities were virtually equal to children of native whites in school progress, and only 7 percent more of the children from foreign-language speaking nationalities were behind than were those of native whites. (Table 2)

TABLE 2

Percent of 10, 11, and 12 Year-olds "Retarded" in School
Progress in 1908, by Parentage and City

City	Native White	Foreign English Lang. Groups	Foreign-Non English Lang. Groups	All Foreign
Twelve Cities	41	40	47	46
Eleven Cities (excludes N.Y.)	42	37	48	46
Boston	11	14	20	17
Buffalo	18	19	37	33
Chicago	36	40	45	44
Cincinnati	40	47	46	46
Cleveland	30	34	43	42
Detroit	38	43	52	49
Newark	54	58	65	64
New York	41	46	46	46
Philadelphia	52	54	61	59
Pittsburgh	55	63	63	63
Providence	25	29	45	39
St. Louis	62	65	67	67

Source: U.S. Immigration Commission, *Reports* (Washington, 1911), vols. 30–35, calculated from city by city tables on retardation.

Within individual cities, the picture is more complicated. Promotion practices varied from city to city, so that the proportion of all students that were retarded shows a wide range. In the largest cities especially, immigrants were progressing at close to the same rate as children of the native born. In only five cities was the gap between those children and immigrant children greater than 15 percent of the city's overall retardation rate. Indeed, immigrant school progress was actually more equal to the progress of children of native whites than Table 2 indicates. Immigrant children tended to enter school at a later age than did children of native whites, and since late entrants were classified as retarded even where they were making normal progress through school, some portion of the apparent gap between the two groups was due to disproportionate late entrance among immigrants. There is some indication that almost all of the gap could be due to this factor.

This becomes clear when the Immigration Commission *Summary* data for children over age 8 in a selected subsample is reanalyzed. When foreign language group children are assumed to have the same proportion of normal age entrants as children of native whites, the difference in retardation falls from 15 percent to 2 percent. (6)   This result suggests that the gap of only 6 percent between immigrant children of foreign-language nationalities and children of native whites observed in the dozen major cities would be considerably reduced if age of entrance could be taken into account.

It would be possible, of course, for retardation rates of groups to have been similar, and for the groups to have differed on other measures of school progress. One measure for which we can draw tentative conclusions is the proportion of students completing grammar school. In the Immigration Commission data, children with foreign-born parents were only slightly less likely to have attended eighth grade, providing they had attended seventh grade. (7) This finding reinforces our sense that the progress immigrant children made in the lower grades was little different from the progress that children of native whites made.

At the point of high school entrance, however, sharper disparities become evident, though they were not consistent across cities. Perhaps these disparities resulted from the proportion of school-age population drawn from the immigrant communities or from the varying ethnic composition of the foreign-born population. In three of five major cities in 1908, we found the proportion of eighth graders beginning high school was around 20 percent higher for children of native whites than for immigrant children. (Table 3) Having begun high school, however, the immigrant child in New York and Chicago had about the same chance of reaching the Senior year as did a child of native white parents. In Boston, where a substantially higher proportion of all pupils continued on to the ninth grade, this was not the case. There the proportion of children of native whites who began ninth grade and reached twelfth grade exceeded the proportion of similar children

TABLE 3

Approximate Percent of Eighth Graders Beginning High
School and Percent of Ninth Graders Reaching
Senior Year, by Parentage; 1908

City	Parentage	Ratio of Ninth Graders to Eighth Graders	Ratio of Twelfth Graders to Ninth Graders
Boston	Native White	71	23
	Foreign	54	13
Chicago	Native White	57	25
	Foreign	37	20
New York	Native White	54	20
	Foreign	34	17
Philadelphia	Native White	56	21
	Foreign	50	23
St. Louis	Native White	56	24
	Foreign	41	32

Source: Calculated from U.S. Immigration Commission, *Reports* (Washington, 1911), vol. 33, pp. 190–193, 564–568 and vol. 34, pp. 624–628.

with foreign parents by 10 percent. In Philadelphia, the disparity at the point of high school entrance was trivial, and in both Philadelphia and St. Louis high school persistence slightly favored children of immigrants.

When we thus compare children of foreign parentage to those of native-born parents during the early part of this century, it seems clear that the former were somewhat more disadvantaged on such measures as school attendance, age-grade retardation, high school entry and high school completion. The differences, however, were negligible for the elementary years and were not particularly striking once children entered high school. The line of demarcation appears to have been between completion of grammar school and high school entry.

School Progress and Nationality Groups

Comparisons between children of the foreign-born and children of native, white Americans are important because they permit some generalizations about the degree and manner in which the immigrants responded to the schools. But such comparisons can also be misleading. For example, finding that immigrant school progress at the elementary level was about equal to the progress of children of native whites suggests that adaptation to the public school was proceeding uniformly. That immigrants were also less likely to begin high school suggests that there was some uniform influence which prevented them from taking advantage of the public secondary schools. The problem with such conclusions, however, is that they obscure a more basic finding: there was no single immigrant experience in the schools. Nationality groups varied substantially on such measures as elementary school retardation, grammar school continuance, high school entrance, continuance, and completion, and in the ratio of males to females in high school.

The evidence to support these contentions is striking. Data compiled on elementary school retardation reveal a few immigrant groups at less than the average of children of native whites, and some groups with unusually high rates of retardation. Table 4 shows the percent of 10 through 12 year olds who were two or more years over-age for grade level in three major cities in 1908.

Despite certain anomalies in these results (e.g. why were German-Jews in Boston so advantaged on school progress?), we are most impressed with the consistency of findings across cities. It would be fortunate if we could compare these data to comparable data for subsequent years, separating the children of newcomers from those of long-term residents. We cannot, but what scanty data we do have suggest the persistent impact of nationality background on elementary school progress. For example, the results of a

TABLE 4

Percent of 10, 11, and 12 Year Old "Retarded" in
School Progress in 1908, by Nationality
Group and City

Father's Birth	Boston	Chicago	New York
Native white	11(.64)*	36(.74)	41(.85)
Native black	24(1.39)	64(1.31)	72(1.49)
English	15(.87)	41(.84)	45(.93)
Swedish	12(.70)	30(.61)	36(.75)
German	12(.70)	41(.84)	33(.68)
Irish	13(.75)	45(.92)	49(1.02)
Hebrew-German	06(.35)	36(.74)	33(.68)
Hebrew-Russian	19(1.10)	50(1.02)	46(.95)
Southern Italian	36(2.41)	72(1.47)	69(1.43)
Polish	25(1.44)	74(1.51)	58(1.20)
Average Group Rate**	17	49	48

*Ratio of group rate to average group rate.
**Arithmetic average of separate group rates. Equivalent to city rate standardized for unequal
nationality composition.
Source: U.S. Immigration Commission, *Reports* (Washington, 1911), vols. 31 and 33, calculated
from city by city tables on retardation.

study conducted in New York in 1933 paralleled the findings of the 1908
Immigration Commission. Schools in which Poles and Italians predominated
were characterized by retardation rates higher than the city average, while
schools in which Germans and Jews predominated were characterized by
rates lower than the city average. (8)

We saw earlier that the proportion of seventh graders continuing on to

TABLE 5

Approximate Percent of Seventh Graders Continuing to
Eighth Grade in Boston, Chicago, and New York,
Combined; by Nationality, 1908

Father's Birth	% Seventh Graders Beginning Eighth Grade
Native white	80
Native black	66
English	82
Swedish	81
German	75
Irish	80
Hebrew-German	82
Hebrew-Russian	74
Southern Italian	58
Polish	62

Source: Calculated from U.S. Immigration Commission, *Reports* (Washington, 1911), vol. 31,
pp. 190–193, 564–578 and vol. 34, pp. 624–628.

the last grade of grammar school was only slightly greater for children of native whites than for immigrant children. However, grammar school continuance, like elementary retardation, depended to a considerable extent on nationality. For some groups, over eighty percent of the seventh graders continued on to eighth grade, while for others, the figure was closer to sixty percent. Table 5 shows the ratio of the number of eighth graders to the number of seventh graders in three cities combined in 1908.

Differences between nationality groups were even more pronounced at the secondary level than they were at the elementary level. High school entrance, continuance, and completion varied appreciably from group to group. In 1908, only a minority of grammar school graduates continued on to high school. However, for some groups, close to or more than half of the eighth graders began ninth grade. At the other extreme, for some groups, less than a quarter of the eighth graders began the ninth grade, usually the first year of high school. Table 6 shows the ratio of the number of ninth graders to the number of eighth graders in Boston, Chicago, and New York, combined.

Almost 60 percent of the eighth graders with native white parents began high school in these three cities. Almost half of the black, English, Irish, and German Jewish eighth graders began high school. Around a third of the German, Russian Jewish, and Swedish eighth graders continued, and slightly under a quarter of the Italians did.

Comparing rates of retardation and rates of continuance, it is clear that a precise relationship did not exist between the two. While high retardation

TABLE 6

Approximate Percent of Grammar School Graduates
Entering High School in Boston, Chicago, and
New York, Combined, by Nationality, 1908

Father's Birth	% Eighth Graders Beginning Ninth Grade
Native white	58
Native black	49
English	47
Swedish	33
German	33
Irish	51
Hebrew-German	46
Hebrew-Russian	35
Southern Italian	23
Polish	*

*n less than 200

Source: Calculated from U.S. Immigration Commission, *Reports* (Washington, 1911), vol. 31, pp. 190–193, 564–568 and vol. 34, pp. 624–628.

rates were usually followed by low continuance levels, low retardation rates were not invariably accompanied by high continuance levels. Germans and Swedes did not continue into the ninth grade at the levels expected by their low retardation rates. In part, we believe this is so because retardation studies usually failed to account for age of entrance, and the apparent advantage of some groups might have been inflated due to this factor. Groups that entered school late would appear retarded even if they were progressing at normal rates. This seems to have been the case for Russian Jews. An alternative explanation would focus on the occupational options open to young adolescents. Swedish and German youth might have been attracted away from school by entry into skilled crafts via apprenticeships or family contacts. Our data do not allow us to pursue these possibilities at present.

In the years after 1908, high school attendance rose for everyone. However, nationality groups continued to differ in their rates of attendance. Data which are directly comparable to the Immigration Commission data presented above are not available. However, for at least one city—Cleveland— we can compare the number of students in high school to the number of students in all the elementary grades at two points in time. Table 7 indicates that the rate of high school attendance for Germans and Jews almost doubled, while the rate for Italians and Poles showed no increase between 1908 and 1916. This result could be misleading, however, if the age composition of the Italian and Polish groups was altered by new immigration during those eight years, while that of the other groups was unchanged. Though we doubt its effect, our data do not permit checking this possibility.

We have already seen that children of immigrants were only slightly less likely than children of native whites to reach their senior year if they be-

TABLE 7

Number of High School Students per 100 Elementary School
Students, by Language Groups; Cleveland, 1908 and 1916

Language Group	1908	1916
English	14	17
German	7	14
Yiddish (Jewish)	5	9
Italian	2	2
Polish	2	3

Source: Calculated from U.S. Immigration Commission, *Reports* (Washington, 1911), vol. 31, pp. 780–783 and Herbert Miller, *The School and the Immigrant* (Philadelphia, 1916), pp. 80–81.

The comparison is not exact because the classification of the later data is by home language, and so children of foreign parents who used English at the time of the survey would have been classified with children of native Americans. The comparison also requires combining the English speaking nationality groups of 1908 into one category.

TABLE 8

High School Progress and Nationality; Selected Studies

New York, Boston, Chicago — 1908		Bridgeport, Conn. 1922		Hartford, Conn. 1925	
Father's Birth	Ratio of Seniors to Freshman	Father's Birth	Ratio Seniors to Freshman	Nationality	Ratio of Juniors to Freshman
U.S. white	.22	U.S.	.44	U.S. white	.64
U.S. black	.20	Scand.	.37	Scand.	.48
English	.20	German	.61	German	.44
Swedish	.18	Irish	.48	Irish	.34
German	.18	Russian (Jew.)	.51	Jewish	.80
Irish	.16	Italian	.17	Italian	.28
Heb.-German	.18	Polish	.15	Polish	.24
Heb.-Russian	.19				
South. Italy	.08				
Polish	*				

*n less than 125

Source: U.S. Immigration Commission, *Reports* (Washington, 1911), vol. 31, pp. 190–193, 564–568 and vol. 34, pp. 624–628; George S. Counts, *The Selective Character of American Secondary Education* (Chicago, 1922), p. 108; Gustave Feingold, "Intelligence of the First Generation of Immigrant Groups," *The Journal of Educational Psychology*, 15 (1924).

gan high school. (Table 3)   But as was the case with entrance, progress through secondary school was closely tied to nationality. Table 8 summarizes the results of studies of high school progress from 1908 to 1925.

The results of Table 8 cannot be used to make any firm inferences about the exact proportion of high school students of a given nationality group that completed the four year course. High school persistence, however, rose over time, so that the proportion of entering students who finished went from around a fifth in 1908 to closer to a half in the mid-1920's. It is also clear that only the Poles and the Italians consistently failed to reach the last two years of high school in proportions reasonably close to the average. There is some city by city variation among groups. Compared to other nationality groups, the Irish, for example, were doing considerably less well in Hartford than in Bridgeport. Finally, while the high rate of continuance for Jews in Hartford was exceptional, it does indicate the beginning of a trend in which Jewish educational attainment exceeded that of most other groups. (9)

Another way of viewing the distinctions among nationality groups is by comparing secondary school attendance by sex. If there were no cultural factors that affected attendance in the secondary schools, we would expect that the sex ratios among high school students would be the same from group to group. We would also expect the proportions of males and females among immigrants to be about the same as for native Americans. In fact, the sex ratios among high school students varied substantially from group to group. Table 9 shows the number of female high school students per 100 male students for three major cities in 1908, and for Bridgeport High School in 1922.

For most groups, girls were more likely to have been in high school than boys. This was especially true among the Irish, English, and children of native Americans. There is good economic reason why this should have been the case. Employment opportunities for men without high school training were greater than the opportunities for untrained women. Men could take industrial jobs. The sectors of the economy that were growing which were open to women often required preparation in skills. This was true for secretarial and office work, and for teaching. In Bridgeport, in 1922, well over three-quarters of the high school girls were enrolled in the Commercial and Normal tracks. High School attendance did not offer boys the same specific job preparation. For boys, high school was principally the route to college, and that was a route only a small minority of any group would follow. (10)

It thus made more economic sense, at least in the short run, for boys to take jobs and girls to continue on in school. Yet for Russian Jews, Poles, and Southern Italians, the groups we suspect were economically the most impoverished, males predominate over females in high school attendance. In part, we believe this to be the result of cultural attitudes toward the educa-

TABLE 9

Number of Female High School Students per 100
Male Students, by Parentage; Boston,
Chicago, and New York, Combined,
1908, and Bridgeport, 1922

Boston, Chicago, New York 1908		Bridgeport 1922	
Father's Birth	Females per 100 Males	Father's Birth	Females per 100 Males
Native white	135	U.S.	134
English	161	British Emp.	131
Swedish	131	Scand.	116
German	103	German	122
Irish	137	Irish	135
Hebrew-German	107	Russian (Jewish)	97
Hebrew-Russian	76	Italian	65
South. Italian	48	Polish	92
Polish	64		

Source: U.S. Immigration Commission, *Reports* (Washington, 1911), vol. 31, pp. 190–193, 564–568 and vol. 34, pp. 624–628; George S. Counts, *The Selective Character of American Secondary Education* (Chicago, 1922), p. 113.

tion of the sexes. Russian Jews historically tended to place a high premium on schooling of the male child. (11) In the United States, college attendance leading to professional occupational status replaced religious study as the mark of highest success. Russian Jews were being sent to high school almost exclusively to prepare them for college entrance. In Bridgeport in 1922, for example, 90 percent of the Russian Jewish boys were in the College or Scientific tracks of the high school compared to 75 percent of the males with native-born fathers. (12)

For Italians, male predominance among high school students is probably explained not by a special positive valuation of schooling for boys, but by a strong cultural aversion to sending girls to school. Italian parents felt, more strongly than most, that girls required close parental supervision and that they should be preparing for their future roles as homemakers. (13)

There was, then, no single immigrant experience in the schools. In the absence of statistically reliable and longitudinal studies, our conclusions cannot be precise. Yet it does seem clear that some groups made slower progress through school than others. Some groups were more likely to finish grammar school than others. It also seems evident that going on to and continuing in high school depended to a considerable extent on nationality and that the sex ratio at the secondary level was also related to nationality. Finally, we are struck by the extent to which nationality background continued to influence school achievement over time. This means that group differences in school performance cannot be accounted for solely by differences which existed at the outset of life in the United States. While immigration continually introduced large numbers of people who were beginning the process of assimilation, by the 1920's the school population, particularly the high school population, included large numbers of children whose parents had been in this country for some time. The persistence of nationality differences in the schools over time is strong evidence that groups were adapting to public education at different rates.

Russian Jews and Southern Italians

A number of characteristics tie Russian Jews and Southern Italians together. Both groups arrived in the U.S. at roughly the same time (1880-1930), were poor upon arrival, spoke little English, and settled in close proximity to one another along the Eastern seaboard. But Russian Jews and Southern Italians differed in at least two significant ways: on measures of school performance and in their occupational history. Jews arrived in the new world with higher levels of vocational skill and advanced vocationally more rapidly than did Southern Italians, and they outperformed them in school on measures of retardation and retention, and on standardized tests. The two are

related; doing better vocationally was paralleled by better school performance. Yet we will argue that differences in occupational attainment do not
fully account for differences in school achievement. Russian Jews and
Southern Italians at the same occupational level did not perform equally
well in school. Nor are differences in such variables as length of parental
residence in the U.S., age of school entrance, use of English in the home,
and scores on standardized tests sufficient to explain school differences between the two groups. The failure of either occupational level or the
other variables to account fully for these differences in school performance
leads us to suggest that group cultural values must be taken into account if
we are fully to understand school achievement.

In its summary volume on education the Immigration Commission analyzed the effects of a number of variables on elementary school retardation
rates. (14) The Commission found, for example, that the longer a student's
father had resided in the United States, the less likely the student was to
have been behind. However, ethnic differences persisted in retardation rates
within categories of length of father's residence. In the case of Russian Jews
and Southern Italians, the gap was greatest for children whose fathers had
been here the longest. (Table 10)

While inferences from cross-sectional data to processes over time are risky,
it would appear that longer residence markedly reduced the Russian Jewish
rate of retardation. The Italian rate was also substantially reduced, but not
by nearly as much. One way of showing the differential effect of father's
length of residence is to ask what would happen to the Southern Italian and
Russian Jewish rates of retardation if both groups had been here equally as
long as a third, and particularly long-term group. When the Southern Italians
are assigned the same distribution of length of residence as that of the
Germans in the sample, their overall rate of retardation falls by only 3 percent, from 63 to 60 percent. The Russian Jewish rate, however, falls from
44 to 33 percent, a rate equal to the German rate. Compared to at least one

TABLE 10

Percent Retarded by Father's Length of Residence in
the United States, Pupils Over 8 Years;
Immigration Commission Summary, 1908

	Father's Length of Residence			
Father's Birth	*Less Than 5 Years*	*5 – 9 Years*	*10 or More Years*	*All Groups*
Hebrew-Russian	75	57	31	41
South. Italian	82	75	59	63

Source: U.S. Immigration Commission, *Reports* (Washington, 1911, vol. 29, p. 92.

other group, then, Southern Italians seem to have been exceptionally immune to the effects of longer residence, while Russian Jews seem to have been quite susceptible. (15)

The later a student entered primary school, the more likely he or she was to have been retarded. This follows, of course, even if the student was making normal progress. In the Commission's sample, Russian Jews and Southern Italians were equally likely to have entered school below the age of eight, so virtually none of the Southern Italian-Russian Jewish difference in elementary retardation could be attributed to differences in age of entrance. (16). Moreover, while the vast majority of both Southern Italians and Russian Jews who entered school at 8 years or over were overage for their grade level in 1908 (92 to 83 percent), only 29 percent of the Russian Jews who entered at ages 6 or 7 were retarded, compared to 55 percent for Southern Italians. When Russian Jews are hypothetically equalized to Germans on age of entrance, their rate of elementary retardation falls by one-fifth; after such equalization, the Southern Italian rate falls by only one-tenth.

A student whose family used English in the home was more likely to have been making normal progress than a student whose home language was not English. Over two-thirds of the Southern Italians in the Commission's sample came from homes where English was not used. About half of the Russian Jews came from homes where English was not used. (17) It would be reasonable to expect that the use of English in more Russian Jewish than Italian homes accounts for a large portion of the difference in retardation rates. However, use of English in the home did not sufficiently affect Italian school progress to explain much of the group difference in retardation. When Southern Italians are assumed to have the same proportion of English-speaking homes as the Russian Jews, their rate of retardation falls by only 3 percent, reducing the gap between the groups by less than one-seventh. In the Immigration Commission data, then, Southern Italian-Russian Jewish differences in elementary retardation cannot be accounted for by differences on language use, age of school entrance, or length of father's residence in the United States.

When we turn to consider the effects of standardized test scores on school performance, we are faced with a number of complicated questions. Should a test score be treated as an outcome like any other measure of school achievement, or should it be treated as a measure of prior ability? To the extent that a test measures acquired cognitive skills, general information, and the ability and willingness to take pencil and paper tests, it measures some of the same things that grades and retardation rates measure. Explanations for test score differences could therefore apply as well to school achievement differences. That is, whatever "causes" test score differences probably "causes" school achievement differences. On the other hand, there are ways in which scores can be seen as a "cause" of school performance. If tests measure intellectual ability, and ability is a large cause of grades, then test scores can be said to "cause" school achievement. Moreover, if academic success affects whether or not a student remains in school and if ability affects grades, then test scores can be said to affect school persistence. Finally, teachers might treat students differently depending on their scores. Discriminatory treatment could affect how students feel about school and whether they continue or drop out. With these complications in mind, we will consider the magnitude of Jewish-Italian test score differences, the apparent effect of these differences on school achievement, and the possible sources of group differences on test scores. (18)

In the early part of the century, Italian and Jewish students differed in their performance on standardized tests. The extent of these differences depended upon the tests used and the samples under investigation. Our general impression, based on the few reported studies conducted in the 1920's which separated subjects by nationality, is that Jewish students scored about a half a standard deviation above Italian students. (19) Since the general literature on the relationship between test scores and measures of achievement suggests that less than half the variation in achievement was associated with variation in test scores, we are led to conclude that the advantage Jewish students enjoyed on school performance cannot be attributed solely to their advantage on test scores. (20)

Despite the risks inherent in making inferences from data about differences among individuals to differences between groups, we think that this conclusion is sound. There is a smattering of evidence that bears more directly on the question. In the 1924 study of Hartford High School, ratios between final exam scores and ability scores were calculated for Jewish, Irish, and American students. This controlled for the effect of ability scores on achievement. Jews ranked the highest on this measure of performance. In that same study, the variation in group test scores was not related to the group variation in school retention. Jews scored lower or equal to children of English, Scottish, German, and native white parents, and yet were much more likely to have reached their Junior year than were these groups. (21)

Finally, if we combine data from disparate sources, we can estimate the proportion of the difference in Jewish and Italian educational attainment associated with group test score differences. Jencks has estimated the correlation between standardized test score at age 11 and eventual educational attainment as .58. (22) This estimate is based on a number of studies in which the testing occurred during the 1920's, and so applies roughly to the population with which we are concerned. (23) We have concluded that Italian elementary students were about one half standard deviation below Jewish students on tested ability. This means that if test differences fully accounted for differences in educational attainment, Italians should be .29 standard deviations below Jews on attainment. Duncan and Duncan have reported educational attainment for a national sample of white male workers born between 1898 and 1937, by father's nationality. (24) In the Duncans' sample, a standard deviation on educational attainment was 3.30 years. Therefore, we would expect Jews to exceed Italians in attainment by slightly under a year (0.96 years). In fact, men in that sample whose fathers were born in Russia, (and are presumed to be predominantly Jewish) exceeded men whose fathers were born in Italy by 2.08 years. If our estimates are correct, then less than half of the Italian-Jewish difference in educational attainment is associated with differences in test scores.

Differences in scores, however, are still relevant to our present problem. If we can explain why there were differences in group averages on test scores we may have explained, in part, why there were differences on measures of school performance. Were the differences between Jewish and Italian scores true "nationality" differences? There is considerable evidence, for example, that parental occupational status bore a strong relationship to test scores. If it were also true that parental occupational status and nationality were confounded, we would conclude that at least some part of the apparent differences in test scores was due to group differences on occupational status.

Sorting out nationality from social class influences is exceedingly complex, in part because few studies have measured simultaneously the effects of ethnicity and parental economic status on school performance. Nonetheless, we do have data on the basis of which to posit some tentative conclusions. Though varying widely in approaches and quality, all studies of the effects of parental occupation on school achievement show considerable differences between children from various backgrounds. (25) We know that parental occupation bore a relationship to high school entry and completion, to tracking and curriculum assignment, and to test scores. (26) This suggests that what appear to have been nationality differences may in fact have been economic differences. This is partially true—social class and school success are related—but we are convinced that group differences in parental occupations and incomes are insufficient to explain group differences in eventual educational attainment. Our reasons become clear when we turn to an analysis of Russian Jewish and Southern Italian economic and educational attainment.

Jewish and Italian immigrants had very different occupational histories in both Europe and the United States. Between 1899 and 1910, almost two-thirds of the Jewish immigrants reporting Old World occupations identified themselves as skilled laborers; only 14 percent were classified as unskilled laborers. (27)   Among immigrants from Southern Italy during the same period, 15 percent reported having had skilled occupations, and 77 percent were classified as laborers. This does not necessarily mean that Jews landed any richer than others. It does mean that Jews were more prepared to enter skilled labor jobs in the United States.

Jews entered the American occupational structure at higher levels than Southern Italians did. Table 11 shows the occupational distribution of foreign-born Southern Italians and Russian Jewish men over age 16, in seven major cities in 1910.

A third of the Southern Italian immigrants in these cities had become unskilled laborers. Less than 1 percent of the Russian Jews were classified as general laborers. Over half the Jews had become manual producers. The largest proportion of these were in the needle trades, which paid higher wages than other manufacturing pursuits. (28)   Almost 30 percent of the Italians were similarly classified, but even when Italians worked in the same occupational category, and even within the clothing industry, they earned less than Jewish workers. (29)

Jewish occupational superiority was generally reflected in family incomes higher than those earned by Southern Italian families. Table 12 shows the average annual family income in five cities in 1910 for Russian Jewish and Southern Italian families. (30)

Starting with certain skill advantages, Russian Jews quickly translated these into higher occupational roles and family incomes than Southern Italians were able to achieve. This strongly suggests that ethnic differences in

TABLE 11

Occupations of Foreign-Born Southern Italian
and Russian Jewish Males Over Age 16,
in Seven Cities, 1910

Occupational Category	Southern Italian	Russian Jewish
Professional	01.5	02
Trade	13	34
Transport	09	03
Manufactures and Mechanical	29	55
Domestic and Personal	09	02.5
General Labor	32	00.5
Other	06.5	03

Source: U.S. Immigration Commission, *Reports* (Washington, 1911), vol. 1, p. 761. The cities were New York, Chicago, Philadelphia, Boston, Cleveland, Buffalo, and Milwaukee.

TABLE 12

Average Annual Income, by Nativity of Family Head

Nationality	Boston	Chicago	Cleveland	N.Y.	Phila.
Hebrew-Russian	$ 543	647	501	813	434
Southern-Italian	534	504	412	688	441

Source: U.S. Immigration Commission, *Reports* (Washington, 1911), vol. 26, pp. 226, 318, 404, 423, 577.

school performance may well have been due to economic differences. However, we are persuaded that economic differences themselves may reflect cultural values, and that the available data do not support an exclusively "economic" explanation of group differences on school performance. (31)   For example, if income differences accounted for differences in elementary school progress, we would expect to find that Italian and Jewish rates of retardation were close to equal in those cities where average incomes were equal, and to find the largest differences in retardation in those cities where average incomes were least equal. Instead, we find no apparent relationship between group income differences and differences in rates of elementary retardation. Table 13 shows the differences between the average annual family incomes of families headed by foreign-born Russian Jews and Southern Italians, and the differences in rates of retardation, for five cities.

   In the two cities where the Jewish income advantage was the greatest, Chicago and New York, Jewish students enjoyed no additional advantage in school progress over what they enjoyed in the other cities. In both Cleveland and Philadelphia, the differences in the proportions of Russian Jewish and Southern Italian students who were behind were greater than in either Chicago and New York. In relative terms, the Italian-Jewish difference in retardation was greatest in Boston, where average family income was virtually

TABLE 13

Jewish-Italian Family Income Differences (1910) and

Elementary Retardation Differences (1908);

Pupils aged 10, 11, 12

	Boston	Chicago	Cleveland	N.Y.	Phila.
Jewish Minus Italian Income	$ +09	+143	+89	+125	−07
Jewish Minus Italian Rate of Retardation	−17%	−22	−28	−23	−25
Jewish-Italian Retardation Difference as % of City Retardation Rate	100%	50	67	50	42

Source: Calculated from Tables 4 and 12 above.

equal. There, the difference in retardation of 17 percent represented 100 percent of the city's overall retardation rate. In the Immigration Commission data, then, the advantage Jewish families had over Italians in earnings does not appear to explain the advantage their children held in elementary school progress.

One should, however, make a distinction between parental occupational status and income. The former appears to have had more to do with school progress than did the latter. In some ways, this makes sense. While we would expect lower incomes to lead to early leaving from school, we would also expect that parental occupations, independent of income level, shape aspirations and motivation. Combining data from Jencks et al, and from the Duncans, as we did earlier with respect to the effect of IQ on attainment, we can estimate the effect of Italian-Jewish differences in father's occupation on group differences in educational attainment. In the Duncans' data, Russian parental occupational status exceeded Italian parental occupational status by .59 standard deviations. (32) Jencks gives the correlation between father's occupation and son's eventual education as .49. If the Jewish-Italian differences in attainment were due only to the effect of the group difference in parental occupation, we would expect Jews to exceed Italians by .29 standard deviations, or 0.96 years. This is less than half of the observed differences in attainment of 2.08 years in the Duncans' sample.

It is also exactly the amount of the difference which we found was associated with the Jewish-Italian difference in test scores. This might suggest that differences in test scores and in average parental occupation together account for almost all of the difference in attainment. However, because there is a relationship between father's occupational and test score, as well as between father's occupational status and educational attainment, and between test score and attainment, this suggestion is wrong. When these joint relationships are taken into account, we find that group differences in test scores and in parental occupation together predict a difference in attainment of 1.39 years. (33) This is substantially less than the observed difference of 2.08 years. While inferences from disparate data are suspect, it would seem that around a third of the difference between Russian Jewish and Italian males in school attainment is not explained by differences in test scores or father's occupation.

The measures of school performance that we have utilized *are* related to factors other than ethnicity. Children who entered school on time, had fathers who had been in the United States for some time, and came from homes where English was used, were more likely to have been making normal progress in elementary school than were other children. Children with higher parental occupational backgrounds scored higher on standardized tests, and were more likely to have begun, and, if they had begun, to complete high school.

Jews were more favored on most of these factors than were Italians. Jewish students were more likely to have come from homes in which English was used. They scored higher on tests, and they had fathers whose occupational status was higher than the status of Italian fathers. The differences on on these factors, however, have not proven sufficiently large to fully explain the magnitude of the differences between the two groups on indices of school performance. This leads us to conclude that group cultural values substantially affected the school progress and attainment of Russian Jewish and Southern Italian children. What some of these values were is the focus of our next section.

Ethnic Culture and School Performance

Success and persistence in school require certain capacities and competencies. Some are cognitive or intellectual, others attitudinal and behavioral. They include the ability and willingness to obey and to follow the prescribed regimen, responsiveness to the school's reward system, facility with words and abstraction, and the belief that completing school is important. While tied to immediate social and economic circumstances, these capacities and beliefs also reflect differing cultural values based in part on group histories and traditions. What different groups think about learning, schools, and teachers, how they see public institutions in general, their belief in opportunity and confidence in individual effort, and the character of the demands placed on children are not simply the effects of economic level. In the case of European immigrants, they were patterns, evolved in the Old World, which shaped group responses to American institutions and partially conditioned the manner in which groups adapted to American society.

This does not mean that each family or individual embodied all the cultural traits we discuss. Nor are we talking about innate traits or unchangeable characteristics of group behavior. Cultures are sustained and modified by circumstances, but while almost all groups in America have accepted the dominant value system, the rates and modes of assimilation have differed among groups and for individuals within groups. In our judgment, evidence drawn from anthropological sources, immigrant novels, and sociological studies makes clear that Russian Jewish culture prepared that group to fare very well in terms of educational success, and that Southern Italian culture was at odds with the demands of formal schooling in America.

Study and learning were highly valued and deeply rooted in Russian Jewish society. Orthodoxy required the study and learning of the Holy Law, while social practice institutionalized religious imperatives in an extensive system of Jewish schooling. The conduct of Jewish education trained and reinforced habits of mind that stressed mental agility, close attention to the meaning of words, and lively criticism. While few men in the Jewish town or shtetl achieved the highest levels of study, the ideal of learning and scholarship as a principal criterion of social evaluation permeated the Jewish community.

While the shtetl system of schooling was not reproduced in the United States, the traditional respect for learning seems to have been transplanted and turned to secular purposes. An old Yiddish lullaby expressed the twin hopes of Jewish parents for their sons: "My Yankele shall learn the Law/ The Law shall baby learn/Great books shall my Yankele write/Much money shall he earn." Learning was therefore both important in its own right and for its use in bringing material success. (34)

High regard for schooling did not necessarily mean that Jews would prepare their children to succeed in the public schools. Had Jews been highly suspicious of American institutions—and their experience in Russia gave reason to be wary of state institutions in a Christian country—they might have sought educational success outside the public system. Instead, they embraced America, and enthusiastically entrusted their children to its schools. Most of the literary evidence portrays Jews as "true believers" in American opportunity. Children are told that "in America you can become almost anything you wish—a fireman, a policeman, a mayor, a Congressman," and that this "is a different land we are in now, a better country—the best country on earth. It is not only overflowing with milk and honey, but with opportunities . . . If you study hard you can make anything you want of yourself." (35)

In addition to Jewish values about schooling and a belief in American opportunity, Jewish parental attitudes and practices encouraged successful school performance. Parental attitudes, like beliefs about opportunity, are tied up with attitudes about the future. The view that the conditions of the present can be improved in the future is a central tenet in Judaism. (36) In concrete terms, placing stock in the future means placing stock in the futures of children. This requires a willingness to make sacrifices for the sake of the child. One such sacrifice is to forego greater immediate economic security in order that a child complete school. A Jewish mother wrote of her dilemma as follows: "If I were to withdraw my son from high school, I could dispense with the salesman, but my motherly love and duty to the child do not permit me to take that step, for he is a very good scholar . . . I must have his assistance in order to keep my business going and take care of the other children; but at the same time I cannot definitely take him out of school . . . I lay great hopes on my child." (37) Jewish high school attendance and completion rates early in the century probably exceeded the rates of economically comparable or superior groups because of an atypical willingness on the part of Jewish families to tolerate the economic burdens of keeping their children in school longer.

The other side of the coin of parental duty is pressure on the child to succeed. The literary and the sociological evidence suggest that Jewish children were subjected to high expectations, and to child-rearing practices that demanded early individual mastery. In *Witte Arrives,* Emil thought to himself that "everybody must have an aim in life . . . Since his father had talked to him about school and opportunities, his aim was 'to make something of himself' as his father had put it, a lawyer a judge or teacher. Certainly he must grasp the opportunities which this country offered." In *Journey to the Dawn,* Moses says "the goyim really are different. Their mothers don't shout at their children as much as Jewish mothers do, and I don't think they care so much if their kids get good marks or bad ones. I mean, they care, but not as much as our mothers." (38)

Studies of parental attitudes, child-rearing practices, and achievement motivation during the 1950's and 1960's support the view of Jewish students as unusually motivated and able to meet the demands of formal schooling. In Kohn's recent study of a national sample of fathers of children aged 3 to 15, fathers of Eastern European Jewish extraction were more likely than any other group to place a high value on "self-direction" for their children. Mc-Clelland in the mid-1950's found Jews to expect a variety of individual masteries at an average age of 6.1 years, lowest for any group in his sample, and markedly lower than the average of 8.2 years for Italian Catholics. Work on achievement suggests a relationship between child-rearing practices that stress independence and mastery and achievement motivation, a finding reinforced by Strodtbeck who found Jews more likely than Italians to hold beliefs in an orderly world, amenable to rational mastery and planning, to be willing to leave home to make one's own way in life, and to prefer individual rather than collective credit for work. These differences, he argued, strongly influenced achievement differences. (39)

Whereas Russian Jewish culture seemed readily adaptable to the American educational system, Southern Italian culture stood in marked contrast to many of the values associated with school success. Italians of the *contadino* or peasant class from the *Mezzogiorno,* the southern part of Italy, constituted the vast majority of the Italian immigrants in the United States. Residents of impoverished rural hill towns, the cultural patterns which these newcomers brought with them had been conditioned by chronic poverty, a rigid social structure, and by exploitation of frequently absent landlords. Their lives practically untouched by the *Risorgimento,* the unification of Italy in the mid-nineteenth century, the views the *contadini* held about institutions like the State and schools, their responses to authority and officialdom, and their expectations for and demands on their children were initially inimical to successful advancement through America's public schools. (40)

The central and controlling feature of Italian peasant culture was the division of the world into an "us-them" polarity. "Them" were the outsiders —the State, the schools, the official church; even neighbors were considered *forestrere*, strangers. Living in a Southern Italian district during the 1930's, Carlo Levi reported that to the *contadini*, "the State is more distant than heaven and far more of a scourge because it is always against them." "Us" was the family, the blood relatives who stood together depending on one another for sustenance. In a world heavily stacked against the *contadini*, the family was the sole refuge within which trust and loyalty could be cultivated. The family required complete allegiance, viewed the outside world as off-limits, and discouraged independence and autonomy by its members. (41)

In America, the Italian family's exclusiveness was modified. A peer group society emerged that expanded upon the family structure and extended the boundaries of participation and mobility. However, the central perception of a dichotomized world persisted, and the peer group society continued to restrict its members from pursuing individual goals that would remove them from the group. (42) The conflicts that emerged in the Italian-American community between expanding one's participation in the world and loyalty to kin and peer group were cogently summarized by William F. Whyte in *Street-Corner Society*:

One of the most cherished democratic beliefs is that our society operates so as to bring intelligence and ability to the top. Clearly, the difference in intelligence and ability does not explain the different corners of Chick and Doc. There must be some other way of explaining why some Cornerville men rise while others remain stationary . . .

Chick [the college boy] and Doc [the corner boy] also had conflicting attitudes toward social mobility. Chick judged men according to their capacity for advancing themselves. Doc judged them according to their loyalty to their friends and their behavior in their personal relations . . .

Both the college boy and the corner boy want to get ahead. The difference between them is that the college boy either does not tie himself to a group of close friends or else is willing to sacrifice his friendship with those who do not advance as fast as he does. The corner boy is tied to his group by a network of reciprocal obligations from which he is either unwilling or unable to break away. (43)

In this conflict, most Southern Italian parents were undoubtedly torn; opportunity versus loyalty were not easy choices to make, and most, we suspect, hoped that both could be achieved. Yet as a group Southern Italian parents sought to train their children for family and group membership primarily, and expected that the desire for independence and mobility would be filtered through the family's larger needs. Child rearing was thus dominated by obedience and a philosophy of control: *"i figli si devono domare"*—children must be tamed. Filial obligation, more important than parental obligation, combined with the expectation that the achievements of the children would not exceed those of the parents. An old Southern Italian proverb went, "Stupid and contemptible is he who makes his children better than himself." (44)

These cultural assumptions were reinforced by a negative view of formal schooling. To the Southern Italian peasant, schools were alien institutions maintained by the upper classes at the expense of the *contadini*. In the rigid class structure of Southern Italy education as an agency of upward mobility had little meaning. The adage toward the *contadini* was, "Of what use is school to you anyway? You'll always be a peasant." Few *contadini* children went beyond third grade. School facilities were always in bad repair, while the teachers made little effort to encourage peasant children to pursue their schooling. Nor did formal education receive religious support. Catholicism in Southern Italy was marked by mysticism, the supernatural, and emotional identification with the patron saints. Rarely was the Italian peasant expected to be able to read the prayer book. Knowledge—religious and secular—was based on community folklore not on written texts, to be learned not debated or analyzed. (45)

This background ill-disposed Southern Italian immigrants to respond favorably to American schools. Schooling was seen as a direct challenge to family values and parental control. The dominant concern of many Southern Italian parents seems to have been that the school would indoctrinate their children with ideas antagonistic to the traditional codes of family life. "School education in America, as the southern Italian peasant found it," Leonard Covello observed, "not only had no appeal to him; it was conceived to be an institution demoralizing youth and disorganizing their traditional patterns of family life." Moreover, schooling, especially for adolescents, conflicted with the economic needs and expectations of Southern Italian families. Once old enough to contribute, Italian youth were expected to work. (46)

Southern Italian children may indeed have left school earlier because their families were poorer than others. Certainly the emphasis on the family's economic needs lends credence to this. But had Italian parents seen the world differently, they might have been more willing to tolerate the acute discrimination their children felt in the public schools and the economic disadvantage of continued education, and kept their children in school longer. (47)

Conclusion

Our treatment of the role cultural values played in determining the school performance of immigrant groups has been necessarily brief and methodologically limited. We have focused primarily on only two nationality groups, and we have confined our analysis to the experience of the first and second generations before World War II. We have not charted the extent to which or the reasons why the impact of ethnic cultures diminished—if they did— in the post-War period. We feel, though, that the argument we have made and the data we have presented support the view that immigrant groups were not indistinguishable masses awaiting civic remodelling in the schools. Nor were they merely collections of individuals bound together by common ancestry and present economic plight. In large measure, immigrants acted on group values and preferences in responding to the institutions which touched their lives.

This does not mean that some groups did not want to succeed in America. We believe that the rules of schooling were often insensitive to group differences. Indeed, the growth of parochial schools during the early twentieth century suggests that public educators and their supporters were unwilling to modify in any substantial way their views of the "American way." Nor do our findings lead us to argue that all groups were free to determine their destinies unhindered by the demands and discriminations of the economic and social system. Nevertheless, within that system there were choices, and the kinds of choices groups made, their priorities, how they perceived the trade-offs, and the levels of trauma they experienced were related in large measure to the ethnic culture they brought with them and reordered in the American environment. The limits of toleration within that environment is the other half of the picture, one we expect to pursue in further work.

Notes

1. Contrast Timothy Smith, "Immigrant Social Aspirations and American Education, 1880-1930," *American Quarterly*, 21 (Fall, 1969) with Colin Greer, *The Great School Legend* (New York, 1972).
2. For a critique of the melting pot belief, see Nathan Glazer and Daniel P. Moynihan, *Beyond the Melting Pot* (Cambridge, 1963), and Milton M. Gordon, *Assimilation in American Life* (New York, 1964). Oscar Handlin, *The Uprooted* (New York, 1951) sets out the themes of alienation and disorientation in the immigrant experience.

3. A number of recent studies emphasize diversity among immigrant groups. See Rudolph J. Vecolli, "Ethnicity: A Neglected Dimension of American History," in *The State of American History*, edited by Herbert J. Bass (Chicago, 1970); Vecolli, "Contadini in Chicago: A Critique of *The Uprooted*," *Journal of American History*, 51 (1964); Vecolli, "Prelates and Peasants: Italian Immigrants and the Catholic Church," *Journal of Social History*, (1969); Victor R. Greene, "For God and Country: The Origins of Slavic Catholic Self-Consciousness in America," *Church History*, 35 (1966).

4. For a similar, though more limited example, see David K. Cohen, "Immigrants and the Schools," *Review of Educational Research*, 40 (1970).

5. For example, see Leonard P. Ayres, *Laggards in Our Schools* (New York, 1908).

6. Calculated from U. S. Immigration Commission, "The Children of Immigrants in the Schools," *Reports* (Washington, D.C., 1911), vol. 29, pp. 63-64.

7. Ratios of the number of eighth grade students to the number of seventh grade students were calculated for nativity groups for Boston, Chicago, and New York. The differences were trivial. U. S. Immigration Commission, *Reports*, vol. 31, pp. 190-193, 564-568; vol. 34, pp. 624-628.

8. J. B. Maller, "Economic and Social Correlatives of School Progress in New York City," *Teachers College Record*, 34 (1933): 664.

9. In Detroit, for example, by 1935, 70 percent of the Jewish youth had graduated from high school compared to 40 percent of the non-Jewish youth. Nathan Glazer, "Social Characteristics of American Jews," in Louis Finkelstein, *The Jews* (New York, 1949), II, 1712.

10. George S. Counts, *The Selective Character of American Secondary Education* (Chicago, 1922), pp. 111-112.

11. See Mark Zborowski and Elizabeth Herzog, *Life is with People: The Culture of the Shtetl* (New York, 1952), Part II, ch. 2.

12. Counts, *Selective Character*, p. 112.

13. See especially Leonard Covello, *The Social Background of the Italo-American School Child* (Leiden, Netherland, 1967), p. 292. We believe similar attitudes held true among Poles.

14. U. S. Immigration Commission, *Reports*, vol. 29. The data in the *Summary* volume are suspect. They are drawn from an unrepresentative sample of the cities and schools in the Commission's data, and they exaggerate the differences in performance between nationality groups. Nevertheless, they are the only data which permit attempts to control the effects of independent variables on nationality differences in retardation, and so we have used them.

15. Ibid., p. 92.

16. Ibid., p. 61.

17. Ibid., pp. 98, 92. Italian English-language acquisition continued to lag in subsequent decades; in 1930, at every age level the proportion of Italians who could not speak English exceeded the proportion of Russians who could not:

	Percent Unable to Speak English—1930			
Birth	*Age*			
	10–24	*25–44*	*45–65*	*65 and over*
Russian	2	3	9	28
Italian	7	12	20	41

Source: U. S. Bureau of the Census, *Abstract of the Fifteenth Census* (Washington, 1933).

18. A number of "IQ" issues are not raised here. One is the possible genetic base of group IQ differences. Our presumption is genetic equality between groups with respect to the determinants of IQ scores. That presumption is consistent with the available evidence, provided we also assume that genes play a larger role in determining IQ than they do in determining educational attainment. Put another way, we assume that the impact of cultural differences is relatively greater on educational attainment than it is on IQ differences. If this is true,—and it is difficult to conceive an important effect of genes on educational attainment that is not mediated by IQ*,—and if groups were equal in genetic endowment affecting IQ, we would expect smaller differences on IQ than on educational attainment. Our best estimate for the period in question is that Jews exceeded Southern Italians by one-half standard deviation in tested IQ, but exceeded them by two-thirds of a standard deviation in educational attainment.

A second set of issues concerns the impact of individual IQ scores on individual attainment within ethnic groups. All of our estimates about the role of IQ differences between groups assume that the relationship between IQ and educational attainment is the same within each group. There is reason to believe that this may not be true. We think it is fair to speculate that among Jews IQ differences mattered less for educational attainment than they did among Italians. We suspect that lower ability Jews were more likely to pursue schooling relative to high ability students than were lower ability Italians. Put another way, a high IQ Italian would stand at a greater advantage over his lower IQ peers than would a high IQ Jew, with respect to educational attainment. If this reasoning is correct, our present estimate of the part group IQ differences played in accounting for Jewish-Italian schooling differences is high, and our confidence in the importance of cultural values for explaining differences in educational attainment is strengthened.

* Athletic prowess, musical talent, and physical attractiveness are important to only the lucky few, and add little to explaining variation in educational attainment among the general population.

19. Arine Murdock, "A Study of Race Differences in New York City," *School and Society,* 11 (1920). The first discussion of the test in the literature, reports results for over 1,000 subjects in Bloomington, Indiana. Standard deviations appear to be 24 for 10 year olds, 28 for 11 year olds, and 25 for 12 year olds. Calculated from S. L. Pressey and L. W. Pressey, "A Group Point Scale for Measuring General Intelligence with First Results from 1,100 School Children," *The Journal of Applied Psychology,* 2 (1918): 266. This means that Italians in Murdoch's sample scored well over a half standard deviation below Jewish subjects. These results are at variance with our other evidence, and are discounted on the assumption that the Pressey test was overly reliant on language acquisition. See also Dorothy W. Seago and Theresa S. Koldin, "A Comparative Study of the Mental Capacity of Sixth Grade Jewish and Italian Children," *School and Society,* 22 (1925): 566 and Gustave Feingold, "Intelligence of the First Generation of Immigrant Groups," 15 (February, 1924): 70 cited in Cohen, "Immigrants and the Schools."

20. See Arthur Gates, "The Correlation of Achivement in School Subjects with Intelligence Tests and Other Variables," *The Journal of Education Psychology*, 13 (1922): 281; Maller, "Economic and Social Correlatives," p. 659; Carl W. Ziegler, *School Attendance as a Factor in School Progress* (New York, 1928), p. 26.

21. Feingold, "Intelligence of the First Generation," pp. 77-82.

22. Christopher S. Jencks, *et al., Inequality: A Reassessment of the Effect of Family and Schooling in America* (New York, 1972), p. 337.

23. Ibid., pp. 323-325.

24. Beverly Duncan and Otis Dudley Duncan, "Minorities and the Process of Stratification," *American Sociological Review*, 33 (1968).

25. See, for example, James W. Bridges and Lilian Coler, "The Relation of Intelligence to Social Status," *The Psychological Review*, 24 (1917); Emily Dexter, "The Relation Between Occupation of Parent and Intelligence of Children," *School and Society*, 17 (1923); S. L. Pressey and Ruth Ralson, "The Relation of the General Intelligence of School Children to the Occupation of Their Fathers," *The Journal of Applied Psychology*, 4 (1919).

26. In addition to Bridges and Coler, Dexter, and Pressey and Ralson cited above, see Counts, *Selective Character* and Joseph K. Van Denburg, *Causes of the Elimination of Students in Public Secondary Schools of New York City* (New York, 1911).

27. Samuel Joseph, *Jewish Immigration to the United States from 1881-1910* (New York, 1914).

28. Isaac Rubinow, "Economic and Industrual Conditions—New York," in Charles S. Bernheimer (ed.), *The Russian Jew in the United States* (Philadelphia, 1905), pp. 110-112.

29. United States Industrial Commission, *Reports*, (Washington, 1901), vol. 15, p. 478, pp. 343-369.

30. Not all income was earned by male members of the family, so not all of the Jewish income advantage can be attributed to male occupational superiority. Forty-three percent of the Russian Jewish households in the seven cities surveyed by the Immigration Commission received income from boarders, compared to 27 percent for Southern Italian households; thirty-six percent of the Russian Jewish households received income from offspring, compared to 22 percent for the Southern Italians. These differentials were somewhat offset by the fact that 17 percent of the foreign-born Italian wives worked, compared to 8 percent of the Russian Jewish wives, U. S. Immigration Commission, *Reports*, vol. 1, p. 766.

31. On the impact of cultural values on economic decisions, see Virginia Yans McLaughlin, "Patterns of Work and Family Organization: Buffalo's Italians," in T. Rabb and R. Rotberg, eds., *The Family in History* (New York, 1973), pp. 111-126.

32. Duncan and Duncan, "Minorities and the Process of Stratification."

33. Knowledge of the intercorrelations between educational attainment, test scores, and father's occupation permits the estimation of the regression coefficients in a path model in which attainment is assumed to be determined by scores and father's occupation. These results are maximum effects, unless either test scores or father's occupation is negatively related to an omitted variable that affects attainment positively. We then substituted the average differences in standard

deviations between Russian Jews and Southern Italians on father's occupation and test scores into the resultant equation predicting education. Our prediction of the difference between the two groups on educational attainment fell short by one-third, as the text notes. Inclusion of family size did not alter the results importantly. At least thirty percent of the attainment gap remained unexplained when family size, test scores, and father's occupation were taken into account. For an explanation of the method of path analysis see Otis D. Duncan, "Path Analysis: Sociological Examples," *American Journal of Sociology,* 72 (1966): 1-16.

34. Zborowski and Herzog, *Life is with People*, pp. 118-123; Mark Zborowski, "The Place of Book Learning in Traditional Jewish Culture," *Harvard Educational Review*, 20 (Spring, 1949); Mary Antin, *The Promised Land* (Boston, 1912), pp. 204, 217.

35. Charles Agnoff, *Journey to the Dawn* (New York, 1951), p. 196; Elias Tobenkin, *Witte Arrives* (New York, 1916), p. 16.

36. The Exodus is the central myth exemplifying this theme.

37. From the *Daily Forward,* May 6, 1906, cited in Robert E. Park and Herbert Miller, *Old World Traits Transplanted* (New York, 1921), p. 7.

38. Tobenkin, *Witte,* p. 23; Agnoff, *Journey,* p. 238.

39. Melvin Kohn, *Class and Conformity, A Study in Values* (Homewood, Ill., 1969), p. 63; F. Strodtbeck "Family Interaction, Values and Achievement," in D. C. McClelland, *et al., Talent and Society* (Princeton, 1958); Bernard Rosen, "The Achievement Syndrome: A Psychocultural Dimension of Social Stratification," *American Sociological Review,* 21 (April, 1956). See also George Psathas, "Ethnicity, Social Class, and Adolescent Independence," *American Sociological Review,* 22 (August, 1957): 415-423 where Jews scored higher than Italians on measures of "parental regard for child's judgment."

40. Like most generalizations, these should be treated with care. For example it appears that Southern Italian districts that had undergone some land tenure changes and whose economic base was more oriented toward "economic individualism" sent a larger proportion of migrants to the U. S. than the more feudal districts. J. S. McDonald, "Italy's Rural Social Structure and Emigration," *Occidente,* 12 (September-October, 1956). On Southern Italian life, see Covello, *Southern-Italian Child;* Phyllis Williams, *South Italian Folkways in Europe and America* (New Haven, 1938); Edward Banfield, *The Moral Basis of a Backward Society* (New York, 1958); Rudolph Vecolli, "*Contadini* in Chicago" and "Prelates and Peasants."

41. Carlo Levi, *Christ Stopped at Eboli* (New York, 1947), p. 76, passim; Covello, *Southern-Italian Child,* chs, 6-8; Vecolli, "Prelates and Peasants"; Banfield, *Moral Basis.*

42. Herbert Gans, *The Urban Villagers* (New York, 1962) and William Foote Whyte, *Street-Corner Society* (Chicago, 1943). Jews traditionally characterized the world as a dichotomy, contrasting Jewish with Gentile. In America, however, except for the very Orthodox, that dichotomy did not inhibit participation in secular and civic society.

43. Whyte, *Street-Corner Society,* pp. 105, 107.

44. Covello, *Southern-Italian Child,* pp. 254-273. Gans reported that the actual mode of child rearing among Southern Italians in Boston's West End mitigated against

school success. The West Enders were episodic and impulsive in their responses to children, stressed immediate person to person contact, and showed limited interest in the use of words and concepts.

45. Covello, *Southern-Italian Child*, pp. 241-274; Vecolli, "Prelates and Peasants."
46. Covello, *Southern-Italian Child*, pp. 286-329; Virginia Yans McLaughlin, "Patterns of Work and Family Organization: Buffalo's Italians"; Gans, *Urban Villagers*, pp. 150, 297. Hostility to schooling, especially to compulsory attendance, as being inimical to the immigrants' economic needs was accentuated by the high proportion of Southern Italians who came to the U. S. with the intention of returning home. Youth who could contribute to that goal by working were an economic asset not lightly given up.
47. For an alternative to this assessment of the relationship between school success and Southern Italian-American culture, see Luciano Iorizzo and Salvatore Mondello, *The Italian-American* (New York, 1971), pp. 92-93 and, more generally, Smith, "Immigrant Social Aspirations." Covello notes that a change in attitudes toward schooling became noticeable during the 1920's as more and more Italians began to abandon the idea that they would soon return to Italy. *Southern-Italian Child*, p. 298.

14

Northern Foundations and the Shaping of Southern Black Rural Education, 1902–1935

James D. Anderson

Northern Philanthropists and Their Interest in Black Rural Education

DURING THE FIRST two decades of the twentieth century an educational awakening stirred the American South. Stimulated by Northern philanthropists and their Southern agents, the region experienced a remarkable expansion of its public educational system. In many states laws were changed to strengthen the constitutional basis of public education. The value of schoolhouses increased, illiteracy rapidly decreased, local taxes multiplied, school terms were extended, and teachers' salaries increased considerably. Historians generally view this organized school campaign as the official launching of the Southern education movement. To be sure, white missionaries and black leaders had campaigned for universal education in the South since the Reconstruction era, but in the dawn of the twentieth century white Southerners made their first vigorous, large-scale efforts to improve the region's schools. The success of the Southern education movement was a result of the combined efforts of industrial philanthropists and Southern white educators. These two groups formed a powerful new force in the struggle to determine the purpose of Southern education for both whites and blacks. The alliance between Northern businessmen-philanthropists and Southern white school officials was ratified by the creation of two major educational organizations, the

James D. Anderson is professor of education at the University of Illinois—Champaign–Urbana.

I wish to thank Clarence Karier, Paul Violas and Ronald F. Movrich for their helpful comments on this article, and the Rockefeller Archive Center for permission to quote from their manuscripts. This research was supported by the University of Illinois Center for Advanced Study and the Spencer Foundation.

Southern Education Board in 1901 and the General Education Board in 1902. The policies and programs formed by these boards profoundly shaped Southern black public education during the first half of the twentieth century. (1)

Significantly, the Northern reformers who effectively shaped the policy and programs of the Southern Education Board and the General Education Board were originally involved in Southern school reform through their nineteenth-century connections with Hampton and Tuskegee Institutes. Robert C. Ogden, the man chiefly responsible for bringing Northern philanthropists and Southern white school officials together, had helped to establish Hampton Institute in 1868. He was Hampton's most active trustee from 1874 to 1894, and from then until his death in 1913, he served as president of the board. Of course, Hampton was the original industrial education school for blacks, and Ogden's commitment to the Institute was based on his belief that industrial training was the appropriate form of schooling to assist in bringing racial order, political stability and material prosperity to the American South. He considered Hampton's principal, Samuel C. Armstrong, "the clearest thinker upon Negro education and the race question generally," and viewed Hampton as "one of the greatest successful educational experiments in the country." Hence, Ogden labored from the early 1870s to obtain financial support for Hampton's industrial education program and to publicize the school's cause in Northern philanthropic circles. As a wealthy merchant capitalist of New York City, his business career afforded him the opportunity to know important Northern philanthropists and his connections meant the addition of many new donors for Hampton and, later, Tuskegee Institute. (2)

By 1901, when the Southern education movement was publicly launched, Ogden was generally recognized by Northern philanthropists as the leading reformer interested in the development of Southern education and he soon gained the respect and confidence of Southern white school officials. From 1901 to 1913 he championed the Southern education movement through such various and powerful positions as president of the Conference for Education in the South, president of both the Southern Education Board and the General Education Board, and president of Hampton and Tuskegee Institute's Board of Trustees. In 1906, Ogden was at once president of all these organizations and was ably situated to project the Hampton-Tuskegee program of industrial training into national prominence and favor. (3)

Second only to Ogden in exerting influence over Northern philanthropists and Southern school officials was George Foster Peabody, a wealthy Wall Street banker. He was a full partner in the banking firm of Spencer Trask and Company. As an investment banker with special expertise in railroads and public utilities securities, Peabody worked closely with many of America's wealthy men. He was also very active in politics. In 1904, he was treasurer of the National Democratic Party Committee, and he campaigned for Woodrow Wilson's presidential nomination in 1912. Wilson offered him the position of Secretary of Treasury in 1913, but Peabody declined, maintaining that he could perform greater service outside of public office. In 1914, however, he accepted appointment as deputy chairman of the New York Federal Reserve Bank. (4)

Peabody, like Ogden, became actively involved in Southern education through Hampton Institute. His interest in black industrial education surfaced as early as 1876 when he became impressed with the Hampton program through contact with Samuel Armstrong. Ogden influenced Peabody to join the Hampton Board of Trustees in 1884. Peabody also viewed the Hampton program as the solution to the Southern race problem and contributed his investment banking skills toward placing Hampton and Tuskegee on a solid economic foundation. He served briefly as Hampton's treasurer and a longer tenure as financial manager on Hampton's and Tuskegee's investment and endowment committees. Like Ogden, he succeeded in arousing a great deal of enthusiasm among Northern millionaires for the Hampton-Tuskegee pattern of industrial education. In the 1920s he helped spearhead a successful campaign to raise $8,000,000 for Hampton and Tuskegee Institutes. The money he secured to expand the Hampton-Tuskegee model of industrial education came largely from Northern millionaires such as William E. Dodge, Collis P. Huntington, John D. Rockefeller, and George Eastman, who had come to trust Peabody's judgment on Southern educational matters. Peabody, a key founder of the Southern Education Board and the General Education Board, served as treasurer of the former from 1901 to 1914 and treasurer of the latter from 1902 to 1909. In vital respects, he was the investment banker of the Southern education movement. (5)

William H. Baldwin, Jr., a railroad entrepreneur who employed thousands of black laborers, was the third leading reformer who significantly shaped the direction of the Southern education movement. Born in Boston on February 5, 1863, he was educated in the city's public schools, the Roxbury Latin School and graduated from Harvard in 1885. After one year in Harvard's law school Baldwin entered the railroad business under the tutelage of Charles Francis Adams. He rose rapidly in the railroad industry and was appointed vice-president and general manager of J. P. Morgan's Southern Railway Company in 1894. Baldwin also became a trustee of Tuskegee Institute the same year, and until his premature death in 1905, worked very closely with Booker T. Washington in advancing the growth of that institution. (6) Baldwin went South as an agent of Northeastern capital to take charge of the region's railroads. The centrality of black labor in the railroad industry compelled him to consider the Negro's place in the Southern social economy. Like Ogden and Peabody, he became convinced that the Hampton program represented the solution to the "Negro problem", and he utilized his connections among Northern capitalists and Southern whites to spread the influence of Hampton and Tuskegee. Baldwin's advocacy of the Hampton Idea meant literally thousands of dollars for black industrial education. As an original trustee of the Southern Education Board and first president of the General Education Board he played a major role in committing Northern philanthropy to black industrial education. (7)

Ogden, Peabody, and Baldwin were the key spokesmen for a larger group of philanthropic reformers who were particularly interested in industrial education as a means of training efficient and contented black laborers for the Southern agricultural economy. To be sure, some of these reformers had capital investments in Negro cotton tenancy, but their broad interest in spreading black agriculture and domestic education transcended concerns for personal economic gains. The philanthropic reformers who presided over the Southern education movement were similar to other twentieth century urbanite who demanded an organized and efficient agricultural sector to supplement the emergent industrial nation. In an excellent study of the industrialization of American agriculture from 1900 to 1930, historian David Danbom well illustrates the complex interests which attracted many urban educators, editors, scientists, businessmen and socially conscious ministers to make agriculture conform to an urban standard of productive efficiency. Among other things, high agricultural productivity lowered food prices, dampened workers discontent and resulted in a general quickening of the wheels of industry. As Danbom concluded, urban reformers believed that "Increasing agricultural productivity was necessary if the nation was to maintain commercial and industrial greatness and realize its full economic promise." In short, agricultural organization and efficiency was a national problem with which many early twentieth century urban reformers were particularly preoccupied. (8)

The Northern philanthropic reformers also regarded an economically efficient and politically stable agriculture as a necessary underpinning for national industrial life. Hence, their concern for an efficient and stable Southern agriculture forced a close study of the black laborers who operated many of the region's farms. Southern agricultural prosperity was inextricably bound to a consideration of black farm workers, especially in a period of declining rural population, race conflict and increasing black migration to the urban North. "Our great problem," said Ogden, "is to attach the Negro to the soil and prevent his exodus from the country to the city." In Ogden's view, "The prosperity of the South depend[ed] upon the productive power of the black man." He embraced the Hampton-Tuskegee model of black industrial education as a vehicle to hold blacks to Southern rural society, stating specifically that Tuskegee's "first and large work" was in the area of "industrial leadership, especially in Agriculture." "The purpose of the Hampton school," said Ogden, "is to furnish district school teachers, well equipped with all the necessary knowledge of domestic science for practical missionary work among the colored people." He believed that the Hampton-Tuskegee industrial education program would help fit blacks into the Southern agricultural economy as wage laborers, sharecroppers and domestic workers. Indeed, this adaptation was the purpose of the school which existed on the Southern Improvement Company, the philanthropists' cotton plantation of which Ogden was a major stockholder. (9)

Like Ogden, Northern philanthropist George Peabody endeavored to convince his Southern countrymen that the Hampton-Tuskegee program could help build a strong Southern economy on the backs of submissive, nonpolitical, cheap black laborers. Convinced that industrial training would "help the Negro fit his environment," Peabody attempted to persuade white Southern businessmen of an inseparable relation between black education and the region's material prosperity. "I believe that the South needs their [blacks] labor and would be practically bankrupt without it," he argued. He informed a prominent Georgia planter and politician that industrially-trained black laborers would primarily benefit white investors:

. . . have you the least doubt that if one million Negroes, constituting nearly one-half of the men, women and children of Georgia were rightly educated to the development of their bodily health and strength and facilities and of the application of the same, which means their minds trained, to have their arms and legs work promptly and accurately in coordination, their moral apprehension rightly trained to know and do the right and avoid the wrong, and their affectional nature encouraged to love and not hate their white neighbors, and to respect and honor their own sexual purity, that they would be worth in dollars and cents to the state of George more than three times their present value. If this be true, as I am positively sure that it is, and as the property of the State of Georgia is so largely owned by the white race, would not the gain to the white race, under present methods of distribution, be most incalculable in dollars and cents . . . (10)

Peabody's business and political career brought him into personal contact with some of America's most influential political and economic leaders, and he used his connections to sell the Hampton Idea to the nation's leaders. In 1918 he invited his friend, President Woodrow Wilson, to make the keynote address at Hampton's Fiftieth Anniversary. Based on his "long and wide experience" in Southern education, Peabody explained to Wilson the importance of the Hampton program to the South's cotton production. "One-ninth of our population is of Negro blood, and the prosperity of the South and the world's supply of cotton are intimately bound up with the development of the Hampton Idea of 'Education for Life,' " he wrote to Wilson. According to Peabody, the Negro's place was in the cotton economy and Hampton's industrial education proram was appropriate to fit him for that life. (11)

Baldwin, more than the other reformers, elaborated the philanthropic vision of black workers' role in regional and national economic development. In 1899, at the Second Conference for Education in the South, he spoke to the gathering of Northern philanthropists and Southern educators about the "great black stratum of human beings, with human intelligence, who can be directed to produce infinite wealth for the South." Baldwin, who entered the South to organize the Southern Railroad, remained acutely aware of the region's cotton mills and their relationship to increased industrialization. Likewise, he recognized the centrality of black farm workers to the cotton industry, and this concern underlay his interest in the Hampton-Tuskegee program. As he wrote to the Southern historian, John Spencer Bassett,

. . . I agree with you, also, that the high price of cotton is going to have a great effect upon the Southern white people. I feel sure with you that the reaction has begun, and that the economic value of the Negro is going to prove his salvation. It is for this reason that I have always been so much interested in industrial edcation.

To spread black industrial education, Baldwin urged Northern and Southern whites "to build up a secondary school system under the general control and supervision of Hampton and Tuskegee." (12)

Baldwin also viewed black laborers as a potential force to protect the Southern economy and the nation against "unreasonable" demands by white unionized labor. In the 1930s, W. E. B. DuBois informed historian Merle Curti that there was "a provable correlation between the migration of Northern capital to the South for industry, and industrial education." DuBois recalled that Baldwin stated in 1901 "that his plan was to train in the South two sets of workers, equally skilled, black and white, who could be used to offset each other and break the power of the trade unions." DuBois' memory was good. For Baldwin, the availability of cheap labor in European markets made it necessary for America to have a non-unionized, cheap, efficient, laboring class. Baldwin's position is well illustrated in correspondence between him and N. F. Thompson, the secretary of Huntsville (Alabama) Chamber of Commerce and Southern Industrial Convention, who urged Northern Capital to come into the South whose "labor" made that section "a stranger to riots, strikes and ugly uprisings." Baldwin was particularly preoccupied with black labor as a means to break the power of Southern white trade unions:

The union of white labor, well organized, will raise the wages beyond a reasonable point, and then the battle will be fought, and the Negro will be put in at a less wage, and the labor union will either have to come down in wages, or Negro labor will be employed. The last analysis is the employment of Negro labor in the various arts and trades of the South, but this will not be a clearly defined issue until your competition in the markets of the world will force you to compete with cheap labor in other countries . . . I believe, as a last analysis, the strength of the South in its competition with other producing nations will lie in the labor of the now despised Negro, and that he is destined to continue to wait for that time.

For this and similar reasons, he struggled to keep black workers in the South by offering them an education that would adapt them to their "natural environment" and unfit them for alternative occupations. He praised industrial training because it educated blacks "for their environment and not out of it." (13)

Other philanthropists also made it abundantly clear that white businessmen were to be the main beneficiaries of black industrial training. In 1904, the Armstrong Association of New York City held a conference to discuss the work of Hampton Institute and "the bearing of industrial education on race problems at the South." Andrew Carnegie, a major donor to black industrial education who gave Tuskegee its first large endowment, spoke on the economic necessity of training black workers:

We cannot produce cotton enough for the wants of the world. We should be in the position in which South Africa is today but for the faithful, placable, peaceful, industrious, lovable colored man; for industrious and peaceful he is compared with any other body of colored men on the earth—not up to the standard of the colder North in continuous effort, but far in advance of any corresponding class anywhere. South Africa has just had to admit contracted Chinese labor, although there are between five and six millions of colored people there who will not work. We should be in the same condition but for our colored people, who constitute one of the most valuable assets of the Republic, viewed from an economic standpoint. It is certain we must grow more cotton to meet the demands of the world, or endanger our practical monopoly of that indispensable article. Either the efforts of Europe will be successful to grow in other parts, even at greater cost for a time, or the world will learn to substitute something else for it. We cannot afford to lose the Negro. We have urgent need of all and of more. Let us therefore turn our efforts to making the best of him.

James Hardy Dillard, the Tulane University president who became general agent of the John F. Slater Fund for black industrial education, was similarly impressed with the economic potential of an industrially trained black citizenry. "We of the South," he informed the Southern Educational Association in 1908, "cannot afford to have in our midst any mass of ignorance, and it is to our interest in every way to train the Negroes to thrift and intelligent industry. It will pay us in material advancement." Walter Hines Page, editor of the *Atlantic Monthly* and trustee of the Southern Education Board, said: "I have no sentimental stuff in me about the Negro, but I have a lot of economic stuff in me about the necessity of training him." Similarly, a Tuskegee Institute trustee from New York City declared that black industrial education was "Good business especially for the South, but good business for the entire country." (14)

The General Education Board:
Interlocking Directorate of Northern Philanthropy

The turn of the century witnessed heightened concern by the school reformers for an interlocking directorate of Northern philanthropic funds earmarked for Southern education. They especially wanted to control donations to Southern black education in order to channel resources to educational programs modeled on the Hampton-Tuskegee industrial training curriculum. William H. Baldwin, Jr., at the 1899 Conference for Education in the South, urged school campaigners and Northern capitalists to establish a "general education board" to support schools engaged in the appropriate kind of industrial work. "Now is the accepted time," said Baldwin, "to concentrate with an organization that will be recognized by the whole country as a proper channel through which the Negro Education can be reached successfully." Baldwin reflected the philanthropic reformers' conviction that private philanthropy was the best vehicle to spread industrial education throughout the Afro-American South. Southern states were either too resistant or too poor to appropriate additional funds to expand black education. Black schools controlled by missionary societies and black religious organizations placed top priority on traditional academic education and were generally indifferent or opposed to the Hampton-Tuskegee model of industrial training. Hence, from the reformers' vantage point, the best hope for the rapid spread of black industrial education lay with expanded philanthropic power. (15)

Not surprisingly, the reformers took their idea of a "general education board" to John D. Rockefeller who had long demonstrated an interest in Southern black education through contributions to the Baptist Home Mission Society and to particular black institutions. In 1899, for example, Rockefeller donated $10,000 to Tuskegee Institute. By 1901, the Rockefeller family was ready to increase its financial donations to Tuskegee Institute and black education in general. Frederick T. Gates, the senior Rockefeller's chief advisor in business and philanthropic matters, wrote to Booker T. Washington in February of 1901: "I am desirous of seeing you to confer more broadly than I have yet been able to do on the general subject of Colored education in the South, and to get your views as to the best plan for conducting the work on perhaps a larger scale than any single institution could contemplate." Thus, in April of 1901, seeking to obtain new philanthropy for Southern education, the reformers gladly included John D. Rockefeller, Jr., as a guest on the chartered Pullman train to the fourth Conference for Education in the South. After visits to Hampton and Tuskegee Institutes and from many discussions with the school campaigners, Rockefeller, Jr., became sufficiently impressed with the Southern education movement to approach his father about establishing a new foundation to reinforce the reformers' efforts. Rockefeller, Jr., helped lay the initial plans for a new educational foundation with the aid of Gates and Wallace Buttrick another advisor to the senior Rockefeller. Gates, in his own words, was especially critical in convincing Mr. Rockefeller of the importance of supporting Southern educational reform. "I knew very well that Mr. Rockefeller's mind would not work on mere abstract theories. He required concrete practical suggestions, and I set forth framing them." (16)

In November of 1901, believing that the reformers had found their financial backer in the person of John D. Rockefeller, Baldwin informed Washington that the plans for new philanthropy looked "very encouraging." Baldwin reported that a committee had been established "to take up this whole work in its broadest aspect as a Treasury, a Clearinghouse for information, etc." The committee, which included Baldwin, George Foster Peabody, J. L. M. Curry, Buttrick, and Rockefeller, Jr., met in January of 1902 to finalize plans for the prospective educational foundation. The young Rockefeller originally desired to name the new foundation the "Negro Education Board," but others argued successfully that such an obvious emphasis would further alienate the white South and lessen the reformers' chance of establishing a clearinghouse for all Northern philanthropy earmarked for Southern education. Hence, largely through the aid of U. S. Senator Nelson W. Aldrich, Rockefeller, Jr.'s, father-in-law, the reformers incorporated the new foundation as the General Education Board by an act of Congress in 1903. The charter conferred on the Board the authority to hold limitless capital and to do anything in the United States that could be construed as directly or even remotely educational. Ogden, Baldwin, Peabody, Gates, Curry, Walter H. Page, Daniel C. Gilman, Morris K. Jesup, and Albert Shaw, were the original trustees (February 27, 1902) and Buttrick was added on May 14, 1902. The trustees elected Baldwin as chairman, Peabody as treasurer, and Buttrick as Secretary and Executive Officer. The General Education Board's executive committee consisted of Baldwin, Ogden, Peabody, Curry, and Gates. Between the years 1902 and 1926 the Board was headed by Baldwin (1902-1905), Ogden (1905-1907), Gates (1907-1917), and Buttrick (1917-1926). (17)

The General Education Board soon became a powerful philanthropic trust as John D. Rockefeller, Sr., supplemented his intial endowment of $1,000,000 by another amounting to $53,000,000 by 1909, and by 1921 he had personally donated over $129,000,000 to the Board. Equally important, the reformers established the Board as an interlocking directorate of major Northern philanthropies concerned with Southern education. In June 1903, Baldwin happily informed Washington of the Board's early success in securing the cooperation of the Peabody and Slater Funds:

On Thursday next we have our first meeting under our National incorporation at Washington, D.C., and also we meet the Peabody Board. They have asked us to help them decide important questions, and to cooperate with them. My hopes are being realized, General Education Board, Slater and Peabody. It scares Mr. [Edgar Gardner] Murphy, but I am not afraid of the results of concentration.

Increasingly as the years passed, the reformers extended their influence over other Northern foundations, especially those devoted solely to black education. The General Education Board gained the cooperation of the Anna T. Jeanes Foundation, established in 1907, the Julius Rosenwald Fund, incorporated in 1917, and Jacob H. Schiff's Southern Education Fund which started in 1909. The Board also worked closely with the Phelps-Stokes fund which was directed by Thomas Jesse Jones, a former Hampton professor who was strongly committed to spreading black industrial education. As historian Louis Harlan aptly stated, the General Education Board acquired "virtual monopolistic control of educational philanthropy for the South and the Negro." (18)

Though many of the General Education Board's key officers and trustees were long-time supporters of black industrial education, the new foundation did not accept mindlessly the preachings of reformers like Baldwin, Peabody, and Ogden. Rather, the Board's black educational policy was carefully and purposely planned after an extraordinary amount of research and discussion by the GEB's own field agents and officers. In June 1903, Gates and Rockefeller, Jr., issued guidelines for the development of an independent policy. Their directive called for "a formulated policy, based on accurate knowledge of the educational situation in each [Southern] state as a whole, and its relation to an economic and ideal system for that state." Following this demand, Wallace Buttrick, the GEB's principal executive officer, went South with a team of "School Inspectors" to study and compile reports on the region's educational system. Twenty years later Buttrick recalled his careful examination of Southern educational conditions.

We began work in 1902. I called conferences of state and county superintendents in the general states of the South. We prepared an elaborate questionnaire, which is somewhat amusing to me now, through which we sought to elicit definite information about the public schools. We sent that out through the state superintendent at the state university or at the capital for a three days' session and conference.

In addition to holding conferences of school superintendents, the GEB's School Inspectors prepared hundreds of case studies on individual educational institutions. Nearly every Southern black secondary school and college was inspected and analyzed by the GEB's agents. (19)

Between 1902 and 1904, after many "journeys through the South," Buttrick became convinced that he understood the educational and economic problems of the region. His inquiries into Southern problems included not only educational conferences, "but a careful economic study of the several states." His work led him "to see that the great need of the South was greater economic efficiency." Like Ogden, Peabody, and

Baldwin, his demand for greater economic efficiency in Southern agriculture held specific implications for the development of black education. In a confidential letter to Gates, he stated that the time was ripe for "a new alignment of forces, a readjustment of agencies and a definite directing of our effort for the true education of the Negroes." Writing as the "fire burned" and "hot from the griddle," Buttrick argued that black schools should be "Hamptonized," that they "should teach agriculture and related industries." In short, Buttrick recommended that the GEB promote "such training of the Negro for the life that now is, as shall make of him a producer — a servant — of his day and generation in the highest sense." Significantly, Gates and Rockefeller, Jr., agreed with Buttrick's judgment. "Mr. Rockefeller and myself," replied Gates, "have no doubt of the justice of your observations." "It seems to me that the matter should not stop here," Gates continued, "the funds given for this purpose are so costly and involve so much sacrifice and are capable of being put to so effective service that we ought to use all of our influence to that end." The Board's key trustees agree, then, that the job of the foundation was to further industrial education in Southern black schools in order to train blacks to be producers and servants for the region's agricultural economy. Hence, the promotion of black industrial education became an official policy of the GEB. In a 1914 confidential report to its members, the Board stated that from 1902 to 1914 it had made "intensive and constructive" efforts to accomplish three main goals: to develop a new method and organization in medical education; to train a new type of businessman through the Harvard Graduate School of Business; and "to develop industrial education in Negro schools." (20)

*The Institutionalization of Industrial
Education in Black Rural Schools*

In pursuit of its goal to develop industrial education in Southern black schools and hence to retain blacks as efficient agricultural and domestic workers in rural society, the General Education Board initiated and sustained some extraordinarily active and far-reaching programs. Beginning around 1910, the GEB penetrated the Southern educational structure with three major programs: the establishment of State Supervisors for Negro Rural Schools in all the Southern states; the placing of County Supervising Industrial Teachers (commonly known as the Jeanes Teachers) in hundreds of Southern counties; and the development of County Training Schools, the most important mechanism for translating the GEB's educational concerns into institutional action at the local level. These programs, funded by the GEB, the John F. Slater Fund and the Anna T. Jeanes Fund, significantly determined the forms of education available to Southern blacks during the first half of the twentieth century. The programs became the GEB's official policy in 1911 when a "Special

Committee on the Education of the Negro" was appointed to devise a plan for the comprehensive development of Southern black education. (21)

Through the State Supervisors of Negro Rural Schools the GEB hoped to create and maintain in each Southern state an administrator who would devote his attention mainly to developing and systematizing industrial training. The supervisor's role was modeled on the work of Jackson Davis, the white superintendent of education in Henrico County, Virginia, who became the first State Supervisor of Negro Rural Schools. H. B. Frissell, principal of Hampton Institute and trustee of the GEB, brought Davis' work to the attention of the Board in 1909. Davis was favorably impressed with Hampton's industrial training program and had kept close supervision over the black schools in his county to make sure that they conformed to the industrial curriculum. The GEB's Special Committee on Negro Education noted that an aggressive state official like Davis could "stimulate and direct state, county, and local effort in developing an effective system of public schools for the training of the Negro children of the state." This position, the Committee further recognized, "would combine the advantage of official authority with freedom from arbitrary political interference." In short, "the State Supervisor would have entree to all counties, communities, and schools of the state; he could transact the state's business with county superintendents, county school boards, local trustees, and teachers." (22)

In 1910, Jackson Davis was appointed the State Supervisor of Negro Rural Schools for Virginia. His appointment was confirmed by the State Department of Education, but he was selected "on the nomination of the State Superintendent of Education and the Secretary of the General Education Board." The GEB paid his salary and travel expenses. Following the Board's decision to pay the salary and expenses of Davis, six other Southern states were given grants to set up State Supervisors: Alabama, Arkansas, Georgia, Kentucky, North Carolina, and Tennessee. All of these states received favorable consideration on condition that a satisfactory white educator was selected by the state superintendent and the GEB's secretary. In some instances, appointments were postponed for several months awaiting the approval of the GEB. The Board exercised considerable influence over the type of men chosen by maintaining the right to veto the nomination. Essentially, the GEB appropriated the grants to particular persons not to the position. In 1913, for example, the Governor of Louisiana replaced State Supervisor Leo M. Favrot and requested the GEB to send the salary check to Favrot's successor. The GEB was dissatisfied that Favrot was removed without its approval and withdrew any further aid for secondary education in Louisana. Three years later, in order to regain the Board's support of black education in Louisiana, the State Superintendent reinstated Favrot. Occasionally, the

GEB encountered problems when State Superintendents viewed the State Supervisors as unwanted agents of Northern philanthropy. In 1919, South Carolina's State Superintendent, J. E. Swearingin, informed the Board that he did not care to have in his office "a man who does not recognize his responsibility to the people of South Carolina and to the elective representatives of our people rather than to the General Education Board." But these were isolated incidents. Generally, the Southern states welcomed the State Supervisor because they shared the GEB's belief in black industrial training and because they needed outside funding to help sponsor a dual school system. (23)

By 1920, all Southern states had Supervisors of Negro Rural Schools and Jackson Davis was appointed by the GEB as general field agent to coordinate the supervisors' work. Horace Mann Bond described the State Supervisors' offices as "central clearing houses for practically all of the activities, state as well as philanthropic, intended to benefit Negro schools on a statewide basis." Since all State Supervisors were required to make monthly reports to the GEB, there exists substantial information on their educational activities. The State Supervisors spent most of their time systematizing industrial education where it was practiced; and advocating its introduction in counties where it was not installed. They endeavored to organize the black principals and teachers in each state and to gain popular support for the industrial education movement. In 1914, North Carolina State Supervisor N. C. Newbold organized the "First North Carolina Conference for Negro Education," which was attended by eighty of the State's "leading Negro educators." Newbold chaired the conference and emphasized the type of industrial training that would prepare black youth for the "sphere of life" to which they were "adapted." In all Southern states, the State Supervisor was the key liaison between black educators and the state office of education. Hence, the supervisors played a major role in determining what forms of education received support from the state. (24)

As the State Supervisors were to organize black industrial training at the state level, the GEB also initiated and supported County Supervising Industrial Teachers who were expected to assist local superintendents in making schools conform to the industrial curriculum. The State Supervisors were white and the Supervising Industrial Teachers, or Jeanes Teachers as they were more often called, were black. It was the duty of these teachers to visit as many schools in their county as possible. In most counties the industrial teacher was a woman. Services varied somewhat with the teacher, but generally the Jeanes Teacher gave lessons in sewing, cooking, housework, laundering, basketry, shuck work, chair-caning, woodwork, broom-making, and gardening. Industrial teachers also organized young boys and girls into "corn and tomato" clubs and school improvement leagues. In its 1918–1919 Annual Report, the GEB stated: "The main factor in enriching the curriculum of the rural school teacher is the supervising industrial teacher." (25)

The Jeanes Teachers increased from two in 1908 to 272 in 1920 and their numbers increased to 500 by 1950. They existed mainly in Southern counties with large black populations. These teachers came to exercise wide-spread influence over curriculum development, particularly in rural black schools. They made regular visits to these schools to hold them to an industrial course. The State Supervisor of North Carolina reported that the State's Jeanes Teachers visited 910 of the 1,046 black schools during the 1915–1916 scholastic year. To these schools the Jeanes Teachers made a total of 3,458 visits. They held 125 county meetings in North Carolina for which they reported an estimated 65,659 persons in attendance. The Jeanes Teachers, recruited largely from Hampton, Tuskegee and similar industrial normal schools, used these meetings to spread the gospel of industrial education. They reported overcoming the opposition of black parents who believed that their children could be taught properly only out of established textbooks and who kept their children away from the industrial work. In order to impress upon the communities the value of industrial education, the Jeanes Teachers organized "Willing Workers Clubs" to draw the community into the school activities. (26)

The Jeanes Teachers extended their efforts to introduce industrial training into the black educational system through their role in the in-service training of black teachers. Beginning in 1914, the GEB supported summer institutes for black teachers throughout the South in order to acquaint them with the methods of industrial education as practiced at Hampton and Tuskegee Institutes. Black teachers considered influential in their communities were encouraged to attend summer school at Hampton or Tuskegee while others went to summer sessions in their home states. The number of North Carolina black teachers attending summer schools in 1916 amounted to slightly more than one-third of the State's black teaching force. During the summer of 1921, Arkansas held seven summer institutes enrolling 54 percent of its black teachers. These institutes expanded in number and influence. By the summer of 1926, fourteen states held 112 summer schools, enrolling 23,686 black teachers, which equaled 54 percent of the total black teaching body in the South. The course of study for the summer normal schools was worked out by the State Supervisor and the Jeanes Teachers. Reports on the educational activities in the summer schools reveal that the instructions were mainly in "domestic science" and "manual training." (27)

The County Training School was the most important mechanism whereby Northern philanthropic reformers translated their sociopolitical ideas into educational programs. Basically, it was an elementary school located in rural areas designed to offer industrial training, laying particular emphasis upon subjects pertaining to agriculture and domestic work. Some of them evolved into "secondary schools" primarily to train industrial teachers for rural black schools. It was also a type of consolidated school development as some Training Schools possessed dormitory facilities to attract students throughout the county. The Training School movement began with the construction of the Tanyipahoa Parish Training School of Louisiana in 1911. In that year the GEB and the Slater Fund supported four such schools. By 1921, Training Schools had multiplied from 4 to 142 in number, the teaching corps from 20 to 848 teachers, and the amount expended annually for salaries from $5,344 to $478,334. The amount invested in Training Schools increased in 10 years from $28,760 to $1,590, 262, and the average expenditure was $2,781 per session in 1911, as against $7,097 in 1921. The rapid spread of the Training School evidences its growing value to the GEB as the most effective means to institutionalize industrial training in black schools. In its 1917-1918 Annual Report, the GEB stated:

There is perhaps no more promising movement in Negro education than the development of the county training schools, which offer seven years of elementary work, with suitable industrial courses, and in addition three years of high school work emphasizing the arts of home making and farm life; the last year includes a simple course in teacher training. (28)

In order for local authorities to receive County Training Schools, the GEB demanded them to meet certain minimum requirements. It was necessary for the school property to belong to the state, county, or district, and for the institution to be a part of the public school system. The state, county, or district had to tax itself for an annual appropriation for teachers' salaries of not less than $750. The GEB (and the Slater Fund) encouraged a school term of at least eight months and required that the course work extend through the eighth year. Local school officials were expected to add at least two years of high school work primarily to train teachers for the first seven grades. (29)

It was the policy of the GEB and the Slater Fund to appropriate $500 a year to each County Training School to be used for teachers' salaries. This appropriation was made on a diminishing scale, in the hope that it would be supported eventually by local school authorities. Usually there was no definite agreement as to the length of time aid would be given, but the practice was to appropriate $500 per year for a minimum of three years, $250 per year for next two years, and $100 per year for needed equipment afterward. The GEB assisted in maintaining the County Training Schools by giving aid to purchase industrial and other equipment. The Board also contributed funds for the erection of industrial buildings, teachers' homes, and dormitories for boarding students. Generally, $500 was appropriated for industrial equipment. When aid was given for purchasing blackboards, desks, etc., the county school boards were required to spend an amount equal to that given by the GEB. In the case of industrial buildings and teachers' homes, individual projects were considered and aided on their "own merits," and in proportion to the response from local authorities. In 1920, the GEB increased its assistance to the County Training Schools by appropriating funds to raise teachers' salaries to a minimum annual salary of $1,000 for principals and of $500 for assistant teachers. This appropriation was made on a diminishing scale, the original amount being decreased one-fifth each year, and wholly disappearing at the end of the fifth year. It was assumed that state, county, or district school boards would compensate for the amounts withdrawn by the GEB. (30)

The letters and unpublished reports of the Board's agents reveal that the Training Schools were designed primarily to train efficient agricultural and domestic workers for the rural South. The State Supervisors, besides assisting local authorities in selecting suitable locations for the Training Schools, helped in planning the educational activities and in choosing the "right kind" of teachers. Alabama State Supervisor James L. Sibley wrote that the State's Training School gave "definite instruction in home economics to girls; in agriculture to boys; and in teacher training to both." Similarly, Georgia State Supervisor George D. Godard viewed the Training School movement as a campaign "to make the Negro a more economical, industrious, and profitable citizen." So important was the Training School, in Leo M. Favrot's view, that upon its institutionalization depended to a large degree the restoration of Southern economic efficiency as a whole:

The fact that the great mass of the Negroes in our rural district is ignorant is no argument in favor of leaving them in ignorance. Under the industrial system that prevailed in slavery times the Negroes were not left in ignorance, but were carefully trained along industrial lines. In those days the industrial slave-holder assumed a responsibility which in our day and time, the state can ill-afford to shun. In those days it was to the interest of the slave-holder to train the slave Negro to become efficient. It is no less to the interest of the South today to train the Negro for efficiency.

Favrot, who was chosen by the GEB to preside over the development of the Training Schools, made a detailed study of them in 1923. He reported that all the Southern counties were "making the training schools distinctly industrial and agricultural all the way through the course offered." (31)

A major complaint of the philanthropic reformers was that black rural schools had separated themselves from the demands of the agricultural economy and the "needs of Negro life" by emphasizing the classical aspects of the curriculum, and hence encouraging farm youths to disdain physical labor. Tennessee State Supervisor S. L. Smith repeated a common criticism when he sneered that he had met a black boy who attended school to avoid hard work:

I addressed the colored school at Bolivar on my return in company with the county superintendent. During my talk I asked one Negro boy why he was going to school. He said, "I'se gwine to get an education so I won't have to work." This little boy voiced the sentiment of the school. I took a few minutes to tell them that they should go to get an education which should enable them to work better than before.

Consequently, the County Training School, stated Leo Favrot, placed heavy emphasis upon "character building and learning to work." Usually, the State Supervisors, as J. A. Presson of Arkansas, emphasized the Training School as a vehicle to "prepare the girls and boys for more efficient work and happier lives in the home and on the farm." In some instances, however, State Supervisors were more specific about the social and economic purposes of the Training School. S. L. Smith equipped the Dyersburg County (Tennessee) Training School with a kitchen "as nearly like a well-ordered kitchen of the city as possible." "This will," Smith contended, "better prepare the girls to do cooking for the white people of the town." Interestingly, Smith took special pains to accomplish this in a county where the Southern white president of the board of education desired "that Negro children learn Latin, Greek, and Higher Mathematics." Smith's actions were consistent with the GEB's position. Ten years earlier Buttrick had maintained that black schools should "eliminate Latin, Greek, etc., to say nothing of piano music and the like." (32)

The Northern reformers, using their own vision of black people's place in the Southern economy as the primary yardstick, probably convinced themselves that simple agricultural and domestic training was good for black youth. Moreover, they attempted to convince themselves that there was a general demand for industrial education arising from the black rural community itself. The GEB's agents stated publicly that the Training School curriculum grew out of the practical experiences of the teachers and the needs of rural life as defined by rural citizens and the county officials. Jackson Davis, who headed the Board's Southern black education program, said: "No attempt has been made to dictate what shall be taught." Likewise, Leo M. Favrot wrote: "There has never been a serious effort to make uniform the training school course of study." Yet, despite the pronouncements of the GEB's agents, agricultural and domestic training had much less relevance for rural blacks. By the post-World War I period, when Training Schools were rapidly expanded, it was the ambition and determination of many young blacks and their parents to get away from the farm with its drudgery, isolation, inadequate financial returns, and limited outlet for talent. Even for those who remained in rural society, agriculture and domestic training could be learned at home as it always had been. Black rural residents, therefore, did not always cooperate with the Training School movement. Indeed, the active participation of blacks in shaping their own school system prevented all but the most naive reformers from concluding that blacks desired only industrial training. (33)

Early on the philanthropic reformers discovered that many rural blacks preferred a more liberal education which prefigured a life away from the poverty, isolation, and drudgery of Southern tenant farming. In some cases, reformers found that black teachers were not willing missionaries of industrial education. Leo Favrot stated that black teachers' indifference to industrial training made it difficult for Arkansas Supervising Industrial Teachers to accomplish their goals. "A Jeanes Fund teacher," Favrot complained, "frequently visits a rural school and has each pupil to work for an hour or two one day in one week and comes again two weeks later and finds that no work of this kind has been done by the pupils during her absence." Four years later, John A. Presson, who succeeded Favrot as State Supervisor of Arkansas, gained some insight as to why the State's black teachers were indifferent to industrial training. He visited the black colleges in the State to learn "their ideas of what kind of education the Negroes need." Presson found that these colleges, which trained most of the State's black teachers, were not teaching industrial education. "They seem to pride themselves on their academic work," wrote Presson, "and take great credit to themselves for work offered in traditional courses, such as are given by leading colleges of the country." (34)

One of the principal reasons for black opposition to the County Training School was its limited and narrowly defined curriculum. Probably for the vast majority of rural blacks, education meant ability to read, write, and calculate, and not the ability to cook and plow for white landlords. Thus, in the early years many black teachers attempted to restructure the Training School curriculum to meet the ambitions of the black community. State Supervisor S. L. Smith visited the Haywood County (Tennessee) Training School in 1914 and discovered black teachers' "attempting to teach four years of Latin, and neglecting a great deal of the most important part of the [industrial] school work." Smith used financial inducements to encourage the acceptance of industrial training and to discourage the inclusion of classical education. Smith offered "$500 aid on condition that they would put in a good industrial department and readjust their course of study to a sound working basis." Tactics of voluntarism, however, were insufficient to stop the broader movement by blacks to subvert the Training School curriculum. In September 1915, James H. Dillard, General Agent of the Slater Fund, corresponded with N. C. Newbold (North Carolina State Supervisor) about black attempts to restructure the Training schools. Dillard wrote to Newbold:

I have just received your letter of yesterday in regard to the course of study and the actual work in the County Training Schools. I have just written to Mr. Godard about a school down in Georgia which proposes to be a County Training School, and had a lot of stuff in the programme, including economics. They had Greek also, I believe, and a lot of other pretentious and impossible subject until Mr. Godard had them taken out.

The following month, Jackson Davis wrote Abraham Flexner, the GEB's Assistant Secretary, about the Ben Hill County (Georgia) Training School that had divided itself "into four departments, and four schools, embracing Caesar, Psychology, Moral Philosophy, Ethics, German, Economics, Evidences of Christianity, and seemingly culminating in 'Marginal Educational Activities.'" Of course, the philanthropic reformers quickly removed these courses from the curriculum and introduced the industrial program. By June 1916, the Ben Hill or Queensland Industrial Training School had an agricultural department that produced 2-½ bales of cotton, 1655 pounds of cotton seed, 35 bushels of sweet potatoes, 2 bushels of rice, 15 gallons of syrup, 25 bushels of corn and 500 pounds of hay. The students in grades 3 to 7 built a cow stall, one stock barn, and a laundry. (35)

In the face of black attempts to subvert the County Training Schools the philanthropic reformers were forced to recognize privately that many rural blacks desired an academic curriculum in contrast to agricultural and domestic training. Jackson Davis admitted to Abraham Flexner that "so many of the principals are not able to resist the popular demand of the colored people for pretentious and high sounding courses." Davis and his colleagues ignored the "popular demand" for academic education. They were convinced that black people did not understand rural life well enough to perceive its requirements or their own educational needs. Consequently, the philanthropists redoubled their efforts to hold the Training Schools strictly to an industrial curriculum. After several incidents in 1915, the reformers began to eschew voluntarism for compulsion. David informed the members and agents of the GEB that "it is quite evident that we shall have to use more pressure in having the proper kind of work done in these school." Abraham Flexner, on behalf of the GEB, informed the State Supervisors in October 1915 that "Dr. Dillard has just been in to see me and has urged the importance of a separate meeting of the Negro Rural School Supervisors, in order to agree upon a program for the development of the county training schools and in order to discuss further the situation with which you all are dealing." In March 1916, Dillard convened the State Supervisors in New York City "to discuss and work out a good, sensible course of study for County Training Schools." (36)

The New York City conference resulted in the appointment of Leo Favrot and Jackson Davis to write a course guide for the Training Schools, which they modestly called a "Suggested Course for County Training Schools." The course booklet outlined an academic and industrial curriculum consistent with the GEB's aims to train an efficient and contented black laboring force for the Southern agricultural economy. For grades five and six, the end of schooling for most rural blacks, the course guide recommended that Training School teachers devote one-half of their time to teaching academic subjects and the other half to industrial education. The academic course consisted mainly of reading, writing, arithmetic, spelling, and history. The industrial subjects were agricultural, cooking, woodwork, and drawing or simple designs for articles to be made in the shop. In addition to the industrial courses, it was recommended that each boy organize a "pig club" and each girl cultivate a home garden. The secondary course was basically the same as the elementary course. (37)

Two kinds of sources reveal the extent to which the Training Schools conformed to the curriculum recommended in the philanthropists' course guide. Favrot and Edward Redcay made detailed studies of the Training Schools in 1923 and 1935. More importantly, however, State Supervisors made monthly and annual reports of educational activities in the Training Schools. Favrot's 1923 study of 107 Training Schools demonstrated that the schools in general placed heavy emphasis on industrial and agricultural subjects. "It is known among state agents of Negro schools," reported Favrot, "that practically all girls and boys over fourteen years of age in the training schools spend from 180 to 750 minutes per week in practical agriculture, the shop, the home economics laboratory, or in some industrial pursuit." The emphasis on industrial training was even greater when rural Training Schools were examined separately from those located in urban communities. In rural schools "from one-third to one-half of the school day is devoted to the vocational subject." Even the teacher training program devoted ample time to instructions in "agriculture, gardening, cooking, sewing, housekeeping, canning, and things of a similar nature." The academic subjects in the teacher training course, according to Favrot, did not go beyond "what is required for a first grade county teachers' license which is very little beyond the subjects of the common school course." In short, the Training School offered an elementary academic course combined with simple training in sewing, basketry, woodwork, agriculture, cooking, blacksmithing, and like subjects. (38)

Clearly, the County Training Schools translated the philanthropists' educational ideology into educational programs. Of course, it's virtually impossible to determine how these programs affected the beliefs and behavior of the students who attended these schools. But solid evidence exists on the centrality of the Training Schools in the Southern black educational system and hence their impact on the forms of education that were available particularly for blacks in the rural South. In 1930, slightly more than two-thirds of all Southern blacks lived in rural areas. Public schooling, expecially at the secondary level, was often nonavailable to this population. Of the 1,077 Southern black high schools reported to the

United States Office of Education in 1933-1934 only 508, fewer than one-half, were rural schools. Of the 1,413 counties in 15 Southern States in 1930, there were 230 whose populations were 12.5 percent or more Afro-American, with 158,939 black children of high school age, which afforded no public high schools for blacks. In 195 other such counties, containing 197,242 black children of high school age, no four-year high schools for blacks were provided. Significantly, these 425 counties were concentrated chiefly in States with large black populations, notably Florida, Georgia, Mississippi, Virginia, Arkansas, Louisiana, and Alabama. (39)

Under these conditions, the County Training School became a far-reaching and dominant institution in Southern black secondary education. Training Schools increased from four in 1911 to 356 in 1933. In 293 of 912 counties in 15 Southern and border states, the Training School was, for blacks between the ages of 15-19, the sole source of public secondary education. The centrality of the Training School in black education is further revealed by the fact that 44.2 percent of all Southern black pupils of high school age were located in counties where Training Schools were either the only secondary schools or the ones with the most number of grades. In states with large black populations, the Training School provided the only or most advanced secondary education for 64.9 percent of black youth in Mississippi, 59.2 percent in Virginia, 54 percent in Louisiana, 52.5 percent in Alabama, 48.4 percent in Florida, 47.9 percent in South Carolina, and 40.2 percent in Georgia. These percentages increase when rural schools are considered separately. In 1933, 66 percent of rural Southern black high school pupils attended Training Schools. Thus, Northern philanthropists had greatly influenced the forms of education available to blacks in the rural South. (40)

To be sure, Northern philanthropists were undoubtedly motivated by a mixture of sentimentalism, humanitarianism, and sociopolitical interests. Historian Henry Snyder Enck has documented several motivations which guided Northern philanthropists' interest in black industrial education. The GEB and its associate foundations, however, were primarily motivated by practical interests in the relationship of black industrial education to the development of Southern agriculture and national industrial life. We know that the Board was motivated by practical considerations from its own testimony. In October 1922, the GEB formed a special committee to consider the fundamental question: "What is the theory or principle underlying the Board's policies in dealing with Negro education?" According to the committee's report, a "clear answer" was obtained: "The Board's interest is neither sentimental nor merely humanitarian; it is practical." Among other practical interests, the committee noted that "Economically, he [the Negro] is an increasingly important productive factor. ' Consequently, "Aside from any concern which may on humanitarian grounds be felt for the Negro for his own sake, it is clear that the welfare of the South, not to say of the whole country — its prosperity, its sanitation, its morale — is affected by the condition of the Negro race." The Board essentially understood the fundamental relationship between Afro-America and the American nation as a whole. However, the conservative means through which the reformers attempted to resolve these problems gave the Southern education movement its particular character. The philanthropists' policies and programs were designed primarily to develop an economically efficient and politically stable Southern agricultural economy by training efficient and contented black laborers while leaving the Southern racial hierarchy intact. (41)

NOTES

1. Louis Harlan, *Separate and Unequal: Public School Campaigns and Racism in the Southern Seaboard States 1901–1915* (Chapel Hill, North Carolina, 1958, [1968 Atheneum edition]), p. 79; Charles W. Dabney, *Universal Education in the South,* Vol. II (Chapel Hill, North Carolina, 1936); Edgar W. Knight, *Public Education in the South* (New York, 1922), p. 433; C. Vann Woodward, *Origins of the New South, 1877–1913* (Baton Rouge, 1951, [1974 edition]), pp. 395–400.

2. Woodward, *Origins of the New South,* p. 401; Robert C. Ogden, *Samuel C. Armstrong: A Sketch* (New York, 1894); Samuel C. Mitchell, "Robert Curtis Ogden: A Leader in the Educational Renaissance of the South," unpublished Biography, Ogden Papers; Henry S. Enck, "The Burden Borne: Northern White Philanthropy and Southern Black Industrial Education, 1900–1915" (Ph.D. Dissertation, University of Cincinnati, 1971), pp. 47–60; For a detailed analysis of the Hampton program of industrial education see James D. Anderson, "The Hampton Model of Normal School Industrial Education, 1868–1900," forthcoming in Vincent P. Franklin and James D. Anderson (editors), *New Perspectives on Black Educational History* (Boston: G. K. Hall, 1978).

3. Enck, "The Burden Borne," pp. 41, 51, 60; Harlan, *Separate and Unequal,* pp. 75–76, 79–82, 85–87; Robert C. Ogden to Mrs. Arthur Gilman (May 12, 1903), Box 6, Ogden Papers, Library of Congress; Louis Harlan, *Booker T. Washington: The Makings of a Black Leader, 1856–1901* (New York [1975 edition] 1972), pp. 62, 284.

4. Louise Ware, *George Foster Peabody: Banker, Philanthropist, Publicist* (Athens, Georgia, 1951), pp. 162, 170, 215; Enck, "The Burden Borne," pp. 72–81.

5. Enck, "The Burden Borne," pp. 77–78; Ware, *George Foster Peabody,* p. 214; Harlan, *Separate and Unequal,* pp. 75–76; Harlan, *Booker T. Washington,* p. 238.

6. John Graham Brooks, *An American Citizen: The Life of William Henry Baldwin, Jr.* (Boston, 1910), pp. 33–38, 53–54, 80, 191, 204–215; Dabney, *Universal Education in the South,* Vol. II, pp. 145–149; Enck, "The Burden Borne," pp. 60–71; Harlan, *Separate and Unequal,* pp. 76–78; James D. Anderson, "Education for Servitude: The Social Purposes of Schooling in the Black South, 1870–1930" (Ph.D. Dissertation, Urbana, University of Illinois, 1973), see Chapter 5 for an extended discussion of the Baldwin-Washington relationship.

7. Enck, "The Burden Borne," p. 60; Woodward, *Origins of the New South,* p. 292; Dabney, *Universal Education in the South,* Vol. II, p. 149; Anderson, "Education for

Servitude," pp. 214-216; see Anderson pp. 190-210 for more specific information on Baldwin's role in raising funds for Tuskegee and industrial education.

8. For the philanthropists' investment in the Southern cotton economy see Enck, "The Burden Borne," pp. 152-164; James D. Anderson, "The Southern Improvement Company: Northern Reformers' Investment in Negro Cotton Tenancy 1900-1920," *Journal of Agricultural History,* Vol. 52 (January, 1978): pp. 111-131; for an excellent treatment of urban interest in organizing American agriculture, see David Byers Danbom, "The Industrialization of Agriculture, 1900-1930" (Ph.D. Dissertation, Stanford University, 1974), pp. 77, 84.

9. Robert C. Ogden to Mrs. Arthur Gilman (May 12, 1903), Box 6, Ogden, "Speech on Negro Education" (1900), Box 22, Ogden Papers; Anderson, "Education for Servitude," p. 217; Anderson, "The Southern Improvement Company"; Ogden to H. W. McKinney (April 30, 1898), Box 6, Ogden Papers.

10. George F. Peabody to Henry R. Goetchius (January 30, 1911), Box 57; Peabody to G. G. Jordan (December 18, 1907), Box 6; Peabody to Colonel James Smith (March 20, 1906), Box 57, George F. Peabody Papers, Library of Congress; Anderson, "Education for Servitude," p. 217.

11. George F. Peabody to President Woodrow Wilson (May 20, 1918), Box 75, Peabody Papers.

12. William H. Baldwin, "Present Problem of Negro Education," *Proceedings of the Second Capon Springs Conference for Education in the South* (Capon Springs, West Virginia, 1899), pp. 104-106; Baldwin to John Spencer Bassett (May 27, 1904), Booker T. Washington Papers, Library of Congress.

13. William H. Baldwin, Jr., to N. F. Thompson (April 15, 1900), Box 792, Washington Papers; Baldwin, "Present Problem of Negro Education," pp. 105-107; Anderson, "Education for Servitude," pp. 206-210; Herbert Gutman, "The Negro and the United Mine Workers of America," in Julius Jacobson, *The Negro and the American Labor Movement* (New York, 1968), p. 411; Herbert Aptheker (ed.), "Some Unpublished Writings of W. E. B. DuBois," *Freedomways,* Vol. 5 (Winter, 1965): 128.

14. See Andrew Carnegie's address in "The Work and Influence of Hampton," *Proceedings of a Meeting held in New York City (February 12, 1904) by the Armstrong Association,* p. 7; Andrew Carnegie, "The Education of the Negro: A National Interest," *Address at the Twenty-fifth Anniversary of the Founding of Tuskegee Institute* (April 5, 1906), Box 253, Andrew Carnegie Papers, Library of Congress; James H. Dillard as quoted in Enck, "The Burden Borne," p. 156; Walter H. Page as quoted in Robert Jay Rusnak, "Walter Hines Page and *The World's Work: 1900-1913*" (Ph.D. Dissertation, University of California, Santa Barbara, 1973), p. 260; William G. Wilcox, "The Builder of Tuskegee," The Trustees of the John F. Slater Fund, *Occasional Papers* No. 17 (Lynchburg, Virginia, 1916), p. 18.

15. Baldwin, "The Present Problem of Negro Education," 104-106; this address was also given at the 1899 American Social Science Association in Saratoga, New York and printed in the *Journal of Social Science,* No. 37 (December, 1899): 52-58.

16. Frederick T. Gates to Booker T. Washington (December 15, 1899), Washington Papers; Gates to Washington (February 9, 1901), Washington Papers; Raymond B. Fosdick, *Adventure in Giving: The Story of the General Education Board* (New York, 1962), pp. 4-7; Frederick T. Gates, "Autobiography of Frederick T. Gates," p. 459, unpublished in the General Education Board Papers in the Rockefeller Foundation Archives (hereafter listed as the GEB Papers).

17. William H. Baldwin, Jr., to Booker T. Washington (November 6, 1901), Washington Papers; Fosdick, *Adventure in Giving*, pp. 9, 13, 338; The Buse Notes, pp. 30-34 (an incomplete manuscript on the history of the GEB), Box 338, GEB Papers; Waldemar A. Nielson, *The Big Foundations* (New York, 1972), pp. 333-336.

18. William H. Baldwin, Jr., to Booker T. Washington (June 23, 1903), Washington Papers; Fosdick, *Adventure in Giving*, pp. 12-13, 327; Harlan, *Separate and Unequal*, pp. 86-87; Horace Mann Bond, *Negro Education in Alabama: A Study in Cotton and Steel* (Kingsport, Tennessee 1939 [1969 Atheneum edition]), p. 272; Thomas Jesse Jones, *Negro Education: A Study of Private and Higher Schools for Colored People in the United States* (Washington, D. C., 1917), pp. 81-95.

19. *The Minutes of the General Education Board from January 1902 to November 1960*, pp. 142-143. GEB Papers; Wallace Buttrick, Address to Harvard University Graduate School of Education (April 29, 1922), Box 303, GEB Papers; Buttrick's reports on conferences with Southern school superintendents, Boxes 209 and 304, GEB Papers; For a sampling of the School Inspectors' reports see David E. Cloyd, William H. Heck and W. T. B. Wiliams' reports in Boxes 200, 209, 260, and 718, GEB Papers.

20. Wallace Buttrick, Address to Harvard University Graduate School of Education, Box 303, GEB Papers; Wallace Buttrick to Frederick T. Gates (October 14, 1904) and Gates to Buttrick (October 20, 1904), Box 716, GEB Papers; Jerome D. Green, Wallace Buttrick and Abraham Flexner, Confidential Report to the Members of the General Education Board (October 22, 1914), Box 331, GEB Papers.

21. Report of the Special Committee on the Education of the Negro (May 25, 1911), Box 722, GEB Papers; Wallace Buttrick to John D. Rockefeller, Jr. (February 5, 1914), Box 203, GEB Papers.

22. Report of the Special Committee on the Education of the Negro; Jackson Davis to Abraham Flexner (July 29, 1919), Box 36, GEB Papers; Fosdick, *Adventure in Giving*, pp. 90-91; S. L. Smith, *Builders of Goodwill: The Story of the State Agents of Negro Education in the South 1910 to 1950* (Nashville Tennessee, 1950).

23. Smith, *Builders of Goodwill*, pp. 11, 17-18; Report of Special Committee on the Education of the Negro; J. E. Swearingin to E. C. Sage (June 6, 1919), Box 131, GEB Papers.

24. Smith, *Builders of Goodwill*, p. 9; Bond, *Negro Education in Alabama*, p. 272. For information on the educational activities of the State Supervisors there are hundreds of reports in the GEB Papers: Mississippi, Box 98; Virginia Boxes 187 and 188; Arkansas, Box 25; North Carolina, Box 115; South Carolina, Box 131; Tennessee, Box 158; Georgia, Box 67; Alabama, Box 17; Louisiana, Box 88.

25. Annual Report of the General Education Board 1918-1919 (New York: GEB, 1920), p. 54; Leo M. Favrot, "Report of Arkansas State Supervisor of Negro Schools for November 1913" (December 8, 1913), Box 25, GEB Papers; N. C. Newbold, "The Jeanes Supervising Industrial Teachers: Some Things They Helped to do Last School Year" (October 25, 1917), Box 115, GEB Papers.

26. "North Carolina Biennial Report of the State Agent of Negro Rural Schools-1917," Box 115, GEB Papers; "Annual Report of Arkansas Supervisor of Negro Schools," Box 25, GEB Papers; *General Education Board: Review and Final Report, 1902-1964*, (New York, 1964), pp. 20-21.

27. Ibid.; For information on summer school activities see reports for Arkansas, Box 25; Hampton Institute, Box 176; Tuskegee Institute, Box 6; Georgia, Box 68; Alabama,

Box 13; "Summary of Reports from Summer Schools for Negro Teachers—1921," Box 302; "Summary Reports. . . . 1930," Box 302; "Report on Special Teachers and In-Service Training of Rural Teachers in Summer Schools for Negroes—1935," Box 302, GEB Papers.

28. Edward E. Redcay, *County Training Schools and Public Secondary Education for Negroes in the South* (Washington, D.C., 1935), pp. 24–45; Leo Mortimer Favrot, *A Study of County Training Schools for Negroes in the South* (Charlottesville, Virginia, 1923), pp. 8–26; John A. Presson, *Annual Report of Educational Activities in Negro Schools* (Little Rock, Arkansas, 1922), pp. 22–23; *Annual Report of the General Education Board* (New York, 1918), p. 51.

29. Ibid.

30. Favrot, County Training Schools For Negroes in the South, pp. 12, 31–32; Presson, *Report of Educational Activities in Negro Schools,* pp. 22–23.

31. Redcay, *County Training Schools,* p. 38; James L. Sibley to Abraham Flexner (January 16, 1915), Box 17, GEB Papers; Leo M. Faurot, "The Industrial Movement in Negro Schools" (June 9, 1913), Box 25, GEB Papers; George D. Godard, "Report of Georgia State Supervisor of Negro Rural Schools for February 1914" (March 2, 1914), Box 67, GEB Papers; Fosdick, *Adventure in Giving,* p. 101; Favrot, *County Training Schools for Negroes in the South,* p. 9.

32. S. L. Smith, "Report of Tennessee State Supervisor of Negro Rural Schools for September 1914" (October 5, 1914), Box 158, GEB Papers; Favrot, County Training Schools for Negroes in the South, p. 27; Presson, *Report of Educational Activities in Negro Schools,* p. 21; S. L. Smith, "Report of Tennessee State Supervisor of Negro Rural Schools for October 1914" (November 5, 1914). Box 158, GEB Papers; Wallace Buttrick to Frederick T. Gates (October 14, 1904), Box 716, GEB Papers.

33. Jackson Davis, *County Training Schools,* Reprinted from the *Southern Workman* (October 1918), p. 8; Favrot, *County Training Schools for Negroes in the South,* p. 27.

34. Leo M. Favrot, "The Industrial Movement in Negro Schools" (June 9, 1913), Box 25, GEB Papers; John A. Presson, "Report of Arkansas State Supervisor of Negro Rural Schools for January 1917" (February 5, 1917), Box 25, GEB Papers.

35. S. L. Smith, "Report of Tennessee State Supervisor of Negro Rural Schools for October 1915" (November 5, 1915), Box 158, GEB Papers; James H. Dillard to N. C. Newbold (September 25, 1915), Box 286, GEB Papers; Jackson Davis to Abraham Flexner (October 2, 1915), Box 286, GEB Papers; See Reports on Georgia County Training Schools for June 1916 and May 1918, Box 68, GEB Papers.

36. Jackson Davis to Abraham Flexner (October 2, 1915); Jackson Davis to James H. Dillard (September 28, 1915); Jackson Davis to Abraham Flexner (October 14, 1915); George D. Godard to Abraham Flexner (October 15, 1915); Arthur D. Wright to Abraham Flexner (October 16, 1915); Abraham Flexner to Jackson Davis, George D. Godard and Arthur D. Wright (October 8, 1915); Jackson Davis to E. C. Sage (March 11, 1916), all above letters in Box 286, GEB Papers.

37. John F. Slater Fund, *Suggested Course for County Training Schools* (Lynchburg, Virginia, 1917).

38. Favrot, *County Training Schools for Negroes in the South,* pp. 36–38; Redcay, *County Training Schools,* 33–37; Favrot, "The Industrial Movement in Negro Schools"; For detailed information on subjects taught in the Training School see Summary Reports from County Training Schools, Box 294, GEB Papers.

39. Doxey A. Wilkerson, *Special Problems of Negro Education*, United States Advisory Committee on Education, Staff Study Number 12 (Washington, D.C. 1939), pp. 39–40.

40. Redcay, *County Training Schools*, pp. 78–84. 100.

41. Henry Snyder Enck, "The Burden Borne: Northern White Philanthropy and Southern Black Industrial Education, 1900–1915" (University of Cincinnati, Ph.D. dissertation, 1970), see chapter 4 on "Philanthropic Motivation"; James H. Dillard, Wickliffe Rose and Raymond Fosdick to Members of the General Education Board (October 6, 1922), Box 331, GEB Papers, p. 24.

15

The Admission and Assimilation of Minority Students at Harvard, Yale, and Princeton, 1900–1970

Marcia G. Synnott

ACCESS to higher education was and is an essential factor in the economic and social mobility of minority groups within the United States. Prominent among the groups to take advantage of educational opportunities were Catholics and Jews, the children and grandchildren of the Irish immigration of the mid-19th century and of the "New Immigration" from eastern and southern Europe at the century's end. Today, however, other groups — blacks, Hispanic-Americans, Indians, and Orientals — are knocking on the door of admissions offices at colleges, universities, and professional schools. It is still too soon to assess their rate of educational mobility and determine whether it will parallel or even exceed that of Jews and Catholics. The role of quotas, both discriminatory and benign, have played a crucial role in retarding and encouraging the educational mobility of both the earlier and contemporary aspirants to advanced degrees. In studying this area of educational and social history, the focus has been limited, at least for the time being, to elite private institutions, to the so-called Big Three of Harvard, Yale, and Princeton. Although admission and assimilation at these colleges would be more difficult than at most public institutions, once attained, success would be noteworthy and could help to open doors elsewhere.

From their colonial beginnings, Harvard, Yale, and Princeton had provided the most prestigious academic ladder — training proportionately more leaders than any other undergraduate colleges in the United States. The demand of upwardly mobile sons of Jewish and Catholic immigrants for admission to each of these universities precipitated an institutional crisis, involving not only the existing limitations of classroom space and

Marcia Synnott is associate professor of history at the University of South Carolina.

campus housing, but also questions of educational purpose — of whom to educate and why. It erupted with World War I, although its earliest signs had appeared before the turn of the century when children of the New Immigration boarded streetcars for their daily academic pilgrimage across the Charles River from Boston to Harvard or uptown to Morningside Heights and Columbia University. (1)

The era of tremendous business and industrial expansion from the Civil War to the 1920's brought with it an influx of over thirty million immigrants, most of them the New Immigration. Pouring into cities, they formed voting blocs, manipulated by party bosses. Together with the Irish, who gained political control of New York and Boston, the masses of newer immigrants might in some not distant future shift the balance of power nationally away from the native-born. At the same time, the native-born felt that the competition of cheaper immigrant labor jeopardized their economic security. Once immigrants had sufficient political and economic leverage, they would be in a position, the native-born feared, to impose alien cultural norms on American society.

The perceived dangers from internal aliens fused with the failed international crusade of President Woodrow Wilson to produce an intense nativist reaction among old-stock Protestant Americans. During the period between the First and Second World Wars, many of them turned their attention away from the world community and reaffirmed their loyalty to their American nation and to people of similar Anglo-Saxon ancestry (their "tribe"). For some, even the United States was too alien and heterogeneous. To protect themselves within their own country, they adopted various restrictive practices, if not downright quotas — aimed at barring the newcomers' access to such important economic, cultural, and social institutions as the corporation, the private, endowed college, and the gentleman's club. Of the three, the denial of educational opportunity hurt aspiring immigrants the most. At stake was more than just petty social snobbery: it was no less than the right to enter the most lucrative professional and managerial positions and even high appointive and elective government offices. (2)

The children of the immigrants would not, in large numbers, be able to surmount these barriers until the post-World War II era brought a vast expansion of both higher educational facilities and scholarship aid (notably, the G.I. Bill and the National Defense Education Act). The United States could remain a superpower only if it utilized the talents of all individuals, regardless of ethnic, racial or social background. In addition to funds from the federal government, states now had the revenues to expand public institutions, while keeping tuition costs low. To attract and educate the most promising candidates, private universities, like Harvard, Yale, and Princeton, had to enter the talent search and offer more scholarships and financial aid. The first minority groups to benefit conspicuously from these opportunities were Catholics and Jews, but vigorous recruitment programs also opened up the educational ladder to newer groups, especially to blacks. (3)

After World War II, then, the Big Three had to broaden and diversify their student body in order to maintain educational leadership, both within the United States and among the international community of scholars. Such had not been their practice during the "tribal twenties." With considerable tolerance, Harvard, Yale, and Princeton had catered to their clientele, almost exclusively middle and upper middle-class old-stock Protestant Americans. Students of good character who could pay the tuition were usually admitted, even if sometimes on academic condition. Sons of men of inherited wealth, the old college families, were joined by sons of nouveaux riches businessmen. This new national upper class came to college as much, if not more, for its social contacts and extracurricular activities as for its classroom instruction. Their days of campus pleasure were threatened, however, by a large and rapid rise in the number of applicants following World War I. In the competition for places, grade-hungry immigrants might jostle aside the Big Three's traditional clientele. (4)

College officials had several choices: they could raise their rather modest academic entrance requirements, but admit the most qualified, whether native-born or immigrant, Gentile or Jew, rich or poor, up to their capacity to educate and to house. Or they could somewhat arbitrarily limit the size of the freshman class and introduce character tests to weed out the socially undesirable, specifically Jews. Or they could frankly impose admissions quotas on Jews and any other immigrant groups which might become too numerous. Harvard, Yale, and Princeton resorted to all three options. As a concession to the brightest of the immigrant sons, they admitted those with the highest scores on entrance examinations. At the same time, they limited enrollments so that they could discriminate among the qualified candidates on the basis of social characteristics. And finally, a quota on Jews was introduced to keep the most academically aggressive of the immigrant groups within bounds. Thus the Big Three and the other universities adopting similar practices were in concert with certain national trends during the 1920's that resulted in the Immigration Quota Laws of 1921 and 1924 and the National Origins Law of 1929. Eastern and southern Europeans were considered less desirable than those of northern European origin not only as collegians but also as citizens. It was no coincidence that President A. Lawrence Lowell, the instigator of the movement to impose a 15 percent Jewish quota at Harvard College, was also a strong advocate of immigration restriction. (5)

Jewish applicants were singled out because they, more than Catholics, sought admission to such private institutions as Harvard, Yale, and Columbia. Although Catholics had arrived earlier than the bulk of Jewish immigration, they did not enter the mainstream of secular higher education until at least a generation later. Whereas Catholics often believed that religious training was an integral part of education itself, Jews largely separated the former from the function of the latter. Consequently, Catholics built an educational system extending from parish schools through universities. Jews did not found denominational colleges. According to President James R. Angell of Yale, neither the Jewish students themselves "nor their families would be likely to look upon a Jewish university as satisfactorily meeting their requirements, unless it were notably more liberally endowed, staffed and equipped than other existing institutions." (6) (See Table 1)

At first this "foreign element," as it was called, was too small to cause concern, but by the late 1910's, administrators at private, eastern colleges began to show alarm at what seemed to be an immigrant invasion of their old-stock educational institutions. Meeting at Princeton University, May

Table 1

Percentage of Jewish Students at Thirty Colleges and
Universities, 1918–1919

College	Enrollment Jewish	Total	Percent
College of Dental & Oral Surgery, New York	477	589	80.9
College of the City of New York	1,544	1,961	78.7
Long Island Hospital Medical College New York	189	343	55.0
New York University	2,532	5,536	45.7
Hunter College	502	1,295	38.7
St. Lawrence University	169	532	31.7
Polytechnic Institute of Brooklyn	97	329	29.4
Fordham University	290	1,247	23.2
Columbia University	1,475	6,943	21.2
Tufts University	310	1,635	18.9
University of Chicago	761	4,106	18.5
Johns Hopkins	322	1,983	16.2
Armour Institute of Technology	95	605	15.7
Western Reserve University	269	1,838	14.6
University of Pennsylvania	596	4,072	14.5
Temple University	266	1,854	14.3
Adelphi College, Brooklyn	42	309	13.5
University of Pittsburgh	443	3,627	12.2
Trinity College, Hartford	29	237	12.2
Harvard University	385	3,843	10.0
Boston University	169	1,714	9.9
Baldwin-Wallace College, Berea, Ohio	55	565	9.8
Cornell University	317	3,505	9.1
Brown University	34	1,140	2.9
Dartmouth College	33	1,173	2.8
Princeton University	30	1,142	2.6
United States Military Academy at West Point	22	994	2.2
Amherst College	8	421	1.9
Bowdoin College	14	774	1.9
Williams College	7	481	1.4

Source: "Professional Tendencies Among Jewish Students in Colleges, Universities, and Professional Schools" (Memoir of the Bureau of Jewish Social Research), *The American Jewish Year Book 5681*, 22 (September 13, 1920, to October 2, 1921), pp. 387-89.

9 and 10, 1918, members of the Association of New England Deans voiced their fears:

Dean Wren [Frank G., Tufts College]
I find that more and more the foreign element is creeping in and now, because of the enlistments, the American boys are getting less and less. . . . How can we get the boys of American parentage to come to college?

Dean Sills [Kenneth Charles Morton, Acting President, subsequently President of Bowdoin College]
We do not like to have boys of Jewish parentage.

Dean Randall [Otis E., Brown University]
They tried to establish a Jewish fraternity at Brown.
Q. Does Brown feel the effects of Jewish students?
A. Yes.

Dean Jones [Frederick S., Yale University]
I think we shall have to change our views in regard to the Jewish element. . . . If we do not educate them, they will overrun us. . . . A few years ago every single scholarship of any value was won by a Jew. I took it up with the Committee and said that we could not allow that to go on. . . . We decided not to give them any scholarships but to extend aid to them in the way of tuition.

Dean Burton [Alfred Edgar, Massachusetts Institute of Technology]
We always ask of our Jewish students whether or not they will be obliged to leave college if they do not receive assistance. In every case they say they will, but we have found by experience that such is not the case.

There was no evidence that the deans made any collective resolutions at this time. But before the 1920 meeting of the Association of Administrative Officers in New England, held at Middletown, Connecticut, Dean Randall of Brown proposed for discussion the "limitation in the enrollment of Jews and Negroes." Discussion or adoption of a Jewish quota at one private, eastern university soon sparked similar consideration or debate at other institutions. (7)

Not only was each worried about its own actual or potential Jewish enrollment, but all felt threatened by the adoption of Jewish quotas elsewhere. Applicants turned away from the first to institute quotas, particularly Columbia and New York Universities, might apply en masse to those with fewer or no restrictions. Columbia had already cut Jewish enrollment from about forty percent to about twenty, in order to regain its former status as an elite institution for native American sons of local business and professional men, its clientele prior to the move to Morningside Heights. In 1919, Columbia adopted the Tests for Mental Alertness, devised by E. L. Thorndike of Teachers College, partly on the assumption that "objectionable" applicants would not have "had the home experiences which enable them to pass these tests as successfully as the average native American boy." Together with new application blanks, photographs, and a personal interview, the so-called "psychological" tests permitted the introduction of additional social criteria in the admissions process. (8)

To be with more pleasing companions, the socially elite might leave Harvard and Yale, as they had already left Columbia, to enter small colleges, notably the Little Three of Amherst, Wesleyan, and Williams, or Dartmouth. Certain factors aided the latter by limiting the number of potential Jewish applicants. First, their small town locations discouraged both local Jewish residents and outside Jewish applicants. Other deterrents were the required chapel attendance and the exclusiveness of clubs and fraternities. In 1918-19, Jewish enrollment at Dartmouth was 2.8 percent; at Amherst, 1.9; and at Williams, 1.4. Indeed, to discreet inquiries, their officials could confidentially report "no pressing Jewish problem." (9)

While Princeton enjoyed most of the same deterrents as these small-town colleges, Harvard and Yale saw themselves as citadels of Anglo-Saxon culture beleaguered by the urban masses. Nevertheless, by the early 1920's, administrators at all three universities decided that they definitely had a "Jewish problem" and possibly a problem with other ethnic groups. President Lowell, for example, even favored the application of a percentage system in college admissions to

any group of men who did not mingle indistinguishably with the general stream, — let us say Orientals, colored men, and perhaps . . . French Canadians, if they did not speak English and kept themselves apart; or we might limit them by making the fact that men do not so mingle one of the causes for rejection above a certain percentage. This would apply to almost all, but not all, Jews; possibly, but not probably, to other people. (10)

The proportion of Jewish freshmen regularly admitted to Harvard had risen from 7 percent (36 out of 511) in 1900 to 21.5 percent (150 out of 698) by 1922. While the numerical increase in Jewish students at Yale was smaller, it caused as much official concern. In 1901-02, there were 18 Jews in the three upperclasses or 2 percent of the enrollment. Twenty years later, 13.4 percent (71) of the 534 members of the Yale College Class of 1925 were Jewish. In 1900, five Jewish undergraduates enrolled at Princeton; in 1922, 25 of the 635 freshmen, or just under 4 percent, of the Class of 1926 were Jewish. By 1911-12, judging from the 250 members of the campus St. Paul's Catholic Club, there were, at the very least, several hundred Catholic students attending Harvard. Yale College had fewer: 30 Catholics were among the 357 members of the Class of 1912. Fewer than 20 Catholics matriculated each year at Princeton until 1908, when 25 enrolled. Although officials at the Big Three may have kept an occasional count of Catholic students, their numbers did continue to increase slightly, even after quotas were imposed on Jewish applicants. (Coincidentally, blacks were totally excluded from Princeton, while Harvard and Yale took only a handful each year.) (11)

Encouraged by the tacit, if not vocal approval of alumni and undergraduates, Harvard, Yale, and Princeton began to apply methods of selection that were not particularly subtle. They ranged from photographs attached to admission forms, specific questions regarding the applicant's race and religion, personal interviews, and a proportionate quota on scholarship aid. Beginning with the Class of 1928, Yale aimed at stabilizing its Jewish representation at around 10-12 percent. The same year, 1924, Princeton almost halved its number of successful Jewish candidates in order to admit no more, and usually less, than the percentage of Jews in the national population, about three percent. Two years later, with the Class of 1930, the Lowell administration began to reduce Harvard's Jewish enrollment (despite considerable faculty opposition to quotas) from about 25-27 percent to about 10-15 percent. (12)

In restricting the admission of Jews, officials at the Big Three expediently acknowledged their dependence upon private preparatory feeder schools (attended almost exclusively by Gentiles) for at least half, if not more, of their undergraduate enrollments. From the early 1900's through the 1940's, about 50 to 60 percent of Harvard and about 70 to 90 percent of Princeton freshmen were private school graduates. Between 40 and 60 percent of Yale freshmen were educated in private preparatory schools, with another 10 to 20 percent adding a year or two at a private school to their public education. Of these percentages, however, only about half or less were really part of the so-called "prep school crowd" of the socially elite. The other half were the sons of middle-class business and professional families, who attended a local or neighboring private school of modest social reputation for a few years before going off to college. College officials were solicitous about protecting their more privileged clientele from both unpleasant social contacts and from too much academic competition. (13)

The prep school crowd chose to attend the Big Three because of alumni connections, college reputation, or private school affiliation. They were the graduates of the twenty or so best private schools, most of which were located in New England. At the top of the social hierarchy were the five Episcopal boarding schools known as the "St. Grottlesex" group: St. George's, St. Mark's, St. Paul's, Groton, and Middlesex. Together with about a dozen others, these prep schools provided the candidates for Harvard's ten "final" clubs, about 11 or 12 percent of the sophomore, junior, and senior classes. Similar groups of private schools sent to Yale future junior fraternity and senior society men and to Princeton the candidates for the dozen or so upperclass eating clubs. (14)

Knowing precisely what they wanted, the prep school crowd created collegiate life. For the most part, they shunned honor grades in order to devote themselves to extracurricular activities: editorships, managerships, and athletic competitions. And not only were they paying customers, but they could usually be counted on to contribute generously both their time and money to alumni activities and fund-raising campaigns (the expectation of future support was less certain from students from lower income families).

While the prep school crowd could largely ignore the presence of social inferiors and disdain to compete with them (protected, as if in a medieval keep, by their clubs and fraternities), this did not hold true for the sons of the native-born, Protestant, "solid middle class," who comprised the rank-and-file of the student body. Increasingly, they had to compete for financial aid with the Catholic and Jewish graduates of the urban public feeder schools, such as Boston Latin and Boston English Schools for Harvard and Hillhouse High School for Yale. And the native-born resented it. In fact, Dean Frederick S. Jones of Yale explicitly blamed the declining interest in scholarship among private school graduates (Gentiles) upon the academic success of the Jews:

Some men say they are not disposed to compete with Jews for first honors; they do not care to be a minority in a group of men of higher scholarship record, most of whom are Jews. It is also cited that the recent vote that the "Y" is preferable to Phi Beta Kappa is indicative of a change of feeling which may be attributed in part to the feeling that the Jew is properly the 'greasy grind' and that other students may hesitate to join the group. (15)

At the same time, the future careers of middle class sons more often than not would depend upon academic performance in college. But their families were hard pressed to educate several children. As sympathetic Yale officials noted, this salaried class of "people of education and refinement" (from whom also came most of the professoriate) needed scholarships to compensate for a loss of purchasing power. As early as 1907, Dean Byron S. Hurlbut of Harvard had expressed concern for the plight of the middle classes after reviewing the applications for financial aid. The cases of greatest appeal, and they were "abundant," were what he called

'the old-fashioned College cases' — sons of families that have been American for generations, — farmers and ministers, and most of all those of families with traditions of refinement and liberal education. Usually this last sort of case is the son of a widow who, used to surroundings of comfort and refinement, finds herself, on the death of her husband, with almost no support. There is another — an increasing class — also interesting, — that is, the foreigners, and especially the Russian Jews. They, however, as a rule accept help with a readiness which cannot but lessen one's interest in them, in comparison with that American spirit which seeks to conceal need. (16)

Interestingly enough, Hurlbut was more sympathetic toward needy students of Welsh or Irish stock. He recalled a Welshman, who as a boy had supported his family by jobs in the Pennsylvania coal mines. In spite of having to work his way through college and developing an occasional " 'miner's cough,' " the Welshman was "jolly, full of fun, cheerful in the darkest days." To match the Welshman's story was that of an Irish mother, who was "one of the 'brave.' " Deserted by her husband, she labored long hours in the mills to support her family. The son, "a cheerful

Irishman," worked as a policeman during the summer. The dean thought that he would "some day be heard from in politics" and hoped that "his Harvard education will help him to stand for what is right." (17)

Of course, these favorable stereotypes of Irish (Catholics) and Welsh students, in contrast to the generally negative ones of Jews, were due in part to the difference in numbers. Catholics still preferred their own denominational colleges. While most Catholic students came to be fairly well received at the Big Three by the mid-1920's, those Jews who passed the required academic and character tests found little or only a begrudging reception. Occasionally, the Protestant-dominated extracurricular and social structure would admit a few students of different ethnic and racial background if they were athletically talented and personable. Some Catholics even made the social club rosters, but Jews were almost entirely absent. Jews, moreover, were often excluded from athletic teams of the major sports, debating societies, editorial boards, and musical clubs. Consequently, they formed parallel cultural and social organizations, such as the Menorah Society, begun at Harvard in 1906. By 1918, there were six Jewish social clubs or fraternities at Harvard, and three at Yale. On the other hand, Negroes were too few in number even to form such supportive organizations. President Charles W. Eliot commented in 1907 that in "a few cases . . . negroes were taken into athletic organizations on account of their remarkable athletic merit," but that he "never heard of negroes being admitted to the fraternities or clubs at Harvard." Indeed, Eliot showed little concern that undergraduate organizations excluded many Catholics, most Jews, and virtually all blacks. Somewhat optimistically he maintained that discrimination by individuals did not matter as long as "the university, like the state, leaves its members completely free to do their own social sorting." It was enough that "all students in Harvard University — as students — are treated by the University precisely alike without regard to class, caste, or race." (18)

In contrast, both President A. Lawrence Lowell, Eliot's successor, and President Woodrow Wilson of Princeton believed that colleges had a social as well as an academic responsibility toward their students. But official involvement in undergraduate social relations — through the assumption of greater obligations for the feeding and housing of students — could cut both ways. On the one hand, courageous administrative enforcement of genuine mixing of undergraduates in campus housing could reduce social snobbery and ethnic or racial prejudice. On the other, given the cost of expanding residential units and dining facilities to accommodate increasing numbers of students, administrators might decide to restrict or exclude from them those who ostensibly did not mingle well with their classmates. In short, Jews and Negroes, and to some extent, Catholics might find it even harder to assimilate into undergraduate life at a residential college than at one which permitted a large number of commuters.

Drawing in part upon Oxford and Cambridge Universities as models, Wilson and Lowell independently developed residential housing plans for their respective colleges. New residential units were necessary at Princeton, Wilson believed, to provide sufficient on-campus housing and to counteract the undemocratic practices which had become entrenched in undergraduate society. By denying membership to one-third of each class, the upperclass eating clubs effectively excluded those students from equal and complete participation in the Princeton community. Only through a system of residential quadrangles would there be a "reintegration" of the academic and social life of the University. No student would be permitted to reside outside this community of young scholars and their mentors (in contrast, Harvard would allow students, in particular its final clubmen, to escape the houses to live with friends in Cambridge rabbit-warrens). There would be no second-class collegians (neither commuters nor the unclubbed) at Princeton. Free of artificial barriers, such a community would be democratic, Wilson maintained, because, by his definition, "democracy [was] made up of unchosen experiences." (19)

Wilson's Quadrangle Plan was defeated because most Princeton alumni and students wanted their college to preserve social distinctions, not to soften them. For example, trustee Bayard Henry argued against the plan on the grounds that "Wilson's idea of uniformity as to food is socialistic and not natural." Food, clothing, and social club affiliation were marks of status. "In a University," Henry maintained, "as well as elsewhere in America, men like to be on their own level, or else to be in a position where they can better themselves. They will not be put on a level with those below them." As long as selective upperclass eating clubs embodied ultimate undergraduate ambition, Princeton would, by its very nature, discourage, if not reject, students of diverse ethnic backgrounds. Not until the late 1950's and 1960's did the university begin to offer alternative facilities for the non-clubmen. (20)

Whereas Wilson envisioned his Quadrangle Plan primarily as a means of elevating intellectual standards, Lowell stressed the social benefits of his Freshman Halls and House Plan—congenial associations in pleasant surroundings. And the Princetonian's failure reinforced the Harvard president's own convictions about the potential alumni and student opposition to enforced residential mixing.

When Harvard opened three Freshman Halls in 1914, College officials handled dormitory and roommate assignments carefully to avoid parental and student objections. By intermingling most freshmen in these units, except those permitted to live off-campus, President Lowell hoped to prevent the formation of cliques based upon schools and economic or geographical distinctions. But he believed that black students should be *persuaded* to seek other accommodations, since it would be *unreasonable* to "compel" whites to live in the same halls with them. In 1922, he personally turned down the application of Roscoe Conkling Bruce on behalf of his son, a student at Phillips Academy Exeter. (Bruce himself was a Phi Beta Kappa and magna cum laude graduate of the Class of 1902 and the son of a former United States Senator, Blanche K. Bruce of Mississippi.) Under pressure — a petition signed by 143 alumni opposing the exclusion of black freshmen from the Halls — Lowell and the Harvard Corporation reversed their stand. But if a black student could not afford the cheapest single nor find a black roommate, he would be unable to live in any one of the Freshman Halls. The number of blacks at Harvard remained small — about 5 or 6 enrolled each year — until the university began seriously to recruit them in the 1960's. (21)

In the early 1930's, through the generous gifts of Edward S. Harkness, Yale '97, Harvard and Yale opened residential units which could accommodate two-thirds or more of the three upperclasses. The masters of the Harvard Houses and of the Yale Colleges selected applicants in such a way that each unit represented cross-sections of secondary school groups and academic fields of concentration. At Harvard, for example, students were sorted by academic rank and grouped into five categories. The first four were by schools; the fifth was by race (by "X" or "*"). Initially, a 10 percent quota limited the number of Jewish applicants admitted to each house. (22)

In his remarks, delivered on Harvard Class Day, June 11, 1975, Professor John Kenneth Galbraith revealed that when he joined the staff of Winthrop House in the autumn of 1935, he was briefly appointed to the house admissions committee and "told to admit only students of the highest quality." He was given a five-columned chart with the following symbols as a guideline: "St. GX" (St. Grottlesexers); "E & A" (Exeter and Andover); "O.P." (Other Private Schools); "H.S." (public high schools); and "X" (Jewish students). "One maximized the number of inmates in the left-hand columns, and most of all the St. GX's," Galbraith was informed, "and minimized, at any cost, those on the far right. No H.S.'s. No X's." He proved himself "intellectually incapable of mastering the further niceties that were involved" and was dropped from the committee as "incompetent." Galbraith concluded, however, that during his forty-one year professorial career at Harvard University "the greatest change for the better [had been] the conversion of its undergraduates from a slightly ludicrous aristocracy to a somewhat serious meritocracy." (23)

World War II released forces which ultimately undermined quota systems. Victory brought the United States world leadership — and into the court of international opinion. Its commitment to democracy abroad was inevitably tested against ethnic prejudice and racial segregation at home. Four important reports, published from December, 1947, to July, 1949, attacked discrimination in higher education: they were drafted by President Truman's Commission on Higher Education, New York State Commission on the Need for a State University, Connecticut State Inter-Racial Commission, and the American Council on Education. Under the combined pressures of state laws and new practices by certain major institutions, most northern colleges and universities dropped from their application blanks questions as to nationality, race, and religion. (24)

Veterans, college-bound with their G.I. Bill benefits, and secondary school seniors flooded admissions offices with applications. As younger men, themselves veterans, joined university faculties and administrations, they began to encourage a shift in student composition by requiring higher academic standards for admission and graduation and by expanding scholarship aid programs. The Big Three — beginning with Harvard and then Yale in the 1950's and Princeton in the 1960's — also accepted their obligations to educate a new elite. They expanded their recruitment of talented high school students outside the East and began to tap the best black applicants from urban centers. By the early 1960's, most students at the Big Three would rank in the highest 5 to 10 percent in intellectual ability of all American college students. At the same time, the number of students from Catholic and Jewish middle- and lower-middle class families almost doubled (more than doubled at Princeton), while those from the upper class, predominantly Anglo-Saxon Protestant families, correspondingly declined. (25)

By 1952 Cornell University sociologists estimated Harvard's undergraduate Jewish enrollment at 25 percent, larger than at ten other universities surveyed, including Dartmouth (15 percent), Cornell (23 percent), and Yale (13 percent). As of 1971, sociologist David Riesman thought that Jews were still roughly about a fourth of the Harvard student body, but Jewish professors had attained a third of the faculty positions. A similar rise in Jewish representation occurred at Princeton and Yale, although a decade or so later. By the early 1970's, probably over 20 percent of entering Princeton freshmen and perhaps as many as one-third of Yale's were Jewish. Catholics, too, totaled about 20 percent, if not more. But at the same time, almost 30 percent of the undergraduates now professed no religious affiliation. Whatever the percentages of the various religious preferences among their students, the Big Three had opened wide its doors. (26)

These changes at Harvard, Yale, and Princeton are important indications of major national shifts in student composition at higher educational institutions. According to a recent study on *Ethnicity, Denomination, and Inequality,* sponsored by the Center for American Pluralism — National Opinion Research Center, Jews are "the best educated Americans," with an average of 14 years of education. Episcopalians and Presbyterians, though ousted from first place in educational achievement, are next with, respectively, 13.5 and 12.7 years. But Catholics (11.5 years of education) rank just below Methodists and somewhat above Lutherans and Baptists. Of all the Catholic ethnic groups, moreover, the Irish (12.5 years of education) outstrip even the British Protestants (12.4 years) to become "the best educated Gentile group in American society." These educational advances are reflected in economic gains; Jews are the most affluent Americans with an average family income of ($13,340; Irish Catholics are second with $12,426, while Episcopalians ($11,032) and Presbyterians ($10,976) trail even the Italian, German, and Polish Catholics ($11,748–$11,298). Education has thus been one of the significant factors in the postwar status revolution benefiting Jews and Catholics. (27)

On the other hand, it has been far more difficult for universities to recruit qualified non-white minorities. Although an increasing number of middle-class blacks qualify for admission to the best colleges and graduate and professional schools, the majority of blacks still lag behind whites in terms of grade point averages and certain aptitude test scores. The social aura of prestige colleges may also discourage black or Hispanic-American applicants. To overcome a legacy of discrimination and failure to recruit, many institutions of higher or professional education have developed special programs and admissions procedures for non-white applicants.·

Harvard, Yale, and Princeton, for example, have adopted "target numbers" for blacks and such other racial minorities as Puerto Ricans, Mexican-Americans, and American Indians as well as for "disadvantaged" white students. At Harvard, the percentage of blacks rose from 2 percent in the early 1960's to 7 percent in 1969. Yale showed similar gains: it had attracted only 37 black applicants in 1960 for the Class of 1964, of which 11 were admitted and 10 matriculated. Ten years later, 755 blacks applied, of whom 270 were women (Yale College became coeducational in 1969); 146 blacks were admitted and 83 came. Yale's director of minority admissions was spending about $17,000 a year in the early 1970's for national recruiting. And to increase the number of Mexican-American and American Indian students at Princeton, the minority students themselves put pressure on the Admissions Office to fund travel expenses for eight undergraduate recruiters (up to $600) to visit high schools in their home communities. In the fall of 1972, there were only 20 Mexican-American and 18 American Indians at Princeton, less than .01 percent of the total undergraduate enrollment. On the other hand, like Harvard and Yale, Princeton had considerable success in recruiting black applicants. The number of blacks (only 5 in 1963) rose to 150 in 1969-70 (the year Princeton began coeducation) and almost doubled to 283 two years later, to about 7 percent of the undergraduates. Among incoming freshmen, the percentage was even higher—slightly over 9 percent. The degree of preferential treatment accorded to minority applicants was hard to gauge. At Harvard, for example, the admission rate for black applicants was only about 60 percent of what it was for alumni sons and athletes, but it was perhaps 5 percent higher than the overall rate. Advantaged whites were still given preference, but were enough disadvantaged whites? (28)

Reverse discrimination may indeed substantially increase minority representation in colleges and professional schools, but, in so doing, it raises tough questions. Today's benign quotas attempt, in a way not unlike the Big Three's earlier discriminatory quotas against Jewish students, to justify race as the key selective factor in the admissions process. On the other hand, there is a major difference in the method of selection imposed by each quota. Whereas the earlier discriminatory quotas required that Jewish students first qualify on the basis of academic achievement and then pass certain social tests of desirability, the current benign quotas may admit minority students with lower academic records or even establish a separate track for them. To protest these new racial quotas, representatives of such white ethnic groups as Jews, Greeks, Italians, Poles, and Ukrainians have filed "friend of the court" briefs on behalf of the suit of Allan Bakke, who claimed that he was denied admission to the University of California Medical School at Davis because he is white. Many professional associations (American Association of University Professors, American Bar Association), liberal organizations (American Civil Liberties Union, Americans for Democratic Action), and institutions have filed briefs in support of the principle behind the Davis Medical School's special admissions program for minority applicants. Among them are four of the nation's leading private universities: Columbia, Harvard, Stanford, and the University of Pennsylvania. In a joint brief, these four institutions argued that racial diversity should be a permissible component in selecting a student body. To protect their own admissions policies from possible challenge, they urged that the United States Supreme Court reverse the 1976 ruling of the Supreme Court of California against the University of California. (29)

In the light of historical evidence, it is ironic that Justice Lewis F. Powell, Jr. cited the Harvard College admissions program as a model of discretion and fairness in the recently decided *Regents of the University of California v. Allan Bakke.* On June 28, 1978, the United States Supreme Court, by a 5-to-4 majority, ruled that race may legitimately be considered as one factor in the selection of students. But by another 5-to-4 vote (with Powell again the pivotal justice), the Supreme Court upheld the judgment of the California Supreme Court against the two-track admissions system at the Davis Medical School. Powell claimed that an important, although fine, line existed between the Harvard and the Davis admissions programs. In expanding its "concept of diversity to include students from disadvantaged economic, racial, and ethnic groups," Harvard had not, Powell contended, insulated any "person from comparison with all other candidates for the available seats." While taking into account their disadvantaged status, Harvard offered minorities neither the inducement nor the protection of an obvious quota. (30)

By contrast, under the system instituted at Davis in 1969, 16 of the 100 slots each year were open only to applicants from "economically and educationally disadvantaged backgrounds," specifically to blacks, American

Indians, Chicanos, Asian-Americans, Puerto Ricans, and Cubans. Although both whites and minorities had applied for the special program, no disadvantaged whites had been admitted. After he was twice denied admission to the regular track, Bakke brought suit against the university under the Equal Protection Clause of the Fourteenth Amendment. The California Supreme Court agreed that the university admissions system "violated constitutional rights of nonminority applicants since it afforded preference on the basis of race to persons who, by the university's own standards, were not as qualified for the study of medicine as nonminority applicants denied admission." The university, moreover, had not demonstrated that its "basic goals" of increasing the number of minority doctors could not be accomplished by means "less detrimental" to the white majority. Since the university could not prove that Bakke would have been denied admission even without the special program, the California Supreme Court ordered him admitted to the medical school. (31)

Vindicated by the United States Supreme Court, Allan Bakke entered the Davis Medical School on September 25, 1978, five years after he initially applied for admission. Other universities which have special admissions programs for minorities now risk similar lawsuits, unless they bring them into conformity with the Bakke decision. On the one hand, the Supreme Court allowed universities some discretion, under the First Amendment, to select a student body which will contribute diverse perspectives to the educational process. On the other, universities must not deny any individual the right, protected by the Fourteenth Amendment, to be evaluated on his or her own merits against all other candidates. Because Harvard apparently "treats each applicant as an individual in the admissions process," its program is constitutional. Quotas, even those which purport to be benign, are outlawed. As the California Supreme Court unequivocally stated:

> No college admission policy in history has been so thoroughly discredited in contemporary times as the use of racial percentages. Originated as a means of exclusion of racial and religious minorities from higher education, a quota becomes no less offensive when it serves to exclude a racial majority.

But the area of legitimate discretion remains indeterminate — until universities are tested, as indeed they will be — by new court cases. (32)

Institutions of higher learning should retain a certain right of discretion in admissions. Course grades and test scores do not infallibly predict future success in college, graduate school, or the professions. Nor do they measure such personal qualities as motivation, dedication, and compassion. Today's admissions officers may be in a better position to decide what kinds of students will benefit, in terms of backgrounds and range of interests, from the education offered and who, consequently, will go on to make the greatest contribution in their careers. But applicants, alumni, the public, and the courts have a right to know the assumptions and guidelines upon which admissions decisions are made. While no institution could ever prove that every student it admitted was better qualified than everyone it rejected, universities may have to submit their standards of admission to periodic public or semi-public reviews. After all, universities are claiming to educate for the future by their recruitment, admissions, and scholarship aid policies. Through a combined process of self-examination and external evaluation, universities may determine more precisely that area in the selection process between legitimate discretion and "unequal" discrimination.

NOTES

* For further documentation and elucidation of this topic, consult my overall study, *The Half-Opened Door: Discrimination and Admissions at Harvard, Yale, and Princeton, 1900–1970* (Westport, Connecticut, 1979).

1. The core of this article is based upon my dissertation: "A Social History of Admissions Policies At Harvard, Yale, and Princeton, 1900–1930" (Ph.D. dissertation, University of Massachusetts, Amherst, 1974). See George W. Pierson, *The Education of American Leaders*, Comparative Contributions of U.S. Colleges and Universities, Praeger Special Studies in U.S. Economic and Social Development (New York, 1969), pp. xix–xxi, 240–51.

2. John Higham, *Strangers in the Land: Patterns of American Nativism 1860–1925*, Corrected and with a new Preface (New York, 1968), ch. 10, "The Tribal Twenties," pp. 264–99; and E. Digby Baltzell, *The Protestant Establishment: Aristocracy & Caste in America* (New York, 1966), ch. 9 "The Anglo-Saxon Decade: Success without Leadership," pp. 197–225.

3. Paul Starr with James Henry & Raymond Bonner, *The Discarded Army: Veterans After Vietnam*, The Nader Report on Vietnam Veterans and the Veterans Administration (New York, 1973), ch. 9 "Education and the G.I. Bill," pp. 226–61. Starr disputes the extent to which the G.I. Bill actually raised the economic and social class level of veterans who took advantage of it (n. 24, pp. 291–92, and n. 41, p. 293).

4. Higham, *Strangers in the Land*, p. 264; Gene R. Hawes, "The Colleges of America's Upper Class," *Saturday Review Magazine* (Nov. 16, 1963): 68–71; and Garland G. Parker, "50 Years of Collegiate Enrollments: 1919–20 to 1969–70," Pt. 1. *School & Society*, 98 (March, 1970): 150.

5. Barbara Miller Solomon, *Ancestors and Immigrants: A Changing New England Tradition* (Cambridge, Mass., 1956), pp. 204–07.

6. Stephen Steinberg, *The Academic Melting Pot: Catholics and Jews in American Higher Education*, A Report Prepared for The Carnegie Commission on Higher Education (New York, 1974), pp. 1–3, 30–31, 33–37.
   James R. Angell to Conrad Hoffman, Jr., Dec. 7, 1933, Records of the President, JRA, Box 84, J.-JOH, file Jewish Problem, Etc., Yale University Archives (hereinafter cited as YUA).

7. "Professional Tendencies Among Jewish Students in Colleges, Universities, and Professional Schools" (Memoir of the Bureau of Jewish Social Research), *The American Jewish Year Book 5681*, 22 (Sept. 13, 1920, to Oct. 2, 1921), pp. 381–93; Minutes of

Meeting of Association New England Deans Held In Princeton, 9th and 10th of May [1918], pp. 21–22, Records of the Dean, Frederick S. Jones, Box 6, file War, YUA; and Topics Proposed For Discussion, Association of Administrative Officers in New England, Middletown, Conn., May 21–22, 1920, Dean of Harvard College — Correspondence, #22 Deans' Association, 1920-27, Harvard University Archives (hereinafter cited as HUA).

8. Frederick Paul Keppel, *Columbia*, American College and University Series (New York, 1914), pp. 179–81; Joel H. Spring, "Psychologists and the War: The meaning of Intelligence in the Alpha and Beta Tests," *History of Education Quarterly*, 12 no. 1 (Spring 1972): 3–15; H.E. Hawkes to Robert N. Corwin, Oct. 16 and 20, 1922, and Corwin to Hawkes, Oct. 18, 1922; YUA. See especially, Harold S. Wechsler, *The Qualified Student: A History of Selective College Admission in America* (New York, 1977), ch. 7 "Repelling the Invasion: Columbia and the Jewish Student," pp. 131–85.

9. Memorandum on Limitation of Numbers; and George Edwin Howes, Dean of Williams College, to Robert N. Corwin, Oct. 16 and Dec. 26, 1922, Com. on Limitation of Numbers, 1922; "Professional Tendencies Among Jewish Students in Colleges, Universities, and Professional Schools," pp. 387–89.

10. A. Lawrence Lowell to William E. Hocking, May 19, 1922, Papers of A. Lawrence Lowell (hereinafter cited as ALLP), #1056 Jews, HUA.

11. Statistics on the Percentage of Jews in various Departments of the University, 1921-22, ALLP, –1056 Jews; *Reports of the President and the Treasurer of Harvard College, 1911-12* (hereinafter cited as *Harvard President's Report*, with date), "Appleton Chapel and Phillips Brooks House," p. 172; A.K. Merritt to Robert N. Corwin, April 11, 1922, copy, Records of the President, JRA, Box 84, file Jewish Problem, Etc. For religious affiliations of Yale College students from the 1870s to the early 1900s, see Appendices D (1) and (2) "Church Members In Academic Classes 1873-1904" and "Religious Composition of Yale University Jan. 1, 1901" *(Two Centuries of Christian Activity at Yale*, edited by James B. Reynolds, Samuel H. Fisher, Henry B. Wright, Committee of Publication (New York, 1901)); also "Yale College 1912 Statistical Blanks," filled out by seniors for *History of the Class of 1912*, Yale College, vol. 1, YUA. For Princeton, see the following in the Princeton University Archives (hereinafter cited as PUA): *College of New Jersey, President's Entrance-Book*, 1 (1871-1893), and *Matriculation Book*, 2 (1893-1903); "Reports of the Dean of the Faculty to the Committee on Morals and Discipline of the Board of Trustees," *Minutes of the Trustees*, 9 (Dec. 1898-Mar. 1901), and 10 (June 1901-Jan. 1908); Radcliffe Heermance, Office of the Supervisor [in 1925, Dean] of Freshmen, "Preliminary Analysis of Freshmen Class," in September, 1921-29, Trustees' Papers; *Annual Report of the President of Princeton University for the year ending December 31st*, 1909-1923 (hereafter cited as *Princeton President's Report*, with date); and *The Nassau Herald, Class of Nineteen Hundred and Twenty-Three* (Princeton, 1923).

12. Robert N. Corwin, Chairman, Board of Admissions, to James R. Angell, Jan. 3, 1933, enclosing table, dated Oct. 19, 1932, "showing our Jewish population for the last ten years," Records of the President, JRA, Box 2 and file Board of Admissions; Preliminary Analysis of Freshman Class," in September, 1921-29, Trustees' Papers, and *The Freshman Herald*, 1930-49. See also Dean's Office to President Lowell, Oct. 25 and Nov. 9, 1925, six tables dated either Nov. 23 or 24, 1925, and Lowell to Henry James, Nov. 3 and 6, 1925, ALLP, #184 Jews — Limitation of Numbers; and [Dean Clarence W. Mendell], report "Harvard," stamped "Dec. 8-1926 Rec'd," Records of the President, JRA, box Mar-Clarence W. Mendell, file Clarence W. Mendell, YUA.

13. *Harvard President's Reports*, 1900-40; George Wilson Pierson, *Yale: College and University 1871-1937*, vol. 2: *Yale: The University College 1921-1937* (New Haven, 1955), pp. 669-71; and *Princeton President's Reports, 1900-40*.

14. Cleveland Amory, *The Proper Bostonians* (New York, 1947), ch. 13 "Harvard and Its Clubs," pp. 291-310; and James McLachlan, *American Boarding Schools: A Historical Study* (New York, 1970), in general; and Loomis Havemeyer, *"Go To Your Room": A Story of Undergraduate Societies and Fraternities at Yale* (New Haven, 1960).

15. "Memorandum on the Problems Arising from the Increase in the Enrollment of Students of Jewish Birth in the University," May 12, 1922, Records of the President, JRA, Box 84, J.-JOH, file Jewish Problem Etc.; Frederick S. Jones to R.N. Corwin, May 6, 1922, Records of the Dean, FSJ, Box 5, file Jews.

16. "Memorandum on the Problems Arising . . . Increase . . . Enrollment of Students of Jewish Birth. . . ." May 12, 1922, see n. 15; B. S. Hurlbut to Joseph Warren, Oct. 16, 1907, Charles W. Eliot Papers (hereinafter cited as CWEP), Box 221, file Hurlbut, Byron Satterlee, HUA.

17. Hurlbut to Warren, Oct. 16, 1907, see n. 16.

18. *Harvard College, Class Reports, First Report*, 1900-40; *Yale College History of the Class*, vol. 1, 1900-40; *Yale Banner and Pot-Pourri*, 1900-40; *The Nassau Herald*, 1900-40; *Z.B.T. 1898-1923, The First Twenty-Five Years* [New York, 1923]; Charles W. Eliot to Bruce L. Keenan, August 9, 1907, CWE Letter Book #96, Dec. 11, 1906 to Oct. 26, 1907, p. 128, HUA. See also Frederick Rudolph, *The American College and University, A History* (New York, 1962), ch. 18 "The Rise of Football," pp. 373-93, and pp. 287-90; and Laurence R. Veysey, *The Emergence of the American University* (Chicago, 1970), "The Mind of the Undergraduate," pp. 268-94.

19. Woodrow Wilson, "The Country and the Colleges" [c. Feb. 24, 1910], *The Papers of Woodrow Wilson*, edited by Arthur S. Link et al., 20: 1910 (Princeton, N.J., 1975), pp. 161, 165, 157-72; "Report on the Social Coordination of the University" [c. June 6, 1907], in the Trustees' Papers, PUA, and in *Princeton Alumni Weekly* (hereinafter cited as *PAW*), 7, no. 36 (June 12, 1907), 606-11.

20. [Bayard Henry] to Henry Burling Thompson, July 13, 1907, *Papers of Woodrow Wilson*, edited by Arthur S. Link et al., 17: 1907-1908 (Princeton, N.J., 1974), pp. 305, 303-06; Henry Wilkinson Bragdon, *Woodrow Wilson: The Academic Years* (Cambridge, Mass., 1967), pp. 408-09; Paul Sigmund, "Princeton in Crisis and Change," *Change: The Magazine of Higher Learning*, 5, no. 2 (March 1973): 37, 34-41.

21. A. Lawrence Lowell to Roscoe Conkling Bruce, Dec. 14, 1922 and Jan. 6, 1923; Bruce to Lowell, Jan. 4, 1923; and clippings from the Boston *Transcript*, Jan. 11, 1923, and New York *World*, Jan. 12, 1923; Robert C. Benchley "To the President and Fellows of Harvard College," Sept. 25, 1922, the Memorial, and "Alumni Signing the Inclosed Memorial"; copies of the *Corporation Records* and the "Book of Understanding," March 26, 1923, ALLP, #42 Negroes. See also "Harvard Men Here Fight Ban Against Negro," *New York Sun*, June 16, 1922, clipping on the Memorial circulated among Harvard alumni in New York, protesting the exclusion of blacks from the Freshman Halls, ALLP, #981 Freshman Dormitories; and Nell Painter. "Jim Crow at Harvard: 1923," *The New England Quarterly*, 44, no. 4 (December, 1971): 627-34.

22. Henry Aaron Yeomans, *Abbott Lawrence Lowell 1856-1943* (Cambridge, 1948), ch.

13 "Housing the Undergraduates, The 'Houses,' " pp. 180-98; Pierson, *Yale: The University College 1921-1937*, ch. 10 "Mr. Harkness and the Quadrangle Plan—I," pp. 207-30; ch. 19 "Planning the Residential Colleges," pp. 420-21, 400-22; Christopher S. Jencks and David Riesman, ch. 22 "Patterns of Residential Education: A Case Study of Harvard," in Nevitt Sanford, editor, *The American College* (New York, 1962), pp. 737-39, 746, 752-59, 764-65.

23. Harvard University News Office, For Release, June 10, 1975, "Text of remarks delivered by John Kenneth Galbraith, Paul M. Warburg Professor of Economics at Harvard University on Harvard Class Day, June 11, 1975," 10 pp.

24. Francis J. Brown, Floyd W. Reeves, Richard A. Anliot, editors, *Discriminations in Higher Education: A Report of the Midwest Educators Conference in Chicago, Illinois, November, 3-4, 1950*, Sponsored by the Midwest Committee on Discriminations in Higher Education and the Committee on Discriminations in Higher Education of the American Council on Education, American Council on Education Studies, Series 1 — Reports of Committees and Conferences, vol. 15, no. 50 (Washington, D.C., August, 1951), pp. 11-22, 35-39. See also R. Freeman Butts, Lawrence A. Cremin, *A History of Education in American Culture* (New York, 1953), pp. 522-23.

25. Francis Bertrand McCarthy, *A Study of the admission of veteran students in Harvard College (1945-1947) and their college records*, 1954, 131 pp. (mimeographed), HUA; Hawes, "The Colleges of America's Upper Class," *Saturday Review Magazine* (Nov. 16, 1963), 70-71; E. Digby Baltzell, "The Protestant Establishment Revisited," *The American Scholar*, 45 (Autumn 1976): 505-06, 511-15.

26. Seymour Martin Lipset and David Riesman, *Education and Politics at Harvard*, Two Essays Prepared for The Carnegie Commission on Higher Education (New York, 1975), pp. 179-80, 307-08; "A Survey of Princeton Freshmen," *PAW*, 71, no. 17 (Feb. 23, 1971), 6-9; Rabbi Arnold Jacob Wolf, "Jewish Experience Is Vividly Present at Yale, " *Yale Alumni Magazine*, 36 (Jan. 1973): 14-15; and Mark Singer, "God and Mentsch at Yale," *Moment*, 1 (Av/Elul 5735, July/August 1975): 27-31.

27. Andrew M. Greeley, *Ethnicity, Denomination, and Inequality*, Sage Research Papers in the Social Sciences (Studies in Religion and Ethnicity Series, No. 90-029) (Beverly Hills and London, 1976), pp. 18-19, 44-46, 70-72.

28. Lipset and Riesman, *Education and Politics at Harvard*, pp. 180, 220; E.J. Kahn, Jr., *Harvard: Through Change and Through Storm* (New York, 1968), pp. 109-11; Penny Hollander Feldman, "Recruiting an Elite: Admission to Harvard College" (Ph.D. dissertation, Harvard University, 1975), "Table 5.5 Admissions Rates of Applicants in Preferred Categories," p. 111; Orde Coombs, "Making It At Yale, The Necessity of Excellence," *Change*, 5, no. 5 (June 1973): chart, "Black Candidates for Admission to Yale," 52, and 49, 51. See also William McCleery, "The Admission Process at Hard-to-Get-into Colleges," *University: A Princeton Quarterly*, (Summer 1970): 23-30; Denny Chin, "Admissions grants recruiting funds to Chicano, Indian undergraduates," *Daily Princetonian*, Oct. 25, 1972, 1, 6; "A Survey of Princeton Freshmen," *PAW*, 71, no. 17 (Feb. 23, 1971), 6-9; Carl A. Fields, "One University's Response to Today's Negro Student," *University: A Princeton Quarterly* (Spring 1968): 14, 17, 19; George E. Tomberlin, Jr., "Trends in Princeton Admissions" (senior thesis in sociology, Princeton University, 1971), pp. 119, 127-28, 136-52, 159-60; and Sigmund, "Princeton in Crisis and Change," *Change*, 5, no. 2 (March 1973): 35-36.

29. Brief of American Jewish Committee et al. as *Amici Curiae*, Brief of Anti-Defama-

tion League of B'nai B'rith et al. as *Amici Curiae*, and Brief of Columbia University et al. as *Amici Curiae* in *Landmark Briefs and Arguments of the Supreme Court of the United States: Constitutional Law, 1977 Term Supplement: Regents of the University of California v. Bakke* (2 vols.: 99 and 100), edited by Philip B. Kurland and Gerhard Casper (Washington, D.C., 1978), vol. 99, pp. 479-590, 689-738. For a list of Briefs in Bakke Case," see *Chronicle of Higher Education*, 15, no. 3 (Sept. 19, 1977): 4.

30. "What the Court Said in Two 5-to-4 Rulings on the Bakke Case, Text of the Opinion by Justice Powell," *Chronicle of Higher Education*, 16, no. 17 (July 3, 1978): 3-7. For texts of the opinions of Justices William J. Brennan, Jr. and John Paul Stevens, see ibid., pp. 7-12; for those of Justices Thurgood Marshall, Harry A. Blackmun, and Byron R. White, see ibid., 16, no. 18 (July 10, 1978), 11-13.

31. *Bakke v. Regents of the University of California*, 18 Cal. 3d 34, 553 P .2d 1152, 132 Cal. Rptr. 680 (1976), especially, pp. 1152, 1156 (and n. 4), 1166, and 1172.

32. See n. 30, "Text of the Opinion of Justice Powell," p. 6; and *Bakke v. Regents of the University of California*, p. 1171.

16

The Struggle against Separate and Unequal Schools: Middle Class Mexican Americans and the Desegregation Campaign in Texas, 1929–1957

Guadalupe San Miguel, Jr.

Since 1929 Mexican American organizations, headed by middle class leaders, have played a significant and increasing role in challenging discriminatory school policies and practices.[1] Led and inspired by the League of United Latin American Citizens (LULAC)[2] and the G. I. Forum,[3] the challenge to education has been essentially a liberal one. As most liberals, Mexican Americans have perceived discrimination, segregation, inferior schools, and culturally biased curriculum and instructional practices as problems incidental to education, not as specific manifestations of systematic structural inequality. As a result, they have not sought the improvement of the existing educational structure by eliminating those barriers which limit Mexican American access to and participation in that system. Hence, the challenge to education has been limited to abolishing segregated schools and student assignment and classification policies which serve to increase segregation. The following essay is a history of this campaign to eliminate the segregation of Mexican American children in the Texas public schools. Emphasis will be placed on the strategies and tactics utilized by LULAC and the G. I. Forum to desegregate the public schools. The period to be covered will be between 1929 and 1957. The year 1929 marks the period during which the League of United Latin American Citizens (LULAC), the first statewide civic organization of Americans of Mexican descent, was organized in Texas. In the latter year the last of a series of desegregation cases filed by the Mexican American community was won. For the next ten years (between 1957 and 1967) because of political, financial, and organizational difficulties, no further legal

Guadalupe San Miguel is associate professor of education and Chicano Studies at the University of California—Santa Barbara.

challenges to educational segregation were made by the Mexican American community. The campaign to desegregate the public schools by Mexican American organizations from 1929 to 1957 has not received the scholarly attention it deserves. This essay will hopefully contribute to this gap in the history of American minority groups by describing and tracing the nature of this campaign against separate and unequal schools for Mexican Americans in Texas.

Prior to 1929, the Mexican community in Texas did not effectively and collectively challenge discriminatory public policies and practices. Although there were sporadic local efforts aimed at eliminating specific types of discriminatory treatment, especially in the public schools, and journalistic exposes of deprivations of civil liberties of the Mexican communities in south Texas by Anglos, the Mexican community lacked forceful and articulate spokespersons.[4] There are several reasons for this lack of collective effort to influence discriminatory educational policy by the Mexican community. The primary reason for this condition was that there was no state wide organization of Mexican Americans to articulate the group's interests, develop collective positions on important issues confronting the community, or bring pressure on local and state school officials. Although prior to 1929 the Mexican American community did not lack civic or social organizations most of these were either protective or mutual benefit associations, that is, they were formed either to give aid to those Mexicans who had encountered discriminatory treatment at the hands of Anglos and to provide insurance, social activities, and entertainment.[5]

Secondly, and perhaps a more important reason for the lack of collective action on the part of Mexicans, the Mexican community had not been integrated into the American system; that is, it had not yet been socialized into accepting the legitimacy of American social, economic, and political institutions, including public schools. The Mexican community in general did not speak English, nor did they necessarily attempt to participate in the established institutions of this country. In many cases, as the history of the campaign to eliminate segregation in the schools will illustrate, local and state officials sought to exclude or limit participation of those Mexican Americans willing to participate in the existing institutions.

During the 1920's, a fundamental shift in ideological and organizational orientation occurred within the Mexican communities of south Texas which significantly affected the social and cultural development of the overall Mexican population. In response to the deteriorating social and economic conditions caused by the growing anti-Mexican feeling among Anglos in Texas, the first generation of Mexicans born or raised in the United States founded new types of organizations in the communities of south and central Texas.[6] Comprised largely of the college trained, the small businessman, and the skilled craftsman, that is, the incipient Mexican American middle class element, these new organizations formed to eradicate social injustices, to ensure just treatment of the Mexican population under the law, and, most importantly, to promote the integration of the Mexican population into the existing social economic, and political structures of the American society.[7] The formation of the Order Sons of America in the early 1920's, the League of United Latin American Citizens (LULAC) in 1929, and, later, the G. I. Forum in 1948, represented a significant departure from the founding of traditional protective and mutual benefit organizations for a number of reasons. First and foremost was the basic shift from largely protective and self-help to assimilative activities. For example, the Constitution of LULAC illustrated this fundamental transformation. According to the Constitution, one of the central aims of the organization was "to develop within the members of our race, the best, purest, and most perfect type of a true and loyal citizen of the United States of America."[8] The making of citizens itself was not a major concern for the middle class Mexican Americans since over half of the Mexican population living in South Texas were already citizens.[9] Rather, from their rhetoric and based on their actual behavior it appears that they were more concerned with the making of active citizens who would practice their citizenship by participating in the dominant political, economic, and social institutions of the land. For this reason, LULAC felt that the members of the Mexican community had to "be aroused to a consciousness of that citizenship and then must be educated as to what are his civil and political rights."[10]

Another reason why these new organizations represented a significant departure from the past concerned their membership. The *mutualista* organizations of the past welcomed both Mexican immigrants and Mexican citizens of the United States. The Order Sons of America and LULAC, on the other hand, initially limited its membership to U.S. citizens of Mexican ancestry. Alonso S. Perales, one of the founders of LULAC, stated that only by using the rights they had as citizens could the socioeconomic problems of all the Mexicans living north of the border be solved. "The day the Mexican American betters his own conditions and finds himself in a position to make full use of his rights of citizenship," he stated, "that day he will be able to aid the Mexican citizen in securing what is due him and to help him assure himself of his own welfare and happiness."[11]

In pledging allegiance to the United States government, the middle class Mexicans in these organizations also de-emphasized dependence on the mother country for moral sustenance. Instead of looking to Mexico for guidance, advice and intellectual nourishment, the middle class now looked to the political and ideological institutions of the United States. As the LULAC Constitution stated, the organization was formed to "define with absolute and unmistakable clearness our unquestionable loyalty to the ideals, principles, and citizenship of the United States of America."[12] To achieve this end, LULAC adopted English as the official language of the organization and pledged "to learn and speak and teach (the) same to our children."[13]

The middle class Mexicans, as Americans of Mexican descent and conscious of themselves as an emerging middle class, assumed the responsibility of educating, protecting, and incorporating the Mexican population into the dominant institutions of their country. But the integration of the Mexican population into the mainstream of Anglo social, political, and economic life was not to be achieved at the expense of their cultural background. The Mexican American middle class was not calling for the total assimilation of the Mexican population into Anglo cultural society as has been suggested by some authors.[14] Integration into Anglo-American political and social life was to be a selective process. "To assume," declared one of their aims "complete responsibility for the education of our children as to their rights and duties and the language and customs of this country; the latter insofar as they may be in good customs."[15] Cultural pride was not to be neglected either. "We solemnly declare once and for all to maintain a sincere and respectful reference for our racial origin of which we are proud."[16] The English language and Anglo American political and social customs and traditions were to be learned, but not at the expense of the Spanish language and the Mexican traditions. Cultural pride, retention of the Spanish language, and the physical and cultural defense of the Mexican heritage were as much goals of the new organizations as were the acquisition of the English language, the training for citizenship, and the struggle for equality for the residents of Mexican ancestry.

Education in the eyes of many was to play an important role in the general strategy of incorporating Mexicans into the dominant institutions of the land. Most importantly, especially in the initial stages, education was also to assist in the enlargement of this particular group of individuals who would eventually lead this historic mission of incorporating Mexicans into the mainstream of American life. Thus, from its founding, one of the major goals of these new organizations was to promote education for organizational growth.[17] O.D. Weeks, an Anglo political scientist who attended the LULAC founding convention, noted the Mexican American leaders were inexperienced and lacked organizational skills. "Regarding the present leaders of the League, it may be said that the aims of the organization are high," he states. "Most of them" Weeks added, "however capable of leadership, have not previously held important positions in similar organizations."[18] The problem confronting the young organization was that of "appraising and choosing the type of local leadership they can command, before consenting to the creation of new local councils," and in "recruiting additional leaders from among the younger men who are coming on."[19]

Recruitment of capable leaders became essential for the growth and effectiveness of the organization in attaining its goals. A possible solution in resolving this problem was formal training or education. "To make themselves valued and respected," one person noted, "The United Latin American Citizens must affect their own intellectual redemption by fostering education."[20] Alonso Perales believed that the organization should strive for better and more formal schooling for all Mexicans. He believed that more education would increase earning power and indirectly improve the living standards of all Mexicans. This, in turn, would elevate the sociopolitical status of the

Mexican community. An editorial in the LULAC News, the organization's newsletter, stated this educational perspective in 1931. It said:

Again and again at different times our orators of the League have expressed their belief that the fundamental and basic problem of our race in Texas and the United States was education. Educate the children of Mexican extraction and we will have a new generation that will measure up to the requirement of American standards.[21]

But while education for all was favored, LULAC members believed that only the exceptionally endowed should receive a higher education, that is, only those who showed promise should receive a college education.[22] Not all members agreed with this Jeffersonian view of education. Paul Taylor in his study of Nueces County noted that there were differences within LULAC. "Naturally," he stated, "there is a considerable diversity of motive and conception of purposes, even when central aims are agreed upon."[23] These differences, for example, affected membership. Although most that agreed that only American citizens of Mexican ancestry should be admitted into the organization, there was disagreement as to what kind of Mexican American should be eligible for membership. Some wanted to admit all American citizens of Mexican descent, while others wanted to admit only the most advanced element of the Mexican community. No definition was given of what was meant by "advanced" but it was implied that only the educated should be admitted. Many strongly believed that only an educated membership could thwart the efforts of powerful leaders who wanted to manipulate and deliver the organization's vote to existing political machines in South Texas.[24]

Regardless of these differences, most LULAC members agreed that education was important for elevating the general socioeconomic and political condition of the Mexican community. Yet, they also believed education would do more than elevate the status of the community. It would increase the size of the middle class within the Mexican community. By receiving more education, especially higher education, the Mexican middle class would enlarge itself as a class. This enlargement of the educated and upwardly mobile elements within the Mexican community would ensure the continued existence and further growth of organizations such as LULAC by providing them with future leaders and members. But in order to achieve more schooling, it was necessary to struggle against obstacles impeding the educational progress of Mexicans. For this reason, their struggle became twofold. On the one hand, they had to modify existing discriminatory educational policies and practices in order to improve the accessibility to more and better schooling for Mexicans. On the other hand, they had to go among their own people and disseminate their faith in public education. To a large extent, LULAC members believed that the problem confronting the Mexican community consisted both of Anglo prejudice as well as Mexican American inaction. "The problems with which they and their racial brothers are faced in

Texas and the United States," one observer commented, "have been created quite as much by their own deficiencies as by the deficiencies of the Anglo-American in his dealings with them."[25] With respect to education, LULAC believed that Mexicans had to adopt the national language, treasure public schooling and learn to demand equal treatment in schools. "We try to impress upon them first, the importance of the English Language," stated a local LULAC member, and "second, the importance of educating their children, even if it is too late for them."[26] In addition to eliminating the "linguistic handicap" the members in LULAC also aimed at raising the standards of personal hygiene among the Mexican American population and creating a more positive attitude toward public education.

The G.I. Forum was ideologically similar to LULAC. Politically liberal, highly patriotic, and pragmatically oriented, it espoused LULAC's faith in the power of education. During the 1950's the G.I. Forum considered education to be of utmost importance. "Education," stated a pamphlet describing what the organization stood for, "is the principal weapon to fight the many evils affecting our people."[27] Education for Mexicans was looked upon with such high regard that the motto for the organization became "Education is Our Freedom and Freedom Should be Everybody's Business." Unlike LULAC, however, the G.I. Forum did not elaborate its philosophy towards education. Their primary concern was struggling against the influx of Mexican immigrants into Texas and their blatant exploitation by agricultural interests.[28] Still education for Mexican Americans was not neglected. Fighting discriminatory school policies occupied much of their time. In general, the G.I. Forum promoted more and better education for Mexican Americans and fought against the provision of separate and inferior schooling.

Mexican American leaders in LULAC and the G.I. Forum were not so concerned with challenging the content of formal instruction or with modifying the structures of governance as were social reformers in other parts of the country.[29] Rather, they were concerned with the denial of educational services and with the right to receive equal treatment by local school districts. The primary target of LULAC's and the G.I. Forum's reform activities centered on challenging the legality and practice of separate and unequal schooling for Mexican American students. School segregation of Mexican Americans and denial of access to elementary and secondary education were perceived by most leaders to be the major obstacles to educational equality. Most importantly, separate and inferior schools for Mexicans was symbolically the most vicious manifestation of the denial of educational opportunity and the most visible aspect of discriminatory treatment in the public schools; it was also the most personal reminder of institutional racism.[30]

The initial response by Mexican American organizations to discrimination and segregation in the public schools began several months after the founding of LULAC in 1929. At first, their efforts were aimed at challenging the legality of using national origin as a basis for providing separate and inferior schools for Mexicans. For example, in 1930, a group of Mexican American parents with the professional, financial, and organizational support of LULAC filed a suit against the Del Rio Independent School District in Southwest Texas.[31] In this court case the community sought to prove that the local school officials of Del Rio, Texas, segregated school children of "Mexican and Spanish descent" from the school children of all other white races in the same grade. Although the Texas Court of Civil Appeals agreed in theory that "school authorities had no power to arbitrarily segregate Mexican children, assign them to separate schools, and exclude them from schools maintained for children of other white races, merely or solely because they are Mexican,"[32] in practice it did not find the Del Rio school officials guilty of such actions. Lacking financial resources, an adequate professional staff, and an atmosphere conducive to legal change, LULAC lessened its stress on legal challenges to segregation and instead emphasized other measures. Informal consultations and persuasion was strongly emphasized as a more effective strategy for changing conditions in the public schools. "We would get acquainted with superintendents, principals and teachers" stated one of the original founders of LULAC, "and we tried to persuade them to do away with segregation and with discriminatory educational practices." According to this person, "we gained more by getting acquainted with administrators and elected officials than by demonstrations."[34]

The soft approach to education reform was illustrated in 1939 during Ezequiel Salinas' term as state president of LULAC. In that year he took several steps to improve the deplorable condition of Mexican children in the public schools. As president of LULAC, he voiced the concerns of Mexican children in school to the state superintendent of public instruction, L. A. Woods, and encouraged him to take action against local school districts.[35] He also appeared before an education conference attended by 100 school superintendents of Texas and spoke in favor of eliminating racism and distortions of Mexicans in the history textbooks. Before his term expired, Salinas worked and supported a Works Project Administration school construction project aimed at solving overcrowded conditions in the public schools of Hondo, Texas. In certain cases where the local school officials failed to eliminate discriminatory educational practices, LULAC conducted boycotts of the public schools and established temporary bilingual schools in the community.[36]

During the 1940's organizational efforts at challenging discriminatory educational policy increased. These new efforts were influenced by two federal court cases declaring that segregation based on national origin was unconstitutional, by administrative responses of different state agencies to the segregation of Mexican American children, and by the emergence in 1948 of the G.I. Forum, a militant and vocal Mexican American veteran's organization.

On April 8, 1947, in response to a California Federal District Courts case which found segregation of Mexican students to be unconstitutional, the

Attorney General of Texas, Price Daniel, issued a legal opinion forbidding the separate placement of Mexican children in the state's public schools.[37] Segregation based on national origin of racial ancestry was prohibited, Daniel reported, but if "based solely on language deficiencies or other individual needs or aptitudes, separate classes or schools may be maintained for pupils who, after examinations equally applied, come within such classifications."[38] Gus Garcia, a LULAC member, sought clarification of the Attorney General's opinion on segregation in the public schools. Garcia inquired whether the opinion prohibited all segregation except that based on scientific tests that were equally applied to all students regardless of national origin, and whether it also prohibited provision of inferior facilities to Mexicans. The Attorney General replied in the affirmative, saying, "We meant that the law prohibits discrimination against or segregation of Latin-Americans on account of race or descent, and that the law permits no subterfuge to accomplish such discrimination."[39] But the legal opinion on segregation was ineffective for no mechanism to secure compliance was established nor guidelines for implementing these steps provided to local school officials.[40]

Consequently, additional legal efforts aimed at the establishment of the unconstitutionality of segregation practices were pursued by LULAC. In 1948, it filed a desegregation suit aimed at clarifying the constitutional issues involved in the segregation of Mexicans in the public schools.[41] In *Delgado v. Destrop Independent School District*, the parents of the school aged Mexican American children charged that school officials in four communities in central Texas were segregating Mexicans contrary to the law. As in the case of California, the United States District Court, Western District of Texas ruled that the placing of students of Mexican ancestry in different buildings was arbitrary, discriminatory, and illegal. The court declared that:

The regulations, customs, usages, and practices of the defendants, Bastrop Independent School District of Bastrop County, et al., and each of them insofar as they or any of them have segregated pupils of Mexican or other Latin American descent in separate classes and schools within the respective school districts heretofore set forth are, and each of them is, arbitrary and discriminatory and in violation of plaintiffs constitutional rights as guaranteed by the Fourteenth Amendment to the Constitution of the United States, and are illegal.[42]

Of additional significance, especially for the continued anti-segregation efforts of LULAC and the G. I. Forum, was the stipulation by the District Court that permanently restrained and enjoined the local school boards and the superintendents

from segregating pupils of Mexican or Latin American descent in separate schools or classes within the respective school districts of said defendants and each of them, and from denying said pupils use of the same facilities and services enjoyed by other children of the same age or grades . . .[43]

Exception, however, was granted in cases where children did not know English and were placed in separate classes on the same campus for the first grade only. The placement of non-English speaking students in separate classes would be determined on the basis of "scientific and standardized tests, equally given and applied to all pupils."[44] The sanctioning of segregation of Mexican American children in the first grade "solely for instructional purposes" weakened the potential impact of this federal decision. As Carl Allsup noted in his study of the G.I. Forum, "even though this decision undermined the rigid segregation of the pre-1948 Texas school system," the Delgado proviso provided a legal loophole "that gave school districts opportunities to circumvent the goals of Gus Garcia, LULAC, and the G.I. Forum."[45]

In response to the Delgado case, the State Superintendent of Public Instruction and the Texas State Board of Education issued regulations regarding the illegality of discriminatory school practices such as segregation. The new instructions to the school districts stipulated that segregation as mandated by the State Constitution and by judicial and legislative decree only applied to blacks and not to members of any other race.[46] These instructions and regulations also stated the following three major points: (1) segregation practices based on national origin were unconstitutional, arbitrary and discriminatory; (2) separate classes would be formed in the first grade only for instructional purposes, "for any students who have language difficulties whether the students be of Anglo American, Latin American or any other origin;" and (3) all educational agencies, including the State Department of Education "will take all necessary steps to eliminate any and all segregations that may exist" in these districts.[47]

One year after this desegregation policy was issued, the Mexican American community embarked on a plan to enforce the ruling by seeking the disaccreditation of the Del Rio School District for failure to comply with the new policy. On January 7, 1949, a Mexican American student group at the University of Texas filed a complaint with the Department of Education against the segregated school district in Del Rio, Texas.[48] Within a month, T. M. Trimble, the Assistant State Superintendent of Public Instruction personally inspected the Del Rio public schools. In his report to the State Superintendent, Trimble recommended that accreditation be withheld. According to the report "the elementary children of the two races were, by board regulation, not permitted to mix."[49] On February 12, 1949, Superintendent Woods cancelled Del Rio's accreditation. The Del Rio school officials requested a reconsideration, but after reviewing their practices, the Superintendent re-affirmed the earlier decision to withdraw accreditation. During the summer, Superintendent Woods, the initiator of the desegregation policy, was replaced by J. W. Edgar as head of the state educational agency.[50] Del Rio school officials then appealed the decision to withdraw accreditation to the State Board of Education. This time they were successful. The Woods decision to withdraw accreditation was reversed. Mexican American efforts to enforce court ordered desegregation policy in Del Rio were blunted. Undaunted by these state actions, Mexican American leaders in Del Rio resorted to mobilizing the community in that particular city and in circumventing specific discriminatory practices aimed at maintaining segregation in education.[51]

Besides increasing public awareness of existing patterns of racial discrimination and segregation in schools and filing legal challenges the Mexican American middle class also attempted to document the extent of segregation in Texas during the late 1940's and early 1950's. For instance, a year after the Delgado case, the Corpus Christi chapter of the G.I. Forum conducted a survey of fourteen school districts adjoining Corpus Christi.[52] The survey indicated that although segregation was still the rule in all of the school districts, it had now assumed new forms. According to the report the response of local school officials to the decree issued by the State Superintendent forbidding discrimination ranged from indifference to helplessness. Of the fourteen school districts visited, six did not make an effort or did not even promise to eliminate segregation. One school district promised to do away with separate educational facilities for Mexicans and Anglos but at a later date. Another one stated that segregation was too far advanced to do anything about it. The rest of the school districts used various evasive schemes to maintain segregated facilities. These included the following: (1) three districts resorted to segregating Mexican children by allowing Anglo but not Mexican American children the option of choosing the school they wished to attend, (2) one district provided token transfers of Mexican children to the Anglo schools whenever there were any vacancies available, (3) one district had established separate classes for Mexicans within the Anglo school, and (4) one district had segregation based on the "language handicap" of the non-English speaking children.[53] The G.I. Forum charged that through the development of evasive schemes local school districts in south Texas were circumventing the decisions of the court and the antisegregation decree of the State Superintendent of the Public Schools. As the Mexican American educational survey stated:

It is the consensus of opinion of the Latin leaders and myself to conclude that the school board officials are purposely and stubbornly trying to get around the law by many rules, actions, etc., which are not only unconstitutional, but also done on purpose to deprive the Latin American children of their God given right of the advantages to which they are entitled to under our great liberal constitution.[54]

The leader of the Corpus Christi chapter of the G.I. Forum, Dr. Hector P. Garcia, continued his attacks on segregation in the months to follow. In a sworn affidavit dated April 13, 1950, Dr. Garcia alleged that segregation existed in ten south Texas cities which he had personally surveyed. The affidavit plus a letter listing twelve other school districts in south Texas found to be segregated was sent to the Commissioner of Education.[55]

These investigations, however, only exposed the inherent weakness of the existing regulations and instructions regarding segregation. Hence, both LULAC and the G.I. Forum moved to strengthen the policy of desegregation. On May 8, 1950, Gus Garcia of G.I. Forum and George I. Sanchez of LULAC, appeared before the State Department of Education and discussed the continued existence of segregation despite the *Delgado* case. They recommended that a state policy of desegregation be declared and that the appropriate mechanisms be established to ensure the implementation of that policy.[56] In response to Garcia's and Sanchez's presentation, the State Board of Education issued a "Statement of Policy Pertaining to Segregation of Latin American Children." This policy recognized the illegality of segregation, but it asserted the right to local districts to handle the complaints and grievances of local citizens alleging discriminatory treatment. "Consistent with this board's belief in local self government to the fullest extent possible," the policy statement read,

this board deems it proper, in cases where it has alleged there exists a practice of segregating Latin American children from Anglo American children that the local boards of school trustees be given the opportunity to eliminate such segregation prior to the bringing of such cases to the Commissioner of Education where such matters would be handled only on the basis of appeal.[57]

The State Board of Education's desegregation policy led to the creation of an elaborate bureaucratic redress mechanism whereby Mexican Americans could voice their complaints to their local schools. If these local school officials failed to eliminate segregation, the Mexican American community could appeal to the State Department of Education, which would then investigate the charges and issue an opinion. The entire process, which was challenged by Mexican Americans in 1952, was tedious, time consuming, extremely bureaucratic, and intended to impede efforts to eliminate school segregation of Mexican American children.[58] Between 1950 and 1957, nine local school districts were brought to the Commissioner of Education for special hearings,[59] although hundreds of school districts throughout the state were segregating Mexican American students.[60] Of the handful of cases heard by the Commissioner of Education, little was done to eliminate the assignment of Mexican American children to separate schools or classes. In fact, evidence indicated that the state's actions in two particular cases actually had the effect of contributing to rather than eliminating segregation based on national origin.[61]

While willing to abide by the State Board's administrative remedies, the Mexican American organizations did not hesitate on taking recalcitrant school districts to court, although they preferred not to. "Reluctantly," said two Mexican American lawyers,

we have been compelled to resort to litigation in federal courts . . . We have waited a long time to file these lawsuits, we do so with a heavy heart. But we have no recourse except to appeal to the public conscience of our Anglo American friends and to the justice of our federal judiciary.[62]

Approximately 15 cases of discrimination in the public schools were filed during the first seven years of the 1950s. Although some of these were dismissed by the courts for various reasons[63] the decisions reached in all of the desegregation cases supported the Mexican American community's claims of discrimination based on national origin.[64] The nature of the arguments made by school officials favoring separate classes for Mexican American children and community persons favoring the elimination of segregation in the grades is best illustrated in the Driscoll case of 1957.[65]

Driscoll, Texas was a rural community in the southwestern part of the state with an average attendance of 288 in all grades. Approximately 70 per cent of the students were of Mexican extraction; many of these came from families who were migratory workers. With the exception of one, none of these children spoke or understood the English language when they enrolled.[66] Spanish was spoken by the parents in the home. In order to solve the serious teaching problems presented by the enrollment of large numbers of non-English speaking students in to the Driscoll public schools the local school officials had established separate classes for all students of Mexican descent. Between 1949 and 1955, when litigation was threatened, the District maintained a system whereby all children of Mexican extraction were kept in the first two grades for four years and permitted to enter the regular third grade with English speaking students who had completed the same grade in two years.[67] In 1955, LULAC and the American G.I. Forum filed a suit claiming that the practice by local school officials of placing school children of Mexican descent in separate classes for the first and second grades of school and of requiring their attendance in these two grades for a period of four years was discrimination based on "race or ancestry" and a deprival of their rights under the Fourteenth Amendment to the United States Constitution. The school officials answered that the segregation of Mexican American students was not done on the basis of race or ancestry. Rather Mexican American students were placed in classes separate from Anglos solely because of their inability to speak or understand English. According to the local school officials the decision to group students of Mexican ancestry in the first two grades was "the result of a decision made in good faith by the school authorities in solving a difficult pedagogical problem . . ."[68] After listening to the arguments on both sides the federal district court on January 11, 1957, entered a final judgement declaring that

1. the Districts's separate grouping of students of Mexican extraction is arbitrary and unreasonable because it is directed at them as a class and is not based upon individual capacities
2. any grouping, whether in the beginning or subsequent years, must not be based upon racial extraction but upon individual ability to speak, understand and be instructed in the English language,
3. individual capacities and abilities in this respect must be determined in good faith by scientific tests recognized in the field of education.[69]

The finding of discrimination against Mexican Americans in the public schools in Driscoll, Texas was welcomed by LULAC and the American G.I.

Forum. Unfortunately, the federal district court's rulings on the unconstitutionality of segregation in Driscoll and other Texas cities had little impact on local school practices. Local school districts managed to circumvent the findings of segregation based on national origin by formulating and implementing creative discriminatory practices which maintained and in some cases strengthened school segregation. The mid and late 1950s can probably be called the era of subterfuges, since it was during this period that a multitude of evasive practices, e.g. "freedom-of-choice" plans, selected student transfer and transportation plans, classification systems based on language or scholastic ability, and others, were utilized by local school districts to maintain segregated schools.[70] Although some small school districts, e.g., Driscoll, did eliminate separate schools for Mexican Americans, the LULAC and the G.I. Forum leaders perceived further litigation to be futile, since "there were so many subterfuges available to bar effective relief."[71] No further desegregation litigation was initiated by LULAC or American G.I. Forum until political and economic circumstances changed in the late 1960s.

Results were disheartening three decades after the first desegregation case was filed in 1930. As late as 1968, a nationwide survey on the education of Mexican Americans in the southwest reported that while ethnic isolation of Mexican Americans in general was high, it was most pronounced in Texas. Approximately 40 percent of the Mexican school age population was attending schools which were 80 percent or more Mexican American.[72] Segregation thus continued to be a way of life for many Mexican American students in Texas. Promises were made to end segregation, but little was actually done. In fact, local school officials managed to expand segregation to the secondary level after the late 1940s. The creation of junior and senior high schools attended primarily by Mexican American students in different parts of the state during the 1950s and 1960s, testifies to the expansion of the segregated public school system.[73] Yet, despite setbacks, Mexican American organizations like LULAC and the G.I. Forum between 1929 and 1957 played an extremely important role in challenging existing patterns of educational inequality at the local and state level. They were instrumental in filing complaints against segregation practices, in encouraging the Mexican community to take advantage of the public schools, and most importantly, in establishing the unconstitutionality of discriminatory practices based on national origin. Encountering racism, indifference, and hostile attitudes, Mexican American organizations, led by middle class members, played an important role in keeping the spirit of resistance alive within the barrio by struggling for equal access to public schooling. Guided by the ideals of political liberalism, Mexican American leaders demonstrated a commitment to American institutions and to their eventual improvement. While the inculcation of liberal thought among Mexican American leaders can be considered a positive step forward in that it inspired individuals to challenge existing patterns of educational inequality it was also a negative ideological development. Solutions framed within the context of political liberal thought served to deflect serious analysis of the source of inequality in the society. Failure to raise basic questions concerning the nature of existing social, economic, and political institutions and the role they play in maintaining and perpetuating inequality also tended to limit the number of possible strategies for dealing with the issues of segregation and school discrimination. In essence, efforts to use the legal system to dismantle school segregation failed to bring about substantive changes. The obstacles which LULAC and the G.I. Forum perceived to be limiting access to and participation in American life, that is, discriminatory school policies, inferior and separate schools, etc., were still present decades after the first legal challenge to educational segregation. As the community entered the tumultuous sixties the changing politics of the nation dictated a strengthening of the campaign against separate and unequal schools. But failure to seriously ponder the sources of inequality and to develop revolutionary strategies to eliminate them led to the development of innovative but ineffectual legal and political challenges to the placement of Mexican Americans in separate and inferior schools.

NOTES

1. For a useful and insightful account of the legal campaign to desegregate the public schools in Texas see Carlos M. Alcala and Jorge C. Rangel, "Project Report: De Jure Segregation of Chicanos in the Texas Public Schools," *Harvard Civil Rights-Civil Liberties Law Review*, 7 (March, 1972): 307-391. For a history of G.I. Forum's participation in the desegregation campaign see Carl Allsup, "Education is our Freedom: The American G.I. Forum and the Mexican American School Segregation in Texas, 1948-1957," *Aztlan*, 8(1977): 27-50.

2. For a general history of these organizations see Miguel David Tirado, "Mexican American Community Political Organization: The Key to Chicano Political Power," in F. Chris Garcia (ed.), *La Causa Politica: A Chicano Politics Reader* (Notre Dame, 1974). For a comprehensive view of LULAC see Edward D. Garza, "LULAC: League of United Latin American Citizens," Unpublished M.A. thesis, Southwest Texas State Teachers College, San Marcos, Texas, 1951 and Moises Sandoval, *Our Legacy: The First Fifty Years* (Washington, D.C., 1979).

3. The American G.I. Forum was originally founded in 1948 in Corpus Christi, Texas by Dr. Hector P. Garcia. The name G.I. Forum meant that the organization was primarily a veteran's group (G.I. refers to an enlisted man in the U.S. armed forces) aimed at discussing the issues facing them in an open and democratic fashion, i.e., forum. Thus the G.I. Forum would be a veteran's group organized for the purpose of openly discussing issues confronting them in order to reach consensus on resolving them. For a brief historical overview of the organization see *The American G.I. Forum and What It Stands For*, (1950), 8 pp. The American G.I. Forum Central Office Files, Corpus Christi, Texas. (Hereinafter to be known as the AGIF Files).

4. Jose E. Limon writes in "El Congreso Mexicanista de 1911: A Precursor to Contemporary Chicanismo," *Aztlan*, 5 (Spring and Fall 1974): 85-118, that *La Cronica*, a Mexican American community newspaper was writing about racial school discrimination and segregation in Laredo and other areas of south Texas as early as 1910. He also notes that at the Congreso Mexicanista a delegation from Houston, Texas, urged the conference participants to make formal protests to the State Superintendent of Public Schools concerning the mistreatment of Mexican Americans in the public schools.

5. See for example, Kay Lynn Briegal, "Alianza Hispano-Americana, 1894-1965," Unpublished Ph.D. dissertation, University of Southern California, 1974.

6. O. D. Weeks, "The League of United Latin American Citizens: A Texas-Mexican Civic Organization," *The Southwestern Political and Social Science Quarterly*, 10 (December, 1929): 257-278, argues that the founders of LULAC were either born or raised in the United States. LULAC was the first organization founded by American citizens of Mexican ancestry.

7. Concrete evidence concerning the social origins of the leaders and members of these new types of organizations is lacking, but scattered information from historical sources strongly support my contention. For

instance, of the seven central individuals responsible for organizing LULAC, four were lawyers, one was a businessman, and two were newspaper editors. See O. D. Weeks, "The League of United Latin American Citizens: A Texas-Mexican Civic Organization," p. 263. Also, out of the total number of 20 Mexican Americans who have been president for the statewide LULAC between 1929 and 1950, over 50 per cent have been either lawyers, judges, small businessmen, or persons with college degrees. The list of state officers can be found in Garza, "LULAC: The League of United Latin American Citizens," p. 12-13.

8. *The Constitution of the League of United Latin American Citizens*, Article LL. LULAC Office Files, Bonilla Building, Corpus Christi, Texas. (Herinafter known as LULAC Files).

9. Dr. George I. Sanchez estimated that 20 percent of the Mexicans in Texas were not citizens. Quoted in Edgar G. Sheldon, Jr. "Political Conditions Among Texas Mexicans Along the Rio Grande," Unpublished M.A. thesis, University of Texas, Austin, Texas, 1946, p. 4. In a study of Mexicans in the public schools H T Manual, *The Education of the Spanish-speaking Children in Texas*. (Austin, Texas, 1930), p. 5, also estimated that nearly 52 percent of the total number of Mexicans in Texas were citizens.

10. *The Constitution of the League of United Latin American Citizens*, Article II. LULAC Files.

11. Alonso S. Perales, "La Unificacion de los Mexico-Americanos," *La Prensa* [San Antonio, Texas] (September 7, 1929), n.p.

12. *The Constitution of LULAC*, Article II. LULAC Files.

13. Ibid.

14. Tirado, "Mexican American Community Political Organization: The Key to Chicano Political Power," for example argues this point.

15. *The Constitution of LULAC*. Article II. LULAC Files

16. Ibid.

17. Weeks, "The League of United Latin American Citizens: A Texas-Mexican Civic Organization:" 257-278, provides an excellent discussion of the problems and issues confronting the organizational development of LULAC see Garza, "LULAC: League of United Latin American Citizens," pp. 5-7.

18. Weeks, Ibid: 268, also stated that organizational growth and the nature of the membership were two other major problems LULAC faced in 1929.

19. Ibid.

20. Perales, "La Unificacion de los Mexico-Americanos," quoted in Weeks, Ibid: 268.

21. "The Segregation of Mexican Children at Del Rio," *LULAC News*, I, No. 1 (August 1931): 12-13, quoted in Garza, "LULAC: League of United Latin American Citizens," p. 27.

22. Perales, "La Unificacion de los Mexico-Americanos," quoted in Weeks, "The League of United Latin-" American Citizens: A Texas-Mexican Civic Organization:" 269.

23. Paul S. Taylor, *An American Mexican Frontier: Nueces County*, Texas (Chapel Hill, North Carolina, 1934), p. 246.

24. For an analysis of the political machines in south Texas see Sheldon, Jr., "Political Conditions Among Texas Mexicans Along the Rio Grande."

25. Weeks, "The League of United Latin American Citizens: A Texas-Mexican Civic Organization:" 277-278.

26. Paul Taylor Collection. Interview with a LULAC member in Corpus Christi, Texas, 1929. Bancroft Library, Berkeley, California, n.p.

27. *The American G.I. Forum and What It Stands For*, p. 2

28. Letter, Ed. Idar, Jr. to H. T. Manual. AGIF Files, n.p.

29. For a brief discussion of the goals of social reformers in education see Michael B. Katz, *Class, Bureacracy, and Schools: The Illusion of Educational Change in America* (New York, 1971), especially chapter 3. David Tyack, *The One Best System* (Cambridge, Mass., 1974), also illustrates the nature of the structural reforms sought by what he labels the "administrative progressiveness" between 1890 and 1940.

30. Most Mexican Americans regardless of their social standing in the community or their length of residence in Texas attended segregated schools and experienced some form of discrimination. For an historical analysis of the impact public school attendance with Anglos had on Mexican Americans in one school district see Guadalupe San Miguel, Jr., "Endless Pursuits: The Chicano Educational Experience in Corpus Christi, Texas, 1880-1960," Unpublished Ph.D. dissertation, Stanford University, 1978, pp. 184-223.

31. *Independent School District vs. Salvatierra*, 33 S. W. 2d 790 (Texas Civ. App., 4th Dist., 1930), *cert. denied* 284 U.S. 580 (1931).

32. Ibid., p. 795

33. Personal interview. Louis A. Wilmot. May 3, 1977.

34. Ibid.

35. In 1939, L.A. threatened to cut state aid from the Ozona School District in South Texas for segregating Mexican children. See Sandoval, *Our Legacy*, chapter 8 and 9, for more information concerning LULAC's educational activities.

36. Ibid., pp. 36-37
37. The California federal court district court case was decided on February 19, 1946. See *Mendez v. West-minster School District.* 64 F. Supp. 544 (S.D., Cal. 1946), *aff'd* 161 F. 2d 774 (9th Cir. 1947)
38. Digest of Opinions of the Attorney General of Texas, V. 128. p. 39 (1947), quoted in Alcala and Rangel, "Project Report," p. 335.
39. Ibid., p. 336.
40. Allsup, "Education is Our Freedom," p. 32, also notes that on October 1947 three University of Texas student groups—the Laredo Club, the Alba Club, and the American Veterans Committee—charged local school districts in Beevile, Sinton, Elgin, Bastrop, and Cotulla with segregation. The local and state school officials dismissed their charges after conducting an investigation and no further action was undertaken either by the student groups or the school officials. Allsup does not discuss the ethnic composition of the student groups but implies that they were Mexican American in origin.
41. For a discussion of some unanswered questions raised by the California court case see George I. Sanchez, *Concerning Segregation of Spanish-speaking Children in the Public Schools* Inter-American Education, Occasional Papers, IX (Austin, 1951), pp. 10-13.
42. *Delgado v. Bastrop Independent School District.* (1948). Civil Action No. 333, District Court of the United States, Western District of Texas (Abstract of Principal Features), p. 1, quoted in *Ibid.*, pp. 68-73.
43. Ibid., p. 1
44. Ibid.
45. Allsup, "Education is Our Freedom," p. 34.
46. Texas State Board of Education, "Instructions and Regulations of the Texas State Superintendent of Public Instruction," Texas State Board of Education Correspondence, AGIF Files. (1948).
47. Ibid.
48. Cristobal Alderete. Personal interview. July 26, 1979
49. Del Rio Decision of L. A. Woods, State Superintendent of Public Instruction, April 23, 1949, p. 1.
50. Alcala and Rangel, "Project Report," p. 339.
51. Cristobal Alderete. Personal interview. July 26, 1979.
52. American G.I. Forum, "School Inspection: Report on Fourteen Schools," 1950, AGIF Files, p. 1.
53. Ibid., p. 2.
54. Ibid., p. 1.
55. Dr. Hector P. Garcia, "Report of Personal Inspection Trip," April 13, 1950, AGIF Files, found that the following twelve cities segregated Mexican American students: Alpine, McAllen, Edinburg, Nixon, Sequin, Beeville, Edcouch, Lubbock, Sonora, Marathon, Pecos, and Rockspring. "Segregation is still the general rule and not the exception," states the report. "School officials and school boards are not abiding by the Delgado Decision and is (sic) more important they have no intentions of abiding by this decree unless they are penalized in one way or another," added Garcia in his report p. 1.
56. Agenda, *State Board of Education Minutes,* April 14, 1950, Texas Education-Agency Library Austin, Texas, p. 3.
57. Texas Education Agency, "Statement of Policy Pertaining to Segregation of Latin American Children," May 8, 1950. State Board of Education Correspondence, AGIF Files.
58. G.I. Forum, *News Bulletin,* 1, No. 4 (December 15, 1952): 3. states that LULAC and the G.I. Forum asked the Commissioner of Education, J. W. Edgar, to revise the procedure in appealing school segregation cases to his office. They sought to eliminate appeals to the local school officials "on grounds that it is like asking a jury to reconsider the case of a man it has already found guilty." Allsup, "Education is Our Freedom," p. 38, also argues that the intent of the state official's actions "was to impede the attempts of the G.I. Forum and other organizations to eliminate segregation."
59. The nine local districts brought to the Commissioner of Education for special hearings were the following: Kyle, Nixon, Hondo, Sanderson, Pecos, Carrizo Springs, Kingsville, Mathis, and Driscoll. The first five cases were decided by the Commissioner in 1953. The Carrizo Springs, Kingsville, and Mathis cases were decided in 1955, and the Driscoll case in 1957. The latter four cases were taken to court by Mexican American organizations but with the exception of the Driscoll case, they were all dismissed before the court reached a final decision. Alcala and Rangel, "Project Report," pp. 340-342: Allsup, "Education is Our Freedom," pp. 40-45.
60. Editorial, *News Bulletin,* v. 5, No. 12 (December, 1957): n.p.
61. Alcala and Rangel, "Project Report," pp. 340-341.
62. Gus C. Garcia and Homero M. Lopez, "Statement," Attorneys for the plaintiffs in the Salinas School Segregation Case, April 28, 1955. AGIF Files, p. 1
63. For example *Cortez v. Carrizo Springs Independent School District* (Dimmit County) Civil No. 832 (W.D. Tex., filed April 20, 1955) was dismissed on June 13, 1955 on plaintiff's motion after the local school

board agreed to cooperate "in every respect." In *Villarreal et al. v. Mathis Independent School District* (San Patricio County) Civil Action No. 1385 (S.D. Tex. May 2, 1957) the expert witness was afraid to testify and so the case was dismissed.

64. Editorial, *News Bulletin*, v. 5, No. 12 (December, 1957): n.p.
65. *Herminia Hernandez et. al. v. Driscoll Consolidated Independent School District*, et. al., Civil No. 1384 (U.S.D.C. So. Distr., Tex., Jan 11, 1957, 2 Race Re. L. Rep. 329)
66. In September 1955 Linda Perez, a young Mexican American child who spoke no Spanish, was denied the opportunity to enroll in the Anglo section of first grade, until she acquired the assistance of a lawyer. According to the court findings "In the twelve years that the present superintendent had been at Driscoll this is the only Mexican child that had been placed in the Anglo section and then only after the lawyer's intervention." Ibid. p. 331.
67. Prior to 1949 the school district placed pupils of Mexican descent in separate buildings and on separate campuses through the sixth grade. Ibid. p. 331.
68. Ibid., p. 329.
69. Ibid., p. 333.
70. For a discussion of these practices and the legal challenges to them see Alcala and Rangel, "Project Report," pp. 326-333.
71. Ibid., p. 345.
72. See data in U.S. Commission on Civil Rights, *Mexican American Education Study*, Vol. I. (Washington, D.C., 1970)
73. For an example of the extension of the segregated school system into the junior and senior high school grades see San Miguel, Jr., "Endless Pursuits: The Chicano Educational Experience in Corpus Christi, Texas, 1880-1960," pp. 82-86.

17

The Volunteers and the Freedom Schools: Education for Social Change in Mississippi

Mary Aickin Rothschild

FROM THE BEGINNING of direct action work in the South, the student civil rights movement constantly evolved new programs and tactics. While the goals of the programs were always to work toward desegregation and voter registration, the programs often stressed varied approaches to those goals and had different tactical components.

Nowhere was this evolutionary process of multidimensional programs more clear than in civil rights work in Mississippi. From the first Student Nonviolent Coordinating Committee (SNCC) voter registration project which precipitated the murder by whites of two local blacks, Mississippi represented the strongest bastion of white racism and resistance in the South.

Direct action work in Mississippi was dominated by SNCC. However the other three major civil rights groups, the Congress of Racial Equality (CORE), the National Association for the Advancement of Colored People (NAACP), and the Southern Christian Leadership Conference (SCLC), were also represented in the state and, contrary to the fragmentation and competition among the groups at the national level, they all tried to support each other. By 1962, the four groups joined together to form an umbrella organization called the Council of Federated Organizations (COFO).

White violence against blacks increased almost daily and included jailings, beatings, shootings, bombings and murder. The Mississippi movement was nearly stymied.

By November of 1963, despite Freedom Days, Freedom Votes, marches, sit-ins and boycotts, few Mississippi blacks were registered to vote, yet the nation seemed unaware of the situation. The Mississippi movement needed a new direction. COFO proposed a massive summer project aimed at recruiting college students as temporary civil rights workers. The Freedom Summer Project was a direct response to the Mississippi experience.

In 1964, more than 650 students from around the country responded to COFO's call to "give a summer to civil rights," and they were called "the volunteers." Overwhelmingly urban and upper-middle class, most were in

---

Mary Aickin Rothschild is associate professor of history at Arizona State University.

college and had exceptionally well-educated parents. The volunteers hailed from the best universities and colleges in the country, and they tended to value education highly. Roughly ninety per cent were white; nine per cent were black and one per cent was Asian-American. Men comprised fifty-four per cent of the group and women were forty-six per cent. The vast majority considered themselves "liberals," while fewer than five per cent identified themselves as "radicals." They were children of the American Dream, and they were enormously naive about the problems and dangers of civil rights work.[1]

While COFO staff assumed from the beginning that volunteers would work in voter registration, Charlie Cobb, a black member of SNCC, also proposed volunteers staff a freedom school program. In a prospectus, Cobb outlined his premise that Mississippi schools were inadequate, that black students in them received an education in every way inferior to that available elsewhere, and that, in consequence, they were victims of a pervasive "social paralysis." He argued that COFO needed to organize students around the state to work in educational programs and that students needed ". . . to articulate their own desires, demands, and . . . to stand up in classrooms around the state, and ask their teachers a real question." He proposed those needs could be met with Freedom Schools which would benefit both COFO and Mississippi students and which could be staffed by the student volunteers and professionals from colleges in the North.

Cobb's initial proposal envisaged a two month session for tenth and eleventh grade high school students to achieve three things:

(1) Supplement what they aren't learning around the state;
(2) Give them a broad intellectual and academic experience during the summer to bring back to fellow students in the state, and
(3) Form the basis for statewide student action, such as school boycotts, based on their increased awareness.

Since these students were still in high school, they would remain in the state to put their knowledge to work.

Compensatory education in basic areas, in addition to skills like typing, would be combined with cultural programs. Social studies and political education would be a "prominent" part of the curriculum. Special projects combining curricular areas, such as writing a newspaper or planning a conference, would stimulate learning and build practical skills.

As part of the rationale for his proposal, Cobb stressed his belief that Freedom Schools would have a "special appeal" to the volunteers. Primarily students themselves, they would be able to try out their educational philosophy and experiment pedagogically with new ways of teaching. Under Cobb's plan, the ratio of volunteers to Freedom School Teachers would be small to ensure dialogue, with perhaps four or five students per teacher.

Summarizing the purpose of the program, Cobb wrote, "The overall theme of the school would be the student as a force for social change in Mississippi."

Freedom Schools were to be a training ground for the next generation of local civil rights workers. The background the schools would supply to students would clarify issues, nurture new skills and strengthen them for their future movement work. As Cobb argued:

If we are concerned with breaking the power structure, then we have to be concerned with building up our own institutions to replace the old, unjust, decadent ones which make up the existing power structure. Education in Mississippi is an institution which can be validly replaced . . .

From the first proposal, then, Freedom Schools were seen as a political organizing tool for COFO which could ably use the skills of northern volunteers. The schools would become what SNCC called a "parallel institution" and would produce students able to work for social change.[2]

The National Council of Churches held a meeting in late March to organize a curriculum for the schools. Four main areas of concern were identified: (1) leadership development; (2) remedial academics; (3) contemporary issues; and (4) nonacademic curriculum which would emphasize fieldwork and projects designed to encourage student organization. Dr. Staughton Lynd, a northern white professor and civil rights activist then teaching at Spelman College, was chosen to be Director of Freedom Schools. During the ensuing months, various individuals worked on curriculum and teaching aids. Since COFO was always strapped for money, materials were generally mimeographed or dittoed, often by the departments of interested individual faculty or student groups in northern colleges. The "core citizenship curriculum," especially, benefited from the work of several notable American historians, including Martin Duberman, Staughton Lynd, Otis Pease, Norman Pollack, and Howard Zinn.

Starting from Cobb's first premise that education is political, the "core citizenship curriculum" was designed to give students a sense of dignity and a link with their past. Curriculum planners made special efforts to present black history and American government and economics to students at all levels. Planners believed that students should know their black heritage for knowledge's sake and to enhance their self-esteem. Additionally, they believed if students found their past, deprived of them by Mississippi schools, they could work actively for a better future. Learning about American government and economics would help students understand the roots of their oppression. This understanding, in turn, would provide the key to change blacks' position in society.

As information was disseminated in the North, however, a subtle change in the Freedom School rationale occurred. Increasingly, memos and mimeographed announcements discussed the schools as primarily a purely academic endeavor, a kind of educational challenge to the "Closed Society." The COFO staff's initial emphasis on schools as a tool for organization and social action faded into the background and became secondary to a more traditional academic emphasis for the schools.[4]

This happened because those people who took over the planning for the schools, particularly the northern volunteers, acted out of their experience, which was for the most part traditionally academic and light-years away from the Mississippi movement. To the volunteers, mainly college students and professors, schools were not automatically connected with political action and social change. Conversely, Cobb and the other black and white SNCC staff who initially envisioned the schools worked out of their world, which was dedicated to political action for social change. Given the enormity of the problems facing Mississippi blacks, from their point of view, allocation of money and staff to Freedom Schools could only be countenanced if it would lead to substantial political action. When the summer program began, the two strains of thought about Freedom Schools formed the context for tension within the schools and for differing assessments about their usefulness to the movement.

Throughout May, Freedom School teachers received information on the project to prepare them for orientation and the summer. The proposed daily schedule and curriculum were outlined, along with the case studies which would illustrate each topic. The volunteers were informed that some teachers might be holding classes without classrooms and that they almost certainly would not have ideal materials and facilities for teaching. The Jackson staff clearly indicated their belief that:

. . . academic experiences should relate directly to . . . [the students'] . . . real life in Mississippi, and since learning that involves real life experiences is, we think, most meaningful, we hope that the students will be involved in the political life of their communities . . . The way students can participate in local voter registration should be worked out by the teachers and local COFO voter registration staff at a meeting before the opening of school . . . It is important that voter registration staff and teachers stay in close touch with each other so these things can be worked out . . .

Volunteers were encouraged to begin thinking about special areas they would like to teach and to collect visual aids, books and teaching aids for both the "citizenship curriculum" and their special subjects. Above all, they were urged "to think creatively about what could be done in the schools and with small groups."[5]

The 1964 volunteers who were to become Freedom School teachers began their summer at an orientation program in Oxford, Ohio, sponsored by the National Council of Churches. Like the voter registration workers who had preceded them by one week, the volunteer teachers were introduced to each other, the staff and to the problems awaiting them in Mississippi. The volunteers had a crash course in Mississippi politics, race relations and black history. Speakers presented varied views on the purpose of the summer projects and movement philosophy, including the issue of nonviolence as a tactic or life commitment. The volunteers learned intensely practical safety rules, such as how and when to report to headquarters and how to travel safely after dark. Additionally, they acted out sociodramas of possible situations and actively practiced nonviolent techniques to protect themselves against the eventually of violent retaliation to the projects from the white community. The only major planned difference between the two orientation sessions was the substitution of training in Freedom School techniques and curriculum for training in voter registration.

On the second day of the Freedom School orientation, Michael Schwerner and James Chaney, both CORE workers, and Andy Goodman, a volunteer, disappeared from Philadelphia, Mississippi. While the training session continued with the planned program, the Freedom School volunteers began to learn to live with gut-wrenching fear, especially as the search continued with no sign of the missing men except their empty, charred station wagon.

Despite their fears, the majority of the 280 Freedom School volunteers stayed through the orientation and went to Mississippi. But the disappearance, and later the discovery of the three mutilated bodies, framed the summer project in violence. No one ever forgot the tension; rarely did anyone ever feel safe.

For the volunteer teachers, area studies were practical and immediately useful. Sections of the state were analyzed and discussed so the volunteers would know the economic and political background of their geographic areas. They reviewed more specific information when they were assigned to their schools. Thus, volunteers bound for Canton learned about cotton chopping and were warned in advance of the possible necessity of double shift sessions to accommodate their working students. Those designated for Hattiesburg found that they could count on a well-established and active black community with reasonably urban resources and attitudes. Each small group of volunteers, then, was introduced to "their" new community: its power structure, economic situation and physical circumstances.

The intrinsic appeal of Freedom Schools became even greater as the volunteers learned more about the existing educational structure in the state. The staff gave a blistering precis of Mississippi Negro education. The underlying premise, according to them, was repression of all kinds—physical, emotional, psychological and intellectual—to the end of keeping the Mississippi black in his place.

As the volunteers read of the discrepancies in black and white schooling from the 1962 report of the State Superintendent for Education and SNCC reports, they began to comprehend the bitterness of the COFO staff. On the state level, Mississippi paid $81.86 for each white student and $21.77 for each black and in many individual districts the discrepancies were much worse. In Yazoo County with a 59.4 per cent black population, for instance, white schools received $245.55 per student and black schools received $2.92 per student.[6]

After introducing the volunteers to the background of the educational situation, the staff discussed what the Freedom School teachers should do in their new jobs. They pressed the point that the volunteer's most important task was to encourage the students to discuss problems and ask questions. so that students would begin to appreciate their intrinsic importance as people.

Noel Day, a SNCC staff member, gave the volunteers several suggestions about teaching Mississippi black children. He advised the teachers to encourage their students in all possible ways:

The leader should not be critical—particularly at the start. For many of the students, *just being able to verbalize in this situation is progress* that can easily be inhibited by a disapproving remark or facial expression.

He suggested that volunteers simplify their language and learn the student's slang: their job was to communicate and to encourage expression.[7]

Exemplifying the somewhat simplistic COFO staff feeling about their new educational structure, Jane Stembridge cautioned the volunteers "to be trustworthy. It's that simple." She also wrote from the Jackson office: "We can say that the key to your teaching will be honesty and creativity. We can prepare materials for you and suggest teaching methods. Beyond that, it is your classroom . . . "[8]

Along with the staff cautions and explanations, the volunteers were given intensive classes in the core curriculum, especially black history, federal and state government, and the history of the movement. They needed to know facts as well as interpretations. And they struggled to absorb enough information to help students understand their personal experiences in the light of the history of black and poor white people in the world. This forging together of personal experience and academic data was the rationale of the Freedom School method. Only with both emphases could the students realize the goal of the organizers that they see ". . . the link between a rotting shack and a rotting America."

At the end of the one week orientation, most of the volunteers were scarcely prepared for their tasks, but they did have some ideas about what they should do and how they might attempt teaching. They had practical information and teaching ideas for projects and role playing. Further, they could count on support from the resource people based in Jackson who had special skills and who often brought mimeographed teaching aids and book lists.

On the last night of orientation, Bob Moses talked to the group about the prospects, the dangers, and the rewards that the summer might bring. He concluded with a plea to the Freedom School teachers, " . . . to be patient with their students. There's a difference between being slow and being stupid, he said. The people . . . [the teachers would] . . . be working with aren't stupid. But they're slow, so slow."[9]

The volunteers left for their respective schools and began working within the week. The staff had estimated that one thousand black students would attend the twenty-five Freedom Schools located throughout the state. After the second week, however, over two thousand students had registered and by the end of the summer an estimated 2,500 to 2,700 black Mississippians had attended at least some classes. The Freedom School sites expanded from twenty-five to forty-one.

A typical Freedom School day began with the core curriculum of black history and philosophy of the movement. This was usually a history lesson or reading followed by a discussion. For example, many teachers gave lectures on W.E.B. DuBois of whom most of the students had never heard. They compared him to Booker T. Washington, whom they had all studied in school. The discussion period would examine questions like:

Who do you think the Movement is proving right—Booker T. Washington or W.E.B. DuBois? And what comment on your own upbringing is made by the fact that you knew all about Booker T. Washington, but most of you had never heard of W.E.B. DuBois?[10]

Following the core curriculum, there was generally some project or discussion aimed at helping the students examine themselves and their environment. The teachers used various methods for this class which ranged from question sessions to impromptu role-playing. Often the teachers introduced a poem and had their students respond with their own creative writing and some beautiful and expressive pieces came out of those classes.

After a break for the hottest part of the day, the Freedom Schools held afternoon sessions which were generally "special interest" classes requested by the students. The most popular ones were foreign languages, higher mathematics, art, drama, typing and journalism. None of these was taught on a regular basis to black students in Mississippi schools. As in the other classes, the teachers tried to relate these subjects to the students. One teacher who taught a French class discovered the students requested it because foreign language classes, taught only in white Mississippi schools, were a symbol of equality to them. She found, however, that ". . . teaching French turned out to be a good way to develop grammar and phoenetic skills that would bore them in English . . . "[11] Thus, the class was related to the regular program in an academic way. Art and drama sessions gave the students a way of exploring and expressing their emotions. It also made them aware of the art media as an important avenue for protest. Typing was a favorite class and students begged to learn, both to obtain better employment and to help in the movement.

Journalism was the most eclectic class of all; the students produced special "freedom" newspapers and in so doing practiced creative writing, typing, news writing and editing. They also spurred on an indigenous black press. A volunteer wrote about his freedom paper:

Most of that week was spent working on the "Clarksdale Freedom Press." Getting all the interested kids in the basement of Haven Methodist Church, examining possible articles, editing them, typing them, etc., was great! The place looked like a newspaper office with people running in and out, with typewriters going, and newsprint everywhere. It was excellent experience for the kids too . . . They did most of the work and made most of the decisions.[12]

In the evening, classes continued, usually with adults. Informal discussions were held about the movement and what could be done to change Mississippi. Additionally, there were literacy classes which used Dr. Frank Laubach's "Each one-teach one" method. Freedom School students helped the teacher on this one-to-one project, thereby learning to teach others and helping the adult students learn to read. The literacy project aided local people in registering to vote and often used the registration form as a reading text.

The teachers themselves had classes. In informal discussions, the volunteers often taught each other in areas with which they were familiar, and in methods which were successful in their classes. Additionally, several professors who had joined the project were assigned to work with the Freedom School volunteers and to discuss subjects relevant to their teaching. Professor Otis Pease, then at Stanford University, volunteered to work with COFO in Mississippi in July. Before he went down, he prepared a paper on "The Development of the Negro in American Politics Since 1900," which was distributed to Freedom School teachers around the state and which constituted Pease's first research in black history. When Pease arrived in Mississippi, he was assigned to work in Hattiesburg, where, among other things, he led a seminar with local Freedom School teachers and used his paper as a basic text. Addressing the controversial issue of working inside or outside the system, Pease held in the paper that blacks exercised power at the national level as a direct result of having the vote in northern states. Essentially, the paper was an historically accurate brief reflecting Pease's belief that working within the system was the most practical way to obtain real political power. The seminar "sparked a lively discussion" on what the goals of the movement should be. While several teachers agreed with Pease's position on working within the system, even with the risks that entailed, a CORE worker from New York adamantly disagreed because, "The System is corrupt." He believed, instead, that the movement should build a new system and revolutionize America. Before Pease could comment, a second volunteer disagreed: building a new system was impracticable, and it was the movement's duty to get what it could within the system and help blacks now. Waiting for a utopian situation was paralyzing and futile.[13]

While most of the volunteers agreed with the expediency of working within the system for what could be gained quickly, the Hattiesburg Freedom School seminar was a microcosmic form of the major debate within the civil rights movement throughout the country, and staff workers, as well as volunteers, remained divided on the issue for several years. The issue was not, after all, small or "academic," for everyone knew it was a fact that people had lost their lives in Mississippi for movement work and that it was a possibility that people would continue to lose their lives "simply" trying to get into the southern political system. Seminars such as this, with heated debates on topics clearly relevant to real people's lives, helped the volunteers examine major issues in the movement and bring back to their students a new awareness of the facts of the black experience and the various interpretations that could be ascribed to these facts. Additionally, the volunteers often came to question their "ivory tower" academic beliefs of "value-free scholarship" and "objectivity," and to formulate alternative visions of what constituted "real" education for their students and themselves.

For the most part, the volunteers were enthusiastic about their new vocation and found it exciting to be in an unstructured "learning situation." Some realized fond dreams when they were able to test their theories of education, and many others began for the first time to seriously consider alternatives to the traditional academic classroom. The most consistently appealing and rewarding aspect of Freedom School teaching, however, was that the volunteers' efforts clearly helped some children overcome their previous experiences in school and respond positively to their teachers. One volunteer wrote home:

I can see the change. The 16-year-old's discovery of poetry, of Whitman and Cummings above all, the struggle to express thoughts in words, to translate ideas into concrete written words. After two weeks a child finally looks me in the eye, unafraid, acknowledging a bond of trust which 300 years of Mississippians said should never, could never exist. I can feel the growth of self-confidence.[14]

And another exclaimed:

Every class is beautiful. The girls respond, respond, respond. And they disagree among themselves. I have no doubt soon they will be disagreeing with me. At least this is one thing that I am working towards. They are a sharp group but they are under-educated and starved for knowledge. They know that they have been cheated and they want anything and everything that we can give them.[15]

Although the majority of the teachers adapted ably to their tasks, there were some who should not have been teaching and probably should not have been in Mississippi at all. Unfortunately, incapable teachers in several cases materially affected their Freedom School, especially if the school was small or in a rural area.[16]

All of the schools varied in their offerings and their composition. Two case studies illustrate the scope of the schools and the different kinds of experience the volunteers had.

Hattiesburg, which was the home of a strong COFO community center, became, in the words of Director Staughton Lynd, the "Mecca of the Freedom School world." What happened there the first week was illustrative of the predicament in which teachers throughout the state found themselves. One volunteer from Hattiesburg wrote home:

. . . All this week we have been working on curriculum, schedules, registration of students and assembling materials for the Freedom Schools at Hattiesburg. It became evident quite early that we are going to have more than the expected 75 students. We called Jackson and got a promise of more teachers—at full strength we will have 23. This was when we expected 150 students. On registration day, however, we had a totally unexpected deluge: 600 students! They were expecting only 700 for the whole state.[17]

Although it was rewarding to the volunteers to find so many students interested in the schools, it was also frustrating. They had hoped to have a teacher-student ratio of about one to five in order to give necessary personal attention to the students. Instead, they found themselves in some cases with twenty or more. They also discovered that, although the Freedom Schools were originally planned for fourteen to eighteen-year olds, Mississippians of all ages registered, and they had to adjust their programs for the wide age spread.

By the end of the second week, there were some five schools in and around Hattiesburg. The "deluge" of students was the result of strong civil rights activity in Hattiesburg previous to the summer. The success of the schools was due in large part to the excellent organization of Arthur and Carolyn Reese, a black couple from Detroit who supervised the project. Professional teachers themselves, they adapted their knowledge and experience of structured teaching to the ideals inherent in Freedom School education.[18]

Because of their innovation and organization, the Freedom Schools in Hattiesburg remained "bright lights" in the state. The Hattiesburg group were particularly successful in instituting the "Each One-Teach One" method of teaching literacy to older people, generally in community centers. And the students from the Hattiesburg School at Palmer's Crossing wrote a "Declaration of Independence," which paraphrased the American Declaration of Independence and included a list of grievances, which indicated students' awareness of their position in society and how government might change that position.[19]

A Freedom School-Community Center project continued throughout the year at Hattiesburg. Seven volunteers remained in the face of increased white harrassment. And the project instituted a proposal made by the Reeses that older students teach younger students thus expanding teaching capabilities.

In contrast to the Hattiesburg schools, volunteers who went to Shaw, Mississippi, faced many problems. Shaw is a poor rural Delta town. Aside from a teenage group, the movement had scarcely touched Shaw prior to the summer; so the volunteers had to make their own introduction.

The volunteers were all housed in the black community and they rented a house for a community center. After installing electricity, building shelves and tables and scrubbing it all down, they were ready to set up their equipment, arrange the books for a library and begin the Freedom School.[20]

Since Shaw is a cotton town, however, schools ran during the summer to allow students to work in the fields at chopping and harvest time. As the children had to go to school from seven to one o'clock, a volunteer wrote, " . . . they want to sleep, not to have to study in the blazing heat of the Mississippi sun and dust." And he continued, "So would I in their place. Furthermore, they don't see how we can help them be free. At this point, neither do we. Slow change is unthinkable when so much change is needed . . . [21] The Shaw volunteers grew more anxious, uncomfortable and jealous as they read reports of Freedom School successes in other areas.

Well into what should have been the second week of classes, the Shaw Freedom School Director, Wally Roberts, wrote on July 11, 1964, to Professor Staughton Lynd, the statewide director, expressing his discouragement which was compounded by family problems:

. . . I am completely frustrated. Living conditions are so terrible, the Negroes are so completely oppressed, so completely without hope, that I want to change it all NOW. I mean this as sincerely as I can. Running a Freedom School is an absurd waste of time. I don't want to sit around in a classroom; I want to go out . . . shake [the white people] up, destroy their stolen property, convince them we mean business . . . I really can't stand it here . . . [22]

Although local people were beginning to use the library and the center, there were still virtually no students in the school.

Roberts' letter brought Staughton Lynd to Shaw on July 14, three days after it had been written. He and Roberts had a long talk that evening, and the next day Lynd and all the volunteers discussed the situation.

As a result, the volunteers decided to try a new tack and turned to full-time voter registration. They immediately organized a Freedom Day and took forty blacks to Cleveland, the Bolivar County seat, to register. To support the registrants, the volunteers organized teenagers to picket the courthouse and sing freedom songs. As one wrote:

Not only was this the first time *any* picketline has occurred in this county, but the Sheriff ignored a newly passed state law forbidding picketing. He hired 35–40 auxiliary police for the day, and posted them around the block with their helmets and rifles in case of incidents . . . [23]

In giving the young people workshops in nonviolence and picketing, the volunteer teachers found, "They had enjoyed them because they understood and valued the end to which we were directing them . . . It suddenly became clear to us that what we should do was to have special tutoring in anything the students desired."[24]

Through this Freedom Day activity, the Shaw Freedom School began. Over a third of the high school came, some thirty-five students, and the volunteers gave classes in anything the students wanted:

Not only are they having special workshops in leadership and non-violence, but we are sneaking in all kinds of citizenship education, and they are enjoying it. We even have several who are interested in straight Negro history, and not too few who want academics, the normal type. So in this more limited, but under the circumstances healthier extent, we are underway as a Freedom School, the last in the state to do so.[25]

The Shaw school succeeded finally by linking its more academic program to political activity, and in that sense reflected Cobb's original plan and rationale for Freedom Schools. Although it was the hardest to start, the problems it faced and the frustrations of the volunteers were not unique to Shaw. There were upsets and disappointments at other schools too.

The culmination of the Freedom Schools was the state-wide convention held in Meridian in early August. Planned mainly by Freedom School students, elected delegates from each school were to analyze the problems in the state and propose demands they would make on the government if they were a voting majority. Delegates from almost every school attended, although in some instances parents were reluctant to risk their children's safety by letting them be publicly involved in civil rights.[26]

When the Freedom School students assembled in Meridian, they immediately began working on a program. One volunteer wrote:

The purpose of the convention was to formulate a youth platform for the Freedom Democratic Party, and the kids did a fantastic job of it . . . There were eight different committees, each concerning a different area of legislation: jobs, schools, federal aid, foreign affairs, voting, housing, public accommodations, health . . . The kids really learned something from the convention, for the first time, Negro students from all over the state came together to discuss their common aims . . . [27]

The students accepted the Palmer's Crossing Declaration of Independence as an ideological statement. They made guidelines for housing projects and health programs and they advocated swift equalization of public schools and job opportunities. Resolving active support of SNCC's Mississippi Student Union (MSU), they called for a political challenge to the all-white Mississippi Young Democrats and for school boycotts in particularly repressive districts.[28]

As the summer drew to a close, most Freedom School teachers left for the North and home. The schools were initially analyzed a success and Director Staughton Lynd issued a "Final Report" which made confident plans to continue the project. The report proposed that a school be kept in every area and that some of the summer Freedom School volunteers remain in Mississippi to staff them. Additional volunteers were to be recruited by SNCC and CORE to complete the staffing. The report also proposed that community center and Freedom School staffs unify to consolidate their strength and acknowledged that the schools would mainly be held in the evening after public school. Liz Fusco, formerly coordinator of the Indianola and Ruleville schools, was appointed the new director of Freedom Schools, since Lynd was going to Yale University to begin an Assistant Professorship. Lynd's final suggestion was that the schools should allow time for restructuring and not go back into session until October.[29]

Continuing and expanding on Lynd's ideas, in September, 1964, a staff member drew up a "Proposal for a Freedom Education Program," which advocated building a "new community institution, a community center," which would act as the meeting place for educational programs, serve as a social service center and be the home base for political education. The plan called for an integrated model pre-school and Freedom School program which would supplement public schools and it outlined a strong, new adult education program. The physical plans for the building were detailed in the proposal. Since buildings of that sort were not readily available in most black communities, " . . . we must build our centers, symbolic of building a New

South when the old South does not meet our needs.[30] Although each center would initially be staffed by a "trained outsider" and long-term northern and local volunteers, completely local leadership would be the goal of a successful center.

The new, smaller Freedom School program began again in the fall. As it was less formal than the summer project, Freedom School teachers made more of their own curriculum and continued to exchange useful units among themselves. Many more clearly realized and emphasized the importance of experiential knowledge: Mississippi blacks knew how to survive politically whether or not they could read or write. Although the summer experience brought this belief, the stress on the educational validity, and in some cases superiority, of experiential knowledge marked a profound change from the summer program. Indeed, Jimmy Garrett of Los Angeles SNCC wrote exemplifying that feeling, "People are called 'ignorant' if they know nothing but their own lives. Are people 'educated' if they know about everything except their own lives?"[31]

This refocusing which emphasized a more immediate political awareness was an evolutionary process, and it did not automatically happen in all of the schools, although it was accelerated statewide by the dissolution of any pretense of a viable COFO by the winter of 1965. With the ascendence of the more politically radical civil rights groups, SNCC and CORE, over the more ameliorative groups, the NAACP and SCLC, it was obvious that programs would become more critical of local institutions and more oriented toward developing the political awareness necessary to "see the links between a rotting shack and a rotting America." While volunteers continued to teach subjects not taught in the public schools, as the year drew to a close, the subjects taught and the emphasis of the classes became more oriented to the individual local people attending them. The students helped each other to learn and make their own standards for the classes.

The evolution had its difficult moments. The Freedom School staff meeting in November, 1964, was an example. In a discussion about what the new Freedom School program should be, a white volunteer suggested the staff work mainly with the "educated" people, because there were fewer communication problems with them and because they were the ones who would ultimately make important political decisions in the state. In response, Liz Fusco wrote: "An irate Negro girl from Greenwood screamed, 'Yes, I'm ignorant, cause they taken me and putten me in a cotton field." "And so," Fusco continued, "we began discussing who we should talk to—which was our way of beginning to discuss who should make the decisions, and what education is . . . In fact, it became 'local people' year!" The new Freedom School goal was "an education based on people," which would acknowledge the importance of the black community's survival and experience which was the crux of Jimmy Garrett's question, "What constitutes education?"[32]

It became clear to the staff and the remaining volunteers that an evaluation of the Freedom School program had to come to grips with the previous thrust of the program. Supplementary education, while it might well boost the ego and self-image of the students, probably did not in a practical sense help students survive in Mississippi and might even fail to illuminate the reasons why the material was not taught in Mississippi schools. Summer Freedom Schools taught remedial reading: did they confront why people could not read? Also, the staff and remaining volunteers watched students drift away in the fall when specialty subjects, like foreign languages, which had drawn large numbers of people in the summer, no longer were taught because the volunteer teacher with those skills had returned to the North.

Just as the reassessment of the program was accelerated by the staff changes in COFO and the disavowal by the more conservative civil rights groups of SNCC's programs, the change in the volunteers who staffed the Freedom Schools hastened the process. Those volunteers who remained in Mississippi after the summer made a long-term commitment to the movement and tended to be more consistently left-wing in their views and radical in their politics. Dedicated to thoroughgoing social change, they tended to join in the criticism of the intent and content of the previous program and to advocate augmenting experiential knowledge to facilitate blacks' changing their society.

Of course, this re-evaluation of the Freedom Schools—judging "success" by actions taken by the community as a result of the school, rather than by the numbers of school students involved—did not contradict the original intent of the Freedom Schools as they were proposed by Charlie Cobb in early 1964. Rather, the assessment brought the program back to the original idea of Freedom Schools as an organizing tool for action within the movement. No one denied that good experiences had come from the schools, for both white volunteers and black local students, but the staff found the schools had not been as organizationally effective as they first had planned. And their lack of effectiveness seemed in direct proportion to the supplementary, non-experiential nature of their programs. Those schools which were the most "northern academic" in content had the least continuity in the fall and winter.[33]

One action legacy from the summer program was the idea and statewide endorsement of public school boycotts. Several communities proposed or held boycotts. Moreover, in Issaquena and Sharkey counties, students organized a long-term Freedom School, when they began a boycott of their public school after the school principal forbade students to wear SNCC buttons. For the remaining staff, this became the new ideal for Freedom Schools.[34]

By any traditional academic standards, the Issaquena-Sharkey Freedom School "classes" were chaos, but they represented the free expression of students the staff had only theorized could be possible in November. And they showed that Freedom Schools could indeed be what Cobb had initially envisioned: foci for community organizing to bring community change.[35] Although some Freedom School teachers came to help and bring supplies, they stayed in the background. The students themselves discussed what they wanted to discuss: the subjects ranged from major league baseball players, to why the earthworm needs the earth, to math, to "how would you like to see

Issaquena County run." They put ideas together on their own. After examining pictures in *Look* and *Ebony* magazines, and comparing them with what they saw around them everyday, one eleven year old boy reported,

By looking at the magazines it let me *know* that they [rich blacks and whites] didn't care nothing about them [poor blacks and whites].
I learned that rich white people gettin' all the water, and them rich Negroes get all the water from the poor Negros; the poor white, they ain't gettin' no water either.

The longest boycott in the state, the Issaquena action continued until September, 1965, when the majority of the children went back to the Issaquena-Sharkey school, still without the right to wear buttons. The main leaders did not go back; the boys took paying jobs with the Delta Ministry, while one girl went North and the other became the first black in the white Issaquena-Sharkey school. The Freedom School experiment lasted eight months.[36]

A more orthodox work-study program was held by SNCC at the Waveland Institute in Waveland, Mississippi, and many of the finest movement teachers came to teach at least one class. While Jane Stembridge was there, she wrote up a speech class by Stokely Carmichael, who was then on the Mississippi staff. One day he wrote eight sentences on the board with four on each side. On the left side were sentences in the local black dialect like "The peoples wants freedom," and "I wants to reddish to vote." Corresponding to those sentences, he wrote on the right side, "The people want freedom," and "I want to register to vote." He turned and asked the class of teenage Mississippi blacks what they thought about the sentences. While they thought that the ones on the right were "correct," they believed the most commonly used ones were those on the left:

Stokely: If most people speak on the left, why are they [teachers] trying to change these people?

Gladys: If you don't talk right, society rejects you. It embarrasses other people if you don't talk right.

Hank: But Mississippi society, ours, isn't embarrassed by it.

Shirley: But the middle class wouldn't class us with them.

Stokely: Will society reject you if you don't speak like on the right side of the board? Gladys said society would reject you.

Gladys: You might as well face it man! What we gotta do is go out and become middle class. If you can't speak good English, you don't have a car, a job, or anything.

Stokely: If society rejects you because you don't speak good English, should you learn to speak good English?

Class: No!

Alma: I'm tired of doing what society say. Let society say "reddish" for awhile. People ought just to accept each other.

Zelma: I think we should be speaking just like we always have.

Alma: If I change for society, I wouldn't be free anyway.

. . . .

Alma: If the majority speaks on the left, then a minority must rule society? Why do we have to change to be accepted by the minority group?

. . . .

Stokely: Let's think about two questions for next time: What is society? Who makes the rules for society?

In what could have been a commonplace class in language, Carmichael, through directed questions, urged his students to think about language, power, control and politics. With a brilliantly executed pedagogical method, he helped his students make vital connections about their language and their lives.[37]

In these sometimes subtle but real ways, the Freedom Schools became more free-wheeling and politically radical. The best of them—like Stokely Carmichael's class—integrated the personal experiences of the students with the political ideology of the movement. This integration of experience and ideology was concretely action-oriented. Students at the Waveland Institute, for instance, pledged themselves to work in the movement for at least as long a time as they took classes. And students in Issaquena-Sharkey actively tried to change their school system.

Early in 1965, after all the program re-evaluations by the Mississippi civil rights staff, the Freedom Democratic Party formally decided to sponsor a small, decentralized project, as the political branch of the state's civil rights movement. The summer project would be based solely on community needs and requests. Some communities decided to have Freedom Schools; many did not. The COFO enthusiasm of the summer before towards the schools had diminished by 1965, since the criterion for a "successful" school had changed and the movement emphasized the FDP and concrete political action. Indeed, as late as the middle of April, movement staff were still debating whether Freedom Schools taught by whites were any longer appropriate for the movement. Many staff members at the April meeting did not believe there was a place for white teachers in the state, but SNCC leader Jim Forman argued the case for assigning "aware people—white or black," to Freedom Schools, and his view seemed to prevail, although each project would determine its own needs and staff.[38]

The group of volunteers which came to the 1965 FDP Project numbered about 300, and Freedom School teachers were a much smaller percentage of the group than they had been in the 1964 Mississippi Summer Project. Volunteers who taught were requested by the community and were expected to have useful skills. Further, they were seen primarily as "facilitators" for the expression of practical political awareness. Although Liz Fusco continued to hold the title Director of Freedom Schools, the summer classes were much less formal than the previous year's. Compared to 1964, the orientation program was less organized and the teaching emphasis was on the movement and the student's place in it.

The focus had indeed shifted. To many in the movement, the Freedom Schools of 1964 would have seemed anachronistic and irrelevant in 1965. Although some Freedom School classes were quite like the previous summer's, most had become more political. Karel Weisenberg's literacy class in 1965 was an example:

Could I have everyone's attention please? . . . Mrs. Ervy's written something and I thought if she read it we could talk about it some . . .

Mrs. Ervy: Here's one thing: I want to know how come we pay taxes so much and don't get our roads fixed into our houses.

And here's another thing—how come they put the rocky floors in our houses? I just don't understand that.

Cow barns is better than some of these houses. I work hard for what I get. I work from 6 to 6 for three dollars a day. That ain't no money . . . I want more . . . I labor a whole week and don't earn but fifteen dollars. We wants better; we wants food to eat . . .

We cook for a white, we washes, we irons, we bathes the children and when it comes to the real part of it, we are used as a dog . . . something got to be done about it. We got to stick together more.[89]

Thus the classes changed from adult literacy for its own sake, to literacy as a means of political expression.

Light-years away from the simple "good citizenship" basis of the previous summer, the McComb Freedom School blazed a controversial path. McComb was widely known as the most violently anti-civil rights town in the state. More black churches were bombed in McComb than in any other area, and two blacks associated with the movement had been murdered since Bob Moses began working there in 1961. Every civil rights worker in McComb had been beaten and jailed on more than one occasion. In fact, initially in June of 1964, Moses refused to assign any white volunteers to McComb because it was so dangerous, though he later relented and allowed three special white volunteers to integrate the project which hung on in the black community in the face of terrible, violent white harrassment. In the 1965 McComb Freedom School political education classes, students examined racism in American society, studied theories of third party politics and worked for the FDP. Encouraged by their northern volunteer teachers, McComb students began questioning the role of the United States' involvement in Vietnam and the links between the civil rights movement and the peace movement. When a local black, who had supported Bob Moses in 1961, was killed in Vietnam, the teachers and students composed the "McComb Project Position Paper on the War in Vietnam." In a clear and concise statement, the students argued that blacks should not fight in Vietnam for ". . .the White Man's freedom, until all the Negro People are free in Mississippi." Further, they urged black men to avoid the draft and called on mothers to encourage their sons to stay home. Finally, while alleging economic aggrandizement as the reason for American participation in the war, they began to see themselves as allies with what soon became generally called the Third World:

We will be looked upon as traitors by all the Colored People of the world if the Negro people continue to fight and die without a cause.

With their "Statement on the War in Vietnam," McComb students made the first connection between the direct action civil rights movement and the burgeoning peace movement. Their statement was the first of any civil rights groups to condemn American fighting in Vietnam.[40]

The leaflet was printed in the *MFDP Newsletter* and created an enormous controversy. State politicians and the local press charged that the students advocated treason. They predicted that the FDP challenge of Mississippi's congressional delegation, at that moment under consideration by the House of Representatives, would fail because of the statement, and, of course, they argued it should fail, because of the "irresponsibility" of such a stand. FDP leaders, Lawrence Guyot and Edwin King, felt compelled to assert that the statement represented only the views of the McComb branch of the FDP and was not the policy of the statewide Party, but they agreed that " . . . it is very easy to understand why Negro citizens of McComb, themselves the victims of bombings, klan-inspired terrorism, and harrassment arrests, should resent the death of a citizen of McComb while fighting in Vietnam for freedom not enjoyed by the Negro community of McComb."[41] When questioned by the local press, one of the volunteers who helped author the statement explained, "It came from the people, this is how they felt. We just put their feelings into words after talking with them, singing with them and living with them."[42]

The more radical political nature of the majority of the Freedom School classes represented a substantial change from the previous summer. Those volunteers who taught in 1965 drew connections between the peace and civil rights movements and organized their classes around viable local issues. They came much closer to enacting the original "Prospectus on Freedom Schools" than most of the 1964 schools, and they cast aside most notions of integrating Mississippi blacks into a basically "benign" American system.

An important educational and organizational experiment, the schools demonstrated the possibility of integrated education based on the premise that everyone has much to offer the community. The schools at their best showed both black and white Mississippi society that integrated students and teachers could laugh and talk and see together   . . . the link between a rotting shack and a rotting America," and that they could then act on their vision. At their worst, the schools deflected energy from movement work and became a diversion which helped fill up time for students and kept volunteers occupied.

By the end of the 1965 summer, the staff in Mississippi did not believe that

Freedom schools taught by northern whites were relevant to the problems of Mississippi blacks, and the program turned solely to direct political action. The life cycle of the organized Mississippi Freedom School project was complete, but the legacy of the schools endures in the Mississippi black community.[43]

NOTES

1. For more background on the Summer Projects, see Mary Aickin Rothschild, *A Case of Black and White: Northern Volunteers and the Southern Freedom Summers, 1964-1965* (Westport, Connecticut, 1982), Chapters 1-2. These characteristics and basic demographic facts apply to the approximately three hundred 1965 Mississippi volunteers as well, though, by 1965, ten per cent of the Mississippi volunteers considered themselves "radical."
2. *Otis Pease Prs*, Seattle, Washington; Charlie Cobb, "Prospectus for a Summer Freedom School Project," COFO mimeo, April, 1964, pp. 1-2.
3. *State Historical Society of Wisconsin (hereinafter SHSW): Howard Zinn Prs.; SHSW: Staughton Lynd Prs.; Otis Pease Prs. Seattle, Washington. Interviews*: Otis Pease, Seattle, Washington, 1967-1968; Howard Zinn, Boston, Massachusetts, 1969.
4. *Otis Pease Prs*, Seattle, WA: "Prospectus for a Mississippi Freedom School Program," COFO mimeo, no date (probably April, 1964), includes original Cobb Proposal; Ilene Strelitz Melish, *Memoirs*, Unpub. Mss. especially pp. 29-30; *Mary Rothschild Prs*, in possession of author: Prospectus for the Mississippi Freedom Summer," COFO ditto, no date (probably late April), includes only edited version of Cobb's proposal; Liz Fusco, "To Blur the Focus of What you Came Here to Know: A Letter Containing Notes on Education, Freedom Schools and Mississippi," ditto, undated (Spring, 1966), hereinafter Fusco, "To Blur the Focus;" Liz Fusco "Issaquena Freedom: A Play Written in Jail in Mississippi," mss., April, 1965, hereinafter Fusco, "Issaquena Freedom;" *SHSW: Howard Zinn Prs.*: Letter: Dr. Robert L. Zangrando to Zinn, Rutgers University, August 20, 1964, p. 3; SHSW: *Elizabeth Sutherland Prs.*; Unused and Uncatalogued Letters," Letter Series "Judy" to parents and sponsor church in Denver, June 30, 1964 - August 11, 1964, Ruleville and Shaw, Mississippi; *SHSW: Staughton Lynd Prs.*: Kristy Powell, "A Report, Mainly on Ruleville Freedom School Summer Project, 1964;" Florence Howe, "Mississippi's Freedom School Summer Project, 1964;" Florence Howe, "Mississippi's Freedom Schools: The Politics of Education," *Harvard Educational Review*, 35 (Spring 1964): 144-160: Elizabeth Sutherland, *Letters from Mississippi*, (New York: 1964), pp. 100-102 (hereinafter Sutherland, Letters); *Interviews*: Otis Pease, Seattle, Wash., 1967; Paul Lauter and Florence Howe, Seattle, Wash., June, 1972.
5. *Otis Pease Prs*, Seattle, Wash.: Mississippi Summer Project Staff (MSPS), "Memorandum: Overview of the Freedom Schools," COFO ditto, May 5, 1964, Jackson, Mississippi, pp. 1-3; Staughton Lynd and Harold Bardanelli, "Dear Freedom School Teacher," COFO ditto; May 20, 1964, Jackson, Mississippi; MSPS, "Dear Summer Project Worker," COFO ditto, undated (Late May), Jackson, Mississippi; Note the subtle differences in tone and purpose between the MSPS memos and the Lynd and Bardinelli memo.
6. William McCord, *Mississippi: The Long Hot Summer* (New York, 1965), p. 35. These are the figures for the local school district's expenditures per student which are matched, dollar for dollar, by the state. From the report of State Superintendent of Education as cited in the *Memphis Commercial Appeal*, January 15, 1962.
7. *Mary Rothschild Prs*, in possession of author: Noel Day, "Remarks to the Freedom School Teachers about Methods," "Notes on Teaching," p. 5.
8. *Mary Rothschild Prs*, in possession of author: Jane Stembridge, "Introduction to the Summer," "Notes on Teaching," p. 1.
9. Sutherland, *Letters*, p. 39; SHSW: Lise Vogel Prs.: "Orientation Notes," hand-written.
10. Liz Fusco, "Deeper Than Politics," *Liberation*, IX, no. 8 (1964), p. 18. *SHSW: Howard Zinn Prs.*: "Negro History Study Questions: 20th Century," COFO ditto, undated (Spring/Summer 1964), p. 1.
11. Sutherland, *Letters*, p. 95.
12. Sutherland, *Letters*, p. 97.
13. *Mary Rothschild Prs*, in possession of author: Otis Pease, "The Development of the Negro in American Politics Since 1900," COFO mimeo, undated (June 1964); *Otis Pease Prs*, Seattle, WA: Handwritten notes on July 16, 1964; *Interviews*: Otis Pease, February 13, 1967; March 23, 1967. Since that summer experience, Pease has always included a substantial component of black history in his courses. Previously, he did not.
14. Sutherland, *Letters*, pp. 94-95.
15. Sutherland, *Letters*, p. 94.

16. *Interviews:* Otis Pease, February 13, 1967; March 23, 1967; Sally Shideler, February 15, 1967.
17. Sutherland, *Letters*, p. 92.
18. *SHSW: Elizabeth Sutherland Prs.:* "Unused and Uncatalogued Letters;" *Interview:* Otis Pease, 1967.
19. *Mary Rothschild Prs*, in possession of author: "Freedom School Data," including "The Declaration of Independence by the Freedom School Students of St. John's Methodist Church, Palmer's Crossing, Hattiesburg, Mississippi," COFO ditto, p. 6.
20. *WSHS: Lise Vogel Prs.:* Letter from Bonnie Guy to "Friends," July 18, 1964, Shaw, Mississippi, p. 1.
21. Sutherland, *Letters*, p. 100.
22. Sutherland, *Letters*, p. 101.
23. *SHSW: Lise Vogel Prs.:* Bonnie Guy, "Letter to Friends," July 18, 1964, Shaw, Mississippi, p. 3.
24. Sutherland, *Letters*, p. 102.
25. Sutherland, *Letters*, p. 102.
26. Florence Howe, "Mississippi's Freedom Schools:" 148. Interviews: Florence Howe and Paul Lauter, June, 1972, Seattle, Wash.; Florence Howe, Series, Summer 1974, Seattle, Washington.
27. Sutherland, *Letters*, pp. 104-105.
28. Liz Fusco, "Deeper Than Politics," *Liberation*, IX, p. 18; *SHSW: Howard Zinn Prs.:* "Freedom Schools—Final Report, 1964," undated (about August 20, 1964).
29. *SHSW: Howard Zinn Prs.:* "Freedom Schools—Final Report, 1964," undated (about August 20, 1964); Staughton Lynd, Mississippi Freedom Schools: Retrospect and Prospect," July 26, 1964, draft mss.; *SHSW: Staughton Lynd Prs.:* Howard Zinn, "Educational Frontiers in Mississippi," draft mss.
30. *Mary Rothschild Prs*, in possession of author: "Proposal for a Freedom Education Program," Xerox of typed mss., p. 3. I am indebted to Ms. Jan Hillegas of the Mississippi Freedom Information Service of Tougaloo, Miss. for allowing me access to her private files.
31. *Mary Rothschild Prs*, in possession of author: Liz Fusco, "To Blur the Focus," p. 9.
32. Liz Fusco, "To Blur the Focus," pp. 1-4.
33. *Mary Rothschild Prs* in possession of author: Liz Fusco, "To Blur the Focus," "Outlook for the Mississippi Community Center Program," Xerox of typed mss., a position paper, March, 1965; Position papers for COFO Re-evaluation, November-December, 1964, ditto. Again I am indebted to Ms. Jan Hillegas of the Freedom Information Service for giving me a complete packet of these papers just as they were given to all the staff members before the meeting. *Interviews:* Nancy Davis, October, 1973, San Francisco; Linda Davis, October, 1973, Washington, D.C.; Fannie Lou Hamer, November, 1969, Ruleville, Mississippi, Charles Horwitz, November, 1969, Jackson, Mississippi, Barbara Rosen, January, 1967, Seattle, Washington.
34. *SHSW: Staughton Lynd Prs.:* Kristy Powell, "A Report, Mainly on Ruleville Freedom School, Summer Project, 1964," pp. 10-11; Florence Howe, "Mississippi's Freedom Schools:" 155-157. Pat Watters, *Down to Now: Reflections on the Southern Civil Movement* (New York: 1971), p. 302.
35. This boycott-Freedom School tradition continues in the Amite, Mississippi, school boycott over sex-segregation in the Amite schools, which integrated under federal mandate in 1969, but which kept the sexes separate so white girls would not be in the same classrooms as black boys. The boycott began in September of 1977 and is not yet completely resolved. *Newsweek* (September 19, 1977): 97.
36. *Mary Rothschild Prs* in possession of author: Liz Fusco, "Tommy Jr., A SNCC Poster (For Food, For Freedom) and some questions," mss., p. 3. Underlining in original mss. Liz Fusco, "Issaquena Freedom," pp. 5-9, Liz Fusco, "To Blur the Focus," p. 14.
37. Paul Jacobs and Saul Landau, *The New Radicals, A Report with Documents* (New York, 1966), pp. 131-35.
38. *SHSW: R. Hunter Morey Prs.:* Box 5, COFO Staff, "Fifth District's COFO Staff Meeting," April 14-17, 1965, Waveland, Miss., "Freedom School Joint Meeting with 3rd Dist.," pp. 12-15.
39. *KZSU Interview*, Stanford University: 0356, pp. 15-16.
40. JoAnne Grant, *Black Protest: History, Documents, and Analyses, 1619 to the Present* (Connecticut, 1968), pp. 415-16, "The War on Vietnam," A McComb, Miss. Project. *Interview:* Dorothy Smith, January 24, 1979, Lawrence, Kansas.
41. JoAnne Grant, *Black Protest*, p. 415, footnote explanation of the background of the statement.
42. Leslie B. McLemore, "The Mississippi Freedom Democratic Party: A Case Study in Grass Roots Politics." (Unpublished Ph.D. dissertation, University of Massachusetts, 1971), p. 237. Quoted from James Bonney, "Letters Author Recalls Praise of FDP Leaders, " *Greenwood Commonwealth* (Mississippi), August 4, 1965.
43. See the discussion of the Amite boycott, footnote 35. *Interviews:* Fannie Lou Hamer, Nov. 2, 1969, Ruleville, Mississippi; Henry Kirksey, Nov. 11, 1969, Jackson, Mississippi; Dorothy Smith, January 24, 1979, Lawrence, Kansas.